Next–Generation Applications and Implementations of Gamification Systems

Filipe Portela
University of Minho, Portugal

Ricardo Queirós
ESMAD, Polytechnic Institute of Porto, Portugal

A volume in the Advances in Human and Social
Aspects of Technology (AHSAT) Book Series

Published in the United States of America by
  IGI Global
  Engineering Science Reference (an imprint of IGI Global)
  701 E. Chocolate Avenue
  Hershey PA, USA 17033
  Tel: 717-533-8845
  Fax: 717-533-8661
  E-mail: cust@igi-global.com
  Web site: http://www.igi-global.com

Library of Congress Cataloging-in-Publication Data

Names: Portela, Filipe, editor. | Queiros, Ricardo, 1975- editor.
Title: Next-generation applications and implementations of gamification
  systems / Filipe Portela and Ricardo Queiros, editors.
Description: Hershey, PA : Engineering Science Reference, 2021. | Includes
  bibliographical references and index. | Summary: "The main goal of this
  book is to show how to put gamification in action by linking academic
  and informatics researchers with professionals who use gamification in
  their day-a-day work to promote the cross-fertilization of gaming
  information and knowledge across professional and geographical
  boundaries, catalyzing the users engaging in several areas like
  education, healthcare, industry, among others"-- Provided by publisher.
Identifiers: LCCN 2021019438 (print) | LCCN 2021019439 (ebook) | ISBN
  9781799880899 (hardcover) | ISBN 9781799880905 (paperback) | ISBN
  9781799880912 (ebook)
Subjects: LCSH: Gamification--Industrial applications. | Educational games.
  | Game theory.
Classification: LCC T57.92 .N49 2021 (print) | LCC T57.92 (ebook) | DDC
  519.3--dc23
LC record available at https://lccn.loc.gov/2021019438
LC ebook record available at https://lccn.loc.gov/2021019439

This book is published in the IGI Global book series Advances in Human and Social Aspects of Technology (AHSAT) (ISSN: 2328-1316; eISSN: 2328-1324)

British Cataloguing in Publication Data
A Cataloguing in Publication record for this book is available from the British Library.

For electronic access to this publication, please contact: eresources@igi-global.com.

Advances in Human and Social Aspects of Technology (AHSAT) Book Series

Mehdi Khosrow-Pour, D.B.A.
Information Resources Management Association, USA

ISSN:2328-1316
EISSN:2328-1324

MISSION

In recent years, the societal impact of technology has been noted as we become increasingly more connected and are presented with more digital tools and devices. With the popularity of digital devices such as cell phones and tablets, it is crucial to consider the implications of our digital dependence and the presence of technology in our everyday lives.

The **Advances in Human and Social Aspects of Technology (AHSAT) Book Series** seeks to explore the ways in which society and human beings have been affected by technology and how the technological revolution has changed the way we conduct our lives as well as our behavior. The AHSAT book series aims to publish the most cutting-edge research on human behavior and interaction with technology and the ways in which the digital age is changing society.

COVERAGE

- End-User Computing
- Public Access to ICTs
- Cyber Behavior
- Computer-Mediated Communication
- Technology Dependence
- Gender and Technology
- Human Development and Technology
- Human-Computer Interaction
- Philosophy of technology
- Technology and Freedom of Speech

IGI Global is currently accepting manuscripts for publication within this series. To submit a proposal for a volume in this series, please contact our Acquisition Editors at Acquisitions@igi-global.com or visit: http://www.igi-global.com/publish/.

Titles in this Series

For a list of additional titles in this series, please visit: http://www.igi-global.com/book-series/advances-human-social-aspects-technology/37145

Technological Influences on Creativity and User Experience
Joshua Fairchild (Creighton University, USA)
Information Science Reference • © 2022 • 305pp • H/C (ISBN: 9781799843542) • US $195.00

Human Factors Issues and the Impact of Technology on Society
Heather Lum (Embry-Riddle Aeronautical University, USA)
Information Science Reference • © 2021 • 333pp • H/C (ISBN: 9781799864530) • US $195.00

Ubiquitous Technologies for Human Development and Knowledge Management
Hakikur Rahman (Institute of Computer Management and Science, Bangladesh)
Information Science Reference • © 2021 • 396pp • H/C (ISBN: 9781799878445) • US $195.00

Technological Breakthroughs and Future Business Opportunities in Education, Health, and Outer Space
Angus Hooke (Australian Institute of Higher Education, Australia)
Business Science Reference • © 2021 • 353pp • H/C (ISBN: 9781799867722) • US $225.00

Machine Law, Ethics, and Morality in the Age of Artificial Intelligence
Steven John Thompson (University of California, Davis, USA & University of Maryland Global Campus, USA)
Engineering Science Reference • © 2021 • 266pp • H/C (ISBN: 9781799848943) • US $295.00

Examining the Socio-Technical Impact of Smart Cities
Fenio Annansingh (York College, City University of New York, USA)
Information Science Reference • © 2021 • 231pp • H/C (ISBN: 9781799853268) • US $190.00

Human-Computer Interaction and Technology Integration in Modern Society
Hakikur Rahman (Institute of Computer Management and Science, Bangladesh)
Engineering Science Reference • © 2021 • 347pp • H/C (ISBN: 9781799858492) • US $195.00

Information Technology Applications for Crisis Response and Management
Jon W. Beard (Iowa State University, USA)
Information Science Reference • © 2021 • 294pp • H/C (ISBN: 9781799872108) • US $195.00

701 East Chocolate Avenue, Hershey, PA 17033, USA
Tel: 717-533-8845 x100 • Fax: 717-533-8661
E-Mail: cust@igi-global.com • www.igi-global.com

Editorial Advisory Board

Table of Contents

Section 1
Game Design Principles

Chapter 1
Ricardo Alexandre Peixoto de Queiros, ESMAD, Polytechnic Institute of Porto, Portugal
Mário Pinto, ESMAD, Polytechnic Institute of Porto, Portugal
Alberto Simões, Polytechnic Institute of Cávado and Ave, Portugal
Carlos Filipe Portela, University of Minho, Portugal

Chapter 2
Igor Fernandes, University of Minho, Portugal
Pedro Branco, University of Minho, Portugal
Carlos Filipe Portela, University of Minho, Portugal

Chapter 3
Sergio Alloza Castillo, Gecon.es Foundation, Spain
Flavio Escribano, Gecon.es Foundation, Spain
Óscar Rodrigo González López, Universidad de Extremadura, Spain
María Buenadicha Mateos, Universidad de Extremadura, Spain

Section 2
Learning Gamification Strategies

Section 3
Serious Games and Apps

Section 4
Gamification Novel Approaches

Detailed Table of Contents

Section 1
Game Design Principles

Chapter 1

    Ricardo Alexandre Peixoto de Queiros, ESMAD, Polytechnic Institute of Porto, Portugal
    Mário Pinto, ESMAD, Polytechnic Institute of Porto, Portugal
    Alberto Simões, Polytechnic Institute of Cávado and Ave, Portugal
    Carlos Filipe Portela, University of Minho, Portugal

Computer science education has always been a challenging topic for both sides of the trench: educators and learners. Nowadays, with the pandemic state that we are facing, these challenges are even greater, leading educators to look for strategies that promote effective virtual learning. One of such strategies includes the use of game mechanics to improve student engagement and motivation. This design strategy is typically called gamification. Nowadays, gamification is being seen as the solution to solve most of the issues related to demotivation, complexity, or tedious tasks. In the latest years, we saw thousands of educational applications being created with gamification in mind. Nevertheless, this has been an unsustainable growth with ad hoc designs and implementations of educational gamified applications, hampering interoperability and the reuse of good practices. This chapter presents a systematic study on gamification standardization aiming to characterize the status of the field, namely describing existing frameworks, languages, services, and platforms.

Chapter 2

    Igor Fernandes, University of Minho, Portugal
    Pedro Branco, University of Minho, Portugal
    Carlos Filipe Portela, University of Minho, Portugal

Organizations are concerned about how they can increase the motivation and engagement of their employees. Gamification arises in this context as an opportunity to address this issue. Thus, gamification has attracted greater attention from companies. The idea of using game elements to solve problems in their processes is starting to be seen as a solution. This study aims to analyse the gamification concept and its benefits and explain how it can be applied in human resources management. This mechanism can help companies to solve employee motivation and engagement problems in different areas of human resources. This chapter analysed eight studies in the areas of recruitment, training, team building, and administrative processes. So a SWOT analysis able to help understand the different models of gamification applied in human resources, its objectives, and its ability to create advantages for companies and their employees was constructed.

Chapter 3

  Sergio Alloza Castillo, Gecon.es Foundation, Spain
  Flavio Escribano, Gecon.es Foundation, Spain
  Óscar Rodrigo González López, Universidad de Extremadura, Spain
  María Buenadicha Mateos, Universidad de Extremadura, Spain

The preconceived notion concerning negative effects of video games and students' academic performance is a widely known subject. However, some investigations explore the positive impact of video games on academic performance. With a sample of 247 university students, this chapter studies the perception of both gamers and non-gamers about soft skills and their current relevance in academic and professional fields. The possible relationships linking the intensity of the usage of video games, academic performance, and the perception concerning soft skills are investigated. The results expose a generalized positive perception respecting the relation between video games and the development of soft skills, specifically to the video game genre and its relevance and influence on academic performance, as well as gender differences, where women prevail in emotional and social managements, although this influence is not elevated.

Section 2
Learning Gamification Strategies

Chapter 4

  Elena Somova, The University of Plovdiv "Paisii Hilendarski", Bulgaria
  Mariya Gachkova, The University of Plovdiv "Paisii Hilendarski", Bulgaria

The main goal of the chapter is to discuss implementation of the structural gamification in LMS. The overview of pedagogical approaches, theories, models, and systems connected to the serious games and in particular for gamification is presented. The possibilities for using the game elements and techniques in e-learning (incl. possible realization with the standard elements of a non-gamified LMS) are presented. A four-stage cyclical gamified learning model is proposed. For the four categories of learners from the Bartle's classification, the appropriate game elements are determined. Two plugins for the application of structural gamification in Moodle have been designed and developed, which integrates game elements and techniques in the process of e-learning. The first plugin changes the design of the course into a game view. The second plugin allows adding specific game elements, which do not exist in Moodle. Different experiments of structural gamification have been done and presented.

Abdulsalam Salihu Mustafa, University Tenaga Nasional, Malaysia
Gamal Abdulnaser Alkawsi, Universiti Tenaga Nasional, Malaysia
Kingsley Ofosu-Ampong, Business School, University of Ghana, Ghana
Vanye Zira Vanduhe, Üner İnşaat Peyzaj Ltd., Turkey
Manuel B. Garcia, FEU Institute of Technology, Philippines
Yahia Baashar, Universiti Tenaga Nasional, Malaysia

Gamification in education is a strategy of motivating and engaging students by integrating game design features into the instructional process. Although there is a growing body of scientific evidence supporting the effectiveness of gamification in the educational setting, some of the evidence is inconclusive and insufficient, especially in developing nations. The purpose of this study is to integrate the technology acceptance model and task technology fit to investigate instructors' intention to use gamified online learning. A sample of 50 participants across various African institutions was involved in this study. Structural equation modelling implemented via partial least squares (PLS) is used to test the research hypotheses. The results revealed that intention to use gamified online learning was significantly and positively influenced by task technology fit, perceived usefulness, and attitude. Notably, subjective norms, facilitating conditions, and computer anxiety failed to predict behavioural intention. The authors discuss the implications of the findings and propose future directions.

Cornelia Nih Popescu, Capgemini Engineering T.E.C., France
Elodie Attie, Capgemini Engineering T.E.C., France
Laëtitia CHADOUTEAU, Capgemini Engineering T.E.C., France

In the context of the current COVID-19 pandemic, e-learning represents a more and more important concern of all education providers and an inevitable direction for the current context in training and education. This chapter follows the theory of gamified learning and the theory of flow to understand to which extent game characteristics improve engagement and learning outcomes, such as performance and engagement. To do this, two groups of learners (N=20) were randomly assigned: the experimental group followed a gamified learning module, and the control group followed the same content without gamification mechanisms. The game mechanisms chosen involve a game, a challenge, virtual rewards, an avatar, a final badge, and a system of points and levels. Results show that the gamified course increased the time spent on the course and the overall performance. Hence, this chapter demonstrates the relevance of using gamification to improve learning outcomes.

Section 3
Serious Games and Apps

Chapter 7

Rui Macedo, Polytechnic of Porto, Portugal
Claudia Silva, Polytechnic of Porto, Portugal
Bruno Albouy, IRFSS Nouvelle-Aquitaine, France
Alejandro F. San Juan, Universidad Politécnica de Madrid, Spain
Tiina Pystynen, Tampere University of Applied Sciences, Finland

Role play and simulated patients are tools frequently used in undergraduate physiotherapy courses to help students gain familiarity with what they will find in future real-life encounters. However, these approaches have limitations when it comes to delivering diversity and repetition to a large number of students and are mostly bounded to the school's premises. Web-based virtual patient software can help to overcome these shortcomings as they equally require students to go through most of the steps of the physiotherapy process, and simultaneously offer unlimited diversity of cases and repetition opportunities and can be delocalized from physical schools. PETRHA + is an Erasmus+ strategic partnership of European high education institutions aiming at the improvement of a web-based serious game prototype designed to enhance physiotherapy students' clinical reasoning using virtual patients. The objective of this chapter is the presentation of the background context that led to the development of the serious game, its design features, functions, and ongoing and future developments.

Chapter 8

Linda William, Temasek Polytechnic, Singapore
Ruan Yang, Temasek Polytechnic, Singapore

A serious game has been introduced as an alternative tool to support teaching and learning. It integrates entertainment and non-entertainment elements to encourage the voluntary learning of knowledge and skills. One of the essential entertainment elements in the serious game to motivate learning is the enjoyment element. However, studies on models to analyze this enjoyment element are still limited. Most models present isolated and specific approaches for specific games that cannot scale to other games. In this chapter, a generic enjoyment analytics framework is proposed. The framework aims to capture learners' enjoyment experience using open-ended feedback, analyze the feedback using sentiment analytics models, and visualize the results in an interactive dashboard. Using this framework, the lecturers would interpret the learners' experience towards the topic and the game and capture difficulties the learners may encounter during the game. It would help the lecturers to decide follow-up actions required for the learners to improve the learning.

    Ricardo Santos, NOVA School of Science and Technology, Universidade NOVA de Lisboa, Portugal
    Armanda Rodrigues, NOVA School of Science and Technology, Universidade NOVA de Lisboa, Portugal
    Teresa Romão, NOVA School of Science and Technology, Universidade NOVA de Lisboa, Portugal
    Francisco M. N. Gouveia, NOVA School of Science and Technology, Universidade NOVA de Lisboa, Portugal

Despite the importance of recycling in the current and pressing context of preserving the environment, it is still not adopted by all of us. Several mobile tools have become available with the aim of sensitizing and motivating the population towards sustainable behaviours, with limitations in information availability and in integration with formal as well as informal sources. Moreover, persuasive characteristics, such as the use of gamification also need improvement towards raising competitiveness (and awareness) in the targeted community. The authors thus propose a mobile responsive gamified application for motivating recycling attitudes centred around an interactive map, supported by the curated data of one of the reference companies of the environmental sector in the region. The app includes collaborative persuasive elements as well as validation processes for crowdsourced content proposed by the community. The results of an evaluation process, with promising results, are described.

Section 4
Gamification Novel Approaches

    María A. Pérez-Juárez, University of Valladolid, Spain
    Javier M. Aguiar-Pérez, University of Valladolid, Spain
    Miguel Alonso-Felipe, University of Valladolid, Spain
    Javier Del-Pozo-Velázquez, University of Valladolid, Spain
    Saúl Rozada-Raneros, University of Valladolid, Spain
    Mikel Barrio-Conde, University of Valladolid, Spain

A lot of millennials have been educated in gamified schools where they played Kahoot several times per week, and where applications like Classcraft made them feel like the protagonists of a videogame in which they had to accumulate points to be able to level up. All those that were educated in a gamified environment feel it is natural and logical that gamification is used in all areas. For this reason, gamification is increasingly becoming important in different fields including financial services, bringing new challenges. Gamification allows financial institutions to provide personalized and compelling experiences. Big data and artificial intelligence techniques are called to play an essential role in the gamification of financial services. This chapter aims to explore the possibilities of using artificial intelligence and big data techniques to support gamified financial services which are essential for digital natives but also increasingly important for digital immigrants.

Systems that aim to maintain and improve the health of citizens are steadily gaining importance. Digital transformation is having a positive impact on healthcare. Gamification motivates individuals to maintain and improve their physical and mental well-being. In the era of artificial intelligence and big data, healthcare is not only digital, but also predictive, proactive, and preventive. Big data and artificial intelligence techniques are called to play an essential role in gamified eHealth services and devices allowing to offer personalized care. This chapter aims to explore the possibilities of artificial intelligence and big data techniques to support and improve gamified eHealth services and devices, including wearable technology, which are essential for digital natives but also increasingly important for digital immigrants. These services and devices can play an important role in the prevention and diagnosis of diseases, in the treatment of illnesses, and in the promotion of healthy lifestyle habits.

Augmented reality strengthens its ties with the gaming world every day. The fact that smartphones can be used as an augmented reality tool, in particular, shows this interest as a remarkable phenomenon for both gamers and game producers. The development of augmented reality applications is of great importance for the future of the gaming world, as it is not only limited to mobile phones but also covers more sophisticated devices. This research intends to evaluate how augmented reality games interpret gaming concepts and principles, through field research methods, new applications, and studies that deal with gamification, presence, immersion, and game transfer phenomena. It is also aimed to make inferences about how our daily life can be gamified in the near future thanks to augmented reality.

Foreword

Gamification is a rather new term with less than 20 years of widespread use. For someone born in the '80s like me, that was yesterday! However, in such a small amount of time, it has already gathered a wide and massive count of fans, experts and, in equal amount, critics.

Current research tells us that, when done correctly, introducing gamification can improve user experience and interaction in products/services through increasing motivation, improve the experience, raise engagement, immersion, and flow, productivity and even happiness levels. However, when the execution is messy or the goals unclear, it can mean not only a waste of time and resources but a disastrous outcome for everyone. As has been the case of other trends and hypes, we can find good and bad examples in gamification.

Nevertheless, even if we ignore the potential nefarious outcomes of a poorly executed gamification of a service/product, there are other points of discussion, in particular: Is the extra layer of complexity in product or service development, either by gamifying an app, a customer service, a website, or any other part of the user experience, worth it? Do people feel more compelled to use or experiment with something? Or a better outcome?

With time and familiarity, and as we test and experiment with time and familiarity, the number of good outcomes starts to outweigh the bad. You will be able to attest in the following chapters, which presents to the reader several interesting, relevant and most of all, impactful gamification experiences and projects.

While not intended as an extensive analysis of all types and uses of gamification, I believe this book provides something better. It gives an overview of the current state of the art, evaluating impacts and bringing to the reader-selected and practical examples of gamification.

With a specific albeit not limited emphasis on learning scenarios, it also covers topics such as the application and use of gamification in healthcare, financial services, different learning environments and contexts and even recycling, as well as the use of other technology such as augmented reality, big data, artificial intelligence to enhance their impact.

It is presented a systemic review of current gamification standards, practices, and applications in order to identify the current status and frameworks in use, which can provide the reader with a clear view and chart a path for the future of the field.

One of the main issues verified in this subject is the connection between fun or enjoyment during the experience and its impact. A framework is proposed to help identify the connection to interpret the learner's experience using a serious game. This connection is further expanded in a study conducted with the University of Extremadura, where positive connections between video games and soft skills and potential gender differences are developed.

Additionally, concerning the tendency or intention to use gamification in the teaching experience, through a study with African institutions, it was possible to find a connection between task technology fit, perceived usefulness, and attitude can positively influence the intention of using gamification experiences what we can conclude from it.

Still, regarding higher education learning experiences, the authors evaluated how the students struggling with motivation and engagement during online learning moments can benefit from gamification through traditional learning management systems. For testing it, two plugins for the popular LMS Moodle have been analysed, and the results reviewed. They further evaluated it by comparing groups of learners, one of which used a gamified learning module for e-learning purposes. The results showed that learners spent more time and increased their performance using this module.

Moving on to corporate organisational environments, as complex structures, they can benefit significantly from gamification to motivate employees. Thus, the potential benefits associated with different models of gamification related to human resources are presented and compared.

Augmented reality is a field gaining renewed interest due to its ability to be implemented on multiple devices. Its use in gamification brings a new and relevant dimension and increases immersion for the user.

Demonstrating the potential in using gamification in different fields, we can also find a specific chapter focusing on using gamified interactions to increase recycling habits and awareness and reward and motivate users that recycle, having reached promising results.

A chapter was dedicated to evaluating an Erasmus+ project on using a web-based prototype stage serious game by physiotherapy students during online learning by simulating virtual patients and identifying the potential of expanding learning in this field beyond the school premises. Still regarding healthcare, complementing with the use of Big Data and Artificial Intelligence, the chapter displays the possibility of using gamification to provide health systems with the tools to not only motivate and engage citizens to improve on their health and lifestyle habits but also help increase the ability to provide proactive, predictive, and preventive care.

The potential impact of connecting big data and artificial intelligence to gamification is once more explored. This time, in financial services, to generate new possibilities for institutions to create personalised and motivating user experiences.

In sum, in this book, we are presented with possible uses and demonstrations of the immense potential of gamification in a wide range of different scenarios and applications. I believe that Dr Ricardo Queirós and Dr Filipe Portela, through their individual and combined decades of experience in the field and multiple innovations and studies, are the perfect authors for a book that can both enlighten and educate on state of the art regarding this concept. Their enthusiasm demonstrated in projects we have worked on together permeates this book, enriching the reader's experience.

Eduardo Nunes
Polytechnic Institute of Porto, Portugal

Preface

Gamification is being used everywhere; despite its apparent plethora of benefits, the unbalanced use of its main mechanics can end up in catastrophic results for a company or institution. Currently, there is a lack of knowledge of what it is, leading to its unregulated and ad hoc use without any prior planning. This unbalanced use prejudices the achievement of the initial goals and impairs the user's evolution, bringing potential negative reflections. Few specifications and modelling languages currently allow creating a system of rules to serve as the basis for a gamification engine. Consequently, programmers implement Gamification in various ways, undermining any attempt at reuse and negatively affecting interoperability.

The book *Next-Generation Applications and Implementations of Gamification Systems* synthesises trends, best practices, methodologies, languages, and tools used to implement Gamification. It also discusses how to put Gamification in action by linking academic and informatics researchers with professionals who use Gamification in their daily work to disseminate and exchange the knowledge, information, and technology provided by the international communities in the area of Gamification throughout the 21st century. The chapters of this issue address topics like Frameworks, Case Studies, Benchmarking, Video Games, Learning Management Systems (LMS), Artificial Intelligence, and Augmented Reality. This book is ideal for programmers, computer scientists, software engineers, practitioners of technological companies, managers, academicians, researchers, and students.

This book presents relevant achievements and practical examples of using this concept in a full range of gamification mechanisms. Gamification can increase user (e.g., students, collaborators, physicians) engagement and support processes and decisions anywhere and anytime by creating a narrative, crediting the tasks, or combining it with trending areas and tools (e.g., Artificial Intelligence). This book aims to promote the cross-fertilisation of gaming information and knowledge across professional and geographical boundaries, catalysing the users engaging in several areas like education, healthcare, industry, and others.

The book's primary goal is to show how to put Gamification into action by linking academic and informatics researchers with professionals who use Gamification in their day-a-day work. The idea is to disseminate and exchange the knowledge, information and technology provided by the international communities in Gamification throughout the 21st century.

This book synthesises new trends, best practices, methodologies, languages, and tools to implement Gamification. New paradigms and technologies are discussed here, without forgetting aspects related to regulation and certification of Gamification. All twelve chapters help to understand the present and shape the future of Gamification. For accomplishing it, the book is divided into four sections:

1. Game Design Principles
2. Learning Gamification Strategies

3. Serious Games and Apps
4. Gamification Novel Approaches

The first section, "Game Design Principles," presents some studies conducted through theory and surveys and proposes a primer framework for Gamification. Then, the chapters of the second section, "Learning Gamification Strategies," show some innovative strategies for using Gamification in the teaching context. The third section, "Serious Games and Apps," presents game-based solutions and explains how authors practice them. The last section, "Gamification Novel Approaches," addresses some novel approaches like Artificial Intelligence and Virtual and Augmented Reality combined with Gamification.

The twelve chapters addressed several topics like Applied Gamification, Cloud and online Gamification, Employee Onboarding Techniques, Gamification Certification, Frameworks and Strategies, Learning Management Systems (LMS), Game as a Service (GaaS) and Serious Games, Gamification micro-services, Gamified Artificial Intelligence, Open-source gamification tools and libraries and Standardisation and Interoperability in Gamification. Globally, they also mentioned some of the best practices for Gamification, analysed the state of Gamification in several application areas (e.g., health, human resources, education, or finances) and showed new concepts and techniques in gamification design and development.

The target audience comprises professionals and researchers working in the field of Gamification in various disciplines (e.g., intelligent systems, standardisation, gaming, computer science, among others).

Moreover, the book provides insights and supports executives concerned with using Gamification to decide in different work communities, contexts, communities of practices and environments. The following group of people should be highlighted:

- Computer science, informatics and engineering professors and students.
- Communities of practices.
- Public and Private Institutions (e.g., Universities, Libraries or Companies).
- Researchers and academics.
- Practitioners of technological companies.
- Managers and other professionals.

The first section of this book, entitled "Game Design Principles," has three chapters.

This first chapter, entitled "A Primer on Gamification Standardization," was written by Ricardo Queirós, Mário Pinto, Alberto Simões and Filipe Portela and addresses the miss of formalism in Gamification by presenting a systematic study on gamification standardisation aiming to characterise the status of the field, namely describing existing frameworks, languages, services, and platforms.

The second chapter, entitled "An Overview of the Use of Gamification on Enterprises to Motivate Human Resources," was written by Igor Fernandes, Pedro Branco and Filipe Portela and presents a study to analyse the gamification tool and, specifically, the benefits and how it can be applied within the human resources area. This mechanism can help companies to solve employee motivation and engagement problems in different areas of human resources. With this study, it is possible to understand the different models of gamification application in human resources, its objectives and its ability to create advantages for companies and their employees.

The last chapter of this section is titled "Genre Differences in Soft Skills Perception and Video Game Usage in the University of Extremadura." The chapter was written by Sergio Alloza Castillo, Flavio

Escribano, Óscar Rodrigo González López and María Buenadicha Mateos. The chapter studies gamers and non-gamers perceptions of soft skills and their relevance in academic and professional fields. The possible relationships linking the intensity of the usage of video games, the academic performance and this perception concerning soft skills are investigated. The results expose a generalised positive perception respecting the relation between video games and soft skills development, specifically even to video games' genre and its relevance and influence on academic performance and gender differences, where women prevail in emotional and social managements influence is not elevated.

The second section of this book, entitled "Learning Gamification Strategies," has three chapters.

The first chapter of this section, entitled "Strategy to Implement Gamification in LMS," was written by Elena Somova and Mariya Gachkova and discusses the implementation of structural Gamification in LMS, based on a four-stage cyclical gamified learning model. For the four categories of learners from Bartle's classification, the appropriate game elements are determined. Two plugins for the application of structural Gamification in Moodle have been designed and developed, which integrates game elements and techniques in the process of e-learning. The first plugin changes the design of the course into a game view. The second plugin allows adding specific game elements, which do not exist in Moodle.

The second chapter of this section, entitled "Gamification of E-Learning in African Universities: Identifying Adoption Factors Through Task-Technology Fit and Technology Acceptance Model," was written by Abdulsalam Salihu Mustafa, Gamal Abdulnaser Alkawsi, Kingsley Ofosu-Ampong, Vanye Zira Vanduhe, Manuel B. Garcia and Yahia Baashar. The chapter proposes a study to integrate the technology acceptance model and task technology fit to investigate instructors' intention to use gamified online learning. A sample of 50 participants across various African institutions was involved in this study. Structural equation modelling implemented via partial least squares (PLS) is used to test the research hypotheses. The results revealed that intention to use gamified online learning was significantly and positively influenced by Task Technology Fit, Perceived Usefulness and Attitude.

The last chapter of this section is titled "Gamified Learning: Favoring Engagement and Learning Outcomes." The chapter was written by Cornelia Nih Popescu, Elodie Attie and Laetitia Chadouteau. The chapter follows the theory of gamified learning and the theory of flow to understand to what extent game characteristics improve engagement and learning outcomes (i.e., performance, engagement). To do this, two groups of learners were randomly assigned: the experimental group followed a gamified learning module, and the control group followed the same content without gamification mechanisms (i.e., game, challenge, virtual rewards, avatar, final badge, points/levels). Results show that the gamified course increased the time spent on the course and overall performance.

The third section of this book, entitled "Serious Games and Apps," has three chapters.

The first chapter of this section, entitled "Petrha+: A Serious Game to Enhance Physiotherapy Students' Clinical Reasoning," was written by Rui Macedo, Claudia Silva, Bruno Albouy, Alejandro F. San Juan, and Tiina Pystynen. This chapter presents PETRHA +, an Erasmus+ strategic partnership of European High Education Institutions aiming to improve a web-based serious game prototype designed to enhance physiotherapy students' clinical reasoning using virtual patients. This chapter aims to present the background context that led to the development of the serious game, its design features, functions, ongoing and future developments.

The second chapter of this section, entitled "Using Sentiment Analytics to Understand Learner Experiences in Serious Games," was written by Linda William and Ruan Yang. The chapter presents a serious game as an alternative tool to support teaching and learning. It integrates entertainment and non-entertainment elements to encourage the voluntary learning of knowledge and skills. One of the essential entertainment elements in the serious game to motivate learning is the enjoyment element. In this chapter, a generic enjoyment analytics framework is proposed. The framework aims to capture learners' enjoyment experience using open-ended feedback, analyse the feedback using sentiment analytics models and visualise the results in an interactive dashboard.

The last chapter of this section is titled "Motivating Sustainable Recycling Practices Through Persuasive Technologies." The chapter was written by Ricardo Santos, Armanda Rodrigues, Teresa Romão and Francisco M. N. Gouveia and proposes a Mobile Responsive Gamified Application for motivating recycling attitudes, centred around an interactive map of the recycling spots. The app includes collaborative persuasive elements and validation processes for crowdsourced content proposed by the community. The results of an evaluation process, with promising results, are described.

The last section of this book, entitled "Gamification Novel Approaches," has three chapters.

The first chapter of this section, entitled "Exploring the Possibilities of Artificial Intelligence and Big Data Techniques to Enhance Gamified Financial Services," was written by María A. Pérez-Juárez, Javier M. Aguiar-Pérez, Miguel Alonso-Felipe, Javier Del-Pozo-Velázquez and Mikel Barrio-Conde. The chapter explores the possibilities of using Artificial Intelligence and Big Data techniques to support gamified financial services that are essential for digital natives and increasingly important for digital immigrants.

The second chapter of this section, entitled "Can Artificial Intelligence and Big Data Improve Gamified Healthcare Services and Devices?" was written by María A. Pérez-Juárez, Javier M. Aguiar-Pérez, Javier Del-Pozo-Velázquez, Miguel Alonso-Felipe, Saúl Rozada-Raneros and Mikel Barrio-Conde. The chapter explores the possibilities of Artificial Intelligence and Big Data techniques to support and improve gamified eHealth services and devices, including wearable technology, which are essential for digital natives and increasingly important for digital immigrants. These services and devices can play an essential role in preventing and diagnosing diseases, treating illnesses, and promoting healthy lifestyle habits.

The last chapter of this section and of the book is titled "Augmented Reality Games." Baris Atiker writes the chapter that evaluates how Augmented Reality games interpret gaming concepts and principles through field research methods, new applications and studies that deal with Gamification, presence, immersion, and game transfer phenomena. It also aims to make inferences about how our daily life can be gamified soon thanks to Augmented Reality.

This book has a transversal and convergent impact because it addresses the use of Gamification applied to several areas of knowledge. These chapters bring some ideas of how to use Gamification in the day-life. Practical examples can clarify and motivate the researchers to conduct their works in applied Gamification. The book can help to prove that the application of Gamification mechanisms can help to solve many issues. The idea behind it is easy, and the people only need to create a narrative able to represent the entire workflow and show ecosystem interaction.

We hope that this book can be a vital contribution in the area and help engage the community of Gamification by bringing some new researchers and professionals to this trending topic.

Acknowledgment

First of all, we thank all the authors, reviewers and the editorial board who contribute to this book's success. Then, a particular thanks to IGI and their editorial team for the help provided during the editing process.

Finally, this book was also supported by FCT – Fundação para a Ciência e Tecnologia within the R&D Units Project Scope: UIDB/00319/2020".

Section 1
Game Design Principles

Chapter 1
A Primer on Gamification Standardization

Ricardo Alexandre Peixoto de Queiros
iD https://orcid.org/0000-0002-1985-6285
ESMAD, Polytechnic Institute of Porto, Portugal

Mário Pinto
ESMAD, Polytechnic Institute of Porto, Portugal

Alberto Simões
Polytechnic Institute of Cávado and Ave, Portugal

Carlos Filipe Portela
iD https://orcid.org/0000-0003-2181-6837
University of Minho, Portugal

ABSTRACT

Computer science education has always been a challenging topic for both sides of the trench: educators and learners. Nowadays, with the pandemic state that we are facing, these challenges are even greater, leading educators to look for strategies that promote effective virtual learning. One of such strategies includes the use of game mechanics to improve student engagement and motivation. This design strategy is typically called gamification. Nowadays, gamification is being seen as the solution to solve most of the issues related to demotivation, complexity, or tedious tasks. In the latest years, we saw thousands of educational applications being created with gamification in mind. Nevertheless, this has been an unsustainable growth with ad hoc designs and implementations of educational gamified applications, hampering interoperability and the reuse of good practices. This chapter presents a systematic study on gamification standardization aiming to characterize the status of the field, namely describing existing frameworks, languages, services, and platforms.

DOI: 10.4018/978-1-7998-8089-9.ch001

INTRODUCTION

Nowadays, the games industry is responsible for an important part of the financial market worldwide (Mordor Intelligence, 2020). Several reasons can be identified for this fact from the entertainment of playing a game to its capacity to enhance two typically opposite values such as competition and cooperation. To bring the benefits of the games to non-game contexts, the term gamification appeared and, currently, gamification is applied in several digital applications for several purposes. The most notable examples are to foster the learning of complex domains and to facilitate the integration of workers in companies (on-boarding).

Regardless of the application domain, there is an unsustainable development of gamified applications in terms of specifications, standards and good practices used. Without this type of regulation, the way how gamified apps are created hinders the reuse and interoperability between peers while promoting replication of features which can be error prone and time consuming.

This article focuses on the current state of gamification standardization in the scope of the gamified application development life cycle. As methodology for our systematic study, we will organize all the current contributions for the standardization of gamification in a well-known client-server software architecture pattern called three-tier architecture. In this pattern the three tiers, namely, Data, Business/Logic and User Interface are mapped with gamification contributions such as languages, services, and platforms, respectively.

This work is organized as follows. Section 2 presents the most popular gamification frameworks and their common features. In section 3, we start by presenting the methodology for this study and then, for each tier, we present the most mature contributions for gamification formalization. In the last section, we analyze the study done by making considerations about trends and listing a set of best practices in the design of a gamified system.

GAMIFICATION FRAMEWORKS

A framework can be defined as a conceptual structure which acts as an abstract (or concrete) guide for the building of a software product. In the field of game/gamification design there are no consensus on the use of frameworks. In fact, (Crawford, 1984) states that game design is an activity too complex to be reducible to a formal procedure. Other authors (Julius & Salo, 2013) conclude that it should be treated as an agile process which does not always follow a specific design framework.

Despite the existence of dozens of frameworks worldwide, several researchers (Seaborn & Fels, 2015) and (Hamari, Koivisto & Sarsa, 2014) claim that gamification as an academic topic is still young and only a few well-established frameworks can be useful. To achieve a more empirical study, a literature review was conducted, between 8 and 15 of December of 2020, based on works indexed in three databases, namely, Google Scholar, SCOPUS, and Web of Knowledge. In this review, the search keywords were gamification, game, design, framework, and models.

The study identified 52 articles which either present or refer a gamification framework. From those articles, 12 frameworks were obtained. Despite the high number of frameworks identified, 5 frameworks were referred more than 75\% of the total of articles. These five frameworks will be compared in the next subsections. The Octalysis framework (Figure1) was created by (Choy, 2015) recognized that there are eight different types of **core drive** that motivates people to perform any activity. Visually, the framework has an octagonal shape where the core drives are represented in each corner.

Figure 1. Octalysis Gamification Framework

The right drives (**Right Brain**) represent the creative, artistic, and social aspects, while the left drives (**Left Brain**) represent the logical and intellectual aspects. These drives favors either extrinsic or intrinsic motivation. In fact, most companies aspire to design solely for the extrinsic motivation, which is about reaching a goal or getting a reward. However, Chou states that the intrinsic motivation, the use of creativity and socializing, should be the priority in the gamification strategy design to encourage continuous motivation and make the activity itself rewarding. The framework also distinguishes the bottom and top side of octagon and coined both parts as **Black Hat** and **White Hat**, respectively. The former defines negative motivations where people is being motivated to take a certain action because of the fear of losing, the curiosity of upcoming event or the strive for achieving the things he/she cannot have. The later are considered as positive motivations. These positive drives motivate individuals through creativity, makes them feel powerful due to the sense of control and the impression of a greater meaning. In short, to have a balance strategy, Chou highlights that successful gamification requires the consideration of all the core drives.

Marczewski created a framework, called GAME (Marczewski, 2015) based on two phases. Firstly, planning and designing, which includes the gathering, by means of a survey, of key information such as the user's types in the gamification context. Then, the best solution for goals and engagement is designed, measuring user activities and outcomes. He applies an own motivation framework called RAMP (Relatedness, Autonomy, Mastery, Purpose).

MDA stands for Mechanics, Dynamics, and Aesthetics framework (Hunicke, Leblanc, & Zubek, 2004) and is defined as a formal approach to bridge the gap between game design and development. According to this framework, games can be broken down into three elements: rules, system, and fun. These elements are directly translated into the respective design components, which must be defined when designing a game. The MDA framework has been modified by different authors to be suitable to several contexts. One of the modifications has resulted in the MDE framework (Robson et al., 2015), where the concept aesthetics is replaced with emotions to describe the user experience.

The Sustainable Gamification Design (SGD) is an enterprise gamification framework developed by (Raftopoulos, 2014). This human-centered framework intends to value creation benefits, destruction risks, and be also concerned about being ethically correct. Based on its author, this kind of frameworks could, potentially, produce more responsible and sustainable results. Table 1 summarizes all five frameworks based on their context and scope.

Table 1. Comparison of gamification design frameworks

Model	Creation Date	Context	Scope
Octalsys	Chou, Y. (2015)	Gamification Design	Core Drives Left/Right brain Black/White hat
MDA	Ruhi, U. (2015)	Game Design	Mechanics Dynamics Aesthetics
MDE	Robson, K. (2015)	Gamification Design	Mechanics Dynamics Emotions
SGD	Raftopoulos, M. (2014)	Game Design	Discover Reframe Envision Create Values/Ethics Reflect/Act Understand/Make
GAME	Marczewski (2015)	Gamification Design	Relatedness Autonomy Mastery Purpose

A previous study (Mora et. Al., 2015) gathers more information about these (and more) frameworks.

GAMIFICATION SYSTEMATIC STUDY

The previous chapter focused on identifying and comparing gamification design frameworks that will help in the gamification process of a software system. However, there will come a time when it will be necessary to implement gamification. For this, there are several tools, services, platforms, and languages that can help in the process. However, there is a huge dispersion of technologies and, as expected, poor adherence to standards. This chapter presents a model based on 3 layers to organize the types of technologies that we can find in a gamified system and, for each of these layers, current standards and best practices are presented.

Within a gamification ecosystem there are several agents responsible either to produce, process or consume data that is crucial for the correct functioning of a gamification system.

This section presents the current state of gamification standardization in the scope of a gamified application development life cycle. As methodology for the systematic study all the current contributions for the standardization of gamification are organized in a well-known client-server software architecture pattern called three-tier architecture composed by:

- **Presentation:** exposes interaction for the end users through an UI.
- **Logic:** expresses business rules and expose them as services.
- **Data:** defines domain knowledge and persists it in a storage.

Based on this pattern, a gamification multi-tier architecture was designed for this study representing typical components in a gamification ecosystem (Figure 2).

Figure 2. Gamification Mapping Model

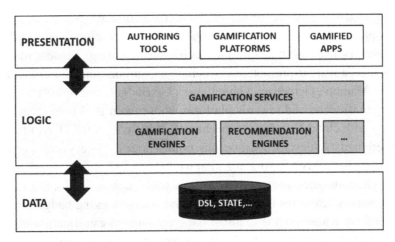

After defining a typical instance of a gamified system, each layer was map to a component. In the next subsection the most popular gamifications platforms in the presentation tier, the most prominent services in the logic tier and the most used domain specific languages for the data tier are presented.

Presentation Tier (Platforms)

Currently, when it comes to develop a gamified application, one of two solutions is chosen: 1) you start creating it from scratch or 2) you use an existing platform to support the gamification features of the application. There are naturally advantages/disadvantages to both approaches.

In the case of the first approach, it requires having a team of multifaceted developers, a deadline not too rigid and servers to store their own game data. On the other hand, flexibility is gained in the development of services and graphical interfaces to be provided to the end user.

In the second approach, it is necessary, firstly, to make a market analysis and identify which platform best supports your needs. Using a platform, weakens flexibility, but development time is saved, as it is not necessary to implement gamification features so developers can focus on business logic.

For the second approach one of the biggest challenges is to choose the most suitable platform considering the current needs.

Gamification platforms can be divided in two main groups:

- Enterprise Gamification Platforms: gathers platforms that implements features typical founded in companies such as worker integration, sales, marketing campaigns, among others.
- Educational Gamification Platforms: dedicated for the teaching-learning process of several domains such as computer programming, math's, medicine, electronics, among others.

The next subsections detail both types of platforms.

Enterprise Gamification Platforms

Gamification is being used with promises results in the enterprise domain (Nah et. al., 2019). In this realm, there are several proprietary business-oriented solutions targeted to client and employee engagement which add complementary features to adapt to a specific business (e.g., content management system, customized rewards, mechanisms to promote social behaviors, on-boarding, reports, and analytics). Some popular examples are Mambo[1], Gametize[2], GameLayer[3], GetBadges, and Spinify[4].

GameLayer is a gamification and rewards platform whose main goal is to create user engagement and consumer loyalty with cloud-based game mechanics. It includes a REST API that exposes several features such as leaderboards, achievements, missions, points, prizes, mystery boxes, teams, and level-ups.

GetBadges.io is more focused on the organization workflow of IT companies allowing the reward of developer teams which more quickly integrate workflow tools such as Trello, Slack, Jira, GitHub, and others. For each integration, teams (or individual workers) start unlocking badges.

Gametize is a platform whose goal is to allow the creation of a gamification experience based on four pillars: interactive challenges, instant feedback, competition \& social and rewards \& redemptions.

Educational Gamification Platforms

Other popular use of gamification is to act as a facilitator for the teaching-learning process of complex domains. Gamification here is typically injected in an ad hoc fashion in so-called open online courses available on the web for several domains.

One of domains that most exploits the use of gamification for enhancing learner's motivation and engagement is the computer programming domain.

In this scope we stress the platforms Coursera[5], Udacity[6], edX[7], Codecademy[8], Khan Academy[9], and Free Code Camp[10] which offer a wide variety of learning material from top universities' courses, with the possibility of get paid certificates.

These platforms typically use gamification to attract learners, adopting elements such as progress indicators, badges, levels, leaderboards, and experience points. For example, Khan Academy uses badges and progress tracking to engage students to enlist and complete courses. Even that it also allows educators to easily create courses for their learners, it is limited to JavaScript-based programming activities

(HTML and CSS are also supported). Codecademy also uses progress indicators and badges. It supports programming languages such as Python, JavaScript, Java, SQL, Bash/Shell, and Ruby. However, creating courses on Codecademy is not yet possible.

In the context of educational institutions, the most widely used approach to create gamified open online courses is to rely on a Learning Management System (LMS) with game mechanics. LMSs were created to deliver course contents and collect assignments of the students. However, many of them evolved to provide more engaging environments resorting to gamification. Some of the most notable examples are Academy LMS, Moodle, and Matrix which include badges, achievements, points, and leaderboards. Moodle also has several plugins which offer a variety of other gamification elements (Paiva, Queirós & Leal, 2015).

One of the most relevant tools is Enki (Paiva, Leal & Queirós, 2016) which is a tool that blends gamification, assessment, and learning, presenting content in various forms as well as delivering programming assignments with automatic feedback, while allowing any stakeholder to create courses freely.

Logic Tier (Services)

Games industry is evolving at an unbridled level. This was one of the reasons for the appearance of Game Backend services.

This trending leveraged the interest of the most important companies (Google, Microsoft, and Amazon) for the creation of gaming integrated development infrastructures. Its architectures are very similar and boils down to a set of tiers responsible for tasks related with the creation, development, storage, and maintenance of a game. In a recent study (Amini et. al., 2018), the tier's architecture was analyzed and organized in five levels depicted in Figure 3:

Figure 3. Levels of Cloud Computing Gaming Services

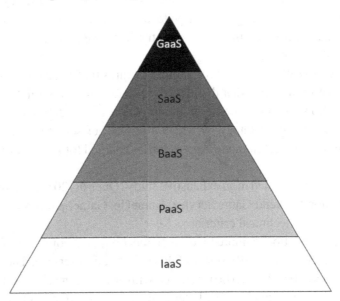

The five tiers are the following:

- **Game as a Service (GaaS)**: revenues model used to deliver game content after its launch (e.g., game subscriptions, gaming on demand and micro-transactions).
- **Software as a Service (SaaS)**: fosters the development, update, and debugging process (e.g., Google Apps, Facebook, YouTube).
- **Backend as a Service (BaaS)**: delivers APIs and SDKs provide many services, such as game elements/mechanics, database management, identity and access management, analysis, and others.
- **Platform as a Service (PaaS)**: offers infrastructure construction and maintenance (e.g., Microsoft Azure, Google AppEngine, Amazon SimpleDB/S3).
- **Infrastructure as a service (IaaS)**: cloud computing that provides virtual computing (e.g., Amazon EC2, GoGrid and Flexiscale).

Based on these tiers we highlighted the BaaS.

The goal of these cloud services is to free the programmer of the implementation of the game infrastructure and give him more time to dedicate in the game logic. The idea is to not replicate the implementation of the game features in each version of the game for several platforms and adhere to a service-oriented architecture providing cross-platform game services that lets you easily integrate popular gaming features such as achievements, leaderboards, remote storage, and real-time multiplayer in games.

A Game-Backend-as-a-Service (GBaaS) is a subset of a Backend as a Service (BaaS) that includes cross-platform solutions for the typical game concepts identified in the previous subsection. During the development process of a game (or a generic application) developers must choose between building their own back-end services

or using an available game back-end platform. This last option is usually preferred since GBaaS include several services specifically tailored for game development. These services allow developers to focus on the game logic by freeing them from implementing boiler plate features.

Typically, a GBaaS includes several gamification features which frees the programmer to the creation of good games rather than reinventing the wheel with the implementation of common gaming features such as leaderboards and achievements.

Most of the GBaaS on the Web offer a set of gaming features through a uniform API and with SDKs in several flavors. One of the features that distinguish GBaaS is regarding its pricing strategy: free or freemium. The former allows the programmer with a previous registration to access all the features of the GBaaS. The latter is a pricing strategy by which a product or service (typically a game or a web service) is provided free of charge, but money (premium) is charged for proprietary features, functionality, or virtual goods.

Most notable examples are detailed in an exhaustive study (Queirós, 2017) where five GBaaS (Google Play Game Services, Yahoo Backend Game Service, GameUp, GameSparks and Photon) are compared based on several on social and technical criteria.

Other services could be mentioned, more focused on the domain of computer programming learning, such as Odin (Paiva, Leal & Queirós, 2015) and FGPE gamification service. The former is a gamification service for learning activities that can be integrated with any learning agent supporting the Learning Tools Interoperability (LTI) specification. The latter is an open-source GraphQL service that transforms a package containing a gamification layer - adhering to a dedicated open-source language (Paiva et.al.,

2021) - into a game. This work was done in the scope of the Framework for Gamified Programming Education Erasmus+ Programme (Swacha et.al., 2020b).

Data Tier (Languages)

The state-of-the-art in the field of gamification currently lacks a main modeling language for gamification concepts. Nevertheless, there are several other established game languages and modeling approaches.

The most notable example of a domain-specific game description language is GaML (Herzig et. al., 2013), a formal and declarative language to define gamification concepts. The language is automatically compliable into gamification platforms without the need to involve IT-experts.

ATTAC-L (Broeckhoven & Troyer, 2013) is a domain specific language which allows the user to specify the game scenario in XML and to build a game using a code generator.

Serious Game Structure and Logic Modeling Language (GLiSMo) is a DSL for serious games. The meta-model includes concepts such as objects, characters, acts, or scenes. Furthermore, the language comprises actions, tasks, and assessments to represent the game's logic.

Other DSL also appeared more tailored to specific aspects of games rather than gamification. This includes the following languages:

- **Card Game Description Language (CGDL)**: focused on the simulation and derivation of novel card games.
- **Strategy Game Description Language (SGDL)**: more specific for the description of emergent strategy games.
- **Video Game Description Language (VGDL)**: used to describe and generate simple video games.

A new language appeared recently to fill the gap of modelling gamification in education called Gamified Education Interoperability Language (GEdIL) (Swacha et. al., 2020). Despite initially designed to fulfil specific requirements of gamification applied in programming courses. These requirements identify a vast collection of rewarding mechanisms such as points, badges, virtual items, and social status (e.g., through leaderboards), to provide extrinsic motivation, but can also affect the educational content directly through unlockable and secret content, different activity modes (e.g., speedup and duels), among others. Nonetheless, GEdIL completely separates the gamification layer from the activities being gamified, which makes it sufficiently generic to be applied to any other educational domains.

Recently several new tools were developed or adapted to help game designers to model, build and analyses games. Unified Modelling Language (UML) is a de-facto standard modelling language used in multiple domains and can be also used to build games. The advantage of UML is that it is well known in the software engineering community. SysML is a general-purpose modeling language for systems engineering applications. That supports specification, analysis, design, and verification of a broad range of systems. SysML has been used for building a training game (Hetherinton, 2014).

Another line of research is the development of modeling languages for formal visual representation of game-based rule systems (Swacha, 2018). In this realm, Machinations and UAREI (Ašeriškis et. al., 2017) are the most popular choices. The models defined in such languages are primarily intended to support the design phase of gamification development. Figure 4 shows a machinations diagram of a Monopoly action scenario.

Figure 4. A Machinations diagram of Monopoly

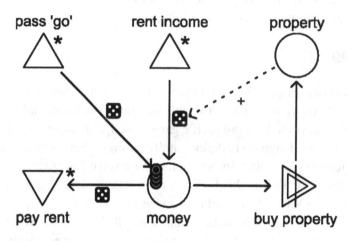

CONCLUSION

In this paper, we present a systematic study on the gamification standardization contributions based on a well-known client-server software architecture pattern called three-tier architecture. For each layer, we shared the most valuable or promising contributions to cover a great part of all gamification design ecosystem.

In the presentation tier, several platforms were depicted that use gamification to empower motivation organized in two flavors: educational and enterprise. In the logic tier, the focus was on services well established in cloud containers known as Game Backend as a Service. Finally, in the data layer, the most popular domain specific languages and modeling approaches were shared.

The paper's contribution is to serve as a synthesis for the contributions that have been shared in the last decade regarding the regulation/formalization of design/implementation strategies in the ecosystem of a gamified application.

Based on this systematic study one can conclude that the gamification ecosystem earns, in this last decade, some contributions trying to fill the huge gap of formalization/regulation in the design of such systems. In this context, several (conceptual) frameworks appeared to give a more formal control to the gamification design strategies. Nevertheless, the efforts are still few requiring more technical contributions and concrete frameworks to shape the future of gamified apps.

REFERENCES

Amini, P., Zahiri Motlagh, S. A., & Nezhadpour, M. (2018). A large-scale infrastructure for serious games services. *2018 2nd National and 1st International Digital Games Research Conference: Trends, Technologies, and Applications (DGRC)*, 27-33. 10.1109/DGRC.2018.8712040

Ašeriškis, D., Blazauskas, T., & Damasevicius, R. (2017). UAREI: A model for formal description and visual representation/software gamification. *DYNA (Colombia)*, 84(200), 326–334. doi:10.15446/dyna.v84n200.54017

Broeckhoven, F., & Troyer, O. (2013). ATTAC-L: A modeling language for educational virtual scenarios in the context of preventing cyber bullying. *2013 IEEE 2nd International Conference on Serious Games and Applications for Health (SeGAH)*, 1-8. 10.1109/SeGAH.2013.6665300

Chou, Y. (2015). *Actionable gamification - beyond points, badges, and leaderboards. Technical report.* Octalysis Media.

Crawford, C. (1984). *The Art of Computer Game Design.* McGraw-Hill, Inc.

Hamari, J., Koivisto, J., & Sarsa, H. (2014). Does gamification work? A literature review of empirical studies on gamification. *2014 47th Hawaii International Conference on System Sciences*, 3025-3034.

Herzig, P., Jugel, K., Momm, C., Ameling, M., & Schill, A. (2013). Gaml - A modeling language for gamification. *2013 IEEE/ACM 6th International Conference on Utility and Cloud Computing*, 494-499.

Hetherinton, D. (2014). Sysml requirements for training game design. *17th International IEEE Conference on Intelligent Transportation Systems (ITSC)*, 162-167.

Hunicke, R., Leblanc, M., & Zubek, R. (2004). Mda: A formal approach to game design and game research. *AAAI Workshop - Technical Report, 1.*

Intelligence, M. (2020). *Gaming Market - Growth, Trends, Forecasts (2020 - 2025).* https://www.researchandmarkets.com/reports/4845961/gaming-market-growth-trends-forecasts-2020

Janssens, O., Samyny, K., Van de Walle, R., & Van Hoecke, S. (2014). Educational virtual game scenario generation for serious games. *2014 IEEE 3rd International Conference on Serious Games and Applications for Health (SeGAH)*, 1-8. 10.1109/SeGAH.2014.7067106

Julius, K., & Salo, J. (2013). *Designing gamification. Technical report.* Marketing.

Marczewski, A. (2015). User Types. In Even Ninja Monkeys Like to Play: Gamification, Game Thinking and Motivational Design (pp. 65-80). CreateSpace Independent Publishing Platform.

Mora, A., Riera, D., Gonzalez, C., & Arnedo-Moreno, J. (2015). A literature review of gamification design frameworks. *2015 7th International Conference on Games and Virtual Worlds for Serious Applications (VS-Games)*, 1-8. 10.1109/VS-GAMES.2015.7295760

Nah, F., Eschenbrenner, B., Claybaugh, C., & Koob, P. (2019). Gamification of Enterprise Systems. *Systems.*, *7*(1), 13. doi:10.3390ystems7010013

Paiva, Haraszczuk, Queiros, Leal, Swacha, & Kosta. (2021). *FGPE Gamification Service: A GraphQL Service to Gamify Online Education.* . doi:10.1007/978-3-030-72654-6_46

Paiva, J. C., Leal, J. P., & Queirós, R. (2015). Odin: A service for gamification of learning activities. In *Languages, Applications and Technologies - 4th International Symposium, SLATE 2015.* Springer. 10.1007/978-3-319-27653-3_19

Paiva, J. C., Leal, J. P., & Queirós, R. A. P. (2016). Enki: A pedagogical services aggregator for learning programming languages. In *Proceedings of the 2016 ACM Conference on Innovation and Technology in Computer Science Education, ITiCSE 2016.* ACM. 10.1145/2899415.2899441

Queirós, R. (2017). A Survey on Game Backend Services. In R. Alexandre Peixoto de Queirós & M. Pinto (Eds.), *Gamification-Based E-Learning Strategies for Computer Programming Education* (pp. 1–13). IGI Global. doi:10.4018/978-1-5225-1034-5.ch001

Queirós, R. A. P. (2017). A survey on game backend services. In Gamification- Based E-Learning Strategies for Computer Programming Education. IGI Global.

Raftopoulos, M. (2014). Towards gamification transparency: A conceptual framework for the development of responsible gamified enterprise systems. *Journal of Gaming and Virtual Worlds.*, *6*(2), 159–178. doi:10.1386/jgvw.6.2.159_1

Robson, K., Plangger, K., Kietzmann, J., McCarthy, I., & Pitt, L. (2015). Is it all a game? Understanding the principles of gamification. *Business Horizons*, *58*(4), 411–420. Advance online publication. doi:10.1016/j.bushor.2015.03.006

Ruhi, U. (2015). Level Up Your Strategy: Towards a Descriptive Framework for Meaningful Enterprise Gamification. *Technology Innovation Management Review*, *5*(8), 5–16. doi:10.22215/timreview/918

Seaborn, K., & Fels, D. I. (2015). Gami_cation in theory and action: A survey. *International Journal of Human-Computer Studies*, *74*, 14–31. doi:10.1016/j.ijhcs.2014.09.006

Swacha, J. (2018). Representation of events and rules in gamification systems. *Procedia Computer Science*, *126*, 2040–2049. doi:10.1016/j.procs.2018.07.248

Swacha, J., Paiva, J. C., Leal, J. P., Queirós, R., Montella, R., & Kosta, S. (2020). GEdIL—Gamified Education Interoperability Language. *Information, 11*(6), 287. doi:10.3390/info11060287

Swacha, J., Queirós, R., Paiva, J. C., Leal, J. P., Kosta, S., & Montella, R. (2020b). A roadmap to gamify programming education. In *First International Computer Programming Education Conference, ICPEC 2020*. Schloss Dagstuhl - Leibniz-Zentrum fur Informatik.

KEY TERMS AND DEFINITIONS

Application Programming Interface: Is an interface that defines interactions between multiple software applications or mixed hardware-software intermediaries.

Backend as a Service: Is a platform that automates backend side development and takes care of the cloud infrastructure.

Domain-Specific Language: Is a computer language specialized to a particular application domain. This contrasts with a general-purpose language (GPL), which is broadly applicable across domains.

Gamification: Application of game-design elements and game principles in non-game contexts.

Interoperability: Is a characteristic of a product or system, whose interfaces are completely understood, to work with other products or systems, in either implementation or access, without any restrictions.

Learning Standards: Are elements of declarative, procedural, schematic, and strategic knowledge that, as a body, define the specific content of an educational program.

Modeling Language: Is any language which can be used to express information or knowledge or systems in a structure that is defined by a consistent set of rules used for interpretation of the meaning of components in the structure.

ENDNOTES

[1]   Link: https://mambo.io/
[2]   Link: https://gametize.com/index
[3]   Link: https://www.gamelayer.co/
[4]   Link: https://spinify.com/
[5]   Link: https://pt.coursera.org
[6]   Link: https://www.udacity.com
[7]   Link: https://www.edx.org/
[8]   Link: https://www.codecademy.com/
[9]   Link: https://pt-pt.khanacademy.org/
[10] Link: https://www.freecodecamp.org/

Chapter 2
An Overview of the Use of Gamification on Enterprises to Motivate Human Resources

Igor Fernandes
University of Minho, Portugal

Pedro Branco
University of Minho, Portugal

Carlos Filipe Portela
iD https://orcid.org/0000-0003-2181-6837
University of Minho, Portugal

ABSTRACT

Organizations are concerned about how they can increase the motivation and engagement of their employees. Gamification arises in this context as an opportunity to address this issue. Thus, gamification has attracted greater attention from companies. The idea of using game elements to solve problems in their processes is starting to be seen as a solution. This study aims to analyse the gamification concept and its benefits and explain how it can be applied in human resources management. This mechanism can help companies to solve employee motivation and engagement problems in different areas of human resources. This chapter analysed eight studies in the areas of recruitment, training, team building, and administrative processes. So a SWOT analysis able to help understand the different models of gamification applied in human resources, its objectives, and its ability to create advantages for companies and their employees was constructed.

DOI: 10.4018/978-1-7998-8089-9.ch002

INTRODUCTION

The term gamification may be new to some, but the idea of using game mechanics and thinking to solve problems and engage audiences is not exactly new (Zichermann & Cunningham, 2011). To date, the term remains without a standard meaning, as different authors ascribe different meanings and typical applications, some of which are contradictory. At the same time, the concept faces division in its academic value, underdeveloped theoretical foundations and a paucity of standard application guidelines (Seaborn & Fels, 2015).

Starting from the idea that Gamification can be a valuable concept when applied within organisations and companies in various areas, this article intends to give an overview of Gamification and show its application in Human Resources (HR). The goal is to describe and compare some existing applications of this concept in real-world companies, understanding its focus on users, the application model and the results obtained. For that, a benchmarking analysis was performed to know how the gamification mechanisms can be implemented in human resources and how they improve employee motivation and engagement at work. This analysis compared different strategies and shows the most suitable solution.

This article has three sections besides introduction and conclusion. It begins by addressing the concepts of Gamification and Human Resources, then presenting a history of combining these two concepts through the presentation of the models in which it can be done and mentioning some practical cases.

Then, it presents the research methods used to carry out this work, moving on to the description and analysis of the practical cases identified throughout the research.

Finally, the study results and the benefits that Gamification can bring to companies, Human Resources Management, and its collaborators are analysed.

This article is part of a project referring to a survey of the current state of Gamification applied to human resources. It will be used to develop a framework and the respective web solution to support it.

BACKGROUND

This section presents the main topics of this chapter with a focus on gamification and human resources management and their relationship.

Gamification

According to the author (Almeida & Simoes, 2019), Gamification is an emerging phenomenon, which stems directly from the popularisation and popularity of games. Its intrinsic capabilities to motivate action, solve problems and enhance Learning in the most diverse fields of knowledge and life of individuals. The author (Reiners & Wood, 2015) defines Gamification as a synonym of rewards, emphasising that to induce more engagement on tasks, most gamification systems focus on leader boards, levels, points, or badges.

Seaborn & Fels (2015) said that Gamification uses game elements and mechanics in non-game contexts. Using this definition and comparing Gamification with games, it is possible to achieve that the primary goal of games is entertainment, while in Gamification, the main goal is to use game mechanisms to accomplish something other than just fun.

An example of the implementation of game mechanisms in a "non-fun" purpose is the concept of Serious Games. Games mechanisms have universal applicability and can be used in various aspects of everyday life such as training and knowledge sharing in all walks of life, like education, defence, health, etc. This kind of games main purpose is to train, investigate, or advertise (Reiners & Wood, 2015).

Figure 1. Serious Games features
according to (Goethe, 2019)

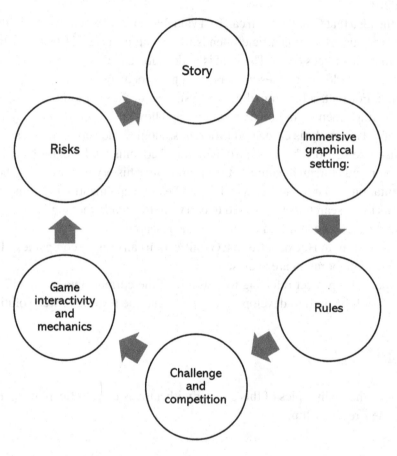

To the author of Figure 1 (Goethe, 2019), the features commonly shared by all games that engagingly reinforce the learning goal are:

- **Story**: every good game has it. It is the narrative behind the game that defines the goals that the player must achieve. In Serious Games, this feature has the accomplishment of reinforcing the company values or adding learning levels.
- **Immersive Graphical Settings**: unlike most popular games, serious games do not need to have immersive graphics. The primary focus of serious games is a learning outcome, so once the purpose is not fun, making an appealing game is more important than gameplay.

- **Rules**: like the story, rules are the feature capable of conduct the game. They deliver a learning goal subliminally. If a player breaks a rule, eventually that will incur a penalty or punishment, which eventually could transform their behaviour.
- **Challenge and Competition**: this feature is essential to motivate the player to the game. At its most accessible form, the player's key challenge is to beat the higher score (Goethe, 2019).
- **Game Interactivity and mechanics**: game mechanics are the tools that make a game functional. These provide elements of interactivity capable of keeping the players involved throughout the entire process.
- **Risks**: in most industries, there is a high risk of errors, like medical, defence, and aerospace. In these cases, serious games offer a risk-free environment where the company's collaborators can improve the necessary skills.

Despite these Gamification and Serious Games terms are distinct, they are related because both try to leverage aspects of games to achieve something beyond playfulness (Reiners & Wood, 2015).

As mentioned before, Gamification can improve motivation to complete a task or achieve an objective, so it is possible to say that Gamification tries to capture motivational power from games to promote participation, persistence, and achievements (Reiners & Wood, 2015).

In summary, the objective of Gamification is not to create a game (Goethe, 2019) but to enhance an existing system to engage users with a task, product or with the company itself.

Human Resource Management

The employees/collaborators are the core of each organisation, and the ability to manage collaborators' interaction inside the company can determine the success of a collaborative environment.

According to Fong et al. (2011), Human Resources Management (HRM) refers to the effective use of people within an organisation for stimulating them to interact, share knowledge and achieve organisational goals. To accomplish it, the HRM practices deployed by organisations are usually staffing, like HR planning (recruitment and selection), HR development (training, development and career planning and development), compensation (direct and indirect financial compensation and non-financial compensation), safety and health, and employee and labour (Fong et al., 2011).

HRM practices are vital for employee evolution. Some are considered effective in encouraging knowledge sharing behaviour, for example, training and development, performance evaluation and compensation (Cabrera and Cabrera, 2005).

In short, according to (Fong et al., 2011), five HR practices have a substantial impact on employees' knowledge-sharing behaviour:

- **Recruitment and selection**: in organisations, recruitment and selection are two activities of HRM's staffing function to ensure employees' correct quantity and quality. In this activity, the recruiter communicates the job description and specifications to potential candidates to attract applications from qualified candidates. In addition, recruiters seek to ensure a match between the candidate and the company, where the candidate's values, beliefs, and characteristics align with the organisational environment and culture.
- **Compensation and reward**: employee motivation can be enhanced through remuneration and reward. Employees are expected to repeat positive behaviour in anticipation of the rewards and

recognition given by the company. Thus, companies use compensation and rewards as tools to entice, enhance and maintain the desired knowledge-sharing behaviour of employees.

- **Performance appraisal**: Performance appraisal is defined as a formal system for reviewing and evaluating the performance of an individual or team tasks. Information collected during this activity can be used for recruitment, training and development, compensation, and internal employee relations. A performance appraisal system can positively encourage employees to perform better through greater knowledge sharing between them.

- **Teamwork**: Teamwork occurs when group members work together to fulfil a common goal. As knowledge sharing involves communicating information and ideas between employees, knowledge sharing can be encouraged by forming work teams in organisations. For knowledge sharing to occur within a company, the company's work environment must be composed of cooperative members. Therefore, a company needs to create and nurture an environment for knowledge sharing to occur.

- **Training and development**: the training process is described as a planned effort by the organisation to assist its employees in the process of learning vital skills for the individual's success at work. Development refers to formal education, improved work experiences, personality assessment and skills that help employees prepare for the future. Training is essential in the context of knowledge sharing, as employees can exchange information and ideas during formal sessions or informal interactions between two or more individuals.

Gamification In Human Resources

In Human Resources, Gamification usually arises on two different models: structural Gamification and serious games. In structural Gamification, game elements typically include emblems, points, leader boards and levels, applied to processes and activities, while serious games are those where activities are carried out in which the purpose is not entertainment but for Learning, training or simulation of activities or processes. Often Gamification is applied to the following areas in HR, as shown in figure 2 (Goethe, 2019):

Figure 2. Applications of Gamification on HR
according to (Goethe, 2019)

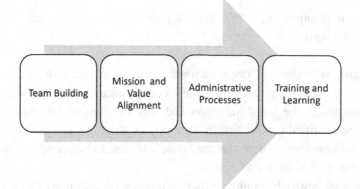

- **Team Building**: by adding collaborative and competitive team elements to activities and events, employees are encouraged to know each other.
- **Mission and Value Alignment**: reward employees with points or badges for living by the company values.
- **Administrative Processes**: specific tasks or activities can become monotonous, so the rewards resulting from the implementation of Gamification can increase efficiency.
- **Training and Learning**: making this activity more appealing encourages workers to obtain points or badges and makes it easier to identify those who are best prepared to take on some tasks or activities.

Otherwise, these are not unique in the implementation of Gamification, as explained by the author (Routledge & SpringerLink (Online service), 2016), who exemplifies the use of this concept in other areas, such as:

- **Recruitment**: this example focuses on the game "Reveal" used by L'O'real, in which candidates can experience a variety of careers available in the organisation. This game combines a behind-the-scenes journey of launching a new product with learning modules designed by experts. It allows the candidate to develop knowledge and enable recruiters to discover potential employees for a particular role in the organisation.
- **Training**: in this example, Videotel[1] used games to address health and safety training on the dangers of enclosed spaces on ships for sailors. This initiative made it possible to overcome the language barrier existing in the sector and ensure that employees understand the risk situations. This barrier is sometimes difficult to overcome because people do not tend to imagine the worst and thus stay focused on training exercises.
- **Health**: this example focuses on the "Freedom HIV / AIS"[2] initiative developed by ZMQ in India and designed to create information, awareness and behaviour change among young people on issues related to interaction sexuality, myths, and misconceptions about HIV/AIDS, combating discrimination and testing and treatment behaviours.
- **Education**: this example focuses on a game developed for the London Science Museum to promote the exhibition "Atmosphere". In this game, players must grow a plant with the resources available in the environment, thus demonstrating the delicate ecological balance of our planet.

MATERIAL AND METHODS

The development of this article includes the analysis of research articles and studies on the concepts of HR and Gamification and the implementation of gamification concepts in Human Resource activities. This research was carried out using indexing services such: Google Scholar, Repository UM, Scopus, and Web of Science (WOS). Articles, books, and dissertations were given prevalence, although some web pages were used.

Thus, the development of this study followed the "Design Science Research" as a research methodology. Given that this paper is included in a global project of developing a Prototype, this study only reflects activity 1.

Design Science Research

According to its authors (Peffers et al., 2007), the Design Science Research Process (DSRP) methodology provides fundamental principles, practices and procedures for car ring out a scientific study based on three main objectives:

- Be consistent with previous literature.
- Provide a nominal process for conducting the study.
- Provide a mental model for evaluating and interpreting study results.

Following the methodology principles, a scientific study is carried out over six stages, as explained in the following image (Figure 3).

Figure 3. DSRP Methodology
adapted from (Peffers et al., 2007)

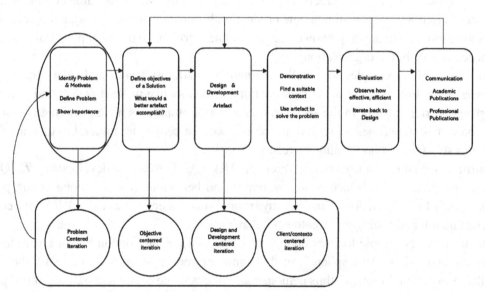

The stage that reflects this paper is Activity 1, denominated "Identification of problem and motivation". This activity seeks a specific definition of the problem under study and justification of the solution value. Since the purpose of the problem is used to create a solution, it is helpful to disaggregate the problem conceptually to capture its complexity. On the other hand, justifying the solution value makes it easier to understand and accept the results. Regarding this work, this task was performed using a benchmarking approach that allowed us to understand existing studies using Gamification and its impact on HR.

Benchmarking

Benchmarking definitions vary, but the main themes include measurement, comparison, identification of best practices, implementation and improvement (Anand & Kodali, 2008). Benchmarking is the search for the best practices applied in the industry to improve the organisation's performance. Anand & Kodali (2008) described benchmarking as "a continuous analysis of strategies, functions, processes, products or services, performances, etc. compared within or between best-in-class organisation's by obtaining information through appropriate data collection method, to assess an organisation's current standards and thereby carry out self-improvement by implementing changes to scale or exceed those standards".

Figure 4. Benchmarking Model
adapted from (Anand & Kodali, 2008)

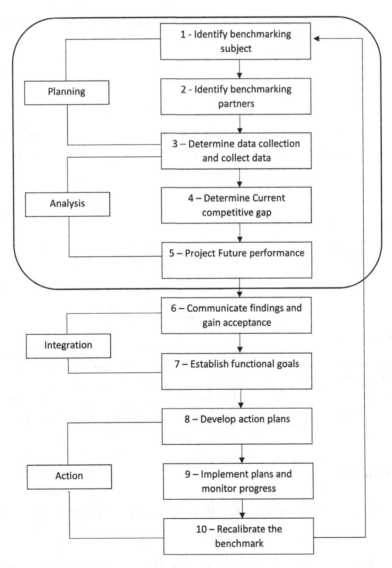

Through these definitions, it can be understood that before a company applies any strategy to improve its performance or one of its products, it must research similar strategies involved in similar organisations. As the authors claim, this data collection would allow organisations to compare different methodologies used and then choose the best among them. It not only facilitates the self-improvement process but also allows companies to match their competitors more easily.

This methodology is divided into ten steps that can be grouped into four major activities: planning, analysis, integration, and action. This study only explored activities of planning and analysis that are the basis of the development of the framework that will be the main contribution of this project.

GAMIFICATION APPLIED TO HUMAN RESOURCES

After the survey of case studies in various human resources areas, those who accomplished implementation of Gamification on HR were chosen.

Context

This study explored eight practical cases, as described in table 1. As can be observed, most of the studies are about recruitment or training, and none is associated with the Mission and Value Alignment of the organisations. For example, study one entitled Virtuoso created a model, and authors applied it to recruitment.

Table 1. Studies found in the literature review

Id	Name	Concept	Results
1	Virtuoso	Recruitment	1 Model
2	My Marriot Hotel	Recruitment	1 Model
3	Google Code Jam	Recruitment	1 Model
4	Deloitte Leadership Academy	Training	1 Model
5	HCL	Training	1 Model
6	Cisco "Social Media Training Program"	Training and Team Building	1 Model
7	Sap Community Network	Team Building	1 Model
8	Live Ops	Training and Administrative Processes	1 Model

Case Studies Analysis

For a better understanding of the studies, the following list addresses each one of the proposals and contributions

1. **Virtuoso**: the Italian-Hungarian company GRaviTalent, design a game where candidates are evaluated in such areas as the resolution of problems, the attitude in work, self-esteem, emotional stability, resistance to stress, impulsiveness, or persistence. According to (Aledo & Gómez, 2016), Virtuoso organises three areas in a total of nine dimensions.
   a. Cognitive Style:

        i.   Problem Solving is the ability to apply or select generic or ad-hoc for ill-defined challenges.

        ii.   Strategical Thinking is the ability to plan what to do to reach a goal.

        iii.   Ingenuity is the ability to think outside the box and searching new ways to solve a problem.

   b.   Work Attitude:

        i.   Perseverance is the ability to focus and try to achieve something.

        ii.   Resilience is the ability to restart repeatedly after every failure.

        iii.   Go-getter is the ability to realise a demand as faster as possible.

   c.   Work Style:

        i.   Speed is the ability to react fast and keep a high pace at work.

        ii.   Precision is the ability to fulfil tasks with minor errors.

        iii.   Efficiency is the ability to achieve a goal using the minimum resources possible.

2.   **My Marriott Hotel** by Marriott International: according to Joy & Assistant (2017), Marriott International was the first company to launch a social media game that targets employees and potential candidates. This game is played on Facebook and allow players to run their own kitchen. The game puts users in various hotel parts, such as the kitchen, reception, bedrooms, etc., setting tasks against the clock so the player can gain points to move through levels or new locations on the hotel. This game was developed from the employees' feedback, sending the message that Marriott International, as an organisation, is essentially its employees. This game aims to give the employees or future employees a better understanding of what is needed to run a hotel. It promotes the work for their organisation as a career rather than just a temporary job.

3.   **Google Code Jam**: Google Code Jam is an international programming competition introduced and run by Google (Joy & Assistant, 2017). This Competition starts in 2013 and is objective is detecting the best talents of engineering for future employment at the company. This Competition includes a set of problems, and participants may use a programming language to solve them in a limited amount of time. According to Joy & Assistant (2017), over 12,000 candidates from more than 129 nations compete in 2008 for prize money of more than $81,000. The numbers have shown that many candidates advanced to the next round. Colours format this Competition; with yellow colour, the candidate ruins the code locally and submit the results to the source; with blue, the candidate submits the code to Google, who will run the code in a distributed environment. According to Google, this is the first competition format this way in the competitive programming world.

4.   **Deloitte Leadership Academy**: "DLA" is an online program for training its own employees as well as its clients (Meister, 2013). The development team found that by embedding missions, badges, and leader boards into a user-friendly platform alongside tests, quizzes, video lectures and in-depth courses, the platform users become more engaged with the company and more likely to complete the online training programs provided. According to Mak (2013), this mechanism achieved tremendous success. Unlike more conventional projects, the company decided to implement mechanisms like a personalised leader board that reflects only the ten closest users instead of a standard table with the top 10 classifieds. The renewing of the scoring system occurred every seven days. It kept users interested and did not give reasons to give up if they fall behind in the rankings due to work travel, vacations, etc.

5.   **HCL**: according to (Aledo & Gómez, 2016), MindTickle helped an IT company building an online community where they can learn how to undertake and prepare new company members across games. To achieve that, candidates must complete tasks related to their future in the company, gain points and overcome levels. This project was a massive success since the abandon between the test

day and of incorporation decreased nine times, helping the company be more precise in its plans of training according to the needs of its employees.

6.   **Cisco** "Social Media Training Program": it seems like another training program; however, Cisco must turn it into a collaborative game. In this program, employees can gain social media skills. For example, sales account managers can learn how to use Twitter to reach their customers, and human resources representatives can learn how to use LinkedIn to get potential candidates. This program also has progression levels and sub-specialisations, but they manage to have a collaborative part. According to (Lau, 2014), this training program has personal and team challenges that smaller groups or the whole company can resolve. It is an effective way for individuals in the organisation to build their skills together.

7.   **Sap Community Network** (SCN): according to (Harbert, 2013) gamification has produced some valuable benefits on SCN. SAP has implemented Gamification by a mechanism of points, badges, and levels that users can earn by helping other users, encouraging users to participate and collaborate. That system became so popular that outsiders are using their SCN status in their profiles on LinkedIn.

8.   **LiveOps**: to reduce operating costs, this call centre company uses a work method in which its agents work directly from home, with more than 30,000 agents distributed worldwide. However, with this work model, some challenges emerged during the standardisation of processes. To overcome this problem, this company implemented a game called Nitro Bunchball LiveOps, to stimulate, train and facilitate the evolution of its employees. This game consisted of small missions, such as completing a call in the shortest time possible or increasing customer satisfaction. Through this, the company was able to assess its employees and create a system in which the highest-ranked would receive more work, thus having the opportunity to earn more money (Aledo & Gómez, 2016).

Strengths, Weaknesses, Opportunities, and Threats (SWOT) Analysis

After analysing the studies, it is possible to observe some common aspects contributing to the Gamification implementation's success or difficulty. Gamification represents an opportunity to engage Human Resources in a company and improve their results.

Strengths

As the case studies proved, it is possible to successfully implement Gamification in the recruitment and training of the company, facilitating the search for the best employees and at the same time ensuring that they have all the Learning needed to carry out their tasks.

In recruitment, it can show the candidates how the company works and experience some tasks or activities. To the candidates, this is an excellent opportunity to understand if they want that job and, if so, motivates them to finish the recruitment process. For companies, this helps to find suitable candidates for the job offer.

In training processes, Gamification allows users to learn in a more appealing and risk-free virtual environment. It will enable not only to keep the user focused on the task he is doing, but the fact that he can make mistakes and try again facilitates Learning. On the other hand, this allows organisations to perceive which employees can perform a specific task and help in the planning process.

Team building also can benefit from this concept. The application of this concept in team training processes or collaborative processes has proved to be a success.

Weaknesses

While successful in their implementation, the examples provided do not address many of the human resources areas. Furthermore, the applied models are all very similar, making it appear that this concept has few possible implementation models.

On the other hand, little published documentation about human resources constitutes an obstacle to searching for different application models.

Opportunities

The existence of few documented application models of this concept reveals itself as an opportunity to create and test new models in other areas of human resources, such as in employee performance assessment.

On the other hand, it also reveals the opportunity to theorise and study different implementations in these areas and to create new scientific documentation capable of promoting the theory of Gamification and helping to idealise new models and new applications of the concept.

Threats

The main threat to this concept is applying a model that does not contemplate the organisation and its employees. Scientific research related to the concept of Gamification as a motivator of people's motivation allows us to understand that applying a specific model in one organisation may not reveal the same results in another. Differences in values, objectives of organisations combined with cultural differences in the surrounding society lead to the application of gamification models being poorly received by people.

It is crucial to build these models based on the environment and, at the same time, prepare people for their application, ensuring that they are at the same level as to the advantages that this type of concept can have in their lives.

CONCLUSION

After the study, it was concluded that if applied correctly, Gamification can play an essential role in different processes and serve as an enhancer for the company and its employees. The examples have shown that its application in recruitment and training processes has promising results. Gamification allows companies to improve the recruitment processes, enhance the training and consequently reduce the cost of time, thus increasing the efficiency of the entire process.

Observing the Google Code Jam example, it is possible to notice that this Competition has joined over 12 000 candidates. It was a vast number of candidates, and records show that many of them advanced to the next round.

By analysing the perspective of users/employees, it is possible to see that using these game mechanics creates a more appealing training environment, which captivates the user. He can complete tasks identical to those performed during his work in a virtual environment, with the possibility of failing and trying again.

Adding to this mechanism is the competitiveness among workers through leader boards. It creates greater motivation in the user (employee) who will seek to have the best ranking and possibly receive rewards. However, as demonstrated in the example of "Deloitte Leadership Academy", the use of these ranking systems can have an adverse effect if the leader board does not match the user's needs and places. For example, people of different levels of education are in the same table, which means that users of lower levels who are further down the table will become discouraged and therefore stop using the system.

Despite the examples found and described during this article, it is necessary to understand better the gamification mechanisms as tools for evaluating the work developed and how the application in this context may or may not be beneficial to companies and employees. This paper cannot assess this issue because the studies mainly found concern recruitment and training processes.

Thus, future work will research, analyse, and compare gamification models in human resources, whose objective is to evaluate the work carried out by the employees of a company. That allows companies to reward these workers with gifts, salary increases or career promotions and at the same time ensure an environment in which workers feel motivated to give their best to achieve the goals created by these rewards. Then, a new framework will be designed, and the IOTECH environment will be used as proof of concept.

ACKNOWLEDGMENT

This work has been supported by FCT – Fundação para a Ciência e Tecnologia within the R&D Units Project Scope: UIDB/00319/2020 and supervised by IOTECH.

REFERENCES

Aledo, S. G., & Gómez, R. C. (2016). GAMIFICATION: A NEW APPROACH FOR. *Human Resource Management*, 60.

Almeida, F., & Simoes, J. (2019). The Role of Serious Games, Gamification and Industry 4.0 Tools in the Education 4.0 Paradigm. *Contemporary Educational Technology*, *10*(2), 120–136. doi:10.30935/cet.554469

Anand, G., & Kodali, R. (2008). Benchmarking the benchmarking models. *Benchmarking*, *15*(3), 257–291. doi:10.1108/14635770810876593

Fong, C., Ooi, K., Tan, B., Lee, V., & Yee-Loong Chong, A. (2011). HRM practices and knowledge sharing: An empirical study. *International Journal of Manpower*, *32*(5/6), 704–723. doi:10.1108/01437721111158288

Goethe, O. (2019). *Gamification Mindset*. Springer International Publishing. doi:10.1007/978-3-030-11078-9

Harbert, T. (2013, Setembro 18). *Case study: 3 heavyweights give Gamification a go*. Computerworld. https://www.computerworld.com/article/2485087/emerging-technology-case-study-3-heavyweights-give-gamification-a-go.html

Joy, M., & Assistant, J. (2017). An investigation into Gamification as a tool for enhancing recruitment process. *Ideal Research, 3*.

Lau, L. (2014, Fevereiro 5). How Cisco Drives Social Media Training with Gamification. *Gamification Co.* https://www.gamification.co/2014/02/05/cisco-drives-social-media-training-gamification/

Mak, H. W. (2013, Janeiro 11). Deloitte Leadership Academy Leads with the Gamification of Training. *Gamification Co.* https://www.gamification.co/2013/01/11/deloitte-leadership-academy-leads-with-the-gamification-of-training/

Meister, J. C. (2013, Janeiro 2). How Deloitte Made Learning a Game. *Harvard Business Review*. https://hbr.org/2013/01/how-deloitte-made-learning-a-g

Peffers, K., Tuunanen, T., Rothenberger, M. A., & Chatterjee, S. (2007). A Design Science Research Methodology for Information Systems Research. *Journal of Management Information Systems, 24*(3), 45–77. doi:10.2753/MIS0742-1222240302

Reiners, T., & Wood, L. C. (Eds.). (2015). *Gamification in Education and Business*. Springer International Publishing., doi:10.1007/978-3-319-10208-5

Routledge, H. (2016). *SpringerLink (Online service)*. Why Games Are Good for Business How to Leverage the Power of Serious Games, Gamification and Simulations.

Seaborn, K., & Fels, D. I. (2015). Gamification in theory and action: A survey. *International Journal of Human-Computer Studies, 74*, 14–31. doi:10.1016/j.ijhcs.2014.09.006

Zichermann, G., & Cunningham, C. (2011). *Gamification by Design*. Academic Press.

ENDNOTES

1   https://videotel.com/
2   http://www.freedomhivaids.in/

Chapter 3
Genre Differences in Soft Skills Perception and Video Game Usage in the University of Extremadura

Sergio Alloza Castillo
https://orcid.org/0000-0002-0149-1433
Gecon.es Foundation, Spain

Flavio Escribano
https://orcid.org/0000-0002-1133-1804
Gecon.es Foundation, Spain

Óscar Rodrigo González López
Universidad de Extremadura, Spain

María Buenadicha Mateos
Universidad de Extremadura, Spain

ABSTRACT

The preconceived notion concerning negative effects of video games and students' academic performance is a widely known subject. However, some investigations explore the positive impact of video games on academic performance. With a sample of 247 university students, this chapter studies the perception of both gamers and non-gamers about soft skills and their current relevance in academic and professional fields. The possible relationships linking the intensity of the usage of video games, academic performance, and the perception concerning soft skills are investigated. The results expose a generalized positive perception respecting the relation between video games and the development of soft skills, specifically to the video game genre and its relevance and influence on academic performance, as well as gender differences, where women prevail in emotional and social managements, although this influence is not elevated.

DOI: 10.4018/978-1-7998-8089-9.ch003

INTRODUCTION

For a number of years now, the scientific community has been studying how video games may affect gamers. The focus of this research has mainly been on the potential negative effects of playing video games, especially in children and adolescents. However, the results of several researches suggest that the popular thinking on the alleged harmful effects of games should be tempered by considering its positive results (Barr, 2017). For that matter, time spent on commercial video games without specific training purposes has repercussions on specific key skills that may positively affect academic and professional development.

Video games seem to offer improvements in a set of cognitive functions. Some of which seem to be generalized to real world contexts (Granic & Engel, 2013) and in professional training results are being obtained, such as the study by Kapustina & Martynova (2020) that demonstrates positive results of the application of video games in the training process, thus it may be recommended to train staff.

Through a descriptive design and cross-sectional study, the relation between the usage of video games by university students and the effects on some soft skills and on academic performance indicators is explored. Previous to the commencement of the research's body, the authors mention some details as a context and *State of the Art* of the following elements to introduce the research hypotheses.

In this chapter the authors work with four hypotheses about the perception that a number of university students (247) of Economics and Human Resources degrees have about video games through various questionnaires. The first three are about video games playing and genre and its relationship with three key soft skills (Complex Problem Solving, Leadership and Organization), the last hypothesis aims to know the perception of the same students regarding the influence (positive or negative) of video games playing and genre in their academic performance. Author's objective is to know the perception of these hypotheses in a sample that represents the general opinion of the subject among the student community.

In the first section of this article you will find a bibliographic review of the main study topics: the effect of video games, the importance of soft skills and academic performance and what is the influence of video games on them. In the second section the authors explain the methodology: study focus groups, materials used and their justification. In the third section the authors show the tables with the results and equivalences in the form of graphs and interpretation. Finally in the fourth section discussion and conclusions can be found as usual in these cases.

University Students

The previous research in relation to video games and academic performance has frequently focused on primary and secondary education; therefore, it is required to execute specific activities focused on university students due to their short-term professional projection. The university period is characterized by being a period in which young adults begin their higher education stage with the aim of obtaining an academic degree that permits ideal access to specific job positions (Martínez et al., 2016).

The results obtained in previous educational stages may —on occasions— not be extrapolated to university students since a greater standard of maturity and responsibility are assumed, as indicated in their work by Burgess et al. (2012). University students conventionally have superior self-regulation mechanisms to invest time in digital leisure than younger students; hence the negative consequences of the usage of video games associated with academic results are inferior in this circumstance, permitting to benefit from the positive effects of these devices.

The research results contribute to the game-based learning literature by revealing the value of video games to students in university and contemplating gaming as a valuable instrument, therefore, their university degree attributes could be improved (Barr, 2018).

Video Games

The most distinctive feature of video games is interaction. Players cannot passively surrender to a game story, and video games are designed for players to actively engage with their systems —in fact, these systems react to player behaviours (Granic & Engel, 2013)—. In addition, video games provide players a "safe" place where they are able to acquire culture, creating cultural identities in a virtual environment that realistically imitates life off-screen (Zielke et al., 2009). According to Barr's work (2018), the importance of enjoyment is connected to the cause of using high-quality commercial video games —products designed by experts to attract and entertain, unlike the already known *serious games* (Susi et al., 2007)—.

It is arduous to talk about the effects of video games due to the great diversity of genres that exists. Video games research should not talk about video games as a whole either. The video game is divided into such genres, which generate very different interactions with the players.. Therefore, it is relevant to distinguish between different kinds of video games. Two of the most accepted classifications in the present days are Wolf's (2001), which defines up to 42 different categories of video games, although some more have been added since 2001; and Hanna's (2016) classification, which is the classification used in the questionnaire, classifying the genres into 11 different general types: Action-adventure games, Fighting games, Shooter games, Platform games, Puzzle games, Racing games, Role playing games (RPGs), Simulation games, Sports games, Strategy Games (Turn Based + Real Time) and Survival games.

Video Games Effects

In the literature, the effects of playing video games are framed in basic dimensions including cognitive, motivational, emotional and social effects (Granic & Engels, 2013) or cognitive, social and behavioural effects (Ray & Jat, 2010). A small review of some of the research is presented below; classified by effects as a small *State of the Art* in order to display the variety of investigations regarding the usage of the most used digital instrument in recent years.

Negative Effects

The large majority of the Investigations on the effects of video games have been approached from a negative perspective, especially investigations centred on the consequences of excessive usage and harm related to violence, addiction and depression (King et al., 2013; Prochnow et al., 2020; Granic & Engels, 2013; Anderson et al., 2010; Ferguson 2007; Onyemaka et al., 2017), although, also in effects on problems of attention in the youth (Gentile et al., 2012; Bioulac et al., 2008), hyperactivity (Bioulac et al., 2008), sedentary lifestyle (Chacón et al., 2015; Castro et al., 2015), reduced social skills (Anderson et al., 2010; Dickerman et al., 2008; Tejeiro et al., 2009), deficient academic self-concept in students (Chacón et al., 2017; Castro-Sánchez et al., 2019) or deteriorated academic performance (Jackson et al., 2011; Rehbein et al., 2010 ; Schmitt and Livingston, 2015; Chiu et al., 2004; Puerta and Carbonell, 2013; Jackson et al., 2011; Martín et al., 2015; An and, 2007; Chacón et al., 2017; Franco, 2013; Onyemaka et al., 2017).

Nevertheless, it is noticeable that many of these investigations precisely conclude that there are no solid links between the habitual usage of video games and certain negative variables including violence or violent behaviours (amongst others, Kerr et al., 2020; Copenhagen, 2020; Ferguson & Wang, 2019; Abegaz et al., 2019; Kühn et al., 2019), considering the absence of significant data and the theoretical difficulty of defining these variables and hence their study, which leads the authors to centre the current research to relate the usage of video games with direct indicators already defined of academic performance.

Positive Effects

On the other side, much of the recent research has focused on how video games are able to impact and benefit certain aspects of the human psyche, also offering positive effects derived from playing video games that are crucial to assess this phenomenon in a balanced and truthful way, and to be able to explore the different possibilities offered considering video games beyond an entertainment instrument.

Following the mentioned categorization of effects by Granic & Engels (2013) and as a summary in order to not to extend the introduction much further, the usage of video games has —amongst others— the following positive effects: cognitive effects (Martín et al., 2015; Pérez et al., 2011; Camacho & Camilo, 2019; Trick et al., 2005; Boot et al., 2008; Trick et al., 2005; Pérez et al., 2011; Shliakhovchuk & Muñoz, 2020; Green & Bavelier, 2012; Adachi & Willoughby, 2013), motivational effects (Kapustina & Martynova, 2020; Pasch et al., 2009; Biddiss & Irwin, 2010; Klimmt & Hartmann, 2006), emotional effects (Pallavicini et al., 2018; Villani et al., 2018; Camacho & Camilo, 2019; Granic et al., 2014) and social effects (Fuster et al., 2014; Camacho & Camilo, 2019; Prochnow et al., 2020). Finally, as it will be presented below, a positive influence on the development of certain soft skills may also be observed.

Soft Skills

It is relevant to know the effects of playing video games on several competences; on the one hand, due to the interest of this article in improving specific soft skills that lead to academic performance at university, and on the other hand, due to the importance of these competences in other real and close areas, i.g., professional environments. Besides, they could even be applied and deployed in diverse contexts, i.g., workplace or training environment (Barr, 2018). Therefore, the development of certain soft skills may have a notable relevance for a proper performance in various academic and professional fields.

In this context, the competences able to be developed using video games according to the current evidence, are —amongst others— spatial skills (Uttal et al., 2013; Green & Bavelier, 2007; Jackson et al., 2011; Milani et al ., 2019), problem solving (Ventura et al., 2012; Gee, 2005; Adachi & Willoughby, 2013), communication (Barr, 2017; Barr, 2018), creativity (Hall et al., 2019 ; Jackson et al., 2012), recognition of opportunities (Scott et al., 2020), attention (Boot et al., 2008; Barr, 2017; Barr, 2018), social skills (Chamarro et al., 2014) and adaptability (Barr, 2017; Barr, 2018).

Taking the skills of the Spanish Degree in Business Administration and Management curriculum as a reference in the training of university students and being shown the great influence of the video game on similar skills, the following soft skills have been selected for the study:

- Complex Problem Solving.
- Leadership.
- Organization Skills.

These soft skills are becoming more relevant —amongst others— considering the compulsion for adaptation to a VUCA environment (Wolf, 2007) and for profile differentiation in a work context. Increasingly, students have access to a higher academic formation, thus the differentiation that was previously obtained through official academic qualification is in present days not enough to add value to future professional profiles. At this juncture, soft skills emerge as a fundamental factor, bringing that differentiation, added value and specification to the applicant for jobs or to his performance as an entrepreneur.

In relation to the usage of video games, there are several investigations that positively relate this entertainment instrument with the improvement of soft skills, as mentioned above. The study by Buelow et al., (2015) is emphasised, where it is concluded that playing video games —specifically action video games— may have a positive impact on the players' executive functions, including decision making, problem solving and risk taking. Besides, a specific relationship between the usage of video games and the improvement of leadership skills (Lisk, 2012; Hettrick, 2012) and organization skills linked to problem solving (Ventura et al., 2012) has been discovered.

Academic Performance

Academic performance is a subject of great relevance concerning university students; therefore, the influence of video games on players' academic performance is deliberated. The evidence on this subject is vulnerable and contradictory, since some investigations have found a negative relationship between the usage of video games and academic results in students (Jackson et al., 2011; Rehbein et al., 2010; Schmitt and Livingston, 2015; Chiu et al., 2004; Puerta and Carbonell, 2013; Jackson et al., 2011; Martín et al., 2015; Anand, 2007; Chacón et al., 2017; Franco, 2013; Onyemaka et al., 2017; Weis and Cerankosky, 2010). However, other academic researches have not discovered any relation between video games and academic results (Ferguson, 2011; Restrepo et al., 2019; Sanchez et al., 2020; Drummond & Sauer, 2014). Others manifest this relationship as positive (Skoric et al., 2009; Adachi & Willoughby, 2013; Pérez et al., 2011). Therefore, the effects of playing video games in academic performance require more extensive studies to conclude on solid criteria and indicators. The emerging evidence on this subject is mixed (Drummond & Sauer, 2020); despite that matter, the extensive idea that video games may negatively affect students' academic performance has received widespread media attention and it is indispensable to consider that the research to date suggests that the efficiency of video games as learning instruments largely depends on the instructional design in which they pertain(de Aldama & Pozo, 2020).

In addition, several works detail these connections between video games and academic performance, providing results that may be of great interest to adequately understand that relationship and especially to be considered in future research. Thus, Rodríguez and Sandoval (2011) exhibit that the university students who made an average distribution between the hours of video games and the time dedicated to university activities obtained higher academic performance than those who made an irregular distribution of time; justifying that a rational distribution or organization permits the benefit of the positive effects of video games without reducing the required time for academic activities.

Hypothesis

Once exposed the information related to both context of the soft skills and the diverse effects of the usage of video games along with the various indicators of academic performance, the following hypotheses are proposed:

Hypothesis One: Is there a positive relationship between the intensity of playing video games, the genres of video games played and the level of "Complex Problem Solving" soft skill development in players?

Hypothesis Two: Is there a positive relationship between the intensity of playing video games, the genres of video games played and the level of "Leadership" soft skill development in players?

Hypothesis Three: Is there a positive relationship between the intensity of playing video games, the genres of video games played and the level of "Organization" soft skill development in players?

Hypothesis Four: Is there a positive relationship between the intensity of playing video games and academic performance and the perception of how playing affects that mentioned performance development in players?

SOFT SKILLS PERCEPTION AND VIDEO GAME USE

Participants

The sample consists of 247 students who study the 2nd and the 3rd year of the degree "Business Administration and Management" in the University of Extremadura (Spain) during the 2019/2020 academic year, aged between 19 and 41 years. Specifically, most of the participants (66%) are between 20 and 25 years old; the 25.1% of them are under 20 years old; and the rest of the participants (8.9%), between 26 and 41 years old. Regarding gender, 57.9% identified with the female gender and the remaining 41.7%, with the male gender. Hence it is a young and distributed sample in terms of gender with a slight feminine predominance. This population of students was not selected for having specific characteristics but, precisely, for constituting a representative sample of the type of student body that the researchers can find in any faculty of a campus.

University access score was one of the academic performance variables that were questioned, which distribution is similar, presenting very similar percentages at all levels (17.4% passed with a score between 5 and 6; 39.7%, notable, with a score over 6 to 8; 17.4%, outstanding, with a score over 8 to 10; and 25.5%, extraordinary, more than 10). However, the percentages decrease when questioning the current average score in the university studies (53.4% passed, 43.7% notable and 2.8% outstanding). This data is also related to the average percentage of subjects that students have passed at first (4.9% between 0% and 25%; 19.4% between 26% and 50%; 26.3% between 51% and a 75%; and 51.4% more than 75%). Finally, the class attendance data is also presented, being more than 75% in the 80.2% of the sample.

Materials

For data collection, a self-administered questionnaire ad hoc designed on "Google Forms" was set. Both the academic authorities of the centre and the students gave their consent to the procedure and the materials. In the questionnaire, the exploratory objectives of the study are explained along with the voluntary, confidential and anonymous nature of the responses. Besides, students who participated were awarded with an extra-credit score of 0.1 in the final subject score for their collaboration in the study.

On the one hand, in addition to identifying gender to explore possible differences in a cross-sectional manner, the authors wanted to explore the academic performance/attendance of the participants as well as their self-concept, for which a series of items were generated around these concepts. Specifically,

3 items were added referring to academic performance (questioning about the university access score, the average score of current subjects and the success rate on the first try); and a questionnaire related to self-concept: a reduced version of the Self-Concept Test was applied (García & Musitu, 1999; Mella & Bravo, 2011).

On the other hand, the authors desired to discover the perception of video games, the played genres and its relationship with soft skills training, as well as questioning about soft skills. Within the item list related to video games, in addition to general questions relating the usage of them and specific questions to the digital distribution platform Steam, the CERV questionnaire was added. The CERV (Video Game Experiences Questionnaire) is a non-mass video game version of the CERI and CERM questionnaires (Beranuy et al., 2009; Chamarro et al., 2014). Regarding the questions about soft skills, a series of items were generated questioning the knowledge and importance of soft skills and their relationship with video games as a training instrument.

For the measurement of the selected soft skills, certain standard tests previously validated by the scientific community have been used:

- To measure Complex Problem Solving, the questionnaire by Darden et al. (1996): Life-skills development scale.
- Regarding the measurement of Leadership, the "Leadership" subscale of the Kostick test (Kostick, 1977).
- Finally, in terms of Organization Skills, the same Kostick test but using the "Organized" subscale.

Procedure

After designing the online questionnaire, incorporating all the scales and tests mentioned, the professors from the University of Extremadura involved in the project implemented the questionnaires in different classes groups from November 2019 to February 2020, providing the students with the questionnaire link, as well as a QR code access.

Once the questionnaire was applied, the data was statistically processed with the SPSS v.24 program to achieve the objectives and proposed hypotheses. On the one hand, a Pearson bivariate correlation analysis was performed to discover the relation between the variables and, on the other hand, a "t-test" for independent samples, being the gender the grouping variable, in order to explore its influence on the indicators of this research, even if it was not a previously defined hypothesis.

RESULTS

Prior to displaying the results of the statistical analysis, the most relevant descriptive statistics are presented (Table 1) as the basis for the context of the subsequent analysis and interpretation. In relation to the university entrance mark (GEN03), 39.7% obtained a notable and 25.5% more than a 10 in their access mark. Regarding academic performance, just over half (53.4%) have a passing grade (GEN06), almost half (51.4%) have passed more than 75% of the subjects they have taken (GEN05), with high class attendance (GEN06), higher than 75%, of the vast majority of respondents (80.2%). Furthermore, more than half of the participants (58.7%) play (VG03) less than 7 hours a week and only 6.5% more than two hours a day. Furthermore, the majority of gamers (53.9%) do not think that video games negatively affect their academic performance (CERV11). On the other hand, almost half (49.8%) value positively or very positively that, apart from fun, a video game allows you to

Table 1. Descriptive statistics

	N	Minimum	Maximum	Average	Standard D.
Gen03. Access score	247	1	4	2,51	1,055
Gen04. The average score of the degree	247	1	3	1,49	,555
Gen05. Success rate	247	1	4	3,22	,926
Gen06. Attendance	247	1	4	3,70	,698
VG03. How many hours do you play per week?	247	0	4	,73	1,014
CERV11. Do you think that your academic performance has been negatively affected by the usage of video games?	102	1	4	1,67	,848
SS07. When buying a video game, rate from 0 to 5 the importance of —apart from fun— allowing you to acquire or develop certain Soft Skills.	247	0	5	3,35	1,112
Complex Problem Solving	247	1	5	3,57	,676
Leadership	247	1	3	1,80	,523
Organization	247	1	3	1,91	,575

Firstly, various of the most relevant bivariate correlations (Table 2) between the academic performance indicators (Gen03. Access score, Gen04. The average score of the degree, Gen05. Success rate, Gen06. Attendance), the level of self-reported soft skills (CPS as Complex Problem Solving, Leadership and Organization Skills) and the frequency of video game usage (VG03. How many hours do you play per week?) together with the variable "CERV11. Do you believe that your academic performance has been negatively affected by the usage of video games?", are presented.

Table 2. Pearson correlations between indicators of academic performance, frequency of video game usage and level of self-reported soft skills.

	Gen03	Gen04	Gen05	Gen06	VG03	CERV11	CPS	Leadership	Organization
Gen03	1	,255**	,404**	0,076	-0,091	-,204*	0,026	,125*	0,025
Gen04	,255**	1	,481**	0,079	-0,028	-,284**	,139*	,171**	0,043
Gen05	,404**	,481**	1	,261**	-0,035	-0,186	0,106	0,075	,127*
Gen06	0,076	0,079	,261**	1	0,04	-0,125	0,005	0,004	,159*
VG03	-0,091	-0,028	-0,035	0,04	1	,389**	-0,003	-0,01	-0,082
CERV11	-,204*	-,284**	-0,186	-0,125	,389**	1	-,242*	0	-0,122
CPS	0,026	,139*	0,106	0,005	-0,003	-,242*	1	0,025	-0,073
Leadership	,125*	,171**	0,075	0,004	-0,01	0	0,025	1	-0,124
Organization	0,025	0,043	,127*	,159*	-0,082	-0,122	-0,073	-0,124	1

*The correlation is significant at the 0,05 level (bilateral).
**The correlation is significant at the 0,01 level (bilateral).

Table 3. Test of independent samples (t) for gender.

		Average	SD	t	Sig. (bilateral)	Potency
Gen03. Access score (*)	Male	2,33	0,994	-2,348	0,021	0,153
	Female	2,64	1,084			
Gen16. I work extensively in class. (**)	Male	3,41	0,868	-2,614	0,01	0,165
	Female	3,71	0,895			
VG03. How many hours do you play per week? (*)	Male	1,28	1,088	7,638	0	0,508
	Female	0,34	0,741			
CERV03. How frequently do you abandon your activities to spend more time playing video games? (**)	Male	1,99	0,617	3,117	0,002	0,298
	Female	1,57	0,626			
CERV06. Do you get angry or irritated when someone disturbs you while playing video games? (**)	Male	2,42	0,931	3,646	0	0,343
	Female	1,7	0,837			
CERV09. Have you been criticized by your friends or family for spending too much time and money on video games, or have you been told that you have a problem, even if you think it is not true? (*)	Male	1,99	0,971	3,771	0	0,403
	Female	1,33	0,711			
CERV11. Do you think that your academic performance has been negatively affected by the usage of video games? (**)	Male	1,78	0,892	2,083	0,04	0,204
	Female	1,4	0,675			
CERV13. Do you lie to your family or friends about the frequency and time you spend in video games? (*)	Male	1,35	0,715	2,917	0,004	0,282
	Female	1,07	0,254			
CERV17. Do you feel the need to invest more time in video games to feel satisfied? (*)	Male	1,32	0,577	3,072	0,003	0,294
	Female	1,07	0,254			
SS07. When buying a video game, —apart from fun— rate from 0 to 5 the importance of allowing you to acquire or develop certain Soft Skills. (**)	Male	3,05	1,097	-3,804	0	0,237
	Female	3,58	1,071			
Organization (*)	Male	1,83	0,601	-2,051	0,042	0,141
	Female	1,98	0,55			

(*) According to Levene 's test, equal variances are not assumed.
(**) According to Levene 's test, equal variances are assumed.

Secondly, the results of the Student's "t-test" in relation to the gender variable and its most significant influence on the rest of the variables explored in the survey (Table 3), considering —despite the fact that was not considered previously in the initial set of hypotheses— the results display data of interest regarding this variable. In relation to video games, there are significant differences between genders in playing time (VG03), much lower in women; in the abandonment of other activities to play (CERV03), somewhat lower in women; in the irritation before the interruption of the game. game (CERV06), quite lower in women; in criticism received by family or friends (CERV09) somewhat lower in women; in the perception that they negatively affect academic performance (CERV11), somewhat lower in women; in lying about their use (CERV13), somewhat lower in women; in the need to play more (CERV17), somewhat lower in women; and in the importance of the acquisition of soft skills (SS07), somewhat lower in men.

Figure 1. Hours per week

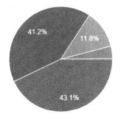

VG03. How many hours do you play per week?

102 responses

- Less than 7h (< 1h per day)
- 7h - 14h (1h-2h per day)
- 14h -21h (2h-3h per day)
- More than 21h (>3h per day)

Figure 2. Video game genres

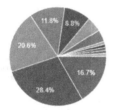

VG07. What genre of games do you usually play?

102 responses

- Sport
- Shooter
- Strategy
- Adventure
- Role Playing Games
- Adventure Game (LucasArt Kind of)
- Puzzle
- MOBA

1/2 ▼

Figure 3. Reason behind video game play

VG08. Why do you play video games?

102 responses

- Competition
- Entertainment
- Distractiont
- For social reasons, to play with friends
- I like to get achievements and trophies
- Exploration
- Personal development, usually playing games developed by Microsoft
- I feel happy when playing videogames

To conclude, various of the most relevant responses from the "Video games" section of the questionnaire (Figures 1, 2, 3) in which a total of 102 responses were obtained after filtering and presenting this section only by the participants who answered "Yes" to the question "Gen22. Do you regularly play video games?"

And the "Soft Skills" section, answered by the entire sample (n = 247), represented by Figures 4, 5, 6, 7 and 8.

Figure 4. The perception of soft skills relevance

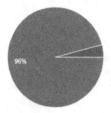

SS04. Do you think soft skills are important?

247 responses

- Yes, in fact I think it is the key when it comes to differentiating yourself from profiles similar to yours
- No, I don't think the world of work gives it importance

96%

Figure 5. The perception of training soft skills with video games

SS06. What do you think of the idea of training soft skills with video games?

247 responses

- It seems to me the best way to train skills
- It would motivate me a lot if it was about playing and also training skills
- I think there are better ways to train those skills
- I do not believe that soft skills can be trained with the use of video games
- I don't think I need to train those skills

64.8%   19.8%   11.3%

Figure 6. Soft skills relevance when buying video games

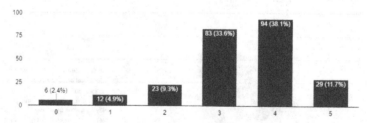

SS07. When buying a video game, value from 0 to 5 the importance that you would give it to, apart from fun, allowing you to acquire or develop certain Soft Skills.

247 responses

6 (2.4%)   12 (4.9%)   23 (9.3%)   83 (33.6%)   94 (38.1%)   29 (11.7%)

Figure 7. The relevance of training soft skills with video games

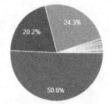

SS10. Do you think it would be useful to add the skills that playing video games trains to the curriculum?

247 responses

- Yes, I think it would better reflect how I am
- No, personally I think it does not contribute
- No, I think the market would not care about
- Yes, I would use it, but alluding to skills
- It depends on the job you want to access
- It would be useful depending on the position
- If you add activities to your resume
- Yes, even if it is not reflected where it comes from

24.3%   20.2%   50.6%

1/2 ▼

Figure 8. The relevance of training soft skills with video games at personnel selection

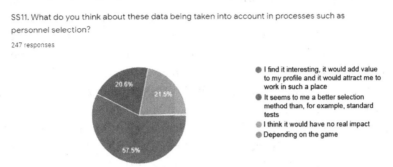

DISCUSSION

From the exposed data, the authors may declare the following items for discussionrelated to the hypotheses initially planned.

Non-significant conclusions have been found in relation to the induced differences by the intensity of playing video games and the level of self-reported soft skills (Complex Problem Solving, Leadership and Organization), hence hypothesis H1, H2 and H3 are rejected. This absence of significance may be due to a non-existent significant relation; possibly, also to the limitations of the present study itself. Specifically, the students were directly questioned if they regularly play video games (question Gen22) to explore if they were video gamers or not, nevertheless the meaning of "a regular gamer" was not specified. It is plausible that a user could not be considered a gamer because it differs from the social profile of "hardcore" gamer (dedicating a massive part of time to video gaming repeatedly, parameter —amongst others parameters— of Poels et al., 2012, classification of hardcore and casual gamers). Regarding the H4 —concerning the relationship of the intensity of video game behaviour and academic performance—, no significant conclusions have been drawn either; rejecting this last hypothesis and supporting the academic works mentioned that have not found a relationship between video games and academic performance (Ferguson, 2011; Restrepo et al., 2019; Sanchez et al., 2020; Drummond & Sauer, 2014). Besides, it is emphasised that users who play seem to perceive a negative influence on their own academic performance (r=.389, p<.01) —although this perception is not supported by the data—. It is probable that the perception is principally based on a social bias belief against video games as an element of interference in education opposed to based on an actual impact on the performance.

However, more quantitative measures involved in the survey display interesting data. Specifically, regarding how gender intervenes in the following processes or events:

Women have a higher access score (M=2.64, SE=1,084) than men (M=2.33, SE=0.994, t(244)=-2,315, p<.05, r=.153) and report that they work significantly more in class (M=3.71, SE=0.895) than men (M=3.41, SE=0.868, t(244)=-2.614, p<.05, r=.165). A greater dedication in the academic field in the female sector of the sample may be assumed, although other indicators including the average score of the degree, success rate or attendance, do not conclude that there are decisive differences in terms of gender. By all means, the low statistical power indicated also is noticeable, which explains a minuscule percentage of the total variance.

On the other hand, a prevalence of video gaming behaviour in men is perceived (M=1.28, SE=1,088), whilst in women the hours of play per week are inferior (M=0.34, SE=0.741, t(244)=8.111, p<.05, r=.50).

This fact could explain why significant differences are obtained, such as men tending to abandon their activities to spend time on video games (M=1.99, SE=0.617) substantially more than women (M=1.57, SE=0.626, t(244)=3.117, p<.05, r=.29) or getting irritated more than women (M=2.42, SE=0.931) due to be disturbed while playing (M=1.70, SE=0.837, t(244)=3.646, p<.05, r=.34). Besides, it is detected that men feel more criticized (M=1.99, SE=0.971) than women (M=1.33, SE=0.711, t(244)=3,324, p<.05, r=.40); they consider that video games have negatively affected their academic performance (M=1.78, SE=0.892) more than women's (M=1.40, SE=0.675, t(244)=2,083, p<.05, r=.20); they lie more in relation to their playing habits (M=1.35, SE=0.715) than women (M=1.07, SE=0.254, t(244)=2.089, p<.05, r=.28); and finally, they feel the need to invest more time in video games (M=1.32, SE=0.577) than women (M=1.07, SE=0.254, t(244)=2.303, p<.05, r= .29).

Nevertheless, it must be considered that these differences are present at a low level considering the range of answers to the questions. For instance, the fact that men lie more than women according to gambling behaviours, it is not decisive that lying is relevant or prevalent, considering the range of answers —from 1 to 4— to the CERV questionnaire, all statistic means shown here, except one, do not exceed score 2, which is considered medium-low. Therefore, all the mentioned variables have a slight prevalence in the global sample; indicating the limited influence of the video game element in the social and emotional life of the students and, specifically, in their academic performance (total average of 1.6 out of 4). Similarly, the low statistical power of the results is also emphasised, concerning significant but minor accentuated differences.

Gender differences are noticeable in two more variables. One of the variable, unanticipatedly, is that women rate higher (M=3.58, SE=1.71) the importance of the presence of soft skills in buying video games, compared to men (M=3.05, SE=1.097, t(244)=-3.804, p<.05, r=.23). Information that may increase in video gaming behaviour in the female gender. In point of fact, it similarly happens with the statistical tests on video gaming behaviour and the same question, concluding that non-gamers consider more relevant (M=3.53, SE=1.007) the presence of soft skills at the time of purchasing a video game than gamers (M=3.10, SE=1.206, t(244)=-3.063, p<.05). It generally seems that the presence of soft skills would increase the perceived value of video games as an entertainment instrument for both regular gamers and non-regular gamers.

The last variable related to gender, the level of "Organization" skill, was scored higher by women (M=1.98, SE=0.55) than men (M=1.83, SE=0.601, t(244)=-2.081, p<.05, r=.14). It is feasible that the levels of organization are the element that positively influences the other differences exposed, explaining that women —having better organization skills— perceive they work more extensively in class and obtain higher access scores, although the impact of this variable would be low considering the statistical power.

Previous to interpreting the statistical charts of the survey's answers, the authors will now discuss various relevant elements related to the soft skills identified in the sample based on the bivariate correlations exposed above.

In relation to the identified levels of the Complex Problem Solving, significant bivariate correlations are emphasised: with Gen04. The average score of the degree (r=.139, p<.05) and with the CERV11 question "Do you think your academic performance has been negatively affected by the usage of video games?" (r=-,242, p<.05). It is logical that users who have scored higher in Complex Problem Solving possess a high academic performance and the usage of video games does not interfere negatively.

By focusing on Leadership and Organization Skills, similar results are concluded, positively correlating Leadership with Gen03. Access score (r=.125, p<.05) and Gen04. Average grade score (r=.171, p<.01) whilst Organization correlates positively with Gen05. Success rate (r=.127, p<.05) and Gen06.

Attendance (r=.159, p<.05). Thus, high levels of soft skills —Complex Problem Solving, Leadership or Organization— would be connected to high levels of academic performance.

On another note, in order to explore all the hypotheses, video game genre data and manifested level in soft skills have been cross-analysed to specifically explore whether the prevalence of a specific gender is related to certain soft skills. As displayed in Table 4, a prevalence of high levels of Complex Problem Solving may be observed in the shooting games genre (as indicated by Green & Bavelier, 2012) and strategy genre (as indicated by Adachi & Willoughby, 2013); as well as in adventure and role-playing genres, whilst the rest of genres and soft skills seem to have a medium level relation. This small approach to the relation between game genres and the presence of soft skills offers an interesting research track that facilitates the range of possibilities for the identification and/or training of particular skills with certain video game genres.

Table 4. Relationship between video game genres and soft skills level mean (Low, Medium, High).

Video Game Genre	Average CPS	Average Leadership	Average Organization
Adventure	Medium	Medium	Medium
Graphic adventure	High	Medium	Medium
Sports	Medium	Medium	Medium
Shooter	High	Medium	Medium
Strategy	High	Medium	Medium
Puzzle	Medium	Medium	Medium
Role Playing Game	High	Medium	Medium

The ratio of people in the sample who play video games is medium-low (41.3%), consequently, it is probable that no more significant conclusions have been detected related to playtime. However, the direct answers to the questionnaire and its distribution indicate a series of factors to be considered.

In relation to the 102 users who answered the video game section, the premise of Steam being a platform known by the majority (82.4%) can be affirmed, which is logical to consider its wide reach, even worldwide. It is detected that almost the entire sub-sample dedicates less than 1-2 hours per day to video games, hence the research sample is a group of casual players or without much time to dedicate to play video games. These results are consistent with the rest of the answers where it can be observed that the playing video games behaviour in the sample tends to be social and online.

Therefore, it may be assumed that male and female players from the study manifest casual online social behaviour (based on the scarce intensity of the playtime, the low investment in video games per month, and entertainment and hanging out as the main reasons to play video games). Besides, it is a conclusion corresponding to the CERV results, where it is noticed that games are used as a distraction method and that "normal" social behaviours, relationships, quality of sleep and family's perception of the players is not affected by the usage of video games.

Now, focusing on the part of soft skills perception, a generalized knowledge about them is noticed, since 76.5% of the total sample know what they are, also indicating that the majority (81.4%) had heard about them in University. Regarding the soft skills training, there is more homogeneity in the answers distribution, hence the three answer options obtained similar relevance ("With some extracurricular course or on their own" with 43.3%, "In formal education such as schools and universities" with 31.6% and "They are not usually trained or promoted" with the remaining 25.1%). Although, regardless of where and how they learned about them or the training methods, 96% of the sample considers soft skills as relevant, emphasising the importance and influence of these skills, specifically in work environments where they are crucial to differentiate professional profiles. Possessing this data, the authors conclude that the collective awareness about soft skills is obtuse, due to the fact that they do consider them meaningful at the work level and they have heard about soft skills but consider they have not arrived at formal academic training environments. Therefore, these results could be manifesting the gap between the current need for soft skills in the labour market and the absence of academic training in this subject.

In relation to soft skills and video games, despite the fact that ambivalence was obtained regarding how to train them (due to absence of academic options), 93.5% of the total sample firmly affirmed that video games are able to train skills, even 20% of participants exemplify this skills improvement in their particular cases. A video game training usage was supported by the majority of the sample (76.1%) when soft skills training with video games is specified and, in fact, 64.8% of the participants emphasised the playful value of such possibility, in addition to the benefit of training. Finally, coincidences between soft skills and video games in purchase indicators can also be noticed, where, as mentioned, 83.4% of the group positively scored the relevance when buying a video game to the knowledge of the associated soft skills enhancement. All this data could indicate a collective awareness concerning the interest and positive impact of video games in the development of soft skills, which in turn is transforming the way they watch video games, giving more value to what was initially just an entertainment instrument, as Barr (2018) argues.

Regarding the usage of the data generated by the players during the playtime, more than half of the students (63.6%) manifest a favourable attitude to the usage of such data as long as it provides added value to the fact of playing, very according to the conclusions of the previous paragraph. Although they state that mentioned data should only be used with an express consent (according to 61.4%). Moreover, the collective consciousness mentioned above also manifests a duality in the professional curriculum value of the addition of soft skills trained by video games, with 50.6% of participants who consider that it would have value and it would reflect better what they are, whilst the remaining percentage displays —amongst other matters— that the labour market itself would not value such data, hence it would not be useful. This last reflection may be the manifestation of the digital gap between the new generations and their perceptions about the positive influence of video games and the global perception of a labour market still controlled by non-gamer generations. Furthermore, when dealing specifically with the usage of this data in selection processes, 78.1% of the participants consider they would value the process and would also be a better selection method than the usage of standard tests, which reinforces the generation gap hypothesis.

The general conclusion of the survey is, in defiance of the absence of significant correlations between video game intensity and other variables, a general positive perception of the relationship between the usage of commercial video games and the development of soft skills. The relevance of soft skills and their influence on academic performance has been observed, as well as the differences in gender, in emotional and social managements regarding the influence of video games in their lives, although this influence is considered insufficient statistically.

CONCLUSION

Data collection work has been carried out through surveys to 247 Business Administration students from the University of Extremadura in Spain to find out their perception of the relationship between the use of video games and academic performance and certain key soft skills. This study has not yielded significant data in this regard, although it has shown interesting conclusions, as they appear in the previous section.

Whilst the mentioned users could dedicate more than an hour per day playing from a mobile device generating micro-experiences throughout the day, therefore, this kind of student should be classified as a gamer (Granic & Engels, 2013). However, answering "No" to "Do you normally play video games?" probably it was excluded from the "Video games" section of the questionnaire. Nonetheless, "normally" is a perceptual measure of quantity that may vary between subjects so, together with the description of the behaviour on video gaming, it should be clarified in future implementations of the survey to work with standardized indicators on gambling behaviour (like in Ventura et al., 2012). For this reason and as a recommendation for future studies, it would be necessary to carry out a research classifying the focus group by type of users (casual, hardcore, pro-gamers) so that the sample would yield results not only in terms of playing time but also by type and by scores obtained in playing.

It is probable that the perception of the influence of video games in certain areas of the student's life was principally based on a social bias belief against video games and that supposes an element of interference in responses, especially those related to academic performance. For this reason the authors should look for ways in which it will be able to extract data on contrasted opinion about video games avoiding the deviations caused by social prejudices that are, in fact, very popular.

The perceptions by gender in the different aspects of the survey have been relatively significant, however it is true that most of the women who responded did not identify themselves as gamers, which of course generates a certain deviation, for example, in the choice of the purchase of a video game based on its relationship with soft skills.

Finally, the relationship between soft skills and video game genres should have a more specific, if not exclusive, approach in future research. Although this first approximation has offered to the authors an interesting research track, the mere manifestation of having been a player of a type of game due to its genre should be complemented with additional data such as recent playing time, recurrency and score received in those games.

REFERENCES

Abegaz, T., Smatt, C., Oakley, R., & Freeman, M. (2019). Win Or Lose: A Study On The Effects Of Video Game Violence. *QRBD, 79.*

Adachi, P. J. C., & Willoughby, T. (2013). More than just fun and games: The longitudinal relationships between strategic video games, self reported problem solving skills, and academic grades. *Journal of Youth and Adolescence, 42*(7), 1041–1052. doi:10.100710964-013-9913-9 PMID:23344653

Anand, V. (2007). A study of time management: The correlation between video game usage and academic performance markers. *Cyberpsychology & Behavior, 10*(4), 552–559. doi:10.1089/cpb.2007.9991 PMID:17711364

Anderson, C. A., Shibuya, A., Ihori, N., Swing, E. L., Bushman, B. J., Sakamoto, A., Rothstein, H. R., & Saleem, M. (2010). Violent video game effects on aggression, empathy, and prosocial behavior in Eastern and Western countries: A meta-analytic review. *Psychological Bulletin, 136*(2), 151–173. doi:10.1037/a0018251 PMID:20192553

Martín, M. D. M. B., Muntada, M. C., Busquets, C. G., Pros, R. C., & Sáez, T. D. (2015). Videojuegos, televisión y rendimiento académico en alumnos de primaria. Pixel-Bit. *Revista de Medios y Educación,* (46), 25–38.

Barr, M. (2017). Video games can develop graduate skills in higher education students: A randomised trial. *Computers & Education, 113,* 86–97. doi:10.1016/j.compedu.2017.05.016

Barr, M. (2018). Student attitudes to games-based skills development: Learning from video games in higher education. *Computers in Human Behavior, 80,* 283–294. doi:10.1016/j.chb.2017.11.030

Bartle, R. (1996). Hearts, clubs, diamonds, spades: Players who suit MUDs. *Journal of MUD Research, 1*(1), 19.

Beranuy, M., Chamarro, A., Graner, C., & Carbonell, X. (2009). Validación de dos escalas breves para evaluar la adicción a Internet y el abuso de móvil. *Psicothema, 21,* 480–485.

Biddiss, E., & Irwin, J. (2010). Active video games to promote physical activity in children and youth: A systematic review. *Archives of Pediatrics & Adolescent Medicine, 164*(7), 664–672. PMID:20603468

Bioulac, S., Arfi, L., & Bouvard, M. P. (2008). Attention deficit/hyperactivity disorder and video games: A comparative study of hyperactive and control children. *European Psychiatry, 23*(2), 134–141. doi:10.1016/j.eurpsy.2007.11.002 PMID:18206354

Boot, W. R., Kramer, A. F., Simons, D. J., Fabiani, M., & Gratton, G. (2008). The effects of video game playing on attention, memory, and executive control. *Acta Psychologica, 129*(3), 387–398. doi:10.1016/j.actpsy.2008.09.005 PMID:18929349

Buelow, M. T., Okdie, B. M., & Cooper, A. B. (2015). The influence of video games on executive functions in college students. *Computers in Human Behavior, 45,* 228–234. doi:10.1016/j.chb.2014.12.029

Camacho Vásquez, G., & Camilo Ovalle, J. (2019). The Influence of Video Games on Vocabulary Acquisition in a Group of Students from the BA in English Teaching. *GIST: Education & Learning Research Journal,* (19).

Castro, M., Martínez, A., Zurita, F., Chacón, R., Espejo, T., & Cabrera, A. (2015). Uso de videojuegos y su relación con las conductas sedentarias en una población escolar y universitaria. *Journal for Educators, Teachers and Trainers, 6*(1), 40–51.

Castro-Sánchez, M., Rojas-Jiménez, M., Zurita-Ortega, F., & Chacón-Cuberos, R. (2019). Multidimensional Self-Concept and Its Association with Problematic Use of Video Games in Spanish College Students. *Education Sciences, 9*(3), 206. doi:10.3390/educsci9030206

Chacón Cuberos, R., Ortega, F. Z., Sánchez, M. C., & Espejo, T. (2018). The association of Self-concept with Substance Abuse and Problematic Use of Video Games in University Students: A Structural Equation Model Relación entre autoconcepto, consumo de sustancias y uso problemático de videojuegos en universitarios. *Adicciones, 30*(3), 179–188. PMID:28492955

Chacón Cuberos, R., Zurita Ortega, F., Martínez Martínez, A., Castro Sánchez, M., Espejo Garcés, T., & Pinel Martínez, C. (2017). Relación entre factores académicos y consumo de videojuegos en universitarios. Un modelo de regresión. *Pixel-Bit. Revista de Medios y Educación, 50*, 109–121.

Chamarro, A., Carbonell, X., Manresa, J. M., Munoz-Miralles, R., Ortega-Gonzalez, R., Lopez-Morron, M. R., Batalla-Martinez, C., & Toran-Monserrat, P. (2014). El Cuestionario de Experiencias Relacionadas con los Videojuegos (CERV): Un instrumento para detectar el uso problemático de videojuegos en adolescentes españoles. *Adicciones, 26*(4), 303–311. doi:10.20882/adicciones.31 PMID:25578001

Chiu, S.-I., Lee, J.-Z., & Huang, D.-H. (2004). Video game addiction in children and teenagers in Taiwan. *Cyberpsychology & Behavior, 7*(5), 571–581. doi:10.1089/cpb.2004.7.571 PMID:15667052

Copenhaver, A. (2020). Violent Video Games as Scapegoat After School Shootings in the United States. In *Handbook of Research on Mass Shootings and Multiple Victim Violence* (pp. 243–266). IGI Global. doi:10.4018/978-1-7998-0113-9.ch014

Darden, C. A., Ginter, E. J., & Gazda, G. M. (1996). Life-skills development scale – adolescent form: The theoretical and therapeutic relevance of life-skills. *Journal of Mental Health Counseling, 18*, 142–163.

de Aldama, C., & Pozo, J.-I. (2020). Do you want to learn physics? please play angry birds (but with epistemic goals). *Journal of Educational Computing Research, 58*(1), 3–28. doi:10.1177/0735633118823160

Dickerman, C., Christensen, J., & Kerl-McClain, S. B. (2008). Big breasts and bad guys: Depictions of gender and race in video games. *Journal of Creativity in Mental Health, 3*(1), 20–29. doi:10.1080/15401380801995076

Drummond, A., & Sauer, J. D. (2014). Video-games do not negatively impact adolescent academic performance in science, mathematics or reading. *PloS One, 9*(4).

Ferguson, C. J. (2007). The good, the bad and the ugly: A meta-analytic review of positive and negative effects of violent video games. *The Psychiatric Quarterly, 78*(4), 309–316. doi:10.100711126-007-9056-9 PMID:17914672

Ferguson, C. J. (2011). The influence of television and video game use on attention and school problems: A multivariate analysis with other risk factors controlled. *Journal of Psychiatric Research, 45*(6), 808–813. doi:10.1016/j.jpsychires.2010.11.010 PMID:21144536

Ferguson, C. J., & Wang, J. C. K. (2019). Aggressive video games are not a risk factor for future aggression in youth: A longitudinal study. *Journal of Youth and Adolescence, 48*(8), 1439–1451. doi:10.100710964-019-01069-0 PMID:31273603

Franco, A. A. (2013). El uso de la tecnología: Determinación del tiempo que los jóvenes de entre 12 y 18 años dedican a los equipos tecnológicos. *RIED, 16*(2), 107–125.

Fuster, H., Chamarro, A., Carbonell, X., & Vallerand, R. J. (2014). Relationship between Passion and Motivation for Gaming in Massively Multiplayer Online Role-Playing Games. *Cyberpsychology, Behavior, and Social Networking, 17*(5), 292–297. doi:10.1089/cyber.2013.0349 PMID:24611801

García, F., & Musitu, G. (1999). *Autoconcepto forma 5*. Madrid: Tea.

Gee, J. P. (2005). Learning by design: Good video games as learning machines. *E-learning, 2*(1), 5–16.

Gentile, D. A., Choo, H., Liau, A., Sim, T., Li, D., Fung, D., & Khoo, A. (2011). Pathological video game use among youths: A two-year longitudinal study. *Pediatrics, 127*(2), e319–e329. doi:10.1542/peds.2010-1353 PMID:21242221

Gentile, D. A., Swing, E. L., Lim, C. G., & Khoo, A. (2012). Video game playing, attention problems, and impulsiveness: Evidence of bidirectional causality. *Psychology of Popular Media Culture, 1*(1), 62–70. doi:10.1037/a0026969

Granic, I., Lobel, A., & Engels, R. C. M. E. (2014). The benefits of playing video games. *The American Psychologist, 69*(1), 66–78. doi:10.1037/a0034857 PMID:24295515

Green, C. S., & Bavelier, D. (2007). Action-video-game experience alters the spatial resolution of vision. *Psychological Science, 18*(1), 88–94. doi:10.1111/j.1467-9280.2007.01853.x PMID:17362383

Green, C. S., & Bavelier, D. (2012). Learning, attentional control, and action video games. *Current Biology, 22*(6), 197–206. doi:10.1016/j.cub.2012.02.012 PMID:22440805

Hall, J., Stickler, U., Herodotou, C., & Iacovides, I. (2020). Player conceptualizations of creativity in digital entertainment games. *Convergence, 26*(5-6), 1226–1247. doi:10.1177/1354856519880791

Hanna, P. (2016). Java Games Programming. Queen's University.

Hettrick, J. (2012). *Online Video Games: Leadership Development for the Millennial College Student*. Johnson & Wales University.

Jackson, L. A., von Eye, A., Fitzgerald, H. E., Witt, E. A., & Zhao, Y. (2011). Internet use, videogame playing and cell phone use as predictors of children's body mass index (BMI), body weight, academic performance and social and overall self-esteem. *Computers in Human Behavior, 27*, 599–604.

Jackson, L. A., von Eye, A., Witt, E. A., Zhao, Y., & Fitzgerald, H. E. (2011). A longitudinal study of the effects of Internet use and videogame playing on academic performance and the roles of gender, race and income in these relationships. *Computers in Human Behavior, 27*(1), 228–239. doi:10.1016/j.chb.2010.08.001

Jackson, L. A., Witt, E. A., Games, A. I., Fitzgerald, H. E., von Eye, A., & Zhao, Y. (2012). Information technology use and creativity: Findings from the Children and Technology Project. *Computers in Human Behavior, 28*(2), 370–376. doi:10.1016/j.chb.2011.10.006

Kapustina, L. V., & Martynova, I. A. (2020). Training Employees in the Digital Economy with the Use of Video Games. In *Digital Transformation of the Economy: Challenges, Trends and New Opportunities* (pp. 444–454). Springer.

Kerr, C., Francis, B., Cross, K., & Guide, G. C. (2020). *Video games, violence, and common sense.* https://www.gamasutra.com/blogs/NicholasMatthews/20130402/189739/Video_games_violence_and_common_sense.php

King, D. L., Delfabbro, P. H., & Griffiths, M. D. (2013). Trajectories of problem video gaming among adult regular gamers: An 18-month longitudinal study. *Cyberpsychology & Behavior, 16*(1), 72–76. doi:10.1089/cyber.2012.0062 PMID:23098213

Klimmt, C., & Hartmann, T. (2006). Effectance, self-efficacy, and the motivation to play video games. *Playing video games: Motives, responses, and consequences*, 133-145.

Kostick, M. (1977). *Kostick's Perception and Preference Inventory.* Applied Psychology Associates.

Kühn, S., Kugler, D. T., Schmalen, K., Weichenberger, M., Witt, C., & Gallinat, J. (2019). Does playing violent video games cause aggression? A longitudinal intervention study. *Molecular Psychiatry, 24*(8), 1220–1234. doi:10.103841380-018-0031-7 PMID:29535447

Lisk, T. C., Kaplancali, U. T., & Riggio, R. E. (2012). Leadership in multiplayer online gaming environments. *Simulation & Gaming, 43*(1), 133–149. doi:10.1177/1046878110391975

Marczewski, A. (2015). *Even Ninja Monkeys like to play.* Blurb Inc.

Martínez-Martínez, A., Zurita-Ortega, F., Castro-Sánchez, M., Chacón-Cuberos, R., Hinojo-Lucena, M. A., & Espejo-Garcés, T. (2016). La elección de estudios superiores universitarios en estudiantes de último curso de bachillerato y ciclos formativos. *Revista Electrónica Educare, 20*(1), 304–321.

Mella, E. R., & Bravo, P. R. (2011). Análisis Psicométrico confirmatorio de la medida multidimensional del Test de Autoconcepto Forma 5 en Español (AF5), en estudiantes Universitarios de Chile. *Psicologia, Saúde & Doenças, 12*(1), 91–103.

Milani, L., Grumi, S., & Di Blasio, P. (2019). Positive Effects of Videogame Use on Visuospatial Competencies: The Impact of Visualization Style in Preadolescents and Adolescents. *Frontiers in Psychology*, 10. PMID:31231275

Onyemaka, S. B., Igbokwe, D. O., Adekeye, O. A., & Agbu, J. F. (2017). "I failed because I was Playing Video games": An Examination of Undergraduate Males Videogame Addiction and Academic Performance. *Covenant International Journal of Psychology, 2*(1).

Pallavicini, F., Ferrari, A., & Mantovani, F. (2018). Video games for well-being: A systematic review on the application of computer games for cognitive and emotional training in the adult population. *Frontiers in Psychology, 9*, 2127. doi:10.3389/fpsyg.2018.02127 PMID:30464753

Pasch, M., Bianchi-Berthouze, N., van Dijk, B., & Nijholt, A. (2009). Movement-based sports video games: Investigating motivation and gaming experience. *Entertainment Computing, 1*(2), 49–61. doi:10.1016/j.entcom.2009.09.004

Pérez-Fuentes, M. C., Álvarez-Bermejo, J. A., Molero, M. M., Gázquez, J. J., & López Vicente, M. A. (2015). Violencia Escolar y Rendimiento Académico (VERA): Aplicación de realidad aumentada. *European Journal of Investigation in Health, Psychology and Education, 1*(2), 71–84. doi:10.30552/ejihpe.v1i2.19

Poels, Y., Annema, J. H., Verstraete, M., Zaman, B., & De Grooff, D. (2012). Are you a gamer? A qualititive study on the parameters for categorizing casual and hardcore gamers. *Iadis International Journal*, (1), 1–16.

Prochnow, T., Patterson, M. S., & Hartnell, L. (2020). *Social support, depressive symptoms, and online gaming network communication.* Mental Health and Social Inclusion.

Puerta, D. X., & Carbonell, X. (2013). Uso problemático de Internet en una muestra de estudiantes universitarios colombianos. *Avances en Psicología Latinoamericana, 31*(3), 620–631.

Ray, M., & Jat, K. R. (2010). Effect of electronic media on children. *Indian Pediatrics, 47*(7), 561–568. doi:10.100713312-010-0128-9 PMID:20683108

Restrepo Escobar, S. M., Taborda, A., Magdaly, L., & Arboleda Sierra, W. (2019). School Performance and Video Games among Middle School Students in the Municipality of La Estrella-Antioquia (Colombia). *Review of Education, 43*(2), 122–134.

Rodríguez, H. G., & Sandoval, M. (2011). Consumo de videojuegos y juegos para computador: Influencias sobre la atención, memoria, rendimiento académico y problemas de conducta. *Suma Psicologica, 18*(2), 99–110.

Sánchez-Alcaraz Martinez, B. J., Sánchez-Díaz, A., Alfonso-Asencio, M., Courel-Ibáñez, J., & Sánchez-Pay, A. (2020). Relationship between physical activity level, use of video games and academic performance in university students. *Espiral-Cuadernos Del Profesorado, 13*(26), 64–73. doi:10.25115/ecp.v13i26.2900

Schmitt, Z. L., & Livingston, M. G. (2015). Video game addiction and college performance among males: Results from a 1 year longitudinal study. *Cyberpsychology, Behavior, and Social Networking, 18*(1), 25–29. doi:10.1089/cyber.2014.0403 PMID:25584728

Scott, S., Niemand, T., Kraus, S., & Oberreiner, R. (2020). Let the Games Begin: Finding The Nascent Entrepreneurial Mindset of Video Gamers. *Proceedings of the 53rd Hawaii International Conference on System Sciences.*

Shliakhovchuk, E., & Muñoz García, A. (2020). Intercultural Perspective on Impact of Video Games on Players: Insights from a Systematic Review of Recent Literature. *Educational Sciences: Theory and Practice, 20*(1).

Skoric, M. M., Teo, L. L. C., & Neo, R. L. (2009). Children and video games: Addiction, engagement, and scholastic achievement. *Cyberpsychology & Behavior, 12*(5), 567–572. doi:10.1089/cpb.2009.0079 PMID:19624263

Steinkuehler, C., & Duncan, S. (2008). Scientific habits of mind in virtual worlds. *Journal of Science Education and Technology, 17*(6), 530–543. doi:10.100710956-008-9120-8

Susi, T., Johannesson, M., & Backlund, P. (2007). Serious games: An overview - Taiwan. *Cyberpsychology & Behavior, 7*(5), 571–581.

Tejeiro, R., Pelegrina, M., & Gómez, J. L. (2009). Efectos psicosociales de los videojuegos. *Comunicación (Cartago), 17*(1), 235–250.

Trick, L. M., Jaspers-Fayer, F., & Sethi, N. (2005). Multiple-object tracking in children: The "Catch the Spies" task. *Cognitive Development, 20*(3), 373–387. doi:10.1016/j.cogdev.2005.05.009

Uttal, D. H., Meadow, N. G., Tipton, E., Hand, L. L., Alden, A. R., Warren, C., & Newcombe, N. S. (2013). The malleability of spatial skills: A meta-analysis of training studies. *Psychological Bulletin, 139*(2), 352–402. doi:10.1037/a0028446 PMID:22663761

Ventura, M., Shute, V., & Kim, Y. J. (2012). Video gameplay, personality and academic performance. *Computers & Education, 58*(4), 1260–1266. doi:10.1016/j.compedu.2011.11.022

Villani, D., Carissoli, C., Triberti, S., Marchetti, A., Gilli, G., & Riva, G. (2018). Video games for emotion regulation: A systematic review. *Games for Health Journal, 7*(2), 85–99. doi:10.1089/g4h.2017.0108 PMID:29424555

Weis, R., & Cerankosky, B. C. (2010). Effects of Video-Game Ownership on Young Boys' Academic and Behavioral Functioning: A Randomized, Controlled Study. *Psychological Science, 21*(4), 463–470. doi:10.1177/0956797610362670 PMID:20424084

Wolf, D. (2007). *Prepared and Resolved: The Strategic Agenda for Growth, Performance, and Change.* Dsb Pub.

Wolf, M. J. (2001). *The medium of the video game.* University of Texas Press.

Zielke, M. A., Evans, M. J., Dufour, F., Christopher, T. V., Donahue, J. K., Johnson, P., Jennings, E. B., Friedman, B. S., Ounekeo, P. L., & Flores, R. (2009). Serious games for immersive cultural training: Creating a living world. *IEEE Computer Graphics and Applications, 29*(2), 49–60. doi:10.1109/MCG.2009.30 PMID:19462634

Section 2
Learning Gamification Strategies

Chapter 4
Strategy to Implement Gamification in LMS

Elena Somova
The University of Plovdiv "Paisii Hilendarski", Bulgaria

Mariya Gachkova
The University of Plovdiv "Paisii Hilendarski", Bulgaria

ABSTRACT

The main goal of the chapter is to discuss implementation of the structural gamification in LMS. The overview of pedagogical approaches, theories, models, and systems connected to the serious games and in particular for gamification is presented. The possibilities for using the game elements and techniques in e-learning (incl. possible realization with the standard elements of a non-gamified LMS) are presented. A four-stage cyclical gamified learning model is proposed. For the four categories of learners from the Bartle's classification, the appropriate game elements are determined. Two plugins for the application of structural gamification in Moodle have been designed and developed, which integrates game elements and techniques in the process of e-learning. The first plugin changes the design of the course into a game view. The second plugin allows adding specific game elements, which do not exist in Moodle. Different experiments of structural gamification have been done and presented.

INTRODUCTION

The current generation in the education system has grown up with Internet access and early use of computers, mobile devices and gaming devices. This group of learners has a different pattern of behavior in media consumption, communication and therefore different expectations in the educational environments. Passive consumption of learning content and traditional pedagogical methods "face to face" and "distance learning" are no longer sufficient for the new generation of learners (Chang & Guetl, 2010).

The modern generation of learners is active, searching and demanding, they want fast, attractive, quality and effective training that uses the latest technologies and tools. Contemporary learning must

DOI: 10.4018/978-1-7998-8089-9.ch004

change / adapt pedagogical methods, approaches and strategies to meet the needs of these learners, as well as to use the technologies of learners.

Recently, one of the most studied pedagogical approaches is the application of games in the implementation of learning and more precisely the so-called serious games. This is no coincidence, because games are widespread in all age groups. Serious games are increasingly being integrated into school and university education and business learning.

Many scientists point to their strong motivating power. Moreover, not only the positive motivation (from success and receiving a reward), but also the negative one (from a bad result and not receiving a certain stimulus) are powerful triggers for the actions of the players.

Due to the large number of existing e-courses in the Learning Management Systems (LMS), the fastest and easiest way to apply the game methodology is by realizing the gamification of these e-courses.

The **main goal** of this chapter is to propose means (models, methods and tools) suitable for the organization of gamification of learning in LMSs for users of different types.

The study formulates and proves the following **hypothesis**: a possible approach to conducting gamified learning is the integration of modules (of the "plugin" type) to the appropriate LMS in which to create and use gamified learning e-courses.

In order to achieve the set goal of the research, the following four main tasks are planned and accomplished:

Task 1: Study of theories, models and systems related to the use of games in education and in particular its gamification;

Task 2: Creating a general model of the process for gamification of learning and methodology for developing gamified courses;

Task 3: Creating an approach for designing a system (module) to implement gamified learning in traditional LMS;

Task 4: Design, implementation and testing of software tools (module) for creating a gamified learning course, as well as for organizing and supporting gamified learning.

The second subchapter provides an overview in the following areas: serious games, in particular gamification of learning and examples of serious games in the LMSs, as well as pedagogical approaches, theories and models suitable for the gamification of learning. The possibilities for using the game elements and techniques in e-learning are presented in the third subchapter. The fourth subchapter proposes a four-stage cyclical learning model for structural gamification of learning. The implementation of structural gamification in a LMS is presented in the fifth subchapter, and the conducted gamification experiments are reflected in the sixth subchapter.

BACKGROUND

Serious Games

The use of game elements and techniques in learning aims to make complex theoretical learning more accessible. The practical activities in the games and their repetition lead to a deeper understanding of the learning content (Connolly et al., 2012).

The games used in learning are known as oxymoron *serious games*. Serious games are aimed at achieving the educational, learning and information goals (Abt, 1987). They do not belong to the category of "games" due to the fact that they are not intended for entertainment, pleasure and enjoyment (Michael & Chen, 2005).

Most serious games are simulations of real events or processes designed to reach solutions to problems. These games can also be funny, even though they are primarily aimed at learning or improving a practice. They focus mainly on learners who are not included in traditional education, although there are many examples from traditional school and university education. Serious games can be: educational games, advertising games, political games, etc. (Gachkova & Somova, 2016). According to Cruz-Chunha (2012), the first serious game is considered to be the Army Battlezone for military training from 1980.

There is currently no classification of serious games, but the following categories can be distinguished (Gachkova & Somova, 2016):

- **Gamed-based Learning** – uses video and electronic games to achieve learning goals;
- **Gamification of learning** – integrates game elements and techniques in the learning process;
- **Organizational-dynamic games** – train, reflecting the dynamics in organizations at three levels: individual behavior, group behavior and cultural dynamics;
- **Simulation games** – designed to learn different skills by playing in artificial environments that recreate both the real world and unreal plots;
- **Edutainment** – presents content designed to both educate and entertain (the term comes from the merging of the words education and entertainment).

Gamification of Learning

Gamification refers to the use of elements and techniques from games in activities outside the game context (e.g. shopping, sports or learning) to create a game-like activity (Langendah et al., 2016). In gamification, it is not a question of turning an activity into a game, nor of developing a game, but only of changing the activity by integrating specific game approaches.

Examples of gamification can be found in various areas of application such as:

- predisposition to ecological behavior and higher sustainability (Gnauk et al., 2012) – the so-called green gamification;
- loyalty card from local shop for discounts;
- the game 'Pokémon Go!' from 2016 rewarded its users with high-level Pokémon for walking long distances – as example of the gamification of physical activity and sport;
- the Volkswagen-funded initiative called Fun Theory, where the Odenplan staircase in Stockholm was equipped with piano keys that make a piano-like sound when people step on them – example of the gamification of physical activity which encourage people to use the stairs instead of the escalator;
- tourist booklet for collecting stamps when visiting historical and cultural places and according to number of stamps, participants receive different type of badges;
- planning the resources of the institution, production and logistics (Herzig et al., 2012);
- supporting innovation processes (Scheiner et al., 2012), etc.

Gamification of learning is an educational approach to motivate learners to go through the learning content by means of additional game elements and techniques in the learning environment (Kapp, 2012). The aim of the approach is to increase learners' satisfaction and engagement by capturing their interest and inspiring them to continue studying learning resources (Huang & Soman, 2013).

The gamification of learning, according to Kap (2012), is divided into two main types:

- **Structural** – learners go through the standard learning courses with included additional game elements and techniques. The content of conventional learning resources does not change, the content does not become game-like, only their structuring/organization in the learning course (e.g. awarding with badges for excellent completion of the test);
- **Content** – application of game elements and game thinking to alter the content to make it more game-like (e.g. adding story elements to a course or starting a course with a challenge instead of a list of objectives). Game techniques and abstract rules are used to change the conventional learning content.

Structural gamification is a very appropriate and useful approach because it can be integrated into already designed e-courses without changing their content, which we used in our study.

Pedagogical Approaches, Theories and Models

According to many authors, the key engine in gamification of learning is motivation. Kapp (2012) distinguishes between two types of motivation: **intrinsic (internal)** motivation derived from the learner and **extrinsic (external)** motivation driven by external factors (for example, the teacher sets a high score in fulfilling predefined learning objectives).

Games are a powerful motivating tool that is used in many learning methods and approaches. Some of them are considered (Gachkova & Somova, 2019), elements of which can be used to build a comprehensive gamification model of learning, suitable for computer implementation in an e-learning environment.

ARCS Model

John Keller (2010) presents the four-component ARCS educational model, which is an instructional design approach, with the following components: Attention, Relevance, Confidence and Satisfaction.

Attention can be acquired in two ways: by perception (by using a surprise or an unexpected event to gain interest) or by asking (by stimulating curiosity through asking challenging questions or placing difficult problems that need to be solved). Keller proposes the following methods to attract learners' attention using:

- Active participation – using game strategies, role plays or other practical methods to attract the learners' attention to participate actively;
- Experience – using visual stimuli, illustrating teaching materials with real-world examples, etc.;
- Variability – using a variety of methods to present learning materials (e.g. short lectures, videos, mini-discussion groups) while taking into account the individual differences in the students' learning styles;
- Humour – using a small amount of humour;

- Mismatch and conflict – using the "devil's advocate" approach, which presents those who contradict previous experience;
- Inquiry – asking questions and problems that learners need to solve (e.g. brainstorming activities).

It is advisable to use terminology presented with concrete examples familiar to the learners in order to achieve **relevance**. Keller's possible strategies for achieving relevance are:

- Familiarity – shows how new knowledge is related to the learners' existing knowledge;
- Goal orientation – orientation of the learner about the importance of the learning objective, describing both the importance of achieving an objective and how it will help the learner in the present and in the future;
- Conformity – compliance of the learning motivation with the learner's motivation.

Methods for achieving learner's **confidence** can include the use of:

- Learners' growth – making small steps for growth during the learning process;
- Setting goals and prerequisites – the probability of success can be assessed more accurately if there are clear requirements for the learner's performance and assessment criteria;
- Helping learners understand the probability of success – learners' motivation will decrease if they think their goals are unachievable or the cost to achieve them (effort or time) is too high;
- Meaningful opportunities for learner success – the student must be explained what is the meaning of achieving specific learning objectives;
- Learning control – make learners believe that their success is a direct result of their efforts and provide them the ability to control learning and evaluation;
- Feedback – providing feedback and opportunities to acquire successes in the course for which feedback is received.

The possible strategies outlined by Keller for achieving learners' **satisfaction** can be:

- Rewarding – obtaining awards for achievements;
- Satisfaction – giving learners feedback about their progress and ensuring improvement of results;
- Usefulness – opportunity for learners to feel the usefulness of the learning by using newly acquired knowledge in a real task or a real environment;
- Avoiding underestimation – avoiding overly easy assignments.

Malone's Theory of Learning Through Intrinsic Motivation

Thomas Malone (1981) presents a model of game motivation analysis based on the motivating power of the games, focusing mainly on the elements of entertainment. The model has three key components: fantasy, challenge and curiosity.

Malone determines **fantasy** as an environment that "induces mental images of things that are not present within the real experience of the learner". Fantasies in games mostly satisfy the emotional needs of gamers. Using fantasy in the learning environment can make it more interesting and educational, because fantasy has both emotional and cognitive benefits.

The **challenge** depends on the set goals with unspecified results, because there is no certainty that the final goal will be achieved. Various levels of difficulty, discovery of hidden information, sets of level crossing objectives or game-based challenges can be used. The learning objectives should be leaner relevant and easily attainable. According to Malone, to reinforce the challenge, it is desirable to provide feedback on learner's success in achieving the learning objectives.

Learning environments can arouse the **curiosity** of the learner if they provide an exciting environment and an optimal level of information complexity. According to Malone, curiosity is cognitive (provoked by the prospect of changing cognitive structures to a higher level, which can be achieved by making students to believe that their knowledge is incomplete or inconsistent, thus motivating them to learn more) and sensory (attracting attention by reflecting changes in light, sound or other sensory stimuli of the environment). To engage the learners' curiosity, it is suggested to use surprising and constructive feedback as well as hidden resources in the learning environment.

Motivational Active Learning (MAL)

Pirker et al. (2016) propose a **strategy game-based approach** to design Motivational Active Learning (MAL) in traditional, blended and distance learning, mainly for implementation in primary and secondary education and to increase students' interest and engagement.

Typical MAL learning material is divided into small pieces of information (theoretical units) through which learners are introduced to key concepts. They then use the acquired knowledge to solve small assignments and problems, as well as apply theoretical knowledge in discussions or research. Most of the offered assignments are group ones (in groups of 2-4 students). Learners take an individual test before and after each learning material and compare their knowledge afterwards.

Kolb's Experiential Learning Model

The Kolb's experiential learning model (A. Kolb & D. Kolb, 2005) explores one aspect of learning – the **learning style** (the way in which students most effectively perceive, process, store, and reproduce information) that is completely independent of the other components and is a relatively stable characteristic of the individual.

The model introduces the concept of "learning cycle", which distinguishes four phases of the learning process that require different skills:

- Feeling – gaining experience from personal experiences;
- Watching – based on a specific experience;
- Thinking – collecting observations and turning them into theoretical models;
- Doing – based on what has already been learned, new ideas and solutions are created, which are then tested in practice.

A. Kolb & D. Kolb (2005) distinguish four learning styles resulting from a combination of each of the two phases in the learning cycle:

- The dreamer – specific experience, observation and reflection;
- The thinker – observation, reflection and abstract thinking;

- The decision maker – abstract thinking and active experimentation;
- The performer – active experimentation and specific experience.

A Learning Model Based on Bloom's Revised Taxonomy

Gloria et al. (2014) identify Bloom's revised taxonomy model as the most popular **cognitive approach** used in serious games (including their assessment). The Bloom's revised taxonomy, based on the Bloom's taxonomy for classification of educational goals (Anderson & Krathwohl, 2001), provides a more dynamic concept for classification and distinguishes six cognitive levels of learners' knowledge. Bloom defines educational goals for different cognitive levels through certain actions (through verbs) and objects (through nouns), while the revised taxonomy uses actions – categories and subcategories (through verbs and gerunds).

Anderson and Krathwohl (2001) further develop the idea by identifying 19 specific cognitive subtasks that complement the six basic categories. According to (Gloria et al., 2014), the two pedagogical models of Kolb and Bloom complement each other and can be easily applied together.

Serious Games in Learning Management Systems

Some learning management systems have integrated concepts and approaches from serious games and especially from game-based learning and gamification. Such systems are GENIE, The Knowledge Arcade, TalentLMS, Frog, Expertus One, Moodle, Academy LMS, Axonify and Accord LMS, as some of them are described below.

The application of elements of serious games in the web-based application GENIE (Growth Engineering GENIE) by Growth Engineering is made by means of:

- Rewarding with points and badges for certain learning goals achieved;
- Ranking in leaderboards for stimulating the competitive spirit;
- Setting time goals (deadlines of tasks);
- Learning through gradually passing through levels.

To add a game functionality, the users can custom elements or use the already created templates, provided by GENIE.

Software as a Service cloud-based platform TalentLMS (TalentLMS) implements gamification through:

- Rewarding with points for performed learning actions;
- Obtaining various badges for completed tests;
- Receiving awards and certificates upon completion of a course;
- Participation in re-certification of a certain time period;
- Ranking of learners in leaderboards – they are realized in the form of charts and diagrams;
- Learning the course by levels.

The web-based system Academy LMS (Growth Engineering Academy), which is also available for Android and iOS, is designed specifically for the application of gamification in learning and is suitable for e-learning, mobile learning and blended learning. The system supports the following key elements and techniques related to gamification:

- Earning badges and points after performing certain activities;
- Learning on the base of levels,
- Monitoring by users the progress of the learning process in a course;
- Ranking of participants;
- Colorful design, including cartoons and funny pictures, which distinguishes it from other similar LMS.

The system Accord LMS (Accord LMS) has been upgraded with the following specific elements for gamification realized by Evoq Social:

- Ranking of the leaders;
- Receiving badges when reaching the necessary criteria;
- Point-based reputation system that shows the learner's progress relative to the progress of the other learners;
- Analyzes for teachers about interaction of learners with the game courses.

The system Axonify (Axonify) implements gamification as a basic learning approach, which is applied by a special methodology. In addition to game elements, such as points, awards, badges and rankings, the system also includes a number of short games integrated into the application itself. These games are interrupted by questions that are triggered by certain game actions.

Three of the most frequently downloaded Moodle modules (Moodle Plugins) that self-identify as gamification modules are: LevelUp, Ranking block and Stash. All three modules are of the block type.

Level up provides gamification of learning with the following features:

- Automatically captures and attributes experience points to students' actions;
- Block that displays current level and progress towards next level;
- Report for teachers to get an overview of their students' levels;
- Notifications to congratulate students as they level up;
- A ladder to display the rankings of the students;
- Ability to set the number of levels and the experience required to get to them;
- Images can be uploaded to customize the appearance of the levels.

The plugin Ranking block proposes the following opportunities:

- Captures Moodle events in real time and awards points for them;
- Offers a ranking of the learners with their points obtained for the completed activities;
- Displays performance graphs for group assignments.

In the third plugin Stash, learners have to find certain items placed in different Moodle activities or resources. Course authors can place such items that encourage learners to explore all learning materials.

It is also possible to collect an unlimited number of items from one place, which will encourage learners to return to certain learning parts to collect more such items.

GAME ELEMENTS, TECHNIQUES AND ACTIONS

Table 1. Using game elements in gamification of learning

Element	Description / Usage in Learning
Avatar	The avatar element represents the role of the player during the participation into the game. Avatars have different names, images and may have different skills depending on the game. The avatar presents the different roles of the learners that can be used in missions and other learning activities.
Level	The level of the game is a section or part of the game. Most games are so large that they are divided into levels, so only one part of the game needs to be loaded at a time. To advance to a higher level, the player usually has to achieve specific goals or perform a specific task. The levels represent the sequence of execution. The different levels of the learning process can be considered as game levels.
Bonus	The results in the games are reported by an abstract quantity (most often through acquired bonuses) related to a player or team. Bonuses are expected gains from different types of abstract units (points, virtual objects or resources). Bonuses are usually collected in the game and their amount is an indicator of a successful game play. The events in the game, related to the activities, can increase or decrease the results of the participants. Bonuses represent the receipt of the expected remuneration for completed learning activities.
Badge	Badges are a reward given for particular success that sets a participant apart from others. There are clearly defined criteria for receiving a badge. Badges are usually digital images that symbolize the success achieved. Badges are a distinctive mark of achievement in various learning activities.
Combo	A combo (combination) is a set of actions performed sequentially, usually with strict time constraints, that give a significant benefit or advantage. It is usually given to the player as a kind of reward for the achieved goal. Combos are used to show an aggressive style of play. The combo is a prize that gives an advantage over the other learners. It can be realized by means of additional hints or learning materials, contributing to the solution of a certain task for a shorter period of time, etc.
Reward	The reward is an unexpected prize (under certain conditions) from various stimuli in the game (such as points, rising the levels, receiving special objects, etc.), which inspire, involve and motivate the player. Rewards are received unexpectedly for certain learning successes and can be resources with interesting facts, certificates, virtual objects or other types of virtual prizes.
Leaderboard	Players can be ranked relative to other players based on achievements (e.g. points earned, levels reached, progress, time used, etc.). Leaderboards can provide an incentive for players to improve as they give a sense of superiority or achievement. This element provokes competition between players (Antin & Churchill, 2011). The leaderboard shows the learners ranked by current success, and sometimes the ranking shows only the first by success, for example the first ten.
Team	Cooperation is an act of teamwork with other players to achieve a mutually desired and useful result. This is the social aspect of the games that many players enjoy. In team games, the more players work together, the more they are able to achieve (Kapp, 2012). Teams are used for group learning activities and reporting on the ability of participants to work in a team.
Resource	Game resources can be a variety of items that are used for achieving the game's objectives. Game resources can be considered as different types of learning resources that are used to implement some game techniques and achieve some learning goals.
Time	According to Kapp (2012), time can be used as a motivating element for the activity and actions of the player. For example, when a timer appears on the video game screen and starts counting down, it increases stress levels and motivates actions. Time is used to set time limits for learning activities in order to control the learning process.
Progress	The progress of the game is used to show the advancement of the player in the game, i.e. how far the player has reached in relation to the whole game. Some games offer the ability to keep the current progress so that once the game is over, the players can start again from the recorded position to improve their final score. Progress usually represents the percentage of objectives achieved in relation to all learning objectives.
Status	The status is used to represent the player's current achievements (e.g. chosen avatar, points earned, level reached, badges received and available resources). The status in the learning considers the current state of the learner – current avatar, learning goals achieved, assessments of the learner, completed learning activity, etc.

The appropriate game elements and actions that can be applied in gamification of e-learning are selected. The possibilities for using the game elements and techniques in the learning are presented in Table 1 and

Table 2. The list of selected game elements (see Table 1) contains: avatar, bonus, badge, combination / combo, reward, leaderboard, level, progress, status, team, time, resource, message and various learning elements, and the list of game techniques (see Table 2): change of identity, reward system, progress tracking, current status tracking, teamwork, time constraint, game rules, feedback, communication, challenge, mission, adventure, hidden treasure and story/plot.

Table 2. Using game techniques in gamification of learning

Technique	Description / Usage in Learning
Game rules	The rules of the game are one of the main components of any game. The rules are designed specifically to limit the player's actions and keep the game manageable (Kapp, 2012). The rules of the learning process can be considered as rules of the game.
Time limit	Time limits are a technique used to provoke players. They focus and begin to perform the tasks needed to achieve the level or the current goal. Time limits are an additional but essential part of the learning rules and connected to the determining of the reward system. They can be used for both learning activities and learning resources.
Communication	Communication is used to send messages between two or more players in order to exchange information related to the game and to stimulate the desire for socialization between participants. Communication is an important factor in learning, through it students can share ideas and problems, to collaborate and work on group learning activities and to implement social communication.
Feedback	Feedback is received from the competent party for the actions performed by the player. It can also be used as a type of prompt/ motivation. Feedback in learning is usually used by the teacher to give the learners an opinion or recommendation on their work.
Mission/ challenge/ adventure	The fulfillment of the assigned missions in the games stimulate the satisfaction of the players. Many games use this technique to achieve various goals, most often described with story and supplemented by time constraints. Missions can represent all the learning activities that the learner has to carry out within the learning course. For more complete gamification, a game story can be added to these learning activities to describe the purpose of the mission.
Hidden treasure	Players should meet certain conditions to unlock hidden treasures. Hidden treasures are a technique for unlocking the discovery spirit of the players. Hidden treasures are hidden learning resources (like interesting fact or examples) that can only be discovered/ opened when certain learning conditions are met (e.g. when completing a certain mission).
Reward System	The reward system is a schedule with a quantitative description of the various reward elements (badges, rewards, bonuses, and combos) and the effort required to obtain them. For example, the most effective reward system, is one in which the rewards have a variable ratio of quantity, time interval and effort to receive. The reward system gives additional benefits and incentives to students under different rules and in different forms, which motivate them to carry out more learning activities.
Story / History	The story includes the ongoing plot of the game (e.g. a description of specific sub-scenes for role-playing games). The story gives an interesting context to the learning process. It can describe a story with different missions to complete.

Also in Table 3 (Sharkova et al., 2020), the interrelation between game element, game technique and game action is made.

Table 3. The relationship between game element, technique and action

Game Element	Game Technique	Game Action
Avatar	Changing Identity	Role Playing
Bonus	Reward System	Receiving a bonus
Badge	Reward system	Receiving an award
Combo	Reward System	Gaining an advantage
Reward	Reward System	Rewarding
Resource	Reward System	Gaining resources, exchanging resources
Leaderboard	Reward system	Participation in a competition
Level	Tracking progress	Going to the next level, repeating a level
Progress	Tracking progress	Getting information about the progress in the game
Status	Current status tracking	Receiving current status information
Team	Team work	Participation in group activities
Time	Time limit	Carrying out activity for a certain time
	Rules of the game	Following the rules
Resource, Message	Feedback	Obtaining an opinion from a competent party
Message	Communication	Sending a message, receiving a message
Various Elements	Challenge / Mission / Adventure	Completing a mission
Resource, Combo	Hidden Treasure	Treasure hunt
	Story / History	Creating and entering a different reality

MODEL FOR STRUCTURAL GAMIFICATION OF LEARNING

Based on the research, a four-stage cyclical gamified learning model is proposed with the following stages (see Figure 1):

- **Learning** – Students learn using the learning resources and activities of the gamified course;
- **Assessment** – Some of the learning activities are assessed to determine if some current learning objectives have been achieved, such as assessment of a test or assignment, fulfillment of input requirements, etc.;
- **Rewarding** – On the basis of assessment, learners are rewarded through various incentives: bonuses, badges, awards, combos and hidden treasures;
- **Ranking** – As a result of rewarding, students receive points or some virtual objects, and/or a new higher game level, which directly affect the position of the participant in the ranking.

After the assessment, awarding and ranking stages, learners feel motivated to learn more or do more learning activities to get more points, to be higher in the rankings, to be awarded with badges, to receive additional bonuses, etc., which rotates the cyclically gamified learning process, as illustrated in Figure 1.

The learning model is built on levels with learning materials and activities as well as with gamification elements and techniques. After the assessment stage, where some of current learning goals are assessed, students are rewarded through different means (stimuli): bonus, badge, reward and combo. As a result, they obtain points and/or new higher level, which directly reflect to the Ranking stage – learners move on the leaderboard ranking. After the processes of assessment, rewarding and ranking students naturally feel motivated to learn more, in order to receive more points, be on a better place in the ranking, obtain badges, receive additional extras, etc. Therefore a four-stage cyclical gamified learning model is a motivation learning model. The detailed model of a gamified learning process is given in Figure 2.

Figure 1. Four-stage cyclical gamified learning model

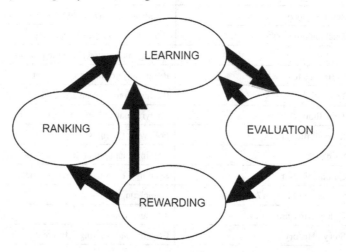

Figure 2. Detailed model of a gamified learning process

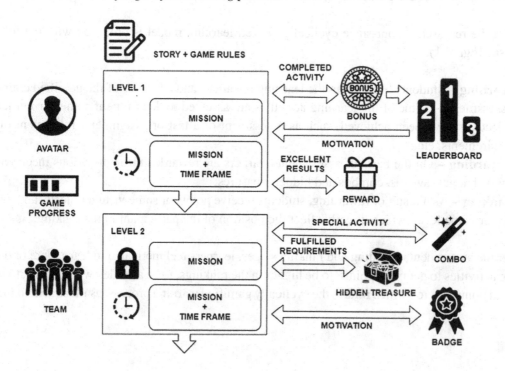

According to Bartle's classification (Bartle, 1996), game players are of 4 types: killers, achievers, explorers and socializers. For these four categories of learners, the appropriate game elements and techniques in the model are determined in Table 4.

It is unlikely to find a learner, a representative of exactly one type. Most learners are usually a combination of more than one type and are therefore motivated by a different variety of game elements.

Table 4. Appropriate game elements and techniques according to the game type of the learner

User's Type	Game Elements	Game Techniques
Killer	leaderboard, bonus, combo, progress, status, time	reward system, progress tracking, current status tracking, time constraint
Achiever	level, badge, bonus, reward, resource, progress	reward system, feedback, challenge/ mission/adventure, progress tracking
Explorer	avatar, reward, resource	challenge/mission/adventure, hidden treasure, story/plot, reward system, feedback, change of identity, game rules
Socializer	team, avatar, message	teamwork, communication, change of identity

IMPLEMENTATION OF STRUCTURAL GAMIFICATION IN LMS

The main purpose of the research is to design and developed a structural gamification of e-learning courses in non-gamified LMS. Two approaches can be used to achieve this goal:

1. Conversion of a standard e-course into a gamified one;
2. Creating a new gamified e-course from "scratch".

Due to the rapid development of e-learning in recent years, as well as the even more widespread blended learning, there are many e-learning environments in which a huge number of already created e-courses are located. That is why the research uses the first approach, in which the already existing traditional e-courses can be used, which can be automatically or with little intervention transformed into gamified ones.

For the implementation of the proposed model and approach, Moodle was chosen as one of the most popular and used LMS in the world, which is a flexible and free open source system with over 250 million users, over 34 million courses, over 173,000 installations on the platform in over 240 countries (Moodle). An important reason for the choice is its wide application in University of Plovdiv, where we do our experiments and where a number of e-courses in various subject areas have already been created. Although Moodle is not a platform for game-based learning, it can easily use game elements and techniques. There is even a special name for the gamification in Moodle – "gamooification", proposed by Henrick (2013).

The LMS Moodle has been analyzed to discover its gamification capabilities and shortcomings. Table 5 shows the implementation in Moodle of the game elements and techniques from the previous section. Most game elements have a full or partial implementation in Moodle or can be presented with other suitable elements.

Table 5. Implementation of game elements and techniques in Moodle

Game Element/Technique	Implementation in Moodle
Avatar	No implementation
Bonus	No exact implementation, but points of activity assessment can be used as one type of bonus
Badge	Implemented, badges can be created and set to be manually or automatically distributed to learners
Combo	No exact implementation, but can be simulated
Reward	No exact implementation, but the awards can easily be realized with other Moodle elements
Resource	Implemented, various learning resources can be added for learning or as a resource for carrying out a learning activity
Rewarding system	Partially, badges and bonus points are fully realized, other awards can be simulated
Ranking	No implementation
Level	No exact implementation, but it is very similar to course section
Progress	No exact implementation of the gamification progress, although there are some statistics in Moodle on learning activities and student assessments
Status	No exact implementation
Team	Implemented, It is possible to create groups of learners to which group assignments/ resources can be assigned
Time	Implemented, it can be used to set a limited period for learning activities and a course
Time limit	Implemented, time limits can be set for submitting assignments and solving tests, as well as for each learning resource and activity in Moodle
Game rules	No exact implementation, but they can be interpreted as learning rules
Feedback	Implemented, there is a functionality for sending feedback from the teacher when assessing learning activities
Communication	Implemented, there is a forum and a chat in Moodle
Mission / Challenge / Adventure	No exact implementation, any learning resource and activity or set of them, possibly with time constraints and including story, can be interpreted as mission
Hidden treasure	No exact implementation, in Moodle, a hidden treasure can be easily simulated by placing various conditional locks on learning resources/activities, and the desire to unlock them by satisfying the set conditions can be interpreted as a search for a hidden treasure
Story/History	No exact implementation, but can be easily created with existing Moodle elements

To implement the model, software (Gachkova & Somova, 2020) for the application of structural gamification of learning in Moodle has been designed and developed, which integrates game elements and techniques in the process of e-learning, without any changes in the learning content of the courses. For this purpose, two plugins have been developed to help the authors of the Moodle courses in creating gamified courses.

We have implemented the missing gamification functionality in Moodle as modules of the "plugin" type so that they can be easily integrated into the environment. For the other game elements that have "partial" implementation, we offer recommendations (see Table 6.) with which existing Moodle elements to be realized. Conditions for a fuller application of gamification are also given.

The first plugin for creating gamified e-courses in the Moodle environment can be used to automatically transform a standard e-course into a gamified one or to initially create a gamified course. This plugin changes the design of the course into a game view – based on game levels (open or locked with input

Table 6. Recommendations for Moodle implementation of game element/techniques

Game Element/Technique	Possible Moodle Elements	Additional Conditions
Bonus	every Moodle resource, points	conditions for obtaining
Badge	badge	conditions for obtaining
Combo	label, page, file, folder, glossary, database, book, lesson, chat, external tool	conditions for obtaining, visible disabled element, time constraint
Reward	page, file, folder, URL, book, lesson, glossary, forum, external tool	conditions for obtaining
Resource	every Moodle resource	conditions for obtaining
Level	course section	conditional entry restrictions
Team	group	–
Time	time	–
Message	message from forum or chat	–
Communication	forum, chat	–
Game Rules	label, page, file	–
Feedback	feedback of Moodle learning resources and activities	depending on student's progress
Mission	page, file, folder, URL, book, lesson, assignment, quiz, glossary, workshop, wiki, database, forum, chat, external tool, survey	possible entry or time constraints
Hidden Treasure	page, file, folder, URL, book, lesson, glossary, forum, external tool	conditional entry restrictions, visible disabled element
Story/History	label, page, file	–

requirements) and offers help on how to implement game elements with standard Moodle elements (on the basis of recommendations in Table 6). Course authors can create a fully gamified course only following recommendations in the plugin and using the familiar Moodle elements, but in the game context.

Figure 3 presents an example of a sample course for a specific learner in game design, containing three (visible) levels of play where the learning has reached level 3. The panel on the right shows information about the participant's current level, progress and menu options: status, leaderboard and rewards.

Moodle supports several basic types of plugins (modules), this module is created by type "course format" and implemented as a specific format for each course.

The second plugin allows adding specific game elements to the standard e-courses, which do not exist in Moodle and cannot be implemented with the standard Moodle elements. This plugin realizes the ranking of learners (leaderboard) depending on the achieved levels and progress, history of the awarded game elements, avatar and game progress.

To comply with EU laws on concealing sensitive information, each learner participates in the leaderboard ranking instead of personal name and photo, with a special name and avatar, which may be different for each course.

The plugin can be used both to create a new course and to modify an existing standard e-course to become gamified. It is designed as a Moodle plugin of the "block" type and is implemented as a separate instance for each course.

The plugin has a menu bar containing three options: status, leaderboard of learners and a diary with awarded activities of the learner, which give the following opportunities to users:

Figure 3. Game view of the course

- To choose an avatar with an image, a special name and a short additional information about the learner;
- To overview the current ranking of learners with the achieved levels and the obtained points (see Figure 4);
- To identify one's place in the ranking of students;
- To view one's current status and progress in the game;
- To examine the reports of personal actions – actions for which the learner has earned points;
- To view the current level reached in the course for all learners;
- To view the current points earned by all learners.

During the learning process, learners collect points for each activity they have performed (opening a text document to study it, completing a test, completing an assignment, etc.). The number of points for each possible action of the learner is configured by the teacher. Students are ranked in the leaderboard based on current points, despite the fact that everyone is moving at their own pace and are currently at a different level.

The learner's progress shows the percentage of points earned in the current level to the total number of points in the level. For example, in Figure 4, the first participant in the ranking ("Angry Bird") has

Figure 4. Leaderboard of learners

achieved only 2% of the points needed to reach the next level (level 6), and the other learner "Jerry" – 67% of the points needed, to move to level 5.

CONDUCTED EXPERIMENTS

Four different experiments of gamification of learning at the University of Plovdiv "Paisii Hilendarski", Bulgaria have been done. The results of the experiments generally prove the thesis that gamified learning is more attractive for learners, students are more motivated to learn and learning outcomes are comparable to standard e-learning, and sometimes higher.

First Example

An example methodology for designing a gamified course based on levels, using rewards, bonus points, badges and a social component (forum or chat) has been experimented (Somova & Gachkova, 2016). The experiment was conducted during traditional learning process of the bachelor course "Web programming", where students use an e-course as addition to face-to-face lectures.

Each learning week, in the e-course, is transformed into a game level. Each course level includes learning resources for study, assessment tests and/or individual or group assignments of different types for implementation, covering certain learning objectives. After the assessment of each assignment, test and some communication activities, students receive points. Based on the points received, students then receive badges and the final grade. If the points received from one assignment are more than 70%, they also receive a reward (additional interesting resource).

The conducted training is compared with the training in the same subject from the previous year. The results (final grades) of the students from the two years are comparable, but the students from the second year have shown a greater desire to get involved in the learning activities of the e-course and motivation to solve the tests and assignments.

Second Example

Second attempt (Gachkova et al., 2018) for structural gamification of the learning have been made on the basis of existing standard e-learning course in Moodle "Modeling and management of business processes", only by using the Moodle resources and activities in gamified context, with which the training has been conducted. A second example of designing a gamified e-learning course has been done, where to the game elements of the first example have been added: input requirements for certain levels, individual or group assignments of different types, combos, leaderboard (as a published list), story/history, status and course progress.

Some of the levels have input restrictions based on the previous assignments (the assignment is completed and submitted, the assignment is assessed with a minimum number of required points and the time limit is met). If the points are not enough for them to go to the next level, they can send the revised assignment again (this is one of the moments when the gamification cycle is triggered).

For encouragement, students can win badges: First Finished, High Score and Best Team (for group assignments). They can also receive combos (additional instructions and help for the next assignment) or unexpected awards such as additional resources with interesting facts, etc.

Although gamification can motivate both at individual and group level, when applied to group assignments, some problems arise that are not directly related to gamification, but rather to the behavior of learners in a group, especially in the automatic distribution of groups: poor organization, insufficient communication and teamwork in some groups, rarely some members of the groups do not get involved at all or enough in the work, very rarely some learners refuse to work in a group and do the assignment alone, and also some conflicting situations appear. Some of these problems can be overcome by enabling learners to form groups themselves and teachers to monitor and control learners' collaboration in a timely manner.

113 students participated in the experiment, and students were given a choice between a standard or a gamified e-course. 41 students choose to participate in the gamified e-course and 27 of them successfully completed all levels of the course. These students who failed during the training continued their education with the standard e-course (as most dropouts were during the first two levels).

The results of the two approaches were compared in the final exam, where the students from the gamified course have 7.13% higher grades than the students from the traditional e-course.

A COLLES (the Constructive On-Line Learning Environment Survey) survey was conducted at the beginning and end of the gamified e-course with the same questions to provide feedback on the effectiveness of some aspects of gamification of learning. First survey find out learner's expectations and the second survey – learner's satisfaction. The COLLES survey is divided into six categories: Practical importance, Self-criticism, Dialogic, Teaching help, Mutual assistance and Understandability, where students answer using the Lycart five-point scale.

The results of this survey can be summarized in the following: students who participate in the gamified e-course spend more time on assignments in the learning environment than students who prefer the standard e-course; students in the gamified e-course have higher grades of assignments than students using the standard e-course; students in the gamified e-course seek fewer explanations than students in the standard e-course; the average understandability of the students in the gamified course is equal to their preferences, expressed before the training, and is higher than 75%.

Third Example

Both created gamification plugins have been tested with real users in third experiment (Gachkova et al., 2020). A total of 50 participants took part in the experiment with bachelor courses "Object-Oriented Design and Programming (C ++)", of which 38 were learners and 12 were teachers.

Two surveys, one for students (with 20 questions) and one for teachers (with 24 questions), have been conducted and analyzed in five areas (practical applicability; motivation; design and accessibility; interactivity and communication; comprehensibility). In general, both students and teachers rate the potential of gamification with very high marks.

The category "Practical applicability" was rated with the highest arithmetic mean of the surveys of teachers and students - 4.49, followed by the categories "Comprehensibility" and "Design and accessibility" - 4.47, "Motivation" – 4.41 and "Interactivity and communication" - 4.26.

The total average grade of all answers of the surveyed students is 4.15 out of a maximum of 5 (the Lycart five-point scale is used). The category "Practical applicability" is rated by students with the highest average grade – 4.25, followed by the categories "Interactivity and communication", "Comprehensibility", "Design and accessibility" and "Motivation" with the lowest score – 4.09.

The total average grade of all answers of the surveyed teachers is 4.71 out of a maximum of 5. The category "Design and accessibility" is rated by students with the highest average grade – 4.79, followed by the categories "Comprehensibility", "Practical applicability", "Motivation" and "Interactivity and communication" with the lowest score – 4.26.

Fourth Example

Fourth experiment (Sharkova et al., 2020) with real students has studied the gamification approach in face-to-face collaborative learning, supported by a cloud environment. The experiment is conducted with two consecutive university level English courses for IT students, "English for ICT: Lifelong writing in the Cloud" and "English for ICT: Learner autonomy in the Cloud". The courses includes the following game elements and techniques: mission, reward, bonus, badge, leaderboard, hidden treasure, team work, avatar, story, progress, status, time limit, team, feedback and communication. The courses are delivered on Google cloud.

Used gamified learning methodology has been proved by conducted survey with 93 participants. Students gave their attitudes towards the different aspects of gamification in descending order, ranging between 97% to 72%: overall effectiveness, game rules, awards, research and problem based tasks and leaderboard.

CONCLUSION

The great motivating role of games and their widespread distribution has naturally led to the increasing use of game methodology for educational purposes and especially in e-learning or blended learning.

In the chapter, the concept of serious games has been discussed and the attempt for their classification has been made with the following categories: game-based learning, gamification of learning, organizational-dynamic games, simulation games and edutainment. Examples of existing LMSs that apply concepts from serious games have been shown.

Gamification, as a motivator of human activities, has been presented in a more general context, with examples in different areas, paying special attention to the gamification of learning and its two types: structural and content.

Pedagogical approaches, theories and models suitable for the design and construction of gamified e-courses have been analyzed: Keller's ARCS model, Kapp's two types of motivation, Malone's theory of learning through intrinsic motivation, an approach for motivated active learning from Pirker et al., Kolb's experimental learning model, and Gloria et al. and Anderson and Krathwohl learning models based on Bloom's revised taxonomy.

The possibilities for using the game elements and techniques in the gamification of learning have been discussed.

Based on the research, a four-stage cyclical gamified learning model has been proposed with the following stages: Learning, Assessment, Rewarding and Ranking, as well as a detailed model of a gamified learning process. For the four categories of learners, from Bartle's classification, the appropriate game elements in the model have been determined.

The game elements and activities and their possible realization with the standard elements of a non-gamifed e-learning environment have been discussed – a specific interpretation of the Moodle LMS has been proposed.

To fully implement the model, two plugins for the application of structural gamification of learning in Moodle have been designed and developed, which integrates game elements and techniques in the process of e-learning, without any changes in the learning content of the courses.

Various experiments for gamification of learning have been performed and presented.

The following directions can be suggested as possible future perspectives for the development of this research: creation of a gamified interactive textbook (based on the EPUB standard) for mobile learning, usage of the gamification methodology in other (non-learning) university activities and systems (e.g. for administrative activities of students, teachers and staff), creation of a specialized gamified environment for e-learning, in the field of green gamification for training users in ecological behavior, etc. These are just a small part of the rich possibilities for using gamification in every field.

REFERENCES

Abt, C. C. (1987). *Serious Games*. University Press of America.

Accord, L. M. S. (n.d.). *Accord LMS*. https://evaluate.accordlms.com/learning-management-system/

Anderson, L. W., & Krathwohl, D. R. (Eds.). (2001). *A taxonomy for learning, teaching, and assessing: A revision of Bloom's taxonomy of educational objectives*. Longman.

Antin, J., & Churchill, E. F. (2011). Badges in Social Media: A Social Psychological Perspective. In *Proceedings of ACM CHI Conference on Human Factors in Computing Systems*. (pp. 1-4). ACM.

Axonify. (n.d.). *Axonify*. https://axonify.com/

Bartle, R. (1996). Hearts, clubs, diamonds, spades: Players who suit MUDs. *Journal of MUD Research, 1*(1).

Chang, V., & Guetl, C. (2010). Generation Y Learning in the 21st Century: Integration of Virtual Worlds and Cloud Computing Services. In *Proceedings of Global Learn Asia Pacific 2010 –Global Conference on Learning and Technology* (vol. 1, pp. 1888-1897). Association for the Advancement of Computing in Education (AACE).

Connolly, T., Boyle, E., MacArthur, E., Hainey, T., & Boyle, J. (2012). A systematic literature review of empirical evidence on computer games and serious games. *Computers & Education, 59*(2), 661–686. doi:10.1016/j.compedu.2012.03.004

Cruz-Cunha, M. M. (2012). *Handbook of Research on Serious Games as Educational, Business and Research Tools*. IGI Global. doi:10.4018/978-1-4666-0149-9

Gachkova, M., & Somova, E. (2016). Game Approach e-learning. In *Proceedings of IX National Conference Education and Research in Information Society*. (pp. 143-152). Institute of Mathematics and Informatics, Bulgarian Academy of Sciences.

Gachkova, M., & Somova, E. (2019). Plug-in for creation of gamified courses in the e-learning environment Moodle. *IOP Conference Series. Materials Science and Engineering, 618*(012079), 1–7. doi:10.1088/1757-899X/618/1/012079

Gachkova, M., & Somova, E. (2020). Moodle plug-ins for design and development of gamified courses. In *Proceedings of 14th Annual International Technology, Education and Development Conference – INTED'2020*. (pp. 2187-2195). IATED Digital Library. 10.21125/inted.2020.0676

Gachkova, M., Somova, E., & Gaftandzhieva, S. (2020). Gamification of learning course in the e-learning environment. *IOP Conference Series. Materials Science and Engineering, 878*(012035), 1–9.

Gachkova, M., Takev, M., & Somova, E. (2018). Learning and Assessment Based on Gamified e-Course in Moodle. *Journal Mathematics and Informatics, 61*(5), 444–454.

Gloria, A., Bellotti, F., & Berta, R. (2014). Serious Games for education and training. *International Journal of Serious Games, 1*(1). Advance online publication. doi:10.17083/ijsg.v1i1.11

Gnauk, B., Dannecker, L., & Hahmann, B. (2012). Leveraging gamification in demand dispatch systems. In *EDBT-ICDT '12: Proceedings of the 2012 Joint EDBT/ICDT Workshops* (pp. 103-110). ACM Digital Library.

Growth Engineering GENIE. (n.d.). *GENIE Authoring Tool*. https://www.growthengineering.co.uk/genie-content-authoring-tool/

Growth Engineering Academy. (n.d.). *Academy LMS*. https://www.growthengineering.co.uk/academy-lms/

Henrick, G. (2013). *Gamification – What is it and what it is in Moodle*. http://classroom-aid.com/2013/11/18/gamifying-learning-with-moodle-gbl/

Herzig, P., Srahringer, S., & Ameling, M. (2012). Gamification of ERP systems – Exploring gamification effects on user acceptance constructs. *Proceedings of the Multikonferenz Wirtschaftsinformatik MKWI*, *12*, 793–804.

Huang, W., & Soman, D. (2013). *A Practitioner's Guide To Gamification Of Education*. University of Toronto.

Kapp, K. M. (2012). *The gamification of learning and instruction: Game-based methods and strategies for training and education*. Pfeiffer.

Keller, J. M. (2010). *Motivational Design for Learning and Performance*. Springer. doi:10.1007/978-1-4419-1250-3

Kolb, A. Y., & Kolb, D. A. (2005). Learning Styles and Learning Spaces: Enhancing Experiential Learning in Higher Education. *Academy of Management Learning & Education*, *4*(2), 193–212. doi:10.5465/amle.2005.17268566

Langendah, P. A., Cook, M., & Mark-Herbert, C. (2016). Gamification in higher education. Toward a pedagogy to engage and motivate. In *Working Paper Series* (vol. 6, pp. 1-43). Swedish University of Agricultural Sciences.

Malone, T. W. (1981). Toward a Theory of Intrinsically Motivating Instruction. *Cognitive Science*, *5*(4), 333–369. doi:10.120715516709cog0504_2

Michael, D., & Chen, S. (2005). *Serious Games: Games That Educate, Train, and Inform*. Muska & Lipman/Premier-Trade.

Moodle. (n.d.). *Moodle*. https://moodle.com/

Moodle Plugins. (n.d.). *Moodle plugins database*. https://moodle.org/plugins

Pirker, J., Riffnaller-Schiefer, M., Tomes, L. M., & Guetl, C. (2016). Motivational Active Learning in Blended and Virtual Learning Scenarios: Engaging Students in Digital Learning. In Handbook of Research on Engaging Digital Natives in Higher Education Settings. IGI Global.

Scheiner, C., Witt, M., Voigt, K., & Robra-Bissantz, S. (2012). Einsatz von Spielemechaniken in Ideewettbewerben. *Proceedings of the Multikonferenz Wirtschaftsinformatik MKWI*, *12*, 781–792.

Sharkova, D., Somova, E., & Gachkova, M. (2020). Gamification in cloud-based collaborative learning. *Journal Mathematics and Informatics*, *63*(5), 471–483.

Somova, E., & Gachkova, M. (2016). An Attempt for Gamification of Learning in Moodle. In *Proceedings of International Conference on e-Learning (e-Learning'16)*. (pp. 201-207). Slovak University of Technology in Bratislava.

Talent, L. M. S. (n.d.). *TalentLMS*. http://www.talentlms.com/

Chapter 5

Gamification of E-Learning in African Universities:
Identifying Adoption Factors Through Task-Technology Fit and Technology Acceptance Model

Abdulsalam Salihu Mustafa
https://orcid.org/0000-0003-3117-062X
University Tenaga Nasional, Malaysia

Gamal Abdulnaser Alkawsi
https://orcid.org/0000-0002-2456-4033
Universiti Tenaga Nasional, Malaysia

Kingsley Ofosu-Ampong
Business School, University of Ghana, Ghana

Vanye Zira Vanduhe
Üner İnşaat Peyzaj Ltd., Turkey

Manuel B. Garcia
https://orcid.org/0000-0003-2615-422X
FEU Institute of Technology, Philippines

Yahia Baashar
https://orcid.org/0000-0002-8004-3929
Universiti Tenaga Nasional, Malaysia

ABSTRACT

Gamification in education is a strategy of motivating and engaging students by integrating game design features into the instructional process. Although there is a growing body of scientific evidence supporting the effectiveness of gamification in the educational setting, some of the evidence is inconclusive and insufficient, especially in developing nations. The purpose of this study is to integrate the technology acceptance model and task technology fit to investigate instructors' intention to use gamified online learning. A sample of 50 participants across various African institutions was involved in this study. Structural equation modelling implemented via partial least squares (PLS) is used to test the research hypotheses. The results revealed that intention to use gamified online learning was significantly and positively influenced by task technology fit, perceived usefulness, and attitude. Notably, subjective norms, facilitating conditions, and computer anxiety failed to predict behavioural intention. The authors discuss the implications of the findings and propose future directions.

DOI: 10.4018/978-1-7998-8089-9.ch005

INTRODUCTION

Described as a strategic attempt to enhance organisations, systems, and services, gamification harnesses game elements and utilises them in a non-game context. (Deterding et al., 2011). Albeit there is no extensive list of game elements, the most commonly utilised ones are points, badges, levels, leaderboards, challenges, and badges (Manzano-Leon et al., 2021; Deterding et al., 2011; Mustafa et al., in press). Applying these game elements in the classroom aims makes learning more appealing while inspiring young learners in the modern age of interactivity and games (Glover, 2013). In its most basic form, gamified learning approaches enhance an existing learning system and transform it into a game-like experience. The strength of interactive gamified learning lies in its potential to influence behaviour towards an intended goal.

Most significantly, in the Coronavirus pandemic (COVID-19) age, gamifying online learning platforms can offer students a degree of commitment to compensate for the lack of classroom activities. This becomes more important, especially that many institutions have implemented blended learning or exclusively online instruction to avoid disruptions in student learning. Nevertheless, in addition to coping with unexpected technical issues, instructors face challenges adapting their lessons to the online environment effectively. A principal challenge with the present online learning systems for educators is encouraging and motivating students to use the system effectively (Cable & Cheung, 2017).

Accordingly, gamification has gained prominence in the education context and is actively being explored (Rodrigues et al., 2021; de la Pena et al., 2021). Several scholars argue that when gamification is designed and implemented appropriately, it can improve students' learning performance through a behavioural change (Sailer & Homner, 2020; Aldemir et al., 2018; Adukaite et al., 2017).

Furthermore, using game elements in online learning can significantly improve educational environments (Antonaci et al., 2019; Alabbasi, 2018). In the case of African universities, however, many are still not ready to gamify their educational programs and, failed to completely leverage the market opportunities of the digital gaming industry (Sawahel, 2020; Ofosu-Ampong et al., 2020). Nevertheless, the World Economic Forum reported that providing adequate education and employment to sub-Saharan citizens will attract an additional USD 500 billion to the region's economy over 30 years (Myers, 2016). Literature also shows that gamifying a university course can improve students' engagement and academic achievement (Manzano-Leon et al., 2021), critical to achieving a high-quality education. A recent study found that teachers have a favourable attitude toward gamification (Martí-Parreño et al., 2016; Sánchez-Mena & Martí-Parreño, 2016). Hence, gamification strategy in learning can motivate students, engage them in the learning process, and minimise dropout rates.

Despite the many potentials of gamification when integrated into online learning, only a limited number of African universities in Kenya, Nigeria, and South Africa currently utilise gamified learning environments (Sawahel, 2020; Ofosu-Ampong et al., 2020). Accordingly, African nations are yet to fully explore the potential of gamification in an online learning platform and its positive impact on students' engagement and performances. In this regard, it becomes crucial to understand factors that will affect the adoption of gamification-based online learning in various African institutions. Determining these factors will provide education leaders with the necessary knowledge to create strategies to encourage more adopters of such modern pedagogy. To make a robust model, and because only a few researchers have integrated information systems (IS) theory in investigating e-learning adoption, Technology Acceptance Model (TAM) was extended by utilising Task Technology Fit (TTF). The study findings will offer practical and theoretical perspectives to improve awareness of the paradigm shift related to gamified online learning.

Preliminary Studies

Initially, to investigate the nature of TAM and TTF and their suitability in determining instructors' intention to adopt gamified learning approach in Africa, the researchers interviewed some respondents to share their experiences. Accordingly, most instructors identified the following reasons for using gamification:

- To expose students to the current motivational technological platforms for online learning
- To provide quick feedback on assignments, quizzes, and discussions
- To motivate learning and improve engagement and communication with and among students
- To promote excitement and fun in teaching and learning

The use of gamification has been centred on assignment creation and quizzes where students are to log in to the gamified system using their identification and attend to the questions. However, most institutions did not employ a generalised gamified system for instructors, implying that instructors relied on free gamification systems. Hence, popular open-source software such as Kahoot and blackboard were customised and used for teaching. However, these open-source gamified systems typically have limited functionality. As a result, the various institutional approaches toward adopting and using gamification in higher education institutions in Africa are still low (Ofosu-Ampong et al., 2020).

Notwithstanding, as previously mentioned, the COVID-19 pandemic also disrupted higher learning in Africa, encouraging more instructors, teachers, and students to embrace gamified online learning systems. Despite the potential benefits of gamification, the challenges faced by instructors in adopting it may account for its low penetration in Africa. These include lack of dedication and time to gamify a course for an academic year and possibly continue the lifecycle, lack of funding and programmers to take gamification agenda in universities (Ofosu-Ampong et al., 2020). Accordingly, this study seeks to identify the factors that are likely to influence instructors' use of gamified online learning systems in African universities.

The rest of this paper is organised as follows. The literature on gamified online learning, TAM, and TTF is reviewed in Section 2. The research model is presented in Section 3, while the research design and methodology in Section 4. The study findings are presented and discussed in Section 5. Section 6 concludes and summarises the study implications. Finally, Section 7 outlines study limitations and future studies.

LITERATURE REVIEW

For a tailored approach to understanding the objective of our study, we conduct a literature review on a selected area. First, we summarise the literature on the development of gamification that justifies the use of TAM and TTF in this area.

Gamification of Learning

Gamification in the past decade has become a widely discussed topic in education. Scholars have defined it in many ways, e.g., applying game design elements to a learning system for use in a non-game context (Deterding et al., 2011). In the learning context, gamification is referred to as gamified learning (Salier and Homner, 2019). In this sense, gamification enhances students' learning processes or activities towards the desired learning outcome. Well-known examples of gamified online learning systems are Coursera, Kahoot, and Udemy. As recent studies show, employing game features in online learning environments can lead to significant benefits. For example, badges positively influenced and improved student engagement (Ibanez et al., 2014), whereas leaderboards resulted in higher learning performance among engineering students (Ortiz-Rojas et al., 2019). In addition, students' attitudes and engagement were enhanced by using points, badges, and a scoreboard (Tan & Hew, 2016).

In the African context, gamification has been used to champion different activities. For instance, in a recent review on dominant gamification in Africa, the authors identified progress, social and immersion as prominent (Ofosu-Ampong & Anning-Dorson, 2020). These include points, trophies, narratives and stories, competition, and social networking. Hence, these affordances generate social learning, feedback, and self-learning experience with embedded videos. Moreover, since social learning is a critical component of gamification systems, researchers have proposed integrated models to advance the quality of learning via gamified forums by championing models that promote the personalisation of learning (Melzer, 2019).

Technology Acceptance Model

Davis (1986) proposed the TAM, which focuses on exploring mediating variables between system attributes and practical system implementation. The model suggests that two significant variables, perceived usefulness (PU) and perceived ease of use (PEOU), are instrumental in explaining the variance in users' intention. PU is the extent to which a person believes that using a particular system will enhance his or her job performance (Davis, 1989). On the other hand, PEOU is the extent to which a person believes that using a particular system will be free of effort (Davis, 1989). Among the beliefs, PEOU is hypothesised to be a predictor of perceived usefulness. TAM is the most influential theory in information systems and is used in several theoretical investigations (Wong et al., 2021; Huang et al., 2019; Wu & Chen, 2017).

Similarly, Lee (2014) stated that TAM is a well-accepted model in IS acceptance that explains consumer behaviour in the context of technology acceptance or rejection. However, researchers have noted that while TAM favours a significant relationship between attitude and adoption intention, this is not always the case (Wong et al., 2021; Shin & Kim, 2015). As such, other factors that inhibit people from adopting technology should be explored. This study considers task technology fit to be one of the most crucial factors influencing users' technology adoption, namely online learning systems.

Task Technology Fit

TTF is one of the most used theoretical models when assessing how information technology impacts performance, usage and evaluating the fit between task and technology characteristics. The fit between a task and technology can be affected by its task and technical. Consequently, this can determine the user's performance or utilisation of the system. TTF represents how a specific technology supports one's effort to perform a task. Since its inception, TTF has been applied to various information systems (Gikas & Grant, 2013).

Additionally, TAM has been generally used to explain the acceptance of new technology in academic settings (Wu & Chen, 2017; Joo et al., 2016). Although studies have examined TTF in various contexts, there is limited research in gamified learning in African institutions to address social factors, limiting its ability to predict social relatedness and learning with technology. Currently, it is unclear whether a good task-technology fit influences a learner's adoption of gamification (Ofosu-Ampong et al., 2020). Accordingly, this study aims to provide a solid theoretical contribution to the acceptance of gamification and bridge the theoretical gap between TAM and TTF.

The Extended Technology Acceptance Model (xTAM)

The current study's research framework is based fundamentally on the integrated model proposed by several authors (Vanduhe et al., 2020; Wu & Chen, 2017; Dishaw and Strong, 1999). However, numerous modifications were made in the present study, including external and contextual factors that explain gamification success in developing nations. Another example was a proposed research model based on the Unified Theory of Acceptance and Use of Technology (UTAUT) and trust to integrate gamification into learning management systems (Ofosu-Ampong et al. 2020). Besides, other scholars combined TAM and motivational theories like self-determination theory to investigate learner's continuance intention to use gamified technology (Fathali & Okada, 2018). Then again, this study focuses on instructors' adoption of gamified technology. However, the primary focus of the task technology fit model in this study is to achieve a favourable result of applying gamification—this result by anticipating a good fit between the task and the technology. Therefore, adopting TTF to investigate instructor acceptance of a gamified online learning system is a highly viable strategy.

Although TAM and TTF are two prominent IS models used to explain user behaviour, they have limitations. TAM, for example, fails to consider task characteristics and how well the technology satisfies the task's requirements. In addition, TTF does not include consumers' attitudes toward technology, a fundamental aspect of TAM. As a result, the weaknesses of the two models can be compensated for by connecting them. Furthermore, integrating technology acceptance models with task technology fit will provide further variance explanation to the use of technology in a given context than when standing alone (Junco & Cotton, 2011). In this study, the proposed theoretical model is used to study instructors' intention to adopt gamification for online learning. In addition, the authors introduce a new construct (task technology fit) to assess the task fit in gamification. Table 1 summarises existing literature integrating TAM and TTF to assess behavioural intention, actual usage, and continuance intention.

THEORETICAL FOUNDATION AND HYPOTHESIS

This study focuses on factors influencing the adoption of game design features in online learning. TAM was extended with TTF to integrate computer use and related support components. TAM and TTF overlap significantly from the related literature and, if combined, can produce a significantly more robust model than either independently (Vanduhe et al., 2020; Dishaw & Strong, 1999). Furthermore, TAM is one of the most widely used models to investigate user acceptance of technology (Davis, 1988). The inclusion of subjective norms and perceived enjoyment construct in the research model allows a better

Table 1. Studies integrating TAM and TTF

Author	Domain	Sample Size & Country	Constructs	Measurement Construct	Findings
Vanduhe et al., 2020	Gamified Online Learning	321 Instructors & Students North Cyprus	TTF, PU, Social Influence, Attitude, PEOU, Social Recognition	Continuance Intention	PU, PEOU, TTF, SR, SI and Attitude significantly influenced CI. GFI=0.87
Rahman et al., 2018	Gamified Online Learning	50 Students Malaysia	Gamification PEOU, Gamification PU, Gamification Attitude	Interaction Engagement, Skill Engagement	Gamification PEOU better indicator of student attitude toward using gamified online learning
Wu & Chen, 2017	MOOC Online Learning	252 Students China	TTF, PEOU, PU, Openness, Reputation, Technology Fit, SI, SR, Attitude	Continuance Intention	PU and Attitude significantly affect CI. PEOU significantly affected by TTF. PEOU and SI do not significantly affect Attitude. GFI=0.92 (95.7% variance)
Yuan et al., 2014	M-banking	434 China	TTF, PEOU, PU, Gender, Perceived Risk, Satisfaction, Confirmation	Continuance Intention	Satisfaction, PU, PTTF, and PR are main predictors of CI. PU significantly affected by PEOU and PTTF GFI=0.89
Shih & Chen, 2011	M-commerce	421 Real estate sales personnel Taiwan	TTF, PEOU, PU, Tool Experience, Tool Functionality, Task Requirements	Behavioural Intention	TTF significantly and directly affects BI, PU and PEOU. Tool Functionality significant predictor of PEOU. Tool Experience not significant determinant of PU. CFI=0.98
Yen et al., 2010	Wireless Technology	231	TTF, PU, PEOU, Task Characteristics, Technology Characteristics	Behavioural Intention	Significant relationship between TAM and TTF. PEOU significantly affected by PU. Tech Characteristics influences PEOU, PU. BI determined by fit between Task and Tech Characteristics, PU and PEOU. GFI=0.89
Klopping & McKinney, 2004	E-commerce	263	TTF, PEOU, PU, BI	Actual Usage (AU)	No significant relationship between TTF and PU. TTF significantly affects PEOU. GFI =0.99 (52% variance)
Dishaw & Strong, 1999	Business Information System	60 United States	TTF, PEOU, PU	Actual Usage (AU)	PEOU significantly affected by TTF. Low correlation between PU and TTF. PU and IT Tool influenced by Tool Functionality. GFI =0.94 (51% variance)

understanding of the impact of these factors. Hence, they can potentially be one of the main predictors of using gamified online learning systems.

Additionally, Computer Anxiety and Facilitating Conditions were considered due to their ability to significantly influence user acceptance of gamified online learning in developing countries. These constructs, considered together, seek to determine instructors' intention and ultimately predict their behaviour. The relationships between these constructs are integrated into the conceptual model depicted in Figure 1.

Figure 1. Proposed theoretical model

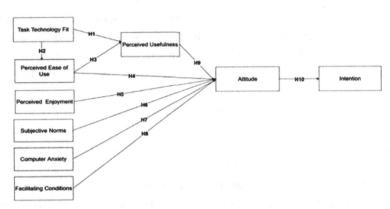

TTF model is used to examine how technology enhances performance. Specifically, TTF is employed to evaluate user performance (Goodhue & Thompson, 1995). The efficacy of technology acceptance is based on user acceptance and how perfect the task fits. Subsequently, researchers have widely used the TTF to forecast the acceptance and usage of new technology (Wu & Chen, 2017). Despite the literature on TTF in IS, there is limited focus on instructors' acceptance of gamified learning systems. A recent related study demonstrated the significance of TTF on user intentions (Vanduhe et al., 2020). To date, TTF's impact on instructors' use of gamified systems remains understudied. Therefore, the authors assume that users are more likely to use the gamified system if technology matches the task. With this understanding, the following is proposed.

H1: TTF will significantly affect the perceived usefulness of using gamified online learning.
H2: TTF will significantly affect the PEOU of using gamified online learning.

Perceived Ease of Use (PEOU) is the extent to which a consumer perceives using a specific system will need no physical or mental effort. Therefore, the system should be simple to use and therefore does not necessitate any specialist skills before application (use). Previous studies indicate that the PEOU directly affects on users' attitudes and the perceived usefulness of technology (Vanduhe et al., 2020, Wu & Chen, 2017). Further, in the gamification context, PEOU is the degree to which the instructors expect the gamified system to be free of effort (Vanduhe et al., 2020; Rahman et al., 2018). Accordingly, PEOU can be a better indicator of students' and instructors' attitudes towards a gamified online system. Based on these, this study hypothesises that:

H3: PEOU will significantly affect the perceived usefulness of using gamified online learning.

H4: PEOU has a positive effect on user attitudes towards intention to use gamified online learning.

Perceived Enjoyment (PE) is a person's overall perceived gratification and satisfaction with using a service (Davis, 1989). TAM may be less robust when applied in hedonic system-use contexts. Hedonic systems are usually more enjoyable, fulfilling, and stimulating to use. Thus, perceived usefulness and PEOU may not be the only important factors influencing the usage of hedonic systems (Wu & Lu, 2013). As such, PE becomes a key variable in hedonic system usage intention. PE is the most widely employed external component in the TAM (Chao 2019; Tsai et al., 2018). Extant literature did not indicate the widespread use of PE in examining instructors' use of gamified learning. However, the limited body of evidence suggests that PE is essential in inspiring students' intentions to use gamified learning (Cabada et al., 2018). From that perspective, this study assumes that instructors are more likely to accept gamification if they perceived that the gamified system to be pleasurable to use. Therefore, the following is proposed:

H4: PE has a positive effect on user attitudes towards intention to use gamified online learning.

Subjective Norms (SN) are the perception that a significant individual or set of people would support a specific behaviour (Ham et al., 2015). The SN is influenced by an individual's perceived social pressure from others to behave in a specific way and their reasons for conforming to those people's opinions. Therefore, individuals who perceive that valued individuals believe they ought to act on behaviour may feel more motivated. In related literature, subjective norms were significant in predicting user intention (Mo et al., 2019; Ham et al., 2015). It is also crucial in developing behaviour change strategies. Thus, in this study, the authors postulated the following hypotheses:

H5: Subjective Norms positively affect user attitudes towards intention to use gamified online learning.

Computer Anxiety (CA) includes invoking uneasy or irrational feelings to performing any computer-related activity (Rizun & Strzelecki, 2020). Indeed, CA plays a significant role in IS adoption (Venkatesh et al., 2003). Among the IT literature, authors affirmed CA is a barrier to technology adoption for academic purposes, particularly in developing nations (Huang & Mayer, 2016). Moreover, gamification literature reported the indirect effects of CA on behavioural intention (Adukaite et al., 2017). It follows that most instructors experiencing computer anxiety may be slower to accept and utilise gamified online learning systems. Based on this, the authors deduced the following hypotheses:

H7: Computer Anxiety positively affects user attitudes towards intention to use gamified online learning.

Facilitating Conditions (FC) is an individual's collective perception that the organisational and technological resources required to use a particular technology are available (Yakubu et al., 2019; Venkatesh et al., 2003). Like most digital learning technologies, instructors use of gamified online learning platforms may suffer from specific issues such as favourable infrastructures, cost, and support tools. In this sense, a favourable set of conditions, such as infrastructure, power supply, IT support personnel, contributes to a greater likelihood to accept and use a system. However, if this infrastructure is unavailable, instructors will be less inclined to utilise the system. Several studies established the importance of facilitating conditions in influencing behavioural intentions and actual use (Alkawsi et al., 2021a; Mensah, 2019;

Kurfali et al., 2017). For example, Mensah (2019) found FC to be a significant predictor of intention to use e-government services and can also fit the context of online learning services. Especially, FC may be critical for developing conditions where the resources (technical and infrastructural support) to sustain gamified systems may be lacking. Therefore, according to the presumptions as mentioned earlier, the following hypothesis was developed:

H8: Facilitating Conditions positively affect user attitudes towards intention to use gamified online learning.

Perceived Usefulness (PU) relates to an individual's belief that using a system will enhance their job performance more than any direct benefits associated with system utilisation (Davis, 1989). For example, the gamification literature suggests instructors perceive that adopting gamified online learning will improve their overall performance. Also, evidence shows that PU can be beneficial in predicting behavioural intention to use gamified learning systems (Vanduhe et al., 2020). It follows that an instructor will be more inclined to accept and use gamified online learning to achieve their academic goals. In this sense, it is assumed that PU will significantly influence the instructors' intention to use gamified online learning systems. Therefore, this study proposes that:

H9: PU has a positive effect on user attitudes towards intention to use gamified online learning.

Attitude (ATT) is the overall feeling of liking or disliking a behaviour (Mo et al., 2019). These attitudes are developed based on the beliefs regarding the consequences (intrinsic and extrinsic rewards) of the considered behaviour (Ajzen, 2005). In gamification, these consequences generally have a positive impact on user acceptance of gamified online learning. Previous studies found attitude as one of the most dominant predictors of technology usage (Wu & Chen, 2017). In related literature, Vanduhe and colleagues (2020) found attitudes to positively affect continuance intentions to use gamification for training. This study, therefore, assumes that attitude will also have a significant effect on instructors' intention to use gamified learning. As such, this study asserts that in a gamified online learning context, the intention to engage with the system is likely to attract a more favourable attitude towards it. Hence, the following hypothesis is proposed:

H10: Attitude has a positive effect on users' intention to use gamified online learning.

METHOD

In this study, a survey is employed to test the hypotheses formulated in the previous sections; questionnaire development and data collection are discussed in the subsequent sections.

Survey Instrument

This study employed a questionnaire survey with two sections to test our theoretical model. The rationale for employing the survey was to collect information and demographic features from a large study sample in a relatively short period (Ponto, 2015). Using the survey method also allows us to obtain data from diverse academics from various African nations. Furthermore, this is an appropriate data collection instrument to employ during the COVID-19 pandemic. A pilot study was presented to 45 African educators before the survey was distributed to produce better questions and eliminate ambiguity, as in previous studies (Alkawsi et al., 2021a; Alkawsi et al., 2021b; Alkawasi & Baashar, 2020). As a result, a response rate of 89% was recorded. Validation testing was performed using expert and content validity to identify items that were likely unclear or redundant in order to verify conceptual equivalence. Participants in this study were instructors from various African institutions. The study was mainly interested in instructors who had not previously utilised gamified online learning platforms.

Data Collection

The participants of this study were instructors at various African institutions. The online test was distributed to approximately 430 prospective participants via Google forms. Email, Facebook, and WhatsApp groups were used to disseminate the questionnaire. The email addresses of the teachers were retrieved from the official websites of their respective universities. To improve the number of responses, reminders and follow-up emails were sent. Data was gathered from February to June 2021; 50 valid replies were received, indicating a poor response rate of 11.6%. The poor response rate could be attributed to instructors not checking their official emails regularly. Furthermore, some instructors, particularly in developing countries, have limited access to the internet (availability). The demographic data of the respondents are summarised in Table 1.

Descriptive Statistics

The sample consisted of 50 participants. The respondents' ages ranged from 26 to 65, and their mean age was 39.5 (SD = 7.8). 18% of the sample was over 45 years old. Over two-thirds (81%) of the sample were male (n= 42) and 16% females (n=8). The majority of respondents are based in Nigerian universities (78%), followed by South African (8%) and Ethiopian universities (4%). Most of the courses taught by the respondents include Sciences (20%), Engineering (18%), Computer/IT (16%), Economics/Financial Management (16%), and Medical (14%). Furthermore, the four main platforms used for online learning in various African institutions were Zoom, Moodle, Google Classroom, and Blackboard. Table 2 presents the demographic information of respondents (n=50).

RESULTS AND DATA ANALYSIS

The evaluation of the study model was done in two steps. First, the measurement model was evaluated by examining the psychometric properties of the variables. Second, the structural model was assessed by looking into collinearity issues, relationships between all the constructs, and the predictive relevance of endogenous variables.

Evaluation of Measurement Model

The reliability of the variables was measured through Cronbach's α (CA) and composite reliability. The acceptable range of internal consistency in exploratory research is 0.6-0.7 (Hair et al., 2016). Likewise,

Table 2. Demographic information of respondents

Characteristics		Frequency	Percentage (%)
Gender	Male	42	84
	Female	8	16
Age	26-35	16	32
	36-45	25	50
	46-55	7	14
	56-65	2	4
Country	Nigeria	39	78
	South Africa	4	8
	Ethiopia	2	4
	Botswana	1	2
	Cameroon	1	2
	Eswatini	1	2
	Ghana	1	2
	Namibia	1	2
Courses Taught	Sciences	10	20
	Engineering	9	18
	Computer Science and Information Technology	8	16
	Economics, Finance and Management	8	16
	Medical Sciences	7	14
	Education, Curriculum and Graduate Studies	6	12
	Social Sciences, Arts and Languages	2	4

Table 3. Psychometric properties (n=50)

Construct	Reliability		Convergent Validity			Discriminant Validity
	Cronbach α	Composite Reliability	K	Loading Range	AVE	HTMT <0.90
Task Technology Fit	0.95	0.96	3	0.94 – 0.97	0.90	No
Perceived Ease of Use	0.87	0.91	4	0.81 – 0.87	0.72	Yes
Perceived Enjoyment	0.90	0.93	4	0.86 – 0.88	0.76	Yes
Subjective Norms	0.82	0.89	3	0.72 – 0.94	0.73	Yes
Computer Anxiety	0.28	0.13	4	- 0.37 – 0.92	0.42	Yes
Facilitating Conditions	0.78	0.87	3	0.82 – 0.85	0.68	Yes
Perceived Usefulness	0.95	0.97	4	0.88 – 0.97	0.87	No
Attitude	0.94	0.95	4	0.89 – 0.95	0.84	No
Intention	0.88	0.92	4	0.76 – 0.91	0.73	Yes

Note: K=number of indicators, AVE=Average Variance Extracted

the convergent validity was measured through AVE (Average Variance Extracted). AVE value 0.5 indicates that the construct explains 50% of the variance of the indicators, whereas the rest of the variance is in error terms. The discriminant validity of the constructs was examined with the Heterotrait-Monotrait Ratio of Correlations (HTMT) criterion. Henseler et al. (2015) suggested that if the value of HTMT is below 0.9 between two constructs, it implies that discriminant validity has been established. The psychometric properties of the constructs are reported in Table 3.

The values of Cronbach's α and composite reliability reported in the above table represent that all the scales have met the criteria for internal consistency. The AVE of all the constructs is above the criterion, which is 0.5 except that of CA. Nevertheless, the AVE value of 0.4 is also acceptable in some of the cases. Given the low reliability of CA based on its acceptable convergent and discriminant validity, it should be excluded from the model. However, CA can be retained in the model as part of scientific theory (Yakubu et al., 2019). All other constructs have acceptable convergent validity. Values of HTMT ratio of all constructs are less than 0.9 except for three factors. Noticeably, the current study is related to the different interlinked features of game design; hence their discriminant validity can be overlooked.

Figure 2. PLS results of the research mode

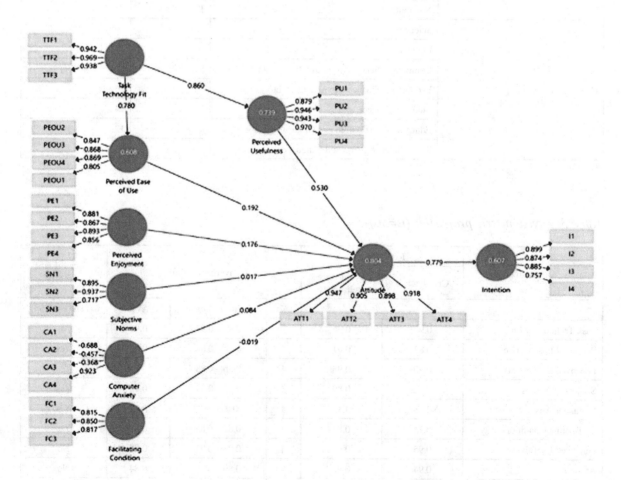

Structural Model

While examining the structural model, collinearity assessment (VIF), Coefficient of Determination (R2), and predictive relevance (Q2) were explored. The PLS results of the research model are presented in Figure 2.

Collinearity Assessment

The correlation between independent variables of the model was assessed to figure out the multi-collinearity issue. It was determined through VIF statistics. According to Hair and colleagues (2016), the value of VIF should be less than 5. Table 4 shows that the VIF value for perceived enjoyment is slightly above the criteria whereas, for all other variables, it is within the acceptable range. Considering the game design features, the inconspicuous correlation of perceived enjoyment with other factors is ignorable.

Table 4. Collinearity statistics (n=50)

Variables	Project Success
Task Technology Fit	2.55
Perceived Ease of Use	2.55
Perceived Enjoyment	5.06
Subjective Norms	2.34
Computer Anxiety	1.40
Facilitating Conditions	1.49
Perceived Usefulness	4.51

Predictive Capabilities of the Model

The predictive capabilities of the model were calculated in two ways. At first, R2 was examined, which means the predictive power of all the exogenous constructs for linked endogenous constructs. It was obtained by Bootstrapping procedure. Secondly, the model's predictive relevance (Q2) was calculated by eliminating specific data points from the model. It was obtained by calculating through Blindfolding Procedure with an Omission Distance of 7. The results are illustrated in Table 5.

Table 5. Coefficient of Determination (R2), Cross-Validated Redundancy (Q2), of the Study Variables (N=50)

Construct	R^2	Q^2
Perceived Usefulness	0.79	0.58
Perceived Ease of Use	0.61	0.39
Attitude	0.80	0.64
Intention	0.61	0.35

Note. $*p<.05, **p<.01, ***p<.001$.

According to Hair et al. (2011), R2 and Q2 values of 0.25 can be considered weak, 0.50 as moderate, and 0.75 as strong. Therefore, values reported in the above table show that all the independent variables are moderate to strong predictors of the dependent variables.

Hypotheses Testing

Path coefficients represent the prediction of specific endogenous constructs by specific endogenous constructs. Its significance is determined by the t value corresponding to the specific significance level (p-value). Confidence intervals can also determine the significance of path coefficients. Notably, the confidence Interval should not include "0" for the significant path coefficient. F2 is effect size. Effect size f2 of less than 0.02 represents that there is no effect. However, 0.02, 0.15, and 0.35 represent small, medium, and large effect sizes.

Table 6. Path co-efficient and effect sizes

Path	Path Coefficient β	p Value	Confidence Intervals		f^2	Supported
Task Technology Fit → Perceived Usefulness	0.86	0.00	0.73	0.96	0.64	Yes
Task Technology Fit → Perceived Ease of Use	0.78	0.00	0.65	0.88	1.55	Yes
Perceived Ease of Use → Attitude	0.19	0.19	-0.09	0.48	0.03	No
Perceived Enjoyment → Attitude	0.18	0.32	-0.24	0.47	0.03	No
Subjective Norms → Attitude	0.02	0.86	-0.20	0.22	0.00	No
Computer Anxiety → Attitude	0.08	0.52	-0.23	0.26	0.03	No
Facilitating Conditions → Attitude	-0.02	0.83	-0.18	0.18	0.00	No
Perceived Usefulness → Attitude	0.53	0.00	0.25	0.94	0.32	Yes
Attitude → Intention	0.78	0.00	0.73	0.85	1.54	Yes

Findings in the Table 6 reveal that only four hypotheses (H1, H2, H9 and H10) were supported. Basically, task technology fit significantly predicted perceived usefulness and perceived use of ease. Furthermore, perceived usefulness significantly predicted attitude. Also, attitude significantly predicted intention. At the same time, perceived ease of use, perceived enjoyment, subjective norms, computer anxiety and facilitating conditions did not affect attitude.

DISCUSSION

A total of ten hypotheses were examined in this study. Accordingly, the authors found evidence for four of the relationships between the constructs. Thus, as in Figure 1, eight independent variables are hypothesised to influence instructors' behavioural intentions to use gamified online learning systems.

Following H1, TTF positively and significantly affected PU, with a large effect size. The indirect effect of TTF on ATT was shown to be significant via the PU of gamified online learning. This outcome supports the conclusion from previous research that task relevance directly affects PU (Dishaw & Strong, 1999).

Nonetheless, our findings contrast those of Vanduhe et al. (2020), who found no significant association between the two variables (TTF and PU). Therefore, the TTF of a gamified learning system improves instructors' behavioural intentions toward its use.

Concerning H2, TTF was found to predict the PEOU of a gamified online system significantly. Furthermore, the findings of our study revealed the critical significance of TTF. According to earlier research, TTF is positively associated with ATT towards using gamified online learning (Vanduhe et al., 2020). As a result, if the gamification learning system fits well with the instructor's task, the technology is more likely to be adopted and used.

Regarding H3, the lack of a strong correlation between PEOU and PU contradicts past research indicating that PEOU has a significant impact on PU (Buabeng-Andoh, 2018). Based on existing literature, if individuals perceive the system as easy to use, they are more likely to view it as beneficial and more inclined to utilise it (Garcia, 2017), notably among inexperienced users (Buabeng-Andoh, 2018, Lau, 2008). Assuming that most respondents are familiar with eLearning systems, they are not considered inexperienced users, and thus PEOU may not be a factor of the perceived usefulness of gamification. Although PEOU and PU are strongly supported in various research, they do not appear to have been validated in the context of gamified online learning. Instead, the current study offers a distinct perspective, and future research may confirm or contradict this conclusion.

In terms of H4, data shows that PEOU is not a significant determinant to instructors as PU despite its prevalence in various studies on technology acceptance. In a recent study (Yakubu et al., 2019), PEOU had the most significant influence on behavioural intentions when using eLearning. Their research focused on students' perceptions of Learning Management Systems (LMS) in the context of a developing country. However, our findings contradict this conclusion. It demonstrates how the discrepancy between instructors' and students' perceptions of a system's ease of use influences their behavioural intention to utilise it. One interpretation is that instructors, unlike students, may not need to be fully engaged with the system. Therefore, they are more concerned with the system's task fit and far less interested in its convenience of use. Another key analysis found that perceived ease of use and perceived usefulness were less significant when predicting technology acceptance among a group of teachers (Chen et al., 2012). It implies that instructors would likely adopt a gamified learning system regardless of how complex the system is to use.

For H5, PE, which should be crucial in influencing instructors' usage of a gamified system, was found to have a non-significant relationship with the intention to utilise the system. Given that gamified systems are hedonic-oriented systems (Oluwajana et al., 2019; Hamari & Koivisto et al., 2015), it is expected that PE will be crucial in predicting their utilisation. This finding, however, suggests that instructors feel they do not need to enjoy using the system or that it must be gratifying (intrinsically motivating) to motivate them to utilise it. Literature provides evidence that, in utilitarian systems, extrinsic motivators are more significant determinants than intrinsic motivators (Wu & Lu, 2013, Fagan et al., 2008). Although gamified systems, as previously stated, are hedonic, an online learning system may be perceived in two states: utilitarian during the adoption stage and hedonic during the post-adoption stage. According to this and earlier research, external motivators are considered sufficient to motivate the adoption of a utilitarian system. Our study did not focus on adherence to the system, which likely depends on users finding using the system fun and interesting (intrinsic motivation), so PE may not be significant in predicting gamification adoption.

According to the empirical findings concerning H6, SN has no effect on instructors' attitudes regarding utilising gamification. Regrettably, our findings cannot be compared to those of other studies, given the limited research on the specific influence of SN in the context of gamified learning. Nevertheless according to the general assumption, individuals are more likely to engage in a behaviour that is considered desirable by significant others. However, in our study, we discovered that instructors do not believe that social pressure from significant others will influence their inclination to use gamified online learning. Therefore, it implies that instructors in developing countries will be willing to utilise gamification regardless of others' opinions. In other words, their intention to use the gamified system will not be swayed or influenced by important persons.

In contrast to our assumptions in H7, the effects of CA on ATT to use gamified online learning is not supported by the data. Because of the nature of our study, this finding could not be compared to prior studies. Notwithstanding, although unexpected, one potential reason for this unexpected finding is that the instructors who completed the survey were more likely to be more proficient with computers, which may have influenced their responses. As a result, they had no difficulty finishing an online survey, whereas those uncomfortable with computers opted not to participate in the online survey. As such, CA's insignificance indicates that aversion to emerging technology usage may no longer be as crucial as it previously was. Surprisingly, our data for H8 revealed no relationship between FC and instructors' intention to use the gamified system. This finding suggests that teachers do not consider FC (internet, technical support) a barrier to implementing gamified systems. Interestingly, instructors in developing nations may have learned to manage with inadequate infrastructures and limited resources (support) and do not consider them significant factors influencing their use of online learning systems.

Following H9, PU significantly predicted instructors' behavioural intention to use the gamified online system. The instructors believe that the system's usability will motivate them to use gamified learning systems. This finding is consistent with prior research in which PU was found to predict behavioural intention significantly (Wong et al., 2020; Rahman et al., 2018; Fagan et al., 2008). According to one study, instructors' attitudes towards adopting gamified systems depend entirely on the PU of gamification (Vanduhe et al., 2020). Our findings support a similar conclusion that gamification is strongly related to users' views of its use rather than ease of use.

For H10, it was found that ATT significantly predicts behavioural intention to use a gamified online learning system. The statistically significant correlation between ATT and Behavioural Intention validates previous research confirming the positive effect of learners' attitudes toward gamification (De-Marcos et al., 2014). This observation shows that an instructor's positive attitude toward gamified online learning is a significant predictor of behavioural intention. A positive attitude would help in building a stronger intention to adopt technology (Davis, 1989).

Implications

In terms of theoretical contributions, the current study adds to existing knowledge in gamification studies by investigating the predictors and intentions of gamified online learning adoption in the educational setting. Overall, little attention has been paid to the factors influencing the adoption of gamified eLearning, particularly in Africa. More specifically, this empirical study aimed to explore the challenges with gamification adoption intentions. Furthermore, it is evident that earlier research mainly focused on students in a non-gamified online learning context. Therefore, this research contributes to the body of knowledge on theory integration such as TTF and TAM. Furthermore, this study provides a more in-depth explanation of the direct and indirect links between the examined constructs and their associated indicators regarding the determinants of instructors' intention to use gamification online learning platforms in African institutions.

This research showed that ATT was the most significant predictor of gamification intention. Thus, it appears critical for institutions to foster positive attitudes on the use of technology among instructors. According to Alzahrani and O'Toole (2017), users who have a positive attitude toward technology are more inclined to use it. Remarkably, PEOU did not affect perceived utility. These findings differ from prior research, suggesting that users likely reject its use despite a technology's usefulness if they regarded it as challenging to use. Most importantly, the gamified online learning should be suited for the instructors' tasks while also being usable and beneficial. Also, the gamified system should support integrated learning. Notably, Computer Anxiety, Subjective Norms, and Facilitating Conditions impacted instructor's intention to engage in gamified online learning. Surprisingly, this implies that instructors are unconcerned with the influence of significant others on them using gamification. Furthermore, they are not worried about facilitating conditions such as a reliable internet connection and electricity affecting their utilisation of gamified learning systems.

Implications for TTF

In TFF, we established that aligning gamification functions to specific tasks allows instructors to perceive its usefulness and ease of use. Similar conclusions were reached by Wu & Chen (2017), confirming that TTF impacts PU, PEOU, and PU in the eLearning domain.

Implications for TAM

In TFF, we observed that matching gamification functionalities to specific tasks will enable instructors to perceive its usefulness and ease of use. Similar conclusions were reached by (Wu & Chen, 2017), indicating that TTF affects PU and PEOU and PU in the eLearning domain. Since instructors prefer to focus on the utility of the system itself rather than its simplicity of use when creating an attitude toward utilising eLearning, PU influence on Attitude is more significant. It appears to be the case for online learning systems that are gamified. As a result, perceived usefulness was significant in predicting the use of gamification. The findings, on the other hand, show that perceived ease of use did not influence PU. Hence, if gamification offers significant functionality, instructors will be ready to accept some difficulty in using it. Consequently, instructors did not value PEOU.

CONCLUSION

Educators should develop more innovative approaches to improve instruction quality, learning experience, and engagement to adapt current learning to new pedagogical needs. In this regard, gamification is offered as an innovative strategy for achieving this goal. Likewise, gamification has the potential to improve student performance and engagement, particularly in developing countries. Given this, it is critical to understand instructors' perspectives on gamification adoption at various African institutions. There is, however, limited evidence in this context, particularly from the perspective of teachers. As a result, the purpose of this study is to determine the predictors of gamified online learning adoption in African institutions.

The application of TAM and TTF to adopt a gamified online learning system presented in this research expands our understanding of the mechanics of technology and attitudinal shift as they pertain to fostering a key area for online learning. In the integrated model, four of the ten offered hypotheses were found to affect behavioural intention positively. TTF, PU, and ATT significantly influence the intention to employ gamification in an online learning environment. However, despite its prominence in many studies on IS adoption, PEOU had no substantial impact on behavioural intention.

Furthermore, SN, FC, and CA did not influence the intention to use a gamified online learning system. The model assists researchers and practitioners in better understanding why people choose to use gamified online learning systems for pedagogy. This insight is especially significant in understanding how individual attributes interact with task features to influence instructors' decisions to utilise or not use the system to improve educational outcomes.

Limitations

Although this work provides several contributions, it does have several limitations that could be addressed in the future. First, as gamification is a novel concept, the initial explicit limitation is the lack of supporting literature for the outcomes. Second, given the low response rate, the results could be affected by a non-response bias. This also limits the findings' generalisability. Hence, prospective studies should involve a larger sample size to increase the findings' significance and generalizability. Second, most respondents appear to be comfortable using computers, which may have influenced the study's conclusions. As a result, further research is required to understand how computer experience influences user intention.

Finally, despite being validated in prior studies, the new variables did not affect behavioural intention. As a result, future research should incorporate more predictive factors from diverse theories and models into the existing theoretical model to improve its predictive power.

ACKNOWLEDGMENT

This research received no specific grant from any funding agency in the public, commercial, or not-for-profit sectors.

REFERENCES

Adukaite, A., van Zyl, I., Er, Ş., & Cantoni, L. (2017). Teacher perceptions on the use of digital gamified learning in tourism education: The case of South African secondary schools. *Computers & Education*, *111*, 172–190. doi:10.1016/j.compedu.2017.04.008

Ajzen, I. (2012). Values, attitudes, and behavior. In *Methods, theories, and empirical applications in the social sciences* (pp. 33–38). VS Verlag für Sozialwissenschaften. doi:10.1007/978-3-531-18898-0_5

Alabbasi, D. (2018). Exploring Teachers' Perspectives towards Using Gamification Techniques in Online Learning. *Turkish Online Journal of Educational Technology-TOJET*, *17*(2), 34–45.

Aldemir, T., Celik, B., & Kaplan, G. (2018). A qualitative investigation of student perceptions of game elements in a gamified course. *Computers in Human Behavior, 78*, 235–254. doi:10.1016/j.chb.2017.10.001

Alharthi, S., & Parrish, J. (2017). The Role of Gamification in Motivating User Participation in Requirements Determinations. *Proceedings of the 12th SAIS*, 7.

Alkawsi, G., Ali, N. A., & Baashar, Y. (2021b). The Moderating Role of Personal Innovativeness and Users Experience in Accepting the Smart Meter Technology. *Applied Sciences (Basel, Switzerland), 11*(8), 3297. doi:10.3390/app11083297

Alkawsi, G. A., Ali, N., Mustafa, A. S., Baashar, Y., Alhussian, H., Alkahtani, A., Tiong, S. K., & Ekanayake, J. (2021a). A hybrid SEM-neural network method for identifying acceptance factors of the smart meters in Malaysia: Challenges perspective. *Alexandria Engineering Journal, 60*(1), 227–240. doi:10.1016/j.aej.2020.07.002

Alkawsi, G. A., & Baashar, Y. (2020). An empirical study of the acceptance of IoT-based smart meter in Malaysia: The effect of electricity-saving knowledge and environmental awareness. *IEEE Access: Practical Innovations, Open Solutions, 8*, 42794–42804. doi:10.1109/ACCESS.2020.2977060

Alzahrani, M. G., & O'Toole, J. M. (2017). The Impact of Internet Experience and Attitude on Student Preference for Blended Learning. *Journal of Curriculum and Teaching, 6*(1), 65–78. doi:10.5430/jct.v6n1p65

Antonaci, A., Klemke, R., & Specht, M. (2019, September). The effects of gamification in online learning environments: A systematic literature review. In Informatics (Vol. 6, No. 3, p. 32). Multidisciplinary Digital Publishing Institute. doi:10.3390/informatics6030032

Buabeng-Andoh, C. (2018). Predicting students' intention to adopt mobile learning: A combination of theory of reasoned action and technology acceptance model. *Journal of Research in Innovative Teaching & Learning*.

Cabada, R. Z., Estrada, M. L. B., Hernández, F. G., Bustillos, R. O., & Reyes-García, C. A. (2018). An affective and Web 3.0-based learning environment for a programming language. *Telematics and Informatics, 35*(3), 611–628. doi:10.1016/j.tele.2017.03.005

Cable, J., & Cheung, C. (2017). Eight principles of effective online teaching: A decade-long lessons learned in project management education. *PM World Journal, 6*(7), 1–16.

Chao, C. M. (2019). Factors determining the behavioral intention to use mobile learning: An application and extension of the UTAUT model. *Frontiers in Psychology, 10*, 1652. doi:10.3389/fpsyg.2019.01652 PMID:31379679

Chen, C. Y., Shih, B. Y., & Yu, S. H. (2012). Disaster prevention and reduction for exploring teachers' technology acceptance using a virtual reality system and partial least squares techniques. *Natural Hazards, 62*(3), 1217–1231. doi:10.100711069-012-0146-0

Davis, F. D. (1989). Perceived usefulness, perceived ease of use, and user acceptance of information technology. *Management Information Systems Quarterly, 13*(3), 319–340. doi:10.2307/249008

de la Peña, D., Lizcano, D., & Martínez-Álvarez, I. (2021). Learning through play: Gamification model in university-level distance learning. *Entertainment Computing*, *39*, 100430. doi:10.1016/j.entcom.2021.100430

De-Marcos, L., Domínguez, A., Saenz-de-Navarrete, J., & Pagés, C. (2014). An empirical study comparing gamification and social networking on e-learning. *Computers & Education*, *75*, 82–91. doi:10.1016/j.compedu.2014.01.012

Deterding, S., Dixon, D., Khaled, R., & Nacke, L. (2011, September). From game design elements to gamefulness: defining "gamification". In *Proceedings of the 15th international academic MindTrek conference: Envisioning future media environments* (pp. 9-15). Academic Press.

Dishaw, M. T., & Strong, D. M. (1999). Extending the technology acceptance model with task–technology fit constructs. *Information & Management*, *36*(1), 9–21. doi:10.1016/S0378-7206(98)00101-3

Fagan, M. H., Neill, S., & Wooldridge, B. R. (2008). Exploring the intention to use computers: An empirical investigation of the role of intrinsic motivation, extrinsic motivation, and perceived ease of use. *Journal of Computer Information Systems*, *48*(3), 31–37.

Fathali, S., & Okada, T. (2018). Technology acceptance model in technology-enhanced OCLL contexts: A self-determination theory approach. *Australasian Journal of Educational Technology*, *34*(4). Advance online publication. doi:10.14742/ajet.3629

Garcia, M. B. (2017). E-Learning Technology Adoption in the Philippines: An Investigation of Factors Affecting Filipino College Students' Acceptance of Learning Management Systems. *The International Journal of E-Learning and Educational Technologies in the Digital Media*, *3*(3), 118–130. doi:10.17781/P002374

Gikas, J., & Grant, M. M. (2013). Mobile computing devices in higher education: Student perspectives on learning with cellphones, smartphones & social media. *The Internet and Higher Education*, *19*, 18–26. doi:10.1016/j.iheduc.2013.06.002

Glover, I. (2013, June). Play as you learn: gamification as a technique for motivating learners. In Edmedia+ innovate learning (pp. 1999-2008). Association for the Advancement of Computing in Education (AACE).

Goodhue, D. L., & Thompson, R. L. (1995). Task-technology fit and individual performance. *Management Information Systems Quarterly*, *19*(2), 213–236. doi:10.2307/249689

Hair, J. F., Hult, G. T. M., Ringle, C. M., & Sarstedt, M. (2016). *A Primer on Partial Least Squares Structural Equation Modeling (PLS-SEM)*. Sage Publications.

Hair, J. F., Ringle, C. M., & Sarstedt, M. (2011). PLS-SEM: Indeed a silver bullet. *Journal of Marketing Theory and Practice*, *19*(2), 139–151. doi:10.2753/MTP1069-6679190202

Ham, M., Jeger, M., & Frajman Ivković, A. (2015). The role of subjective norms in forming the intention to purchase green food. Economic research-. *Ekonomska Istrazivanja*, *28*(1), 738–748. doi:10.1080/1331677X.2015.1083875

Hamari, J., & Koivisto, J. (2015). "Working out for likes": An empirical study on social influence in exercise gamification. *Computers in Human Behavior, 50*, 333–347. doi:10.1016/j.chb.2015.04.018

Henseler, J., Ringle, C. M., & Sarstedt, M. (2015). A new criterion for assessing discriminant validity in variance-based structural equation modeling. *Journal of the Academy of Marketing Science, 43*(1), 115–135. doi:10.100711747-014-0403-8

Huang, C. K., Chen, C. D., & Liu, Y. T. (2019). To stay or not to stay? Discontinuance intention of gamification apps. *Information Technology & People, 32*(6), 1423–1445. doi:10.1108/ITP-08-2017-0271

Huang, X., & Mayer, R. E. (2016). Benefits of adding anxiety-reducing features to a computer-based multimedia lesson on statistics. *Computers in Human Behavior, 63*, 293–303. doi:10.1016/j.chb.2016.05.034

Ibanez, M. B., Di-Serio, A., & Delgado-Kloos, C. (2014). Gamification for engaging computer science students in learning activities: A case study. *IEEE Transactions on Learning Technologies, 7*(3), 291–301. doi:10.1109/TLT.2014.2329293

Joo, Y. J., Kim, N., & Kim, N. H. (2016). Factors predicting online university students' use of a mobile learning management system (m-LMS). *Educational Technology Research and Development, 64*(4), 611–630. doi:10.100711423-016-9436-7

Junco, R., & Cotten, S. R. (2011). *A decade of distraction? How multitasking affects student outcomes.* Academic Press.

Klopping, I. M., & McKinney, E. (2004). Extending the technology acceptance model and the task-technology fit model to consumer e-commerce. *Information Technology, Learning and Performance Journal, 22*(1).

Kurfalı, M., Arifoğlu, A., Tokdemir, G., & Paçin, Y. (2017). Adoption of e-government services in Turkey. *Computers in Human Behavior, 66*, 168–178. doi:10.1016/j.chb.2016.09.041

Lau, J. (2008). *Students' experience of using electronic textbooks in different levels of education.* Academic Press.

Manzano-León, A., Camacho-Lazarraga, P., Guerrero, M. A., Guerrero-Puerta, L., Aguilar-Parra, J. M., Trigueros, R., & Alias, A. (2021). Between level up and game over: A systematic literature review of gamification in education. *Sustainability, 13*(4), 2247.

Martí-Parreño, J., Seguí-Mas, D., & Seguí-Mas, E. (2016). Teachers' attitude towards and actual use of gamification. *Procedia: Social and Behavioral Sciences, 228*, 682–688. doi:10.1016/j.sbspro.2016.07.104

Melzer, P. (2019). A conceptual framework for task and tool personalisation in IS education. In *A conceptual framework for personalised learning* (pp. 47–76). Springer Gabler.

Mensah, I. K. (2019). Factors influencing the intention of university students to adopt and use e-government services: An empirical evidence in China. *SAGE Open, 9*(2).

Mo, D., Xiang, M., Luo, M., Dong, Y., Fang, Y., Zhang, S., ... Liang, H. (2019). Using gamification and social incentives to increase physical activity and related social cognition among undergraduate students in Shanghai, China. *International Journal of Environmental Research and Public Health, 16*(5), 858.

Mustafa, A. S., Ali, N., & Dhillon, J. S. (2021). A Systematic Review of the Integration of Motivational and Behavioural Theories in Gamified Health Interventions. In F. Saeed, F. Mohammed, & A. Al-Nahari (Eds.), *Innovative Systems for Intelligent Health Informatics. IRICT 2020. Lecture Notes on Data Engineering and Communications Technologies* (Vol. 72). Springer.

Mustafa, A. S., & Karimi, K. (2021). Enhancing Gamified Online Learning User Experience (UX): A Systematic Literature Review of Recent Trends. In Human-Computer Interaction and Beyond-Part I (pp. 74-99). Bentham Science Publishers.

Myers, J. (2016). *The world's 10 youngest populations are all in Africa*. Retrieved from: https://www.weforum.org/agenda/2016/05/the-world-s-10-youngest-countries-are-all-in-africa/

Ofosu-Ampong, K., & Anning-Dorson, T. (2020). Gamification Research: Preliminary Insights Into Dominant Issues, Theories, Domains, and Methodologies. In Handbook of Research on Managing Information Systems in Developing Economies (pp. 397-412). IGI Global.

Ofosu-Ampong, K., Boateng, R., Anning-Dorson, T., & Kolog, E. A. (2020). Are we ready for Gamification? An exploratory analysis in a developing country. *Education and Information Technologies*, 25(3), 1723–1742. doi:10.100710639-019-10057-7

Oluwajana, D., Idowu, A., Nat, M., Vanduhe, V., & Fadiya, S. (2019). The adoption of students' hedonic motivation system model to gamified learning environment. *Journal of Theoretical and Applied Electronic Commerce Research*, 14(3), 156–167. doi:10.4067/S0718-18762019000300109

Ortiz-Rojas, M., Chiluiza, K., & Valcke, M. (2019). Gamification through leaderboards: An empirical study in engineering education. *Computer Applications in Engineering Education*, 27(4), 777–788. doi:10.1002/cae.12116

Ponto, J. (2015). Understanding and evaluating survey research. *Journal of the Advanced Practitioner in Oncology*, 6(2), 168. PMID:26649250

Rahman, R. A., Ahmad, S., & Hashim, U. R. (2018). The effectiveness of gamification technique for higher education students engagement in polytechnic Muadzam Shah Pahang, Malaysia. *International Journal of Educational Technology in Higher Education*, 15(1), 1–16. doi:10.118641239-018-0123-0

Ringle, C. M., Wende, S., & Becker, J. M. (2015). *SmartPLS 3*. http://www.smartpls.com

Rizun, M., & Strzelecki, A. (2020). Students' acceptance of the Covid-19 impact on shifting higher education to distance learning in Poland. *International Journal of Environmental Research and Public Health*, 17(18), 6468. doi:10.3390/ijerph17186468 PMID:32899478

Rodrigues, L., Toda, A. M., Oliveira, W., Palomino, P. T., Avila-Santos, A. P., & Isotani, S. (2021, March). Gamification Works, but How and to Whom? An Experimental Study in the Context of Programming Lessons. In *Proceedings of the 52nd ACM Technical Symposium on Computer Science Education* (pp. 184-190). 10.1145/3408877.3432419

Sailer, M., & Homner, L. (2020). *The gamification of learning: A meta-analysis*. Academic Press.

Sánchez-Mena, A., & Martí-Parreño, J. (2016, June). Gamification in higher education: teachers' drivers and barriers. In *Proceedings of the International Conference the Future of Education* (pp. 180-184). Academic Press.

Sawahel, W. (2020, November 26). *Gamification of education could engage students during COVID-19.* Available at: https://www.universityworldnews.com/post.php?story=20201123063309960

Shih, Y. Y., & Chen, C. Y. (2013). The study of behavioral intention for mobile commerce: Via integrated model of TAM and TTF. *Quality & Quantity, 47*(2), 1009–1020. doi:10.100711135-011-9579-x

Tan, M., & Hew, K. F. (2016). Incorporating meaningful gamification in a blended learning research methods class: Examining student learning, engagement, and affective outcomes. *Australasian Journal of Educational Technology, 32*(5). Advance online publication. doi:10.14742/ajet.2232

Tsai, Y. Y., Chao, C. M., Lin, H. M., & Cheng, B. W. (2018). Nursing staff intentions to continuously use a blended e-learning system from an integrative perspective. *Quality & Quantity, 52*(6), 2495–2513. doi:10.100711135-017-0540-5

Vanduhe, V. Z., Nat, M., & Hasan, H. F. (2020). Continuance intentions to use gamification for training in higher education: Integrating the technology acceptance model (TAM), social motivation, and task technology Fit (TTF). *IEEE Access: Practical Innovations, Open Solutions, 8,* 21473–21484. doi:10.1109/ACCESS.2020.2966179

Venkatesh, V., & Davis, F. D. (2000). A theoretical extension of the technology acceptance model: Four longitudinal field studies. *Management Science, 46*(2), 186–204. doi:10.1287/mnsc.46.2.186.11926

Venkatesh, V., Morris, M. G., Davis, G. B., & Davis, F. D. (2003). User acceptance of information technology: Toward a unified view. *Management Information Systems Quarterly, 27*(3), 425–478. doi:10.2307/30036540

Wong, D., Liu, H., Meng-Lewis, Y., Sun, Y., & Zhang, Y. (2021). Gamified money: Exploring the effectiveness of gamification in mobile payment adoption among the silver generation in China. *Information Technology & People.* Advance online publication. doi:10.1108/ITP-09-2019-0456

Wu, B., & Chen, X. (2017). Continuance intention to use MOOCs: Integrating the technology acceptance model (TAM) and task technology fit (TTF) model. *Computers in Human Behavior, 67,* 221–232. doi:10.1016/j.chb.2016.10.028

Wu, J., & Lu, X. (2013). Effects of extrinsic and intrinsic motivators on using utilitarian, hedonic, and dual-purposed information systems: A meta-analysis. *Journal of the Association for Information Systems, 14*(3), 1. doi:10.17705/1jais.00325

Yakubu, M. N., & Dasuki, S. I. (2019). Factors affecting the adoption of e-learning technologies among higher education students in Nigeria: A structural equation modelling approach. *Information Development, 35*(3), 492–502. doi:10.1177/0266666918765907

Yen, D. C., Wu, C. S., Cheng, F. F., & Huang, Y. W. (2010). Determinants of users' intention to adopt wireless technology: An empirical study by integrating TTF with TAM. *Computers in Human Behavior, 26*(5), 906–915. doi:10.1016/j.chb.2010.02.005

Yuan, S., Liu, Y., Yao, R., & Liu, J. (2016). An investigation of users' continuance intention towards mobile banking in China. *Information Development*, *32*(1), 20–34. doi:10.1177/0266666914522140

KEY TERMS AND DEFINITIONS

eLearning: A learning approach based on formalised instruction and uses electronic resources.

Game Elements: The components or characteristics of a game.

Gamification: The introduction of game design features in a non-game context.

Gamified Learning: Integrating game elements in learning to make it more entertaining and exciting.

Information System: A software used to organise and analyse data.

Task Technology Fit (TTF): The extent to which a certain Information System or technology facilitates the task at hand.

Technology Acceptance Model (TAM): A theory of information systems that describes how consumers come to accept and use technology.

Chapter 6
Gamified Learning:
Favoring Engagement and Learning Outcomes

Cornelia Nih Popescu
Capgemini Engineering T.E.C., France

Elodie Attie
Capgemini Engineering T.E.C., France

Laëtitia CHADOUTEAU
Capgemini Engineering T.E.C., France

ABSTRACT

In the context of the current COVID-19 pandemic, e-learning represents a more and more important concern of all education providers and an inevitable direction for the current context in training and education. This chapter follows the theory of gamified learning and the theory of flow to understand to which extent game characteristics improve engagement and learning outcomes, such as performance and engagement. To do this, two groups of learners (N=20) were randomly assigned: the experimental group followed a gamified learning module, and the control group followed the same content without gamification mechanisms. The game mechanisms chosen involve a game, a challenge, virtual rewards, an avatar, a final badge, and a system of points and levels. Results show that the gamified course increased the time spent on the course and the overall performance. Hence, this chapter demonstrates the relevance of using gamification to improve learning outcomes.

INTRODUCTION

The context of Covid-19 has impacted the learning process, and institutions had to transform face-to-face classes into online classes within a short amount of time (Al-Okaily et al., 2020; Kiselicki et al., 2020). Even though the Covid-19 pandemic drives a need for innovation, there is a significant difference between an online and a physical learning experience (Sawangchai et al., 2020). E-learning environ-

DOI: 10.4018/978-1-7998-8089-9.ch006

ments imply a wide range of applications and resources, structured and interactive learning environments without temporal & spatial constraints (Krishnamurthy, 2020; Masie, 2006). Therefore, distance learning is becoming more relevant than ever before with a disrupted learning transition that forces students to modify their learning behaviours (Meade & Parthasaranthy, 2020). E-learning offers advantages such as 24h/7days training, self-pacing, scalability, repeatability and consistency of educational content for all learners across distance and time. However, many educational institutions were not ready for this digital transition and are still trying to create e-learning courses (Abu et al., 2020). The access to a wide variety of tools can facilitate or not the learning process, creating inequalities between students (Bobokhujaev, 2019). Indeed, students can be reticent toward e-learning in general, due to the Internet costs (Hasani & Adnan, 2020), the cognitive overload with the use of different learning tools, and the lack of efficacy perceived (Meade & Parthasarathy, 2020). Yet, for institutions, this context could represent an opportunity to confirm and establish competences and a reputation in the digitalization of training (Sawangchai et al., 2020). However, students and instructors encounter issues of accepting this new way of teaching as they both perceive online instructions as less effective than face-to-face teaching (Al-Okaily et al., 2020; Tartavulea et al., 2020). E-learning environments also emphasize learners' independence and responsibility for learning since Internet applications simplify access to learning resources (Dragomir & Munteanu, 2020). However, online learning is complementary to traditional teaching and learning methods, as it can be used together to reach the best learning outcomes (Dragomir & Munteanu, 2020). For instance, neurolearning has shown that repeating information multiple times increases memory. Gamification is a way to repeat the same information in different playful forms while enhancing learners' interest, and interest can activate an intrinsic motivation for learning (Silvia, 2008). Moreover, games bring out a better development of the intellectual point of view, creativity and intuition (Baisheva et al., 2017). Therefore, gamification is starting to gain interest in various domains, such as business strategies (Kiselecki et al., 2020). Gamification involves implemented motivational affordances, from perceived opportunities for action to intentions of motivation (Huotari & Hamari, 2012). Therefore, the theory of gamified learning links the theory of motivation (Ryan & Deci, 2002), the resulting psychological outcomes (i.e., anxiety, fun, distraction; von der Heiden et al., 2019) and further behavioural outcomes (i.e., engagement, performance; Huotari & Hamari, 2012).

This chapter aims to understand to which extent gamification influences the learning process, such as motivation, engagement, and performance. To study this research question, we created a gamified e-learning module presented via the Moodle training platform as a potential way to improve user engagement. The first part of this chapter presents a literature review of gamification and the theory of gamified learning; then, the second part of this chapter presents an experimental study that deepen the understanding of the role of gamification on engagement; the third part of this chapter highlights solutions and recommendations for teaching institutions; finally, the fourth part of this chapter brings out future research directions.

BACKGROUND

The background of this chapter describes the literature about gamification, which leads to the description of different gamified mechanisms used in learning processes and the theory of gamified learning. This part aims to shed light on the concept of gamification in education.

What Is Gamification?

The term "gamification" appeared in 1966, showing the influence of simulation games on learning (McKenney & Dill, 1966). Since then, the literature displays 30 academic publications on this subject (source: Business Source Ultimate). Table 1 presents the main definitions of gamification from the literature, using the components to suggest a broader meaning.

Table 1. Overview of the definitions of gamification from the literature

Author(s), date	Definition of gamification	Main components
Deterding et al. (2011)	"The use of game-play mechanics for non-game applications"	- Game-play mechanics
Lee & Hammer (2011)	"Mechanics, dynamics, and frameworks to promote desired behaviours"	- Mechanics, dynamics, frameworks - Desired behaviours
Kapp (2013)	"Play mechanics, aesthetics, and thinking engage people, motivate action, promote learning, and solve problems"	- Play mechanics, aesthetics, thinking - Engagement, action
Huotari & Hamari (2012)	"A process of enhancing services with (motivational) affordances to invoke gameful experiences and further behavioural outcomes"	- Experience - Motivation and behavioural outcomes
Dominguez et al. (2013)	"The integration of gaming elements into a non-game software application to increase user experience and engagement"	- Gaming elements - User experience - Engagement

Table 1 highlights the different elements composing the definition of gamification from the literature. Although the main components of these definitions remain close, this chapter contributes to the literature by putting them together to redefine a complete definition of gamification, such as: *"gamification is a pedagogical intention which, to be achieved efficiently and improve experience, motivation, engagement, and behaviours, must be able to think, select, quantify and use game-play mechanisms, aesthetics and dynamics adapted to the right context, target, and learning objective"*. More specifically, the gamification environment represents a complex environment presenting several offshoots and poles part of the same ecosystem (see Figure 1).

Figure 1 shows that several poles and offshoots gravitate around the assessment of gamification and can define a goal for institutions and teachers, namely:

- **Game**: The game applies a set of defined rules, introduces a goal, a purpose for the learner, challenges adapted to the learner's skill level to motivate him and increase his self-esteem. The game uses time pressure as a motivator for the learner's activity and action. In addition, it involves competition and cooperation through interactivity. The game allows building a universe for the players with his characters, rules, reward structures (badges, levels, points, rankings, etc.).
- **Humans**: interactivity, feedback. For example, feedback in gamified learning has several roles. First, it provides information and guides the learner to the correct result. Second, it encourages and stimulates learning by allowing trial and error behaviour and giving control to the learner. As a result, the feedback increases the learner's motivation and engagement.

Figure 1. The gamification environment

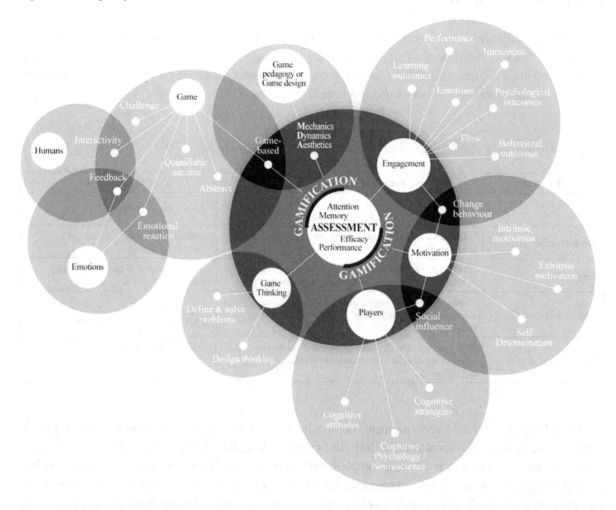

- **Emotions**: feedback, emotional reaction: For example, using storytelling features can help foster emotional connections with learners. According to Lazarro (2004), games evoke powerful emotions, from curiosity to joy to frustration. These emotions activate different levers of engagement involving the main human motivations: social influence, search for meaning, possession, creativity and autonomy, curiosity, etc.
- **Game pedagogy or design**: game-based, mechanics, dynamics, aesthetics. Gamification aims to achieve a higher level of engagement and motivation among learners who are naturally more involved in their activities. To achieve this, gamification takes inspiration from many areas that can explain beliefs, behaviours, limits or ideals, such as the game pedagogy to understand how a game system (Mechanics) and gameplay (Dynamics) create to the player an engaging experience (Aesthetics).
- **Engagement**: learning outcomes, performance, emotions, immersion, psychological outcomes, flow, behavioural outcomes, behavior change.
- **Motivation**: behavior change, intrinsic and extrinsic motivation, social influence. Gamification mechanisms have an impact on several aspects of motivation. For example, using a badge satisfies

the need to consider oneself competent, which is one of the sources of motivation identified in the self-determination theory from Deci and Ryan's (2002).

- **Players**: social influence, cognitive strategies, cognitive psychology and neuroscience, cognitive attitudes. According to Bartle's (1996) and Marczewski's (2016) methodology, each player has a different personality and relationship to the game.
- **Game-thinking**: define and solve problems, design thinking. Gamification influences game thinking, which can help to define and solve problems or do design thinking (i.e., an approach to addressing complex problems) and gamification represents a way to re-design courses through an innovative process (Hung, 2018).

Gamification Mechanisms

Gamification offers various mechanisms to increase students' motivation, engagement, and performance, such as the following ones:

- **Avatars:** Avatars solicit decision-making by the learner and bring the first level of immersion by stepping into the character's skin they decide to create. According to Alsawaier (2018), avatars represent players since they reflect their aspirations, vulnerabilities, and the different roles they could also play in life. Players should choose or create their avatars as manifestations of their needs for autonomy.
- **Quests and challenges:** In a gamified environment, quests and challenges enable learners to practice without the fear of failure, which can reduce the stress associated with a single final assessment challenge. Quests and challenges give players directions and/or a purpose within a gamified environment (Zichermann & Cunningham, 2011). Indeed, adding story elements or beginning a course with some form of challenge is more engaging than a list of learning objectives: both strategies are recommended and implemented by gamification advocates (Lyubomirsky et al., 2011).
- **Points:** Points can accumulate as the participant progresses through the gamified environment. They provide feedback to the participant, represent a reward for the completed activities, and inform the participant about a specific task's progress. This element of the gamification allows the participant to experience the first level of competence.
- **Badges:** Badges are a visual representation of completing an activity and are collected directly in the gamified environment. Badges establish people's reputation in a game environment. Besides, Alsawaier (2018) shows that displaying a badge can highlight learners' qualities linked to their competence and efficiency.

According to Attali and Arieli-Attali (2015), both points and badges are extrinsic rewards for task performance.

- **The leaderboard:** Leaderboards represent lists of participants ranked according to their success in the activity, providing information about the participant's individual performance in relation to the group. It is considered as a motivational element if the participant is at the top of the ranking and conversely positioned at the bottom of the ranking, the participant may feel demotivated (Werbach & Hunter, 2012).

- **Storytelling:** Storytelling is able to challenge the context of higher education, personalizing the learning process while developing learners' skills (Ribeiro et al., 2016). Storytelling is a way to give life to knowledge, leading to quicker and more durable retention of information.

The Theory of Gamified Learning

Education is increasingly using gamification as an educational theory (Bíró, 2014; Kapp, 2012). The theory of gamified learning (Landers, 2014) presents the influence of gamification, such as the characteristics of the game and the instructional content, on learning outcomes (see Figure 2).

Landers distinguishes two processes by which game elements can affect learning: a more direct mediating process and a less direct moderating process.

Figure 2. Theoretical model of gamified learning
(Landers, 2014)

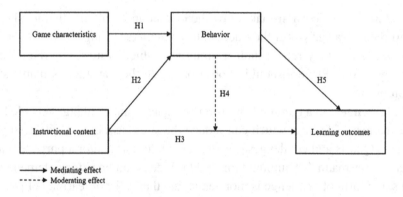

H1 represents the influence of game characteristics on behavior; H2 the influence of instructional content on behavior; H3 the influence of instructional content on learning content; H4 the moderating effect of behavior on H3; H5 the influence of behavior on learning outcomes.

Figure 2 shows a mediation process between game characteristics, behaviour, and learning outcomes, which is the most common application of gamification in the literature (Nah et al., 2013). In the gamified learning theory, gamification is effective through this mediation process if the game characteristics (e.g., badges, points, feedback, challenge) engender the targeted behaviour (e.g., participation, motivation, engagement, enjoyment), and if this behaviour increases learning outcomes (e.g., performance, success rate, memory) (Landers, 2014). Thus, game elements are the initial causal force on the change created in desired outcomes (Landers et al., 2018). For example, a leaderboard could improve employees' motivation to attend training materials, which can enhance efforts, and in turn learning outcomes. Yet, the theory of gamified learning cannot demonstrate which combinations have a stronger impact on learning and the particular outcomes for which they are impactful (Landers, 2014).

The moderating process: the game elements affect the behaviours/attitudes that moderate instructional effectiveness. Landers cites the example of Indiana University (Tay, 2010), where an instructor incorporated fantasy elements into a course. His implicit goal is to improve a learning behaviour. In this case, the goal may be to increase student effort (behaviour) or to make students understand that homework is fun (an attitude). Thus, by incorporating fantasy (a game feature), student engagement (a behaviour/ attitude) should increase, strengthening the relationship between instructional content and learning outcomes. In short, using a game feature increases engagement, which moderates the relationship between instructional content and learning outcomes.

Gamification affects learning through moderation when an instructional designer intends to encourage a behaviour or attitude that will increase learning outcomes, enhancing pre-existing instruction (Landers, 2014).

In summary, Landers' theory provides two specific causal pathways through which gamification can affect learning and a framework for testing these pathways. In one, this behaviour moderates the relationship between teaching quality and learning. In the other, this behaviour mediates the relationship between game elements and learning.

MAIN FOCUS OF THE CHAPTER

The main focus of this chapter addresses the role of gamified elements on learning motivation, engagement, and performance. An experimental study demonstrates how a gamified e-learning module influences engagement and learning outcomes to deepen this question.

Studying the Influence of Gamification on Learning Outcomes

Among other advantages, a gamified course increases students' motivation, interest, and memory (Barna & Fodor, 2019; Huotari & Hamari, 2012). In addition, its creation is low cost compared to a serious game. At the same time, it leads to the same outcomes (i.e., knowledge absorption and retention, increased performance, engagement level, etc.) (Larson et al., 1980). Thus, gamification offers excellent advantages to solving "boring" courses by popularizing complex theoretical concepts thanks to game elements. This study aims to create a gamified course, to study to which game elements improve learning outcomes (i.e., engagement, performance). Another research question is to investigate if isolated game characteristics improve learning outcomes with engagement as a mediator.

The self-determination theory from Deci and Ryan (2002) separates intrinsic and extrinsic motivations:

- **Extrinsic motivation** relies on external rewards (i.e., bonus, awards, etc.) to stimulate successful performance; it is effective if used correctly, but in the long-term, it can become demotivating (Deci & Ryan, 2002).
- **Intrinsic motivation** is linked to autonomy (i.e., willingness to pursue and accomplish a task), competence (i.e., need to overcome challenges and success) and relationships with others (i.e., social status and mutual respect); it creates long-term motivation and represents the basis of engagement.

Hence, engagement implies the simultaneous occurrence of high concentration, absorption into the task, interest, and desire through a state of flow (Csíkszentmihályi, 1975). Motivation represents a fertile ground for cognitive engagement. Research has shown the importance of motivation and engagement in learning, and their separation as independent constructs (Appleton et al., 2006). Indeed, the combination of high motivation and engagement facilitates a successful learning experience (Deci & Ryan, 2002).

Figure 3 presents the link between the self-determination theory and gamification elements (i.e., game elements, mechanisms, dynamics design, structural gamification, content gamification).

Figure 3. The self-determination theory and gamification elements

Self-determination Theory & Gamification

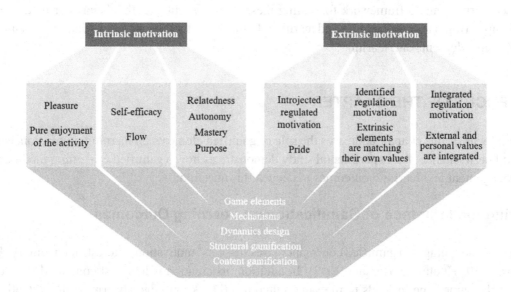

Figure 3 details the states that generate the intrinsic and extrinsic motivations from the self-determination theory. On the one hand, intrinsic motivation includes the notions of pleasure and pure enjoyment of the activity, self-efficacy and flow, and relatedness, autonomy, mastery and purpose. On the other hand, extrinsic motivation includes introjected regulated motivation and pride, an identified regulation motivation and extrinsic elements that match their values, and an integrated regulation of motivation and external personal values. With the differentiation of these motivations, gamification elements can target both types of motivation: game elements, mechanisms, dynamics design, structural gamification, and content gamification. For example, the fun of playing through gamified training content can foster the development of intrinsic motivation. Moreover, the pride of accomplishment can enable one of the components of extrinsic motivation. Furthermore, an introjected regulated motivation in gamification can manifest with rankings and individual rewards (Fulton, 2019).

Methodology

An experimental study targeted two groups of learners randomly assigned to the same pedagogical content about innovative digital training strategies but with different game characteristics. Indeed, the experimental group followed a gamified learning module (i.e., mini-game, challenge, virtual rewards, avatar, final badge, points). The control group followed a non-gamified module containing the same pedagogical content and assessment criteria (see Appendix 2). Both modules were integrated into a

Learning Management System (LMS) environment named Modular Object-Oriented Dynamic Learning Environment (Moodle). Moodle provides many possibilities to create a student-centred, personalised and manageable course interface and is one of the most used open-source LMS environments (Barna & Fodor, 2019). The course presents four levels with a mini-quiz that enables the collection and analysis of learning outcomes. The main task proposed to users is to complete the course through reading the transmissive content, accomplishing the activities, performing the proposed quizzes, and consulting external resources (see Appendix 2). Achieving a minimum score of 70% on the quiz/activities is recommended but not mandatory for completing the course. However, if both conditions are respected (minimum 70% and completion of the course), the learner gets the final badge with the "Super-Engineer" status. Participants have many possibilities during their module, such as viewing the progress of their module ("Overview" plugin), choosing the order of the activities, unlocking higher levels without completing the previous ones, or failing and making multiple attempts (the best score is retained). Based on the theory of learning gamification, we hypothesize that the integration of gamification mechanisms in an e-learning module positively impacts learners' behavior with better results than for a non-gamified e-learning module. (Appendix 1)

Time on Task Indicates The Level of Concentration

Hypothesis One: (a) The gamified group spends more time on the course than the non-gamified group, and (b) the time spent on the course has a positive influence on the average score

Course Access Represents the Frequency of Interactions with the Course

Hypothesis Two: (a) The gamified group is more active on the course than the non-gamified group, and (b) the activity has a positive influence on the average score performance

According to Pastor-Pina et al. (2015), students need an active role to succeed: student motivation and commitment are key factors in the learning process. Gamification is a way to increase action (Landers & Callan, 2011).

Hypothesis Three: (a) The gamified group has a higher completion rate on the course than the non-gamified group, and (b) the completion rate has a positive influence on the final quiz score

According to Deci and Ryan's (1985) theory, individuals need to feel competent, more motivated. Therefore, if students perceive they can improve their competence by trying again, they should be more motivated with an interactive gamified content.

Number of Attempt Below 70%

Hypothesis Four: (a) The number of attempts below 70% on the activities for the gamified group is higher than the non-gamified group, and (b) the number of attempts below 70% has a positive influence on the quiz scores

Total Number of Attempts

Hypothesis Five: The number of attempts at the activities for the gamified group is higher than the non-gamified group

Access to External Resources

Hypothesis Six: The gamified group accesses more the external resources pages than the non-gamified group

Regarding the Isolated Elements, the Number of Attempts with the Mini-Game Super-Engineer

According to Landers and Callan, (2011), an ad-hoc mini-game favors the practice, learning and development of knowledge in a more interesting way (Super-Engineer mini-game, memory).

Hypothesis Seven: The mini-game has a positive influence on (a) the number of attempts, and (b) which has a positive influence on the score

The Score and Duration of the Challenge

Hypothesis Eight: The challenge has a positive influence on (a) the time spent on the challenge, and (b) which has a positive influence on the score

Sample and Measures

This study is conducted exclusively in an online environment in August 2020. The sample is composed of 20 volunteers (20% students, 80% professionals; 85% women, 15% men) who randomly followed during 1h30 a gamified (N1 = 10 participants) or non-gamified (N2 = 10 participants) course. The main target group is made of pedagogical engineers and designers (professionals and students) as well as digital learning project managers. They have prerequisites in training engineering, but a basic knowledge in the field of gamification and its application to educational content.

The learning platform allows for the collection of a wide range of data through reports generated on Moodle:

- The duration of the course with the time spent on the retrievable tasks;
- Quiz results, average score and final quiz score;
- Access to the course with the number of logs/clicks reported
- The number of completed activities indicates the level of completion of the course;
- The number of attempts below 70% and the total number of attempts;
- Access to external resources with the number of logs to the resources.

For isolated items, the Moodle SCORM report allows us to obtain:

- The number of attempts at the mini-game and the mini-game score;
- The time spent on the challenge and the score obtained.

Results

Based on Landers and Callan's model of gamified learning (2014), the effects of gamification on activity performance, through the engagement mediator, are tested. The gamification elements individually tested are the mini-game and the challenge. The quantitative results are analyzed with the gamified learning model from Landers and Callan (2014). More precisely, the main criteria studied is the engagement and performance level with these indicators: duration, frequency, number of attempts (and number of attempts below a 70% score), and access to the different contents of the course (see Table 2). Traces of each learner's behaviour are also collected on the LMS Moodle.

Table 2. Results of the study

Indicators	Gamified Learning	Non-gamified Learning
Duration	864 min	369 min
Number of logs	1267	828
Number of attempts	110	71
Cumulative score	93.3%	31.3%
Final Quiz score	88.4%	82.2%
Number of attempts < 70%	13	2
Number of clicks on optional "external resources" page	27	21
Initial self-assessment	24%	24.4%
Final self-assessment	69%	58.8%
Duration Challenge vs. Quiz	Challenge: 265 min	Quiz 85 min
Score Challenge vs. Exercice	83%	56%
Duration Mini-game vs. Quiz	60 min	22 min
Score Mini-game vs. Quiz	100%	78%
Course completion; number of participants who completed the entire course	100%; 10 participants	68.9%; 0 participant

Table 2 shows that the gamified course increased the time spent on the course with significant differences in the means: M = 86.4 for the gamified group versus M = 36.9 for the non-gamified group; H1a is supported. There are also significant differences for the cumulative score with M = 93.3 (SD = 3.13) for the gamified group versus M = 31.3 (SD = 24.8) for the non-gamified group (see Appendix 5); H1b is supported. The causal relationship between gamification and behavioural indicators (total time and cumulative score) is supported too (see Appendix 6). The descriptive analyses show significant differences between the two groups' means: the correlation matrix applied between the behavioural indicators also shows a highly significant positive correlation (r = 0.752) (see Appendices 7 and 8). Furthermore, the gamified group finished the entire course (M activities = 9), whereas the non-gamified group did not complete the course (M activities = 6.20); H2a is supported. For the final score, there is a small difference in the means between the gamified versus the non-gamified group (respectively M = 88.4, SD = 5.46; M = 82, SD = 5.27); H2b is supported. The completion rate is higher for the gamified group than the non-gamified group (respectively 100% and 68.9%); H3a is supported. Both groups achieved and obtained scores over 70%; H3b is not supported. Then, the number of attempts over 70% are higher for the gamified group than the non-gamified group (respectively 110 and 71); H4a is supported. The quiz score is higher for the gamified group than the non-gamified group (respectively 88.4% and 82.2%); H4b is supported. Moreover, the number of attempts is higher for the gamified group than the non-gamified group (respectively M = 110; M = 71); H5 is supported. Yet gamification does not impact the number of clicks on the external resources page (27 clicks for the gamified group versus 21 for the non-gamified group); H6 is not supported. Regarding the isolated game elements, the activity with the highest number of attempts was the Super-Engineer mini-game, with 21 attempts for the gamified group than 8 for the non-gamified group; the latter completed a traditional quiz with the same content and assessment criteria, but without any game element; H7a is supported. The correlation matrix applied between the number of attempts and the score shows a significant positive correlation (r = 0.487), as well as between the number of attempts below 70% and the score (r = 0.589); H7b is supported. Moreover, the causal relationships between the mini-game, number of attempts and the mini-game score obtained are positive (see Appendix 10). Finally, there are significant differences between the averages of the gamified versus the non-gamified group with the challenge score (respectively M = 83%; M = 45%) and time (respectively M =265 minutes; M = 85 minutes) (see Appendix 10); H8a and H8b are supported.

DISCUSSION

This study supports the theory of gamified learning: random assignment to gamified content supported a causal effect. Researchers usually study gamification with the self-determination theory's psychological foundation, the flow-theory, and the self-efficacy theory (Cherry, 2017; Tandon, 2017). Results show that gamification influences motivation and engagement, global performance of the course, and perceptions of fun and entertainment.

Motivation and Engagement

The comparative analysis of the indicators (i.e., total time, course connections, number of clicks, average score, completion, quiz attempts) shows higher significant differences for the gamified group, which seemed more actively engaged in the course than the non-gamified group (control group). Regarding the time spent on the course, the gamified group spent 864 minutes on the course while the non-gamified group spent 369 minutes. This difference in time (495 min) was related to the number of times the courses were consulted by the gamified and non-gamified group (respectively 543 min and 396 min) and the number of clicks in the course (respectively 1267 and 828). This significant difference in time and activity of the gamified group could be explained by the fact that participants in the gamified experience were more active on the course, and showed a constant interest in the content, which positively impacted on the learning outcomes. This may explain the increased engagement of the participants in the gamified course due to the impactful combination of the applied elements. Furthermore, the mini-game Super-Engineer implied the most attempts for the gamified group than the non-gamified group, and the challenge was 100% completed by the gamified group versus 68% by the non-gamified group—all the other activities were completed just once. The challenge has an estimated duration of 25 minutes, which could explain the relatively low number of attempts. Contrary to our expectations, the number of clicks to the external resources page is insignificant for both groups. This could be due to the limited duration of the experiment and the summer period. Regarding the isolated gamification mechanisms, the mini-game was a success due to the presence of storytelling (score of 100%, 21 attempts (2.1 per participant) and eight attempts below the score of 70%). Therefore, these results are in line with theory indicating that gamification allows teachers to increase their students' motivation, interest, and recall (Huotari & Hamari, 2012).

Performance

The average score obtained by the gamified group exceeded the expectations and guidance for success: there is a highly significant effect of mode on the cumulative scores with an average of 93.5% success for the gamified group compared to 31.3% average obtained by the non-gamified group. The activities were completed entirely by the gamified group, which could be explained by their desire to obtain the badge. Another explanation would be a very high engagement rate driven by their intrinsic motivation (i.e., validating the quizzes for personal satisfaction and self-esteem). In addition, some activities obtained a 100% success rate for the gamified group (i.e., the mini-game "Super-engineer" and the practical assignment). This could be explained by the strong impact of the challenge (i.e., storytelling, virtual rewards, avatar choice) on the gamified group. Moreover, the gamified group completed 90 activities (i.e., 100% completion) compared to the non-gamified group (i.e., 62 activities completed). Both conditions for successfully completing the course were fully met for the gamified group, whereas for the non-gamified group, only 6 out of 10 participants completed and scored over 70% on the final quiz—none of the participants in the non-gamified group completed the entire course. This may suggest that the badge had a significant positive impact on participants with the gamified version. This could explain an increased engagement and determination to complete the course and to even exceed the average quiz score. The non-gamified group, in the absence of the badge, did not show sufficient engagement with the course, which could demonstrate a disengagement from completing the course. Finally, the causal relationship between challenge, time on task and performance scores on the challenge was highly significant. Participants in the gamified group spent three times more time on the challenge than participants in the non-gamified group on the corresponding activity (respectively 265 minutes and 85 minutes) and had higher scores on the practical task (100% with a number of attempts three times higher). This could be explained by all the gamification elements used in the challenge that can facilitate immersion in the game (i.e., storytelling, challenge, virtual goods to be won, avatar).

Fun and Entertainment

In line with the flow theory, engagement involves the simultaneous occurrence of a higher concentration, absorption in the task, interest, and a desire to complete the activity (Larson et al., 1980). Díaz-Ramírez (2020) found similar results, including an increase in the course completion. Similarly, other research highlighted the gamification's educational value and its influence on cognitive strategies for improving task solving, attention, memory, motivation, and the depth of knowledge (Meyniel et al., 2016). Research has shown that students favour gamified courses (Díaz-Ramírez, 2020), leading to greater acceptance and usage (Utomo & Santoso, 2015). Gamified learning is also perceived as a hedonic system in which learners play for their own pleasure (Liu et al., 2013; Malone, 1981). Indeed, enjoyment is an intrinsic motivator (Lowry et al., 2012) that describes the perceived entertaining, enjoyable, and fun nature of an activity (Van der Heijden, 2004). The most functional consequence of this research, along with other implications, is that this study offers an answer to a post-effect of Covid-19 to address different problems relevant to the online learning framework: it shows that gamification encourages user engagement and satisfaction in order to build a more robust user e-learning environment.

SOLUTIONS AND RECOMMENDATIONS

The experimental study brings out some solutions and recommendations. To assess learner engagement in a gamified module, a longitudinal study is recommended. In order to reach statistical significance, a larger sample size and a more extended test period are required.

To isolate the effect of gamification elements, we recommend testing the implementation of a single element to obtain significant results. Focusing future research on one gamification element allows for a more refined observation of its effect. To better measure the impact of a single gamification element, we recommend selecting a gamification element before designing the instructional content and defining how it will be measured

The results of our study lead us to more general recommendations, which we detail below.

How to Better Understand Students' Behaviours During a Gamified Module?

Gamification is a way to appeal and connect to a new generation of students called the digital natives (Prensky, 2001). However, each student is different and behaves differently in front of a gamified course. Bartle (1996) divided students according to a specific typology, game characteristics and motivational outcomes. Teachers can also better understand players' behaviour through Marczewski's (2016) typology to propose gamification elements adapted to different participants' gaming behaviours.

Figure 4 illustrates the link between the type of motivation and the player profiles. This diagram shows the type of players according to Bartle's typology (1996) (Achievers, Explorers, Socializers, Killers) and according to Marczewski's classification (2016) (Philanthropists, Socialisers, Free Spirits, Achievers, Players, Disruptors).

Gamification User Types: Which Gamification Design Elements for Which Player Types?

Identifying player types can lead to the use of gamification mechanisms and design elements. The literature presents two classifications of players: Bartle (1996) and Marczewski (2016).

The classification of players of Bartle (1996) is made according to specific aspects of their personality and their way of understanding the game in a virtual world. This study relies on the four sources of interest identified in a proposed game: acting, players, world, and interacting. Consequently, according to Bartle (1996), there are four types of players:

Figure 4. Motivation and player types

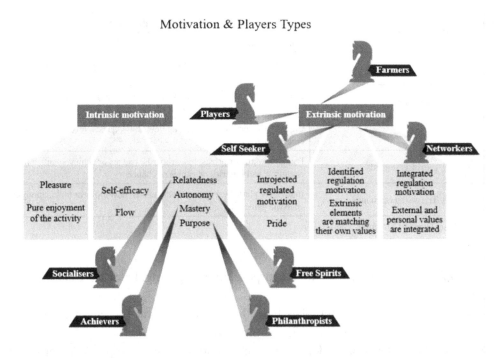

Motivation & Players Types

- **Achievers:** These players are interested in acting on the world (i.e., succeeding in a mission and obtaining the highest score);
- **Explorers:** These players are interested in exploring the world (i.e., discovering and learning new things);
- **Socialisers:** These players are interested in interacting with other players (i.e., chatting and playing with others);
- **Killers:** These players are interested in acting on other players (i.e., taking action over the other players, killing, playing, fighting, manipulating and controlling others).

To find out our player profile, we can take the test proposed by Bartle[1].

However, Bartle's (1996) typology is based on observing the dynamics of player populations in a game, like multi-user dungeons (MUD). It relates to the interrelationships of two dimensions of playstyle: action versus interaction, and world versus player orientation. Thus, it can be difficult to identify these profiles in a gamified pathway. Consequently, Marczewski (2016) used this typology along with the self-determination theory to create the Hexad model which defines different players' profiles according to motivations' personification. This model leads to six user types with game suggestions to meet each user's motivations (Table 3).

Table 3 shows the six main players types according to Marczewski (2016):

Table 3. Suggested design elements according to user types and their motivation type

User Types	Motivation type	Suggested design elements
Philanthropists	Purpose	Collection and trading, gifting, knowledge sharing, and administrative roles
Socialisers	Relatedness	Guilds or teams, social networks, social comparison, social competition, and social discovery
Free Spirits	Autonomy	Exploratory tasks, nonlinear gameplay, Easter eggs, unlockable content, creativity tools, and customization
Achievers	Competence	Challenges, certificates, learning new skills, quests, levels or progression, and epic challenges
Players	Extrinsic rewards	Points, rewards or prizes, leaderboards, badges or achievements, virtual economy, and lotteries or games of chance
Disruptors	Triggering of change	Innovative platforms, voting mechanisms, development tools, anonymity, anarchic gameplay

https://gamified.uk/UserTypeTest2016/user-type-test.php

- **Philanthropists:** These players look for a purpose through gifting, knowledge sharing and administrative roles, etc.
- **Socialisers:** These players look for relatedness through social networks, comparison, competition and discovery, etc. This type of user comes from Bartle (1996).
- **Free spirits:** These players look for a sense of autonomy through exploratory tasks, creativity tools and customization for example.
- **Achievers:** These players look for competence through certificates, learning new skills and quests to reach, etc. This type of user comes from Bartle (1996).
- **Players:** These players look for extrinsic rewards such as points, rewards, leaderboards or badges, among other examples.
- **Disruptors:** These players look for change and innovations through innovative mechanisms and tools, etc.

FUTURE RESEARCH DIRECTIONS

Future research directions show the importance of deepening the concept of adaptive gamification systems, immersive learning technologies, and neurolearning analyses. These techniques are complementary to a gamified learning environment and aim to favour learning processes and outcomes.

Adaptive Gamification Systems

An adaptive gamification system enables to personalize the pedagogical content to each learner profile by adapting game characteristics and learning environments to the behavioural tracking (Stuart et al., 2019). There are two types of adaptive gamification: static gamification according to students' profiles and dynamic gamification based on performance and interaction with the learning system. Also, implementing an adaptive gamification system would allow for the personalization of educational content based on the learner's profile by adapting game features and learning environments to behavioural tracking (Stuart et al., 2019). Indeed, e-learning modules can be too linear and static and they do not foster enough retention among learners. Therefore, adaptive learning technology can overcome these challenges by incorporating artificial intelligence along with evidence-based strategies for optimal learning, engagement and retention in real-time. It can be a powerful tool in any teacher's toolbox, and integrating adaptive learning into the educational program is a great opportunity to respond to learners' needs (i.e., further training, topics to review).

Immersive Technologies

In addition, immersive technologies continue to evolve and innovate in the education market. Artificial intelligence personalizes in real time the learning experience, through chatbots which adoption is rapidly spreading (Smutny & Shreiberova, 2020), and deep learning can provide a tailored solution to specific targets with disabilities such as deaf, blindness, motor problems, etc. Moreover, e-learning 360° videos can use gamification to discover the context, check for different items and interact with the video. Augmented reality is another immersive technology that enables data visualization (i.e., to track, analyze and visualize activity) and virtual reality (VR) allows a highly interactive setting (i.e., learners can perceive, decide and act in virtual environments). Radianti et al. (2020) highlighted researchers' interest in immersive technology, especially for the application of virtual reality in education. VR should bring an added dimension to teaching and learning in order to support learners with the use of controllers, touchpads and haptic feedback. The literature does not indicate the learning theories behind the use of VR and few studies have looked at learning outcomes (Radianti et al., 2020). This indicates that VR has recently been introduced as a learning tool in education. Future research could compare the results from one technology to another, as well as the retention of the information after two weeks for example.

Neurolearning Analyses

Neuroscience has shown that some learning methods, such as gamification, rest periods between each course, or an encouraging environment, can improve learning outcomes. It should be interesting to study to which extent each method is the most efficient. Techniques from neuroscience like eye-tracking and facial coding enable a real-time comparison of the cognitive (e.g., attention) and emotional (e.g., positive versus negative emotions) system activation (e.g., Meyniel et al., 2016). Neurolearning is a method of learning that relies on the way the brain processes information. The learning process requires the activation of several brain areas, including the brain's reward system and the medial structures of the temporal lobes (hippocampal cortex) and the amygdala nuclear complex (Nabar et al., 2018). Gamification is a tool from neurolearning that can increase short-term knowledge retention—up to two weeks—(Putz & Horst, 2019) if people's needs and personality traits are taken into account (Gordon et al., 2020). Through gamification, brain structures in the brain and the circuits that interconnect them are activated by playing the game due to the intrinsic motivation generated by this activity (Nabar et al., 2018). There is an increase in dopamine levels in the reward circuits due to the uncertainty and novelty of each change, the emotions that produce curiosity and stimulate attention to facilitate learning, enthusiasm, creativity, self-confidence, and the feedback received—all enhancing the learner's perseverance (Nabar et al., 2018). The psychology and neuroscience literature provides an emotional cognitive view of gamification to better understand the alignment of cognition, emotions, and desired game mechanics (Mullins & Sabherwal, 2020). This provides game designers with guidance to improve the likelihood of learning success (e.g., integrating an emotion structure map with the types of game mechanics that can elicit various emotions). The literature shows that a gamified learning experience activates neurotransmitters (e.g., dopamine, serotonin), endorphins, and hormones (e.g., oxytocin), which in turn influence learner motivation and mood (Meyniel et al., 2016). For example, continuous feedback keeps the learner interested and motivated (Meyniel et al., 2016). In addition, developing a gamified course is less expensive than a serious game and achieves the same results (e.g., knowledge absorption and retention, increased performance, and engagement level) (Larson et al., 1980).

CONCLUSION

This study was able to demonstrate that combining gamification elements positively impacted performance (through engagement) and that two isolated gamification elements (challenge and mini-game) also increased behavioural indicators (time on task, number of attempts) that improved learning outcomes.

This chapter supports neurolearning research about the influence of gamification on learning, following the theory of gamified learning (Landers, 2014), self-determination (Deci & Ryan, 2002) and the theory of flow (Larson et al., 1980). Gamification offers great benefits by popularizing complex theoretical concepts through game elements. Indeed, gamification has a positive influence on motivation, cognitive system (e.g., attention, reaction times), as well as social skills (e.g., interactions) and emotions (Meyniel et al., 2016). However, computer anxiety is a consequential negative psychological limitation (Igbaria & Parasuraman, 1989), representing a problem for e-learning courses (Saadé & Kira, 2007). The integration of face-to-face time through the use of blended learning could mitigate this adverse effect. In the future, it should be interesting to calculate training expectations through the ROE (Return On Expectations), by analyzing before the training students' needs, expectations, and initial level of satisfaction; and after the training, their behaviours and level of satisfaction (Kirkpatrick, 1959). Neurolearning thus represents a societal and technological evolution that brings out new ways to teach, through gamification. With competition among training centres, differentiation of educational offerings is crucial. According to Rodriguez and Santiago (2015), several pedagogical aspects must emanate from this fusion of gaming and learning to stand out, such as motivation, the active role of the learner, personalization, contextualization, richness of the multimedia support, the possibility of being wrong without risk, or immediate feedback. Furthermore, gamification offers affordable prices and more possibilities to put into practice, offering an accessible way to teach students at school as well as employees in companies of all sizes. To conclude, gamification has become a technology trend to promote desired learning behaviours and boost outcomes, including in business, that continues to evolve according to learners and teachers' needs (Zainuddin et al., 2020).

ACKNOWLEDGMENT

This research was supported by Capgemini Engineering.

REFERENCES

Abu, A., Jusmawati, J., Makmur, Z., Jumliadi, J., & Yusuf, M. (2020). Problems Faced by IAIN Palu Students in Online Learning in the Middle of the COVID-19 Pandemic. *International Colloquium on Environmental Education (ICEE)*.

Al-Okaily, A., Al-Okaily, M., Shiyyab, F., & Masadah, W. (2020). Accounting information system effectiveness from an organizational perspective. *Management Science Letters, 10*, 3991–4000. doi:10.5267/j. msl.2020.7.010

Alsawaier, R. (2018). The effect of gamification on motivation and engagement. *International Journal of Information and Learning Technology*. doi:10.1108/IJILT-02-2017-0009

Appleton, J. J. Christenson, S. L, Kim, D., & Reschly, A. L. (2006). *Measuring cognitive and psychological engagement: Validation of the Student Engagement Instrument*. doi:10.1016/j.jsp.2006.04.002

Attali, Y., & Arieli-Attali, M. (2015). Gamification in assessment: Do points affect test performance? *Computers & Education, 83*, 57–63. doi:10.1016/j.compedu.2014.12.012

Baisheva, M., Golikov, A., Prokopieva, M., Popova, L., Zakharova, A., & Kovtun, T. (2017). The potential of folk tabletop games in the development of the intelligence and creativity of children. *Journal of Social Studies Education Research, 8*(3), 128–138.

Barna, B., & Fodor, S. (2019). A Data-Driven Approach to Analyze User Behavior on a Personalized Gamification Platform. In *International Conference on Games and Learning Alliance*. Springer. 10.1007/978-3-030-34350-7_26

Bartle, R. (1996). Hearts, clubs, diamonds, spades: Players who suit MUDs. *Journal of MUD Research, 1*(1), 19.

Bíró, G. I. (2014). Didactics 2.0: A pedagogical analysis of gamification theory from a comparative perspective with a special view to the components of learning. *Social and Behavioral Sciences, 141*, 148–151.

Bobokhujaev, S. I. (2019). The role of ICT and the problems of organizing distance education in Uzbekistan. *2019 International Conference on Information Science and Communications Technologies (ICISCT)*, 1-4. 10.1109/ICISCT47635.2019.9011876

Buhagiar, T., & Leo, C. (2018). Does Gamification Improve Academic Performance? *Journal of Instructional Pedagogies, 20*.

Calantone, R. J., Chan, K., & Cui, A. S. (2006). Decomposing product innovativeness and its effects on new product success. *Journal of Product Innovation Management, 23*(5), 408–421. doi:10.1111/j.1540-5885.2006.00213.x

Cherry, S. (2017). *Transforming behaviour: Pro-social modelling in practice*. Taylor & Francis. doi:10.4324/9781315084633

Csíkszentmihályi, M. (1975). *Beyond Boredom and Anxiety: Experiencing Flow in Work and Play*. Jossey-Bass.

Davis, F. D. (1989). Perceived Usefulness, Perceived Ease of Use, and User Acceptance of Information Technology. *Management Information Systems Quarterly, 13*(3), 319–340. doi:10.2307/249008

Davis, F. D., Bagozzi, R. P., & Warshaw, P. R. (1989). User acceptance of computer technology: A comparison of two theoretical models. *Management Science, 35*(8), 982–1003. doi:10.1287/mnsc.35.8.982

Deci, E. L., & Ryan, R. M. (2002). Overview of self-determination theory: An organismic-dialectical perspective. In E. L. Deci & R. M. Ryan (Eds.), *Handbook of self-determination research* (pp. 3–33). University of Rochester Press.

Deterding, S., Sicart, M., Nacke, L., O'Hara, K., & Dixon, D. (2011, May). Gamification: Toward a definition. *Proceedings of the CHI 2011 Gamification Workshop.*

Díaz-Ramírez, J. (2020). Gamification in engineering education–An empirical assessment on learning and game performance. *Heliyon, 6*(9), e04972. doi:10.1016/j.heliyon.2020.e04972 PMID:32995639

Domínguez, A., de Navarrete, J. S., de Marcos, L., Fernández-Sanz, L., Pagés, C., & Martínez-Herráiz, J.-J. (2013). Gamifying learning experiences: Practical implications and outcomes. *Computers & Education, 63*, 380–392. doi:10.1016/j.compedu.2012.12.020

Dragomir, C. C., & Munteanu, A. (2020). Impact of online education on economic students' professional training in the context of Covid-19 pandemic. *Review of General Management, 31*(1).

Fulton, J. N. (2019). *Theory of Gamification – Motivation* (PhD dissertation). William Howard Taft University.

Gordon, S., Todder, D., Deutsch, I., Garbi, D., Alkobi, O., Shriki, O., Shkedy-Rabani, A., Shahar, N., & Meiran, N. (2019). Effects of neurofeedback and working memory-combined training on executive functions in healthy young adults. *Psychological Research*, 1–24. doi:10.100700426-019-01170-w PMID:31053887

Hasan, M. M. (2018). Design and Implementation of Gamified Course Contents. Handbook of Research on Mobile Devices and Smart Gadgets in K-12 Education, 32-44. doi:10.4018/978-1-5225-2706-0.ch003

Hasani, L. M., & Adnan, H. R. (2020). *Factors affecting student's perceived readiness on abrupt distance learning adoption: Indonesian Higher-Education Perspectives.* doi:10.13140/RG.2.2.22908.16008

Hung, H. T., Yang, J. C., Hwang, G. J., Chu, H. C., & Wang, C. C. (2018). A scoping review of research on digital game-based language learning. *Computers & Education, 126*, 89–104. doi:10.1016/j.compedu.2018.07.001

Huotari, K., & Hamari, J. (2012). Defining Gamification: A Service Marketing Perspective. In *Proceeding of the 16th International Academic MindTrek Conference.* ACM. 10.1145/2393132.2393137

Igbaria, M., & Parasuraman, S. (1989). A path analytic study of individual characteristics, computer anxiety and attitudes toward microcomputers. *Journal of Management, 15*(3), 373–388. doi:10.1177/014920638901500302

Kapp, K. M. (2012). *The Gamification of Learning and Instruction: Game-based Methods and Strategies for Training and Education.* Pfeiffer.

Kapp, K. M. (2013). *The Gamification of Learning and Instruction. In Fieldbook: Ideas into Practice.* John Wiley & Sons.

Kirkpatrick, D. (1959). Techniques for Evaluating Training Programs. *Journal of American Society for Training and Development, 13*(11-12).

Kiselicki, M., Josimovski, S., Pulevska Ivanovska, L., & Kirovska, Z. (2020). Digital transformation of learning process due to Covid19 crisis in the Republic of North Macedonia. *Journal of Sustainable Development, 10*(25), 53-66. http://fbe.edu.mk/images/stories/JSDv25.pdf

Krishnamurthy, S. (2020). The future of business education: A commentary in the shadow of the Covid-19 pandemic. *Journal of Business Research, Elsevier, 117*(C), 1–5. doi:10.1016/j.jbusres.2020.05.034 PMID:32501309

Landers, R. N. (2014). Developing a theory of gamified learning: Linking serious games and gamification of learning. *Simulation & Gaming, 45*(6), 752–768. doi:10.1177/1046878114563660

Landers, R. N., Auer, E. M., Collmus, A. B., & Armstrong, M. B. (2018). Gamification science, its history and future: Definitions and a research agenda. *Simulation & Gaming, 49*(3), 315–337. doi:10.1177/1046878118774385

Landers, R. N., & Callan, R. C. (2011). Casual social games as serious games: The psychology of gamification in undergraduate education and employee training. In *Serious games and edutainment applications* (pp. 399–423). Springer. doi:10.1007/978-1-4471-2161-9_20

Landers, R. N., & Landers, A. K. (2014). An empirical test of the theory of gamified learning: The effect of leaderboards on time-on-task and academic performance. *Simulation & Gaming, 45*(6), 769–785. doi:10.1177/1046878114563662

Larson, R., Csikszentmihalyi, M., & Graef, R. (1980). Mood variability and the psychosocial adjustment of adolescents. *Journal of Youth and Adolescence, 9*(6), 469–490. doi:10.1007/BF02089885 PMID:24318310

Lee, J., & Hammer, J. (2011). Gamification in education: What, how, why bother? *Academic Exchange Quarterly, 15*(2), 146.

Liu, N. H., Chiang, C. Y., & Chu, H. C. (2013). Recognizing the degree of human attention using EEG signals from mobile sensors. *Sensors, 13*(8), 10273-10286.

Lowry, P. B., Gaskin, J., Twyman, N., Hammer, B., & Roberts, T. (2012). Taking 'fun and games' seriously: Proposing the hedonic-motivation system adoption model (HMSAM). *Journal of the Association for Information Systems, 14*(11), 617–671. doi:10.17705/1jais.00347

Lyubomirsky, S., Dickerhoof, R., Boehm, J. K., & Sheldon, K. M. (2011). Becoming happier takes both a will and a proper way: An experimental longitudinal intervention to boost well-being. *Emotion (Washington, D.C.), 11*(2), 391–402. doi:10.1037/a0022575 PMID:21500907

Marshall, M. (2020). Covid Virus Pushing Education to Online Learning/Teaching Creates Big Challenges: Ethical, Practical & Financial Issues for Teachers/Professors and Administration Leadership; Commentary. *PM World Journal*, 1-4.

Masie, E. (2006). The blended learning imperative. The handbook of blended learning: Global perspectives, local designs, 22-26.

McKenney, J. L., & Dill, W. R. (1966). Influences on Learning in Simulation Games. *The American Behavioral Scientist, 10*(2), 28–32. doi:10.1177/000276426601000205

Meade, J. A., & Parthasaranthy, K. (2020). Did COVID-19 Impact Student Learning in an Introductory Accounting Course? *Business Education Innovation Journal, 12*(2), 18–23.

Meyniel, F., Goodwin, G. M., Deakin, J. W., Klinge, C., MacFadyen, C., Milligan, H., Mullings, E., Pessiglione, M., & Gaillard, R. (2016). A specific role for serotonin in overcoming effort cost. *eLife, 5.* PMID:27824554

Mullins, J. K., & Sabherwal, R. (2020). Gamification: A cognitive-emotional view. *Journal of Business Research, 106*, 304–314. doi:10.1016/j.jbusres.2018.09.023

Nabar, M. J. M. Y., Algieri, R. D., & Tornese, E. B. (2018). Gamification or gaming techniques applied to pedagogy: Foundations of the cognitive neuroscience applied to the education. *Global Journal of Human-Social Science: Linguistics & Education, 18*(2).

Nah, S., & Saxton, G. D. (2013). Modeling the adoption and use of social media by nonprofit organizations. *New Media & Society, 15*(2), 294–313. doi:10.1177/1461444812452411

Pastor Pina, H., Satorre Cuerda, R., Molina-Carmona, R., Gallego-Durán, F. J., & Llorens Largo, F. (2015). Can Moodle be used for structural gamification? *INTED2015: Proceedings of the 9th International Technology, Education and Development Conference*, 1014-1021.

Prensky, M. (2001). The games generations: How learners have changed. *Digital Game-Based Learning, 1*(1), 1-26.

Putz, L. M., & Treiblmaier, H. (2019). Increasing Knowledge Retention through Gamified Workshops: Findings from a Longitudinal Study and Identification of Moderating Variables. *Proceedings of the 52nd Hawaii International Conference on System Sciences.*

Radianti, J., Majchrzak, T. A., Fromm, J., & Wohlgenannt, I. (2020). A systematic review of immersive virtual reality applications for higher education: Design elements, lessons learned, and research agenda. *Computers & Education, 147*, 103778. doi:10.1016/j.compedu.2019.103778

Ribeiro, M. T., Singh, S., & Guestrin, C. (2016). Model-agnostic interpretability of machine learning. *2016 ICML Workshop on Human Interpretability in Machine Learning.*

Rodríguez, F., & Santiago, R. (2015). *Cómo motivar a tu alumnado y mejorar el clima en el aula.* Digital-Text.

Saadé, R. G., & Kira, D. (2007). Mediating the impact of technology usage on perceived ease of use by anxiety. *Computers & Education, 49*(4), 1189–1204. doi:10.1016/j.compedu.2006.01.009

Sawangchai, A., Prasarnkarn, H., Kasuma, J., Polyakova, A. G., & Qasim, S. (2020). Effects of Covid-19 on digital learning of entrepreneurs. *Polish Journal of Management Studies, 22*(2), 502–517. doi:10.17512/pjms.2020.22.2.33

Silvia, P. J. (2008). Interest—The curious emotion. *Current Directions in Psychological Science, 17*(1), 57–60. doi:10.1111/j.1467-8721.2008.00548.x

Silvia, P. J., Winterstein, B. P., Willse, J. T., Barona, C. M., Cram, J. T., Hess, K. I., Martinez, J. L., & Richard, C. A. (2008). Assessing creativity with divergent thinking tasks: Exploring the reliability and validity of new subjective scoring methods. *Psychology of Aesthetics, Creativity, and the Arts, 2*(2), 68–85. doi:10.1037/1931-3896.2.2.68

Smutny, P., & Shreiberova, P. (2020). Chatbots for learning: A review of educational chatbots for the Facebook Messenger. *Computers & Education, 151*, 103–862. doi:10.1016/j.compedu.2020.103862

Soderstrom, N. C., & Bjork, R. A. (2015). Learning Versus Performance: An Integrative Review. *Perspectives on Psychological Science, 0*(2), 176–199. doi:10.1177/1745691615569000 PMID:25910388

Stuart, H., Serna, A., Marty, J. C., & Lavoué, E. (2019). Adaptive gamification in education: A literature review of current trends and developments. *European Conference on Technology, Enhanced Learning (EC-TEL),* 294-307.

Tandon, T. (2017). A Study on Relationship between Self Efficacy and Flow at Work. *International Journal of Indian Psychology, 4*(4), 87–100. doi:10.25215/0404.069

Taylor, S., & Todd, P. (1995). An integrated model of waste management behavior: A test of household recycling and composting intentions. *Environment and Behavior, 27*(5), 603–630. doi:10.1177/0013916595275001

Utomo, A. Y., & Santoso, H. B. (2015). Development of gamification-enriched pedagogical agent for e-learning system based on community of inquiry. *Proceedings of the International HCI and UX Conference in Indonesia,* 1-9. 10.1145/2742032.2742033

Van der Heijden, H. (2004). User acceptance of hedonic information systems. *Management Information Systems Quarterly, 28*(4), 695–704. doi:10.2307/25148660

Von der Heiden, J. M., Braun, B., Müller, K. M., & Egloff, B. (2019). The Association Between Video Gaming and Psychological Functioning. *Frontiers in Psychology, 10,* 17–31. doi:10.3389/fpsyg.2019.01731 PMID:31402891

Werbach, K., & Hunter, D. (2012). *For the win: How game thinking can revolutionize your business.* Wharton Digital Press.

Zainuddin, Z., Chu, S. K. W., Shujahat, M., & Perera, C. J. (2020). The impact of gamification on learning and instruction: A systematic review of empirical evidence. *Educational Research Review, 30*, 100326. doi:10.1016/j.edurev.2020.100326

Zichermann, G., & Cunningham, C. (2011). *Gamification by design: Implementing game mechanics in web and mobile apps.* O'Reilly Media, Inc.

ADDITIONAL READING

Denny, P., McDonald, F., Empson, R., & Kelly, P. (2018). *Empirical Support for a Causal Relationship Between Gamification and Learning Outcomes. University of Otago Dunedin.* Andrew Petersen University of Toronto.

Gordon, S., Todder, D., Deutsch, I., Garbi, D., Alkobi, O., Shriki, O., Shkedy-Rabani, A., Shahar, N., & Meiran, N. (2019). Effects of neurofeedback and working memory-combined training on executive functions in healthy young adults. *Psychological Research*, *84*(6), 1586–1609. doi:10.100700426-019-01170-w PMID:31053887

Hamari, J. (2015). Do badges increase user activity? A field experiment on the effects of gamification. *Computers in Human Behavior.*

Healy, A. F., Kole, J. A., Schneider, V. I., & Barshi, I. (2019). Training, retention, and transfer of data entry perceptual and motor processes over short and long retention intervals. *Memory & Cognition*, *47*(8), 1606–1618. doi:10.375813421-019-00955-z PMID:31215009

Hense, J. U., Klevers, M., Mandl, H., & Sailer, M. (2013). Psychological Perspectives on Motivation through Gamification. *Interaction Design and Architecture(s). Journal*, *19*, 28–37.

Hense, J. U., Mandl, H., Mayr, S. K., & Sailer, M. (2017). How gamification motivates: An experimental study of the effects of specific game design elements on psychological need satisfaction. *Computers in Human Behavior*, *69*, 371–380. doi:10.1016/j.chb.2016.12.033

Ibanez, M., Di-Seio, A., & Delgado Kloos, C. (2014). Gamification for Engaging Computer Science Students in Learning Activities: A Case Study. *IEEE Transactions on Learning Technologies*, *7*(3), 291–301. doi:10.1109/TLT.2014.2329293

Javanbakht, A., Duval, E. R., Cisneros, M. E., Taylor, S. F., Kessler, D., & Liberzon, I. (2017). Instructed fear of learning, extinction and recall: Additive effects of cognitive information on emotional fear of learning. *Cognition and Emotion*, *31*(5), 980–987. doi:10.1080/02699931.2016.1169997 PMID:27089509

Lazzaro, N. (2004). Why we play games: Four keys to more emotion without story. X. E. O. Design, Inc. Retrieved from: http://xeodesign.com/ xeodesign_ whyweplaygames.pdf

Pereg, M., Shahar, N., & Meiran, N. (2019). Can we learn to learn? The influence of procedural working-memory training on rapid instructed-task-learning. *Psychological Research*, *83*(1), 132–146. doi:10.100700426-018-1122-4 PMID:30478608

Tay, L. (2010, March 18). Employers: Look to gaming to motivate staff. itnews for Australian Business. Retrieved from http://www.itnews.com.au/News/169862,employers-look-togaming-to-motivate-staff.aspx

KEY TERMS AND DEFINITIONS

E-Learning: An asynchronous remote training resource, more or less scenario-based, multimedia and interactive, which may include quizzes and different learning paths.

Engagement: The psychological investment and effort directed toward learning, understanding, mastery of knowledge and the development of expected skills or abilities (Newmann et al., 1992).

Extrinsic Motivation: Motivation based on the consequences expected from an action (i.e., rewards, performance, competences).

Flow: A mental state reached when an individual is completely immersed in an activity and is in a maximum state of concentration, full commitment, and satisfaction in its accomplishment (Csíkszentmihályi, 1975).

Gamification: A pedagogical intention which, to be achieved efficiently, must be able to select and quantify gamification mechanisms adapted to the right context, target, and learning objective.

Gamified Learning: The use of game characteristics, including the language of action, assessment, conflict or challenge, control, environment, game fiction, human interaction, immersion and rules or objectives, to influence learning and related outcomes.

Intrinsic Motivation: Motivation based on the achievement of the action (i.e., confidence, self-efficacy, self-determination).

Learning Performance: Relatively permanent changes in knowledge or behaviour that support retention and transfer (Soderstrom et al., 2015).

Performance: Temporary fluctuations in knowledge or behaviour, measures or observed during, or shortly after, instruction to a course (Soderstrom et al., 2015).

APPENDIX 1. INDICATORS AND OPERATIONAL ASSUMPTIONS OF THE STUDY

Table 4.

Indicators	Tracking	Operational Assumptions
Gamified course		
1 - Course duration (time spent on task)	- Time spent on task recoverable (Moodle SCORM report) - Final quiz score	Hypothesis One: (a) The gamified group spends more time on the course than the non-gamified group, and (b) the time spent on the course has a positive influence on the average score
2 - Course access (frequency)	- Number of logs/clicks reported (Moodle logs report) - Average score	Hypothesis Two: (a) The gamified group is more active on the course than the non-gamified group, and (b) the activity has a positive influence on the average score performance
3 - Course completion	- Number of completed activities (Moodle "Course completion" report)	Hypothesis Three: (a) The gamified group has a higher completion rate on the course than the non-gamified group, and (b) the completion rate has a positive influence on the final quiz score
4 - Number of attempts below 70%	- Number of attempts below 70% (Moodle SCORM report) - Quiz scores	Hypothesis Four: (a) The number of attempts below 70% on the activities for the gamified group is higher than the non-gamified group, and (b) the number of attempts below 70% has a positive influence on the quiz scores
5 - Total number of attempts	- Number of attempts (Moodle SCORM report)	Hypothesis Five: The number of attempts at the activities for the gamified group is higher than the non-gamified group
6 - Access to external resources	- Number of logs to resources (Moodle logs report)	Hypothesis Six: The gamified group accesses more the external resources pages than the non-gamified group
Isolated elements		
7 - Number of attempts (Super-Engineer)	- Number of attempts (Moodle SCORM report) - Mini-game score	Hypothesis Seven: The mini-game has a positive influence on (a) the number of attempts, and (b) which has a positive influence on the score
8 - The score and duration (challenge)	- Challenge score - Time spent on the challenge (Moodle SCORM report)	Hypothesis Eight: The challenge has a positive influence on (a) the time spent on the challenge, and (b) which has a positive influence on the score

APPENDIX 2. LEARNING PATH MATRIX: STRUCTURE AND PEDAGOGICAL CONTENT OF THE MOODLE TRAINING COURSE

Figure 5. Learning path matrix: Level 1

Innovative trends in digital learning: playful pedagogy Gamified course	Innovative trends in digital learning: Playful pedagogy Non-gamified course
Level 1 Introduction	
Training objective: Raise the awareness of the pedagogical engineer to new innovative trends in digital learning. **Estimated duration**: 1h30	
Starting questionnaire **Objective:** collect the profile of the participants: age, gender, function	
Introduction module **Objective:** discover the narrative universe and the learning objectives of the course **Estimated duration :** 10 minutes **Format** : Scorm **Initial self-assessment** **Objective**: estimate their initial level of knowledge **Estimated duration:** 1 min **Format :** scorm	

Gamification mechanisms
Gamification of system :
   ❖ 200 points if the activity is completed (plugin Level up)
Content gamification :
   ❖ Storytelling
	Content gamification :
	Storytelling

Figure 6. Learning path matrix: Level 2

Level 2
Vocabulary discovery **Objective :** discover 5 innovative digital learning terms **Estimated duration : 9 min** **Format : Scorm**

Gamification mechanisms <u>Gamification of system</u> : ❖ 200 points if the activity is completed (plugin Level up) <u>Content gamification</u> : ❖ Storytelling	**No gamification mechanisms**
Super-engineer mini-game (3 min) **Objective**: check the knowledge of the latest digital learning vocabulary **Estimated duration** : 2 min **Format** : Scorm	**Quiz (3 min)** **Objective**: check the knowledge of the latest digital learning vocabulary **Estimated duration** : 3 min **Format** : Scorm
Gamification mechanisms <u>Gamification of system</u> : ❖ 200 points if activity is completed ❖ Target : 75 % success rate <u>Content gamification</u> : ❖ Activity based on a mini-game (game created especially for the module (character, rule, conditions, points, sonor background)	**No gamification mechanisms** ❖ Success rate : Target : 75 % success rate

Figure 7. Learning path matrix: Level 3

Level 3
Video introduction (cartoon style) : Playful pedagogy
Objective : introduce the main concepts of game-based pedagogy
Estimated duration: 1min 33
Format : video Powtoon

Gamification mechanisms (system)	No gamification mechanisms
❖ 100 points if the activity is completed	

Focus on Gamification and Serious Game
Objective : explore the concepts of gamification and serious game
Estimated duration : 14 min
Format : Genially presentation

Gamification mechanisms (system)	No gamification mechanisms
❖ 200 points if the activity is completed	

Intermediate quiz
Objective : verify the knowledge acquired at this level
Estimated duration : 5 min
Format : Moodle activity (test)

Gamification mechanisms	No gamification mechanisms
❖ 400 points if the activity is completed	

Challenge	**Exercise: Serious game**
Objective : apply the acquired concepts on the serious game	**Objective :** apply the acquired concepts on the serious game
Estimated duration : 13 min	**Estimated duration :** 12 min
Format : Scorm	**Format :** Scorm

Gamification mechanisms	No gamification mechanisms
Gamification of system :	
❖ 300 points if the activity is completed	
Content gamification :	
❖ Activity based on a **challenge**	
❖ Reward: obtain 3 virtual objects	
❖ Storytelling	
❖ Avatar	

Figure 8. Learning path matrix: Level 4

Level 4	
Homework : exercise	
Objective: consolidate knowledge	
Estimated duration : 4 min	
Format : scorm	
Gamification mechanisms ❖ 200 points if the activity is completed	No gamification mechanisms
Self-assessment	
Objective : estimate the level of knowledge acquired	
Estimated duration : 1 min	
Format : scorm	
Gamification mechanisms (system) ❖ 200 points if the activity is completed	No gamification mechanisms

Figure 9. Learning path matrix: Level 5

Level 5	
Final quiz	
Objective : evaluate the knowledge of the entire course	
Estimated duration : 10 min	
Format : Moodle activity (test)	
Gamification mechanisms (system) ❖ 200 points if the activity is completed ❖ Obtain at least **70% success rate** (linked to the condition of obtaining **the badge)**	No gamification mechanisms
Take away: resources to go further	
Objective: browse sources and additional information on the content of the course	
Gamification mechanisms ❖ 100 points if the activity is completed	No gamification mechanisms
End of the module Gamification mechanisms (system) **Leaderboard** all along the course **Badge requirements** : ❖ 70% success in the final quiz ❖ To have completed or consulted all the activities and resources of the course	**End of the module** No gamification mechanisms

APPENDIX 3. THE LEADERBOARD IN THE MOODLE TRAINING PLATFORM

Figure 10. Leaderboard

Rang	Niveau	Participant	Total	Progression
1	6	Quelqu'un d'autre	6 200 ^{XP}	0 ^{XP} restant
2	6	Quelqu'un d'autre	4 900 ^{XP}	0 ^{XP} restant
3	6	Quelqu'un d'autre	4 500 ^{XP}	0 ^{XP} restant
4	6	Quelqu'un d'autre	4 300 ^{XP}	0 ^{XP} restant
4	6	Quelqu'un d'autre	4 300 ^{XP}	0 ^{XP} restant
6	6	Quelqu'un d'autre	4 100 ^{XP}	0 ^{XP} restant
7	6	Quelqu'un d'autre	3 700 ^{XP}	0 ^{XP} restant
7	6	Quelqu'un d'autre	3 700 ^{XP}	0 ^{XP} restant
9	6	Quelqu'un d'autre	3 500 ^{XP}	0 ^{XP} restant
10	6	Quelqu'un d'autre	3 300 ^{XP}	0 ^{XP} restant
11	6	Quelqu'un d'autre	2 900 ^{XP}	0 ^{XP} restant
12	5	Quelqu'un d'autre	2 300 ^{XP}	200 ^{XP} restant
13	2	Quelqu'un d'autre	500 ^{XP}	100 ^{XP} restant

APPENDIX 4. THE POSITIONING OF GAMIFICATION ELEMENTS IN THE MOODLE TRAINING PLATFORM

Figure 11. Training path home page in Moodle

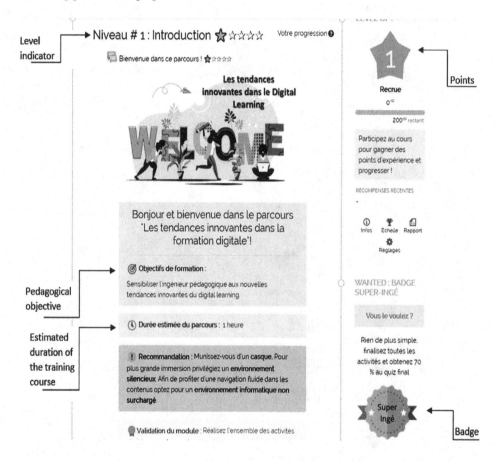

APPENDIX 5. DESCRIPTIVE OF TOTAL TIME ON COURSE AND CUMULATIVE SCORE AVERAGES

Figure 12. Total time on course and Cumulative Score averages

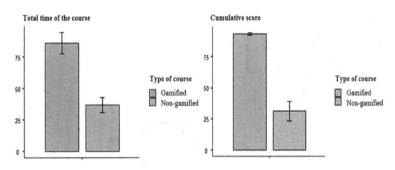

APPENDIX 6. DESCRIPTIVE OF MEANS AND MEDIANS OF THE CUMULATIVE SCORE

Figure 13. Means and medians of the cumulative score

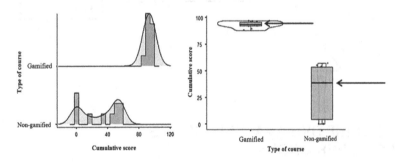

APPENDIX 7. POSITIVE CORRELATION MATRIX BETWEEN THE NUMBER OF LOGS AND THE CUMULATIVE SCORE

Figure 14. Correlation matrix number of logs and cumulative score

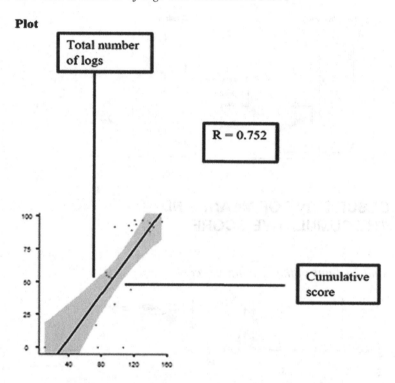

APPENDIX 8. DESCRIPTIVE ANALYSIS OF THE NUMBER OF LOGS PER GROUP

Figure 15. Number of logs per group

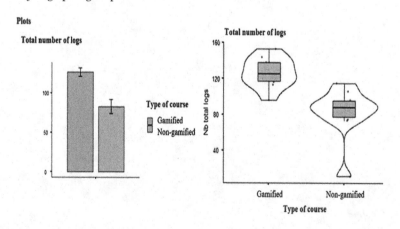

APPENDIX 9. DESCRIPTIVE ANALYSIS OF THE MEANS OF THE SUPER-ENGINEER SCORE

Figure 16. Means of the Super-Engineer score

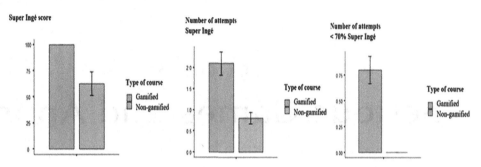

APPENDIX 10. VISUAL REPRESENTATION OF COMPARISONS OF MEANS

Figure 17. Comparisons of means

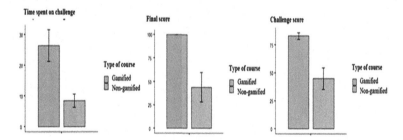

Section 3
Serious Games and Apps

Chapter 7
Petrha+:
A Serious Game to Enhance Physiotherapy Students' Clinical Reasoning

Rui Macedo
Polytechnic of Porto, Portugal

Claudia Silva
Polytechnic of Porto, Portugal

Bruno Albouy
IRFSS Nouvelle-Aquitaine, France

Alejandro F. San Juan
Universidad Politécnica de Madrid, Spain

Tiina Pystynen
Tampere University of Applied Sciences, Finland

ABSTRACT

Role play and simulated patients are tools frequently used in undergraduate physiotherapy courses to help students gain familiarity with what they will find in future real-life encounters. However, these approaches have limitations when it comes to delivering diversity and repetition to a large number of students and are mostly bounded to the school's premises. Web-based virtual patient software can help to overcome these shortcomings as they equally require students to go through most of the steps of the physiotherapy process, and simultaneously offer unlimited diversity of cases and repetition opportunities and can be delocalized from physical schools. PETRHA + is an Erasmus+ strategic partnership of European high education institutions aiming at the improvement of a web-based serious game prototype designed to enhance physiotherapy students' clinical reasoning using virtual patients. The objective of this chapter is the presentation of the background context that led to the development of the serious game, its design features, functions, and ongoing and future developments.

DOI: 10.4018/978-1-7998-8089-9.ch007

INTRODUCTION

PETRHA+ is an ongoing ERASMUS+ project[1] that follows the PETRHA[2] strategic partnership. Drawing from one of the intellectual outputs of the previous partnership, a serious game, PETRHA+ partners are improving it as a clinical process training tool for undergraduate physiotherapy students. Like its predecessor, the PETRHA's+ serious game aims to structure student's clinical reasoning and enhance the assertiveness of their physiotherapy diagnosis by repeatedly playing multiple competitive and collaborative virtual clinical cases of different health-related conditions within the scope of physiotherapy practice. Clinical cases in English, Spanish, Portuguese, and French will be delivered through a free online platform with versions in each of the four European languages. The objective of this chapter is to present PETRHA's+ serious game structure and functionalities.

BACKGROUND AND CONTEXT

Developments in physiotherapy professional competencies (WCPT-ER, 2013) in undergraduate physiotherapy education include a focus on the interactions with patients and clients and the process that spans from the first contact to measure an intervention's results. For teaching purposes, this process can be broken down into several tasks that involve collecting data from patient history, patient files, and physical examination (including assessments of the main functions of the body, activity limitations, participation restrictions). Then, the collected information is processed to establish a physiotherapy diagnosis, rehabilitation goals, choosing rehabilitation means and techniques, implementing therapeutic actions, and re-assessment. Most parts of this process can be emulated using simulation approaches that span from the low-tech, low-budget paper case, through virtual cases or mannequins, right to standardized patients both in mixed and real lab contexts (Jull et al., 2011; Pritchard et al., 2016).

Simulations using actors as patients in undergraduate physiotherapy training courses helps students gain familiarity with clinical encounters or care environments like those they will find in real life, without risk for the patient, for the healthcare professional or for the student (Murphy et al., 2015; Phillips et al., 2017). However, these simulated clinical situations present some limitations. In addition, the scenario of students role-playing with peers might present some limitations, regardless of its usefulness. For example, when roles lack realism, students do not behave as they might in a real situation; they may have poor acting skills, inadequate preparation, uncertainty about the quality of peer feedback, or lack of clarity in instructions that make the experience less believable (Nestel & Tierney, 2007).

Actors as patients can be very realistic and be good for evaluation purposes because of their ability to standardize the assessment environment but are expensive (Paparella-Pitzel et al., 2009). Moreover, because a large number is needed to cover all health conditions, they take a long time to train and get tiered, all of which makes them inadequate for large-scale training. Finally, patients in a class context have the advantage and richness of its reality but must be accompanied by staff, and like with actors, they get tiered, which limits repetition. The approaches described above, although limited as stand-alone solutions, can complement each other if delivered for a specific purpose alongside the curriculum. Despite their value as learning tools, they have similar limitations when it comes to delivering diversity and repetition to a large number of students. Their use is also limited because they are mostly bound to the school's premises.

A learning tool that could be delocalized from physical schools, offer diverse cases, and have unlimited repetition opportunities would fill the gaps in the learning opportunities associated with simulation. Virtual patients can be that missing piece and have been used in education in health professions (Bateman et al., 2012; Consorti et al., 2012; Forsberg et al., 2011; Kononowicz et al., 2019), including physiotherapy (Macauley, 2018) and it's associated with improved outcomes in comparison with no intervention in a variety of health professionals across a range of clinical topics (Cook, Erwin, & Triola, 2010). Using virtual patients for student learning would require going through most of the steps of the physiotherapy process and play a major role in student training. Virtual patients would allow students to fulfill the repetition component of training (Cook & Triola, 2009). Practice can be further reinforced when simulation with virtual patients is delivered in the form of a game played in a competition (Chong, 2019) with fellow students or just for a better score or time. This competition-collaboration approach enhances learning by motivating students to practice and keep on task (Chong, 2019). Practicing with virtual patients promotes clinical reasoning development (Cook & Triola, 2009), which is associated with efficiently gathering and retaining information. This is also associated with developing pattern recognition strategies, which is a characteristic that experts have in their approach to patients (Jensen et al., 2008).

PETRHA+ The Project

PETRHA+ is a 36 month, 448.8 K€ funded ERASMUS+ strategic partnership that is being carried out by an association of five European higher education institutions: the Free High School of Brussels - Ilya Prigogine (HELB) in Belgium, the IRFSS Aquitaine in France, the Polytechnic University of Madrid in Spain (UPM), the Polytechnic Institute of Porto in Portugal (IPP), and the University of Applied Sciences of Tampere (TAMK) in Finland. A French e-health software company, Interaction Healthcare, is also associated with it. Coming from different countries, these partners cover a broad range of cultural and educational backgrounds, which ensures that the intellectual outputs incorporate a multicultural point of view of physiotherapy and serve very different contexts of physiotherapy education.

At the same time, the project aims to harmonize undergraduate physiotherapy training in Europe by incorporating the standards of physiotherapy practice of those European countries. The project's intellectual outputs will be a massive open online course (MOOC) dedicated to structuring a theoretical framework, providing an assessment tool to test students' clinical reasoning, and a serious game to train clinical reasoning in different areas of physiotherapy. The project is being designed to consider the richness of partner's differences, which will allow other non-partner higher education institutions across Europe to take advantage of them and promote the dissemination of the project.

PETRHA's+ Serious Game: Goals, Theoretical Framework, and Strategy

Building a virtual patient delivery tool that is user-friendly and easily scalable for a variety of patients with a diverse range of health conditions was the goal of PETRHA that was kept for the PETRHA+ project. Allowing it to be used free of charge and available in several languages was the strategy used to promote the project's development and dissemination.

Adopting PETRHA's+ theoretical framework from the International Classification of Function (ICF) was another strategy set from the beginning. The game profited from the ICF's association with clinical reasoning and physiotherapy diagnosis and from the ICF's shared theoretical framework with other health professions. These benefits facilitate the game's future adaptation to other professions with undergraduate training.

Description of the PETRHA Serious Game

Not being a finished project and without the integration of all the new features that will be part of the PETRHA+ version of the serious game, this description refers to the game developed under the PETRHA project since it shares technologies, structure, and other components and elements that confer the distinctive characteristics of this game. The serious game is composed of two distinct but interconnected parts. The front end consists of the interface for players, and the back office is where cases are loaded and where administrative tasks related to the game are performed, namely their parameterization and user management. The front end of the host page has a link to the MOOC with game instructions on PETRHA that are available for newcomers.

Starting with the welcome page, the interaction with the game begins immediately through demos[3]. Players can choose one of the four versions of the game that appear in any of the official languages. In doing so, the players have access to the contents (e.g., virtual patients) available in that language. Other existing virtual patients are available and can be accessed by registered players.

Playing

Playing the game consists of interacting with the virtual patient in the front-end, collecting information that is necessary for the formulation of the diagnosis in physiotherapy, and elaborating intervention objectives for that virtual patient. These will be compared with the diagnosis and objectives defined by the creators of the case. The degree of correspondence between diagnosis and objectives proposed by the player and those of the case creator translates into a score.

Gathering Information

The front end features a navigation menu with tabs that refer to different locations where the player can collect information regarding the case they are playing (Figure.1). The tabs correspond to the main sources of information available to clinicians when dealing with real patients. These sources are the clinical file of the virtual patient where their clinical history is stored, the interview with the patient or their caregiver, answers to written questions, and the physical examination (Figure.2) (including testing, associated complementary means of diagnosis, and body functions that are suspected of being impaired). There are also scales measuring the impact on activities and participation to complement the available information. Like in real cases, virtual patients have relevant information that can be retrieved only through watching. Media files and documents stored in the game for that purpose are available and are accessible to the player by hyperlinks.

Establishing Physiotherapy Diagnosis

After collecting the relevant information, the player formulates a diagnosis. To do so, they must select and submit the findings that best support their diagnosis. Physiotherapy diagnosis is multidimensional,

Figure 1. Locations

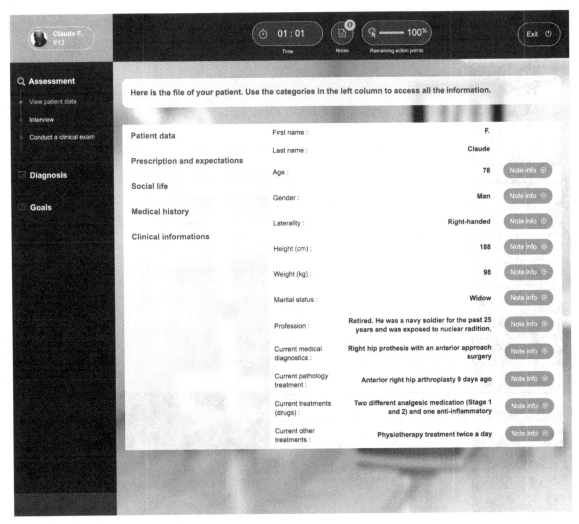

so findings are categorized in different dimensions (i.e., structures, functions, activities, and participation) and consider the positive and negative contextual factors (Figure.3).

Setting Goals and Objectives

This is the third and final phase of the game. Here, the player sets goals, defines their duration (e.g., final, intermediate, or initial) according to the expected time frame for their compliance. If there are several objectives for each period, the player must prioritize them. After this process is completed, the player submits their proposal, and the application returns a performance report with overall and partial scores for each phase of the game.

Figure 2. Physical examination

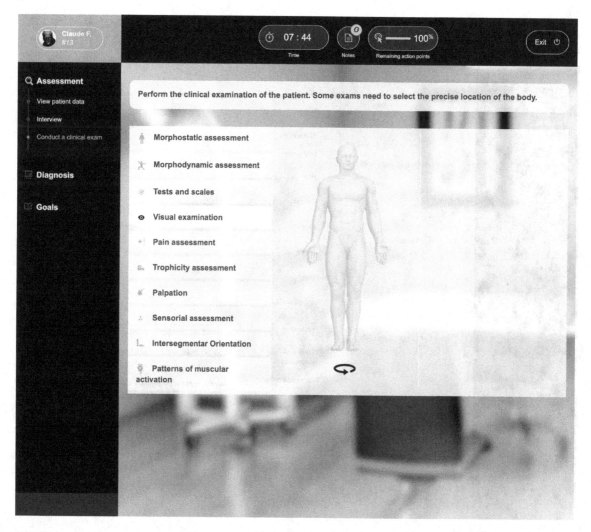

The Back Office

Although the back office exists for administrative tasks, its main use is to upload virtual patients' cases (i.e., a database interface). In it, there are fields for loading information related to virtual patients that will be available to players (Figure.4). Fields for diagnosis and objectives are also available to the case creator. Most fields are already labeled and have predefined the type of information to be loaded. These predefinitions express the consensus of the partners about the information they considered that could be necessary for physiotherapy diagnosis and is in alignment with the best available evidence to date. New fields can also be added and labeled in the back office. This flexibility has been incorporated into the game to accommodate the cultural diversity of partners, allow the adaptation of the needs of other users outside the partnership, and facilitate the scalability of the game. A feature associated with some fields is the possibility to upload or create hyperlinks to media files with content relevant to the game's course.

Figure 3. Positive and Negative contextual factors

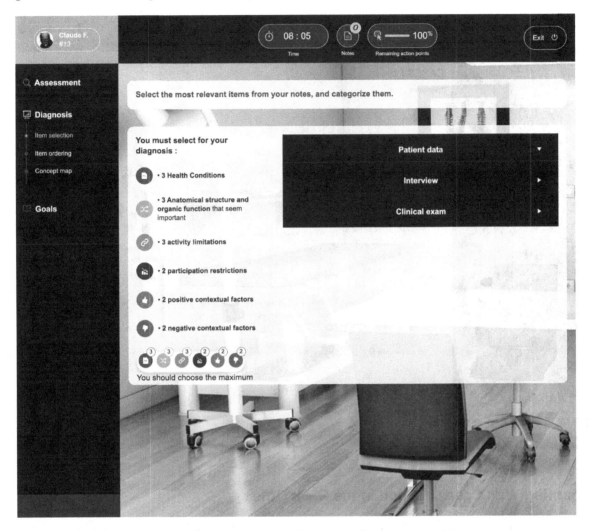

Virtual Patient Customization

In addition to uploading the information, the creator of the case can define the level of relevance of the information for the diagnosis, setting objectives, and setting a particular path for players. They can also define the weight that each part of the game (e.g., data collection, diagnosis, goals) has in the final score. Depending on compliance with a set of requirements and the quality of cases, availability can be just for local users or expand to European users.

Administrative Functions

There are different levels of permissions to navigate and proceed to settings in the Backoffice. Depending on the level, the back-office user can create, duplicate, transform or translate other cases and customize them. Back-office users can add individual or institutional users and create sessions for players.

Figure 4. Information available to players

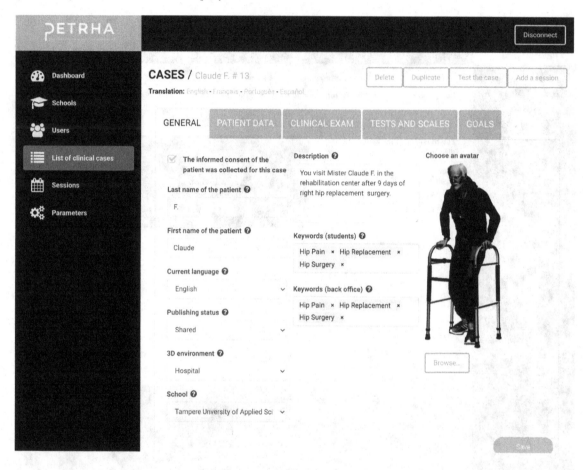

Learning With Case Creation in the Back Office

Like other software, PETRHA's back office has different users' profiles. Therefore, limited access to the back office can be granted to students for case creation. Due to the nature of the cognitive tasks associated with creating and uploading virtual patients, this process has the potential to promote the development of clinical reasoning that underlies the diagnosis in physiotherapy. Also, this way of using the game, especially under the proper supervision, exponentially increases the potential of available cases on the front-end side.

Using PETRHA as a Tool

In the original version developed under the PETRHA project, the functional prototype of the serious game was designed for virtual geriatric patients. However, the transdisciplinary theoretical framework, the complexity of geriatric cases, and the possibility of adding fields were reflected in the addition of functionalities that, with some adaptation, enable the creation of virtual patients with other health conditions.

Even being in the prototype phase, students from schools outside strategic partnership competed in 2017 PETRHA CUP, an event designed to collect players assessments of the game usability and it's performance with simultaneous multiple players. Within PETRHA+ project in 2021 a similar event took place this time with players in different countries and collected data (preliminary unpublished results) show impact in clinical reasoning skills. Between these events the game was used by schools from and outside the partnership in small scale to provide students with new learning opportunities, namely in pre-clinical or even in a clinical context. In fact, some of the eleven schools with a PETRHA account have used the game in in-class learning tasks and to prepare for internships. One of the uses is the adaptation of real patients to virtual patients. This process is a strategy used to promote critical reflection and the development of clinical reasoning. Similarly, exploring the applicability of the game in the teaching-learning process of pre-graduate courses of other health professions has already begun with the creation of cases by speech therapy students.

FUTURE DEVELOPMENTS

The serious game is being perfected under the PETRHA+ and already incorporates virtual patients from the musculoskeletal, neurological, cardiorespiratory, and pediatrics areas. Following the creation of these cases, new features and interfaces are being developed to make the game more comprehensive, robust, and functional and will include the types of cases that physiotherapists find in their daily lives. Higher Education Institutions outside the project were invited to test the new prototype and data relating to its usability, bugs and potential improvements is being collected. Simultaneously its being carried out a study on the short-term effects of the use of the serious game on clinical reasoning skills.

CONCLUSION

PETRHA+ virtual patient's serious game as a set of features and functions that are in line with the evidence relating to the development of clinical reasoning skills and improvement of the ability to do physiotherapy diagnosis. The web-based delivery mode of the learning experiences provides conditions for accessibility and scalability, both for case creation and playing. There seems to be an interest by educators on PETRHA's serious game. Future studies should be caried out to assess PETRHA's game in clinical reasoning development and compare it to other approaches.

ACKNOWLEDGMENT

This research was supported by the European Economic Community: ERASMUS + Strategic Partnership Program [Project n ° 2018-1-BE01-KA203-038581]; European Economic Community: ERASMUS + Strategic Partnership Program [Project n ° 2015-1- FR01-KA203- 015057]

REFERENCES

Bateman, J., Allen, M. E., Kidd, J., Parsons, N., & Davies, D. (2012). Virtual patients design and its effect on clinical reasoning and student experience: A protocol for a randomised factorial multi-center study. *BMC Medical Education*, *12*(1), 62. Advance online publication. doi:10.1186/1472-6920-12-62 PMID:22853706

Chong, D. Y. K. (2019). Benefits and challenges with gamified multi-media physiotherapy case studies: A mixed method study. *Archives of Physiotherapy*, *9*(1), 1–11. doi:10.118640945-019-0059-2 PMID:31139434

Consorti, F., Mancuso, R., Nocioni, M., & Piccolo, A. (2012). Efficacy of virtual patients in medical education: A meta-analysis of randomized studies. *Computers & Education*, *59*(3), 1001–1008. doi:10.1016/j.compedu.2012.04.017

Cook, D. A., & Triola, M. M. (2009, April). Virtual patients: A critical literature review and proposed next steps. *Medical Education*, *43*(4), 303–311. doi:10.1111/j.1365-2923.2008.03286.x PMID:19335571

Forsberg, E., Georg, C., Ziegert, K., & Fors, U. (2011). Virtual patients for assessment of clinical reasoning in nursing - A pilot study. *Nurse Education Today*, *31*(8), 757–762. doi:10.1016/j.nedt.2010.11.015 PMID:21159412

Jensen, G., Resnik, L., & Haddad, A. (2008). Expertise and clinical reasoning. *Clinical Reasoning in the Health Professions*, *3*, 123–136.

Jull, G., Wright, A., Joan, M., Norman, M., Rivett, D., Blackstock, F., … Neads, P. (2011). *Health Workforce Australia National Simulated Learning Project Report for Physiotherapy*. Health Workforce Australia.

Kononowicz, A. A., Woodham, L. A., Edelbring, S., Stathakarou, N., Davies, D., Saxena, N., Tudor Car, L., Carlstedt-Duke, J., Car, J., & Zary, N. (2019). Virtual patient simulations in health professions education: Systematic review and meta-analysis by the Digital Health Education Collaboration. *Journal of Medical Internet Research*, *21*(7), e14676. doi:10.2196/14676 PMID:31267981

Macauley, K. (2018). Evaluating changes in clinical decision-making in physical therapy students after participating in simulation. *Health Profession Education*, *4*(4), 278–286. doi:10.1016/j.hpe.2018.06.001

Murphy, S., Imam, B., & Macintyre, D. L. (2015). Standardized patients versus volunteer patients for physical therapy students' interviewing practice: A pilot study. *Physiotherapy Canada. Physiotherapie Canada*, *67*(4), 378–384. doi:10.3138/ptc.2014-50E PMID:27504038

Nestel, D., & Tierney, T. (2007). Role-play for medical students learning about communication: Guidelines for maximising benefits. *BMC Medical Education*, *7*(1), 3. doi:10.1186/1472-6920-7-3 PMID:17335561

Paparella-Pitzel, S., Edmond, S., & DeCaro, C. (2009). The use of standardized patients in physical therapist education programs. *Journal of Physical Therapy Education, 23*(2). https://journals.lww.com/jopte/Fulltext/2009/07000/The_Use_of_Standardized_Patients_in_Physical.3.aspx

Phillips, A. C., Mackintosh, S. F., Bell, A., & Johnston, K. N. (2017). Developing physiotherapy student safety skills in readiness for clinical placement using standardised patients compared with peer-role play: A pilot non-randomised controlled trial. *BMC Medical Education, 17*(1), 133. doi:10.118612909-017-0973-5 PMID:28797260

Pritchard, S. A., Blackstock, F. C., Nestel, D., & Keating, J. L. (2016). Simulated patients in physical therapy education: Systematic review and meta-analysis. *Physical Therapy, 96*(9), 1342–1353. doi:10.2522/ptj.20150500 PMID:26939603

WCPT-ER. (2013). *WCPT Glossary: TermsUsed in WCPT's Policies.* Author.

ADDITIONAL READING

Cook, D. A., Erwin, P. J., & Triola, M. M. (2010). Computerized Virtual Patients in Health Professions Education: A Systematic Review and Meta-Analysis. *Academic Medicine, 85*(10), 1589–1602. Advance online publication. doi:10.1097/ACM.0b013e3181edfe13 PMID:20703150

Hege, I., Kononowicz, A. A., Kiesewetter, J., & Foster-Johnson, L. (2018). Uncovering the relation between clinical reasoning and diagnostic accuracy - An analysis of learner's clinical reasoning processes in virtual patients. *PLoS One, 13*(10), e0204900. Advance online publication. doi:10.1371/journal.pone.0204900 PMID:30286136

Higgs, J., Jensen, G., Loftus, S., & Christensen, N. (Eds.). (2019). *Clinical reasoning in the health professions* (4th ed.). Elsevier.

Motola, I., Devine, L. A., Chung, H. S., Sullivan, J. E., & Issenberg, S. B. (2013). Simulation in healthcare education: A best evidence practical guide. AMEE Guide No. 82. *Medical Teacher, 35*(10), e1511–e1530. doi:10.3109/0142159X.2013.818632 PMID:23941678

Watson, K., Wright, A., Morris, N., McMeeken, J., Rivett, D., Blackstock, F., Jones, A., Haines, T., O'Connor, V., Watson, G., Peterson, R., & Jull, G. (2012). Can simulation replace part of clinical time? Two parallel randomised controlled trials. *Medical Education, 46*(7), 657–667. doi:10.1111/j.1365-2923.2012.04295.x PMID:22646319

KEY TERMS AND DEFINITIONS

Clinical Reasoning: The cognitive process used by health professionals, to collect and evaluate data and to make judgements about the diagnosis and management of patient problems.

Physiotherapy Diagnosis: The identification of existing or potential impairments, limitations in activities and restrictions in participation and of factors influencing functioning positively or negatively which results from the cognitive process of clinical reasoning.

Serious Game: Serious games are simulations of real-world events thought out for educational purposes and not intended to be played primarily for amusement.

Virtual Patients: A computer program conceived to simulate a real-life individuals with health conditions in which the player acting as a health care provider gathers information from history and physical exam, and makes diagnostic and therapeutic decisions.

ENDNOTES

[1]   PETRHA+ Erasmus strategic partnership 2018-1-BE01-KA203-038581

[2]   PETRHA Erasmus strategic partnership 2015-1- FR01-KA203- 015057

[3]   http://www.petrha.org/game/front/pages/home

Chapter 8
Using Sentiment Analytics to Understand Learner Experiences in Serious Games

Linda William
Temasek Polytechnic, Singapore

Ruan Yang
Temasek Polytechnic, Singapore

ABSTRACT

A serious game has been introduced as an alternative tool to support teaching and learning. It integrates entertainment and non-entertainment elements to encourage the voluntary learning of knowledge and skills. One of the essential entertainment elements in the serious game to motivate learning is the enjoyment element. However, studies on models to analyze this enjoyment element are still limited. Most models present isolated and specific approaches for specific games that cannot scale to other games. In this chapter, a generic enjoyment analytics framework is proposed. The framework aims to capture learners' enjoyment experience using open-ended feedback, analyze the feedback using sentiment analytics models, and visualize the results in an interactive dashboard. Using this framework, the lecturers would interpret the learners' experience towards the topic and the game and capture difficulties the learners may encounter during the game. It would help the lecturers to decide follow-up actions required for the learners to improve the learning.

1. INTRODUCTION

The serious game is defined as a (digital) game designed and created not with the primary purpose of pure entertainment but with the serious intention of using it in training, education and healthcare (Loh, Sheng, & Ifenthaler, 2015). It can be used as an alternative or interactive tool to improve skills/performance as well as to broadcast messages to the learners (Liu, Alexandrova, & Nakajima, 2011; Ma, Oikonomou, & Jain, 2011; De Freitas & Liarokapis, 2011; Loh, Sheng, & Ifenthaler, 2015). Serious game infuses

DOI: 10.4018/978-1-7998-8089-9.ch008

knowledge and skills into the game environment while maintaining the entertainment elements that keeping the learners engaged and interacted with the game. Learners who train and learn with a serious game will "play as they learn and learn as they play". Through the engagement and interaction with information, tools, materials and other learners in the serious game, learners would voluntarily learn and master their knowledge and skills (Kim, Park, & Baek, 2009).

Serious game has been implemented in various areas, including computer programming (Coelho, Kato, Xavier, & Gonçalves, 2011; Muratet, Torguet, Jessel, & Viallet, 2009), healthcare (Garcia-Ruiz, Tashiro, Kapralos, & Martin, 2011; de Freitas & Jarvis, 2008; Graafland, Schraagen, & Schijven, 2012), military applications (Lim & Jung, 2013), city planning (Gómez-Rodríguez, González-Moreno, Ramos-Valcárcel, & Vázquez-López, 2011) and supply chain management (William, Rahim, Souza, Nugroho, & Fredericco, 2018). According to a recent report, about 25% of the Global Fortune 500 companies, particularly from the United States, Britain and Germany, have already adopted serious games for their training and education (Loh, Sheng, & Ifenthaler, 2015). Main objectives for the implementation include broadcasting information related to a specific topic (i.e. refugees (United Nations High Commissioner for Refugees, 2021; United Nations High Commissioner for Refugees, 2005; Canadian Red Cross, 2021)), improving the skills and performance of the learners (i.e. python programming language (CodeCombat, 2021)), and testing and evaluating learner's skills as an assessment tool (William, Abdul Rahim, Wu, & de Souza, 2019).

Numerous studies have revealed the benefits of using serious game (Ma, Oikonomou, & Jain, 2011). The benefits include enhancing and encouraging engagement, curiosity, motivation, self-monitoring and problem solving (Ma, Oikonomou, & Jain, 2011; Rieber, 1996; Knight, et al., 2010; Kumar, 2000) to improving the learner's knowledge and skills for specific topics or subjects. The serious game would encourage active participation and interaction from the learners to eventually increase their understanding of particular knowledge and skills (Hou, 2015). The learners would gain experience implementing the new knowledge and skills by completing tasks and challenges in the game.

One of the serious game's essential entertainment elements is learners' enjoyment (Sweetser & Wyeth, 2005). Enjoyment comes from positive experience while playing the game. This enjoyment element helps to decide whether learners would or would not continue playing the game. In the serious game, the enjoyment element is also believed to intrinsically motivate learners to learn new knowledge and skills (IJsselsteijn, De Kort, Poels, Jurgelionis, & Bellotti, 2007; Sweetser & Wyeth, 2005). Enjoyment allows learners to encounter flow experience for a total absorption or engagement in the game (immersive). During the optimal flow experience, the learners are in a state where they are so involved in the game that nothing else seems to matter (Kiili, 2006). It encourages the learners to complete and win the game by achieving new skills and understanding new concepts voluntarily (Kiili, 2006).

However, studies on models for assessing learners' enjoyment and its impacts to improve the learners' knowledge and skills are still limited (Sweetser & Wyeth, 2005; Giannakos, Chorianopoulos, Jaccheri, & Chrisochoides, 2012). Most of the models present isolated and non-repeatable heuristics approaches for evaluating the enjoyment element. It may only focus on only one specific aspect or concept, such as the interface (game control and display), the mechanism (interaction and feedback in the game world), and the gameplay (game problems and challenges). The main challenges in developing the model are 1) collecting the inputs and feedback from the learners, 2) analyzing the inputs and feedback, and 3) interpreting the enjoyment based on these inputs or feedback. The results of the game alone may be minimal and may not be able to represent the learners' enjoyment in the game. Additionally, for existing games (or serious games) in the industry, learners' inputs are mainly used to improve gameplay quality instead of understanding the learning process.

This chapter aims to design a generic enjoyment analytics framework to tackle these three challenges using machine learning models. The proposed framework focuses on open-ended feedback from learners while they are playing the game. This framework has three main components: 1) feedback gathering component, 2) feedback analytics component, and 3) feedback visualization component. The first component, the feedback gathering component, is embedded in the game itself. It allows the learners to provide open-ended feedback regarding the serious game frequently. The second component, the feedback analytics component, analyzes the feedback using machine learning models to detect favorable (positive) or unfavorable (negative) sentiments. These sentiments would be used to indicate the learners' enjoyment experience toward the topics and game itself. Nine machine learning models were developed to perform sentiment analytics. After comparing the models, the best model with the highest accuracy will be implemented in the enjoyment analytics framework. The third component, the feedback visualization component, provides an interactive dashboard to present the sentiment analytics results. It can be used to interpret the learners' experience. Detailed information about the sentiment analytics results and the learners' information is also provided in an interactive dashboard. The framework was evaluated using semi-structured interviews with several lecturers in Singapore. These interviews captured the usefulness of the framework to understand the learners' learning and experience better. The proposed framework is designed to implement it to different games and different topics with no or limited changes required.

The remaining of the chapter will be organized as follows: Section 2 presents the literature review on serious game design, enjoyment in serious game, and sentiment analytics. Section 3 discusses the overview of the proposed enjoyment analytics framework and its three components. Section 4 captures the evaluation of the framework. Section 5 and section 6 present the future research direction and conclusion.

2. LITERATURE REVIEW

This literature review includes: how a serious game can be designed, the impact of enjoyment in a serious game, how emotion can influence learning, the definition of sentiment analytics, and how sentiment analytics can be applied in text feedback.

2.1. Serious Game Design

The serious game has been defined as games with a purpose to educate (Yu, 2019). There is a consensus that serious game has a significant potential as a tool for instruction (Bellotti, Kapralos, Lee, Moreno-Ger, & Berta, 2013). In recent years, there is a sudden increase in serious game usage in education and training (Cowan & Kapralos, 2014). It is found that learners who had serious games integrated into their curriculum had a remarkable performance compared to those who had only a typical curriculum (Blunt, 2009). Additionally, it is also identified that serious game's learners had a drastic improvement in the topics compared to the non-serious game's learners (Guillén-Nieto & Aleson-Carbonell, 2012).

Serious game needs to balance the entertainment and non-entertainment (i.e. teaching pedagogy) to let the learners enjoy the game and learn from the game. Techniques to balance these two elements have been discussed as practices and frameworks in serious game design (Van Staalduinen & de Freitas, 2011). These best practices and frameworks combine game design and instructional design components to balance the entertainment and non-entertainment components in serious game. A few of these frameworks are the Game Object Model (Amory & Seagram, 2003; Amory, 2007), the Experiential Gaming Model (Kiili, 2005a; Kiili, 2005b; Kiili, 2005c), the Four-Dimensional Framework (De Freitas & Oliver, 2006; De Freitas & Jarvis, 2009), and the Game-based Learning Framework (Van Staalduinen & de Freitas, 2011).

The game object model is based on the object-oriented programming concept (Amory & Seagram, 2003; Amory, 2007). Pedagogy elements are combined with game elements that can implement the pedagogy elements in a game, such as a story, plot, and interaction. In contrast, the experiential gaming model describes the relationship between the gameplay and experiential learning to facilitate flow experience (Kiili, 2005a; Kiili, 2005b; Kiili, 2005c). It uses flow theory, which is defined as a total engagement in the game that motivates players to win the game by acquiring new skills and understanding new concepts voluntarily (Kiili, 2006). The four-dimensional framework introduces four dimensions in game design: learning specification, pedagogy, representation and context (De Freitas & Oliver, 2006; De Freitas & Jarvis, 2009). Lastly, the game-based learning framework explores the relationship between game elements and expected learning outcome (Van Staalduinen & de Freitas, 2011). It includes three components, namely: learning, instruction and assessment.

2.2. Enjoyment in Serious Game

In serious game design, enjoyment is one of the essential entertainment elements to be included. It plays a significant role in the learners' decision to continue playing the game and motivate them to achieve certain tasks, such as learning a specific concept (IJsselsteijn, De Kort, Poels, Jurgelionis, & Bellotti, 2007; Sweetser & Wyeth, 2005). Enjoyment would make the learners immerse and engage with the game entirely. This experience is referred to as a "flow" experience. "Flow" experience is denoted as a state during the game where the learners are so involved in the game that nothing else seems to matter (Kiili, 2006). They are fully concentrating on the tasks in the game and less conscious of the passage of time. The "flow" experience would encourages the learners to complete and win the game and help learners to unknowingly learn new skills and knowledge (Kiili, 2006), which result in a better learning process (Nagle, Wolf, Riener, & Novak, 2014).

The most significant factor in game enjoyment is emotion (Lazzaro, 2009). Emotion is a complex behavioural phenomenon involving many neural and chemical integration levels in the body (Lindsley, 1951) that can be classified into two superset terms, namely: positive and negative (Bower, 1992). Emotions can control conscious thought, such as attention focus (Lazzaro, 2004). It is crucial and drives focus, which drives learning and memory (Sylwester, 1994). Learners' emotions would affect their self-regulated learning and determination, which subsequently affect their accomplishment (Mega, Ronconi, & Beni, 2014).

Emotion can be perceived from facial expressions and communication language (Barrett, Lindquist, & Gendron, 2007). Language, including written language (i.e. text), can express emotions, and it helps with categorizing sensations into emotion categories such as anger, disgust, and fear (Lindquist, Satpute, & Gendron, 2015). Emotions in written language can be identified from different writing style (Hancock, Landrigan, & Silver, 2007).

2.3. Sentiment Analytics

Sentiment analytics has been widely used to study opinions, sentiments, and emotions expressed in the text (Miner, Elder IV, & Hill, 2012). It is generally known as computational identification of opinions, sentiments, emotions, and subjectivity from a given text (Medhat, Hassan, & Korashy, 2014). Sentiment analytics can be used to find out about the point of view of the public regarding a topic or individual (Medhat, Hassan, & Korashy, 2014), context to social conversations (Godsay, 2015), and different emotions (Altrabsheh, Gaber, & Cocea, 2013). The objectives of sentiment analytics are to identify the sentiments expressed in a text and classify their polarity. The sentiments can be categorized into two categories: positive and negative, or into an n-point scale, such as very good, good, neutral, bad, and very bad.

Based on its coverage, sentiment analytics can be divided into three levels, namely: document-level, sentence-level, and aspect-level (Medhat, Hassan, & Korashy, 2014). Document-level sentiment analytics focuses on analyzing the whole document and classifying the sentiments for that document. Sentence-level sentiment analytics only focuses on sentiments for each statement. Aspect-level sentiment analytics aims to identify sentiments for specific aspects of the text.

There are two main approaches to solving sentiment analytics: the lexicon-based approach and the machine learning approach (Sommar & Wielondek, 2015). Lexicon-based approaches use a list of predefined words, where each expression is associated with a specific sentiment (Gonçalves, Araújo, Benevenuto, & Cha, 2013). For example, the term "good" is associated with positive sentiment, while the word "bad" is associated with negative sentiment. In the lexicon-based approach, it is essential to have a complete lexical-based dictionary. Different languages and topics would require a different dictionary. This dictionary will determine the accuracy of the sentiment analytics results. Preparing a suitable dictionary is one of the main challenges in a lexical-based approach.

Machine learning approaches for sentiment analytics generally use a supervised classification approach. In this classification, each sentiment is considered as one label. Machine learning-based sentiment analytics approaches have been commonly used and gained popularity in recent years (Agarwal & Mittal, 2015). These approaches require labelled data as a training dataset (Pang, Lee, & Vaithyanathan, 2002). Machine learning approaches for sentiment analytics would generally train the model using the pre-labelled dataset to find patterns in the data and classify the text into specific sentiments (Sommar & Wielondek, 2015). The model will then be used to predict sentiments in new or "real" text. One main benefit of using machine learning approaches is adapting and creating trained models based on the specific context. It can also adjust to the changes in the "real" dataset in the implementation phase. Machine learning approaches are believed to have better performance than the lexicon-based approach (Pang, Lee, & Vaithyanathan, 2002). One main challenge in these machine learning approaches is preparing the pre-labelled dataset, which can be costly or even prohibited for a particular context.

3. PROPOSED ENJOYMENT ANALYTICS FRAMEWORK

To tackle the above challenges, an enjoyment analytics framework is proposed. This proposed framework aims to collect, analyze, and interpret learners' open-ended feedback while using a serious game. It is used to understand their learning experience through a serious game. It has three main components, namely: 1) feedback gathering during game session, 2) data analytics for the analyzing the feedback using sentiment analytics, and 3) visualization of the feedback and sentiments result for interpreting the learners' experience. The three components are summarized in Figure 1.

Figure 1. Components of the proposed enjoyment analytics framework

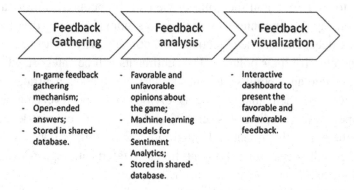

3.1. Feedback Gathering Component

The feedback gathering process is conducted through the serious game itself using open-ended question. The answers will then be stored in a shared database for further processes. This mechanism enables frequent feedback while playing a serious game rather than single feedback at the end of a game. It would help the current learners and act as checkpoints to early identification of learning challenges.

The feedback is collected after each topic for a particular subject. For example, the subject "Introduction to Programming" has two topics, namely: "Condition" and "Loop". The subject would collect two pieces of feedback, one for each topic. The steps for gathering the feedback are as follows:

1. After completing a particular topic, the game will prompt the learners for their feedback. The interface for feedback collection is shown in Figure 2.
2. After they pressed the 'Submit' button, their feedback will be stored in a table of the database for further processes.

Figure 2. Example of one feedback gathering UI interface

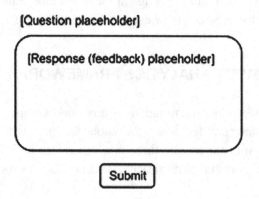

3.2. Feedback Analytics Component

Feedback analytics is conducted for learners' feedback stored in a shared database. It uses a sentiment analytics model to identify learners' enjoyment experience towards the topic and the game itself. The model needs to identify two enjoyment experience categories, namely: positive and negative. The sentiment analytics will allow the lecturers to identify the learners who have a negative experience with the topics and the game. Negative experience may affect learning and indicates difficulties during the game. Lecturers can give more attention and provide extra assistance to learners who have a negative experience to improve their learning.

3.2.1. Machine Learning Models

For this component, sentiment analytics is considered a classification problem with two labels: positive and negative. The feedback text is being classified into these two groups. Nine machine learning models were developed and compared. These nine models are Support Vector Machine (SVM), Logistic Regression, Random Forest Classifier, K-Nearest Neighbour (KNN), Naïve Bayes, Simple Neural Network (SNN), Convolutional Neural Network (CNN), Recurrent Neural Network with Long-Sort Term Memory (RNN-LSTM), and Bi-directional Recurrent Neural Network with Long-Sort Term Memory (Bi-RNN-LSTM). SVM, Logistic Regression, Random Forest Classifier, KNN, and Naïve Bayes are supervised models, while SNN, CNN, RNN-LSTM, and Bi-RNN-LSTM are neural network models. A brief description of these models is as follows.

3.2.1.1. Support Vector Machine (SVM)

SVM is a supervised learning method that generates input-output mapping functions from a training dataset (Vapnik, 1995). An SVM model maps the training dataset to a point in high-dimensional feature space to maximize the gap between categories (i.e. positive and negative sentiment). There are four fundamental concepts of SVM, namely: (1) the separating hyperplane, (2) the maximum-margin hyperplane, (3) the soft margin, and (4) the kernel function (Noble, 2006).

3.2.1.2. Logistic Regression

Logistics regression is a supervised learning method that uses a logistics function to find the best fitting model to explain the relationship between an outcome (dependent) variable and a set of independent (predictor) variables. In logistics regression, the outcome variable usually is binary or dichotomous, such as true and false or positive and negative (Hosmer Jr, Lemeshow, & Sturdivant, 2013).

3.2.1.3. Random Forest Classifier

Random forest is a supervised learning method based on a combination of decision tree predictors. Each tree depends on an independent random vector with the same distribution for all the forest trees (Breiman, 2001). It builds multiple decision trees using some component of randomness and determines the classification using the majority of various trees (Breiman, 2001; Mishina, Murata, Yamauchi, Yamashita, & Fujiyoshi, 2015).

3.2.1.4. K-Nearest Neighbour (KNN)

KKN is a supervised learning method that classifies the input data based on their nearest neighbour's group (Kataria & Singh, 2013). The nearest neighbour's distance can be calculated using any distance measurement such as Euclidian distance and Manhattan distance.

3.2.1.5. Naïve Bayes

Naïve Bayes is a supervised learning method that assigns the most likely group to the data based on its probability (Rish, 2001). Naïve Bayes classifier assumes that the effect of an attribute value on a given group is independent of the other attributes' values.

3.2.1.6. Simple Neural Network (SNN)

SNN is a basic neural network model with interconnected nodes (referred to as neurons) that collectively learn from the input dataset to produce the optimized final output (O'Shea & Nash, 2013). It usually has an input layer, hidden layer and output layer. Each layer would have one or more nodes.

3.2.1.7. Convolutional Neural Network (CNN)

CNN is an extension of SNN that is primarily used in pattern recognition within images (O'Shea & Nash, 2013). It encodes image-specific features into the network.

3.2.1.8. Recurrent Neural Network With Long-Sort Term Memory (RNN-LSTM)

RNN is a neural network with a feedback (closed-loop) connection (Medsker & Jain, 2001). The architecture can be a fully interconnected net to a partially connected net. LSTM is a storing mechanism to save representation of recent input event in the form of activation (Hochreiter & Schmidhuber, 1997). LSTM is implemented in RNN to solve the vanishing gradient problem that significantly increased computational costs by exponentially grows the network.

3.2.1.9. Bi-directional Recurrent Neural Network With Long-Sort Term Memory (Bi-RNN-LSTM)

Bi-RNN LSTM is similar to RNN LSTM. But in Bi-RNN LSTM, the feedback connection can work in both directions (forward and backwards).

3.2.2. Data Preprocessing

Before applying the models, the dataset undergoes data pre-processing to remove any data quality problems and transform the dataset to fit the models. The steps in the data pre-processing are as follows:

1. Change to lower case

    The models might not recognize the same word with different capitalizations, thus changing all words to the lower case can help mitigate the issue.

2.   Remove characters

Several characters, such as special characters, extra white spaces, numbers, single-character word, and punctuations, may not provide much meaning to the sentiment analytics. Hence, these characters are removed. Few research in the literature stated punctuations could provide meaningful sentiment in VADER (Valence Aware Dictionary and sEntiment Reasoner) using specific models (Hutto & Gilbert, 2014). The models in this work are built from scratch and do not have such advanced technology to recognize punctuations' meaning. Thus, punctuations were removed.

3.   Split the dataset

The dataset is split into train and test dataset to evaluate the quality of the models' performance.

4.   Change the feedback text to vectors.

As the models cannot process feedback text in its raw form, changing the feedback text into vectors helps the models process the text.

For supervised models, Term Frequency–Inverse Document Frequency (TF-IDF) was used to transform the feedback text to vector (Roelleke, 2013). TF-IDF put more weight on rare occurring terms and was more suitable for simple machine learning.

Table 1. Examples of changes from feedback text to vector

Method	Text			Vector		
TF-IDF	Term	First document (Term Frequency)	Second Document (Term Frequency)	First document (TF-IDF)	Second Document (TF-IDF)	
				0	0	
	The	1	1	0.043	0	
	Quick	1	0	0	0.086	
	Brown	0	2	0	0	
	Fox	1	1	0	0	
	Jumps	1	1	0	0	
	Over	1	1	0.043	0	
	Dry	1	0	0	0	
	Log	1	1			
Tokenizer	['Well done!', 'Good work', 'Great effort', 'nice work', 'Excellent!']			[[0. 0. 1. 1. 0. 0. 0. 0. 0.] [0. 1. 0. 0. 1. 0. 0. 0. 0.] [0. 0. 0. 0. 0. 1. 1. 0. 0.] [0. 1. 0. 0. 0. 0. 0. 1. 0.] [0. 0. 0. 0. 0. 0. 0. 0. 1.]]		
Padding sequence	[[1], [2, 3], [4, 5, 6]]			[[0, 0, 1], [0, 2, 3], [4, 5, 6]]		
GloVe	The pre-trained version was implemented. There is no additional change using the dataset.					

The following methods were implemented for neural network models: a tokenizer, padding sequence, and GloVe. Tokenizer changes each text into a sequence of vectors where each token's coefficient could be binary based on TF-IDF (Manning, Raghavan, & Schütze, 2008). It fits its internal vocabulary based on the train data and transforms the text to a sequence of integers based on that internal vocabulary. The padding ensures that the sequences of integers generated have the same length as the longest sequences for training (Manning, Raghavan, & Schütze, 2008). The gloVe is an unsupervised learning model for obtaining vector representation of words (Pennington, Socher, & Manning, 2014). It is a count-based model as it learns the vectors by reducing the occurrence counts matrix. It aims to find the lower dimensional that is the best representation of the high dimension data. Examples of these changes are in Table 1.

3.2.3. Comparison Method

3.2.3.1. Dataset

Two different datasets were employed for comparing these models. The first dataset is a movie review dataset from IMDB (Maas, et al., 2011), consisting of current game reviews with pre-labelled sentiments. It has more than 50,000 reviews with a wide variety of vocabulary. Examples of the data are shown in Figure 3. The text column refers to the text review, and the label column is the sentiment label. 0 means negative sentiment, and 1 means positive sentiment. The number of reviews with positive sentiments and the number of reviews with negative sentiments in this dataset are similar.

Figure 3. Part of the data from the movie review dataset

text	label
I grew up (b. 1965) watching and loving the Thunderbirds. All my mates at school watched. We played "Thunderbir	0
When I put this movie in my DVD player, and sat down with a coke and some chips, I had some expectations. I was	0
Why do people who do not know what a particular time in the past was like feel the need to try to define that time	0
Even though I have great interest in Biblical movies, I was bored to death every minute of the movie. Everything is l	0
Im a die hard Dads Army fan and nothing will ever change that. I got all the tapes, DVD's and audiobooks and every	1
A terrible movie as everyone has said. What made me laugh was the cameo appearance by Scott McNealy, giving a	0
Finally watched this shocking movie last night, and what a disturbing mindf**ker it is, and unbelievably bloody and	1
I caught this film on AZN on cable. It sounded like it would be a good film, a Japanese "Green Card". I can't say I've	0
It may be the remake of 1987 Autumn's Tale after eleven years, as the director Mabel Cheung claimed. Mabel emp	1
My Super Ex Girlfriend turned out to be a pleasant surprise for me, I was really expecting a horrible movie that wou	1
I can't believe people are looking for a plot in this film. This is Laural and Hardy. Lighten up already. These two wer	1
If you haven't seen the gong show TV series then you won't like this movie much at all, not that knowing the series	0
I have always been a huge fan of "Homicide: Life On The Street" so when I heard there was a reunion movie comin	1
Greg Davis and Bryan Daly take some crazed statements by a terrorists, add some commentary by a bunch of uber	0
A half-hearted attempt to bring Elvis Presley into the modern day, but despite a sexy little shower scene and a pset	0

Figure 4. Part of the data from a serious game review dataset

feedback	label
it's fine	0
Too easy	1
It is a good game that we are able to learn and play at the same time.	1
A refreshing way to learn and understand python	1
It is an interesting educational coding game, good for beginners.	1
It was a great beginner course	1
It was stimulating	1
I felt that this was the best method to learn coding.	1
I think we need more assignments with the game	1
I felt that the levels did not cover much content in Python in the sense that m	0
Bad Game	0
Great	1
It is a intresting way to learn coding	1
Fun	1
It was fun as it makes me practise with my coding with playing a game	1
It was fun and im able to learn within the game	1

The second dataset is an actual serious game review from learners (William, 2021). The serious game review dataset is a small dataset with an imbalance number of positive and negative reviews. Examples of the dataset are shown in Figure 4. The feedback column is the text feedback from learners, while the label column is the sentiment labels.

3.2.3.2. Preliminary Test

A preliminary test was conducted to eliminate the machine learning models that are not performing well with the given dataset. In this preliminary test, those nine machine learning models were trained and tested using the first dataset (IMDB movie revise dataset) in their default parameter values. No optimization was performed in this preliminary test. The performance of the models was evaluated using accuracy measurement. Accuracy is the ratio of the correct number of observations to the total number of observations. It can be a good indicator for the model's performance when the data is balanced, as in the first dataset. The test results are shown in Table 2.

Table 2. Preliminary test for sentiment analytics models

Method	Accuracy	Prediction Time*
Support Vector Machine (SVM)	89%	75 s
Logistic Regression	89%	61.2 μs
Random Forest Classifier	85%	575 μs
K-Nearest Neighbour	83%	562 μs
Naïve Bayes	79%	7.81 s
Simple Neural Network	72%	1.21 s
Convolutional Neural Network	83%	1.84 s
Recurrent Neural Network with LSTM	83%	1.59 s
Bi-directional Recurrent Neural Network with LSTM	85%	5.83 s

*Timings may differ due to computer specifications.

Table 2 shows that the best-supervised models are Support Vector Machine (SVM) and Logistic Regression, with an accuracy of 89%. The best neural network model is Bidirectional Recurrent Neural Network with Long Short Term Memory (LSTM), with an accuracy of 85%. However, SVM cannot handle large dataset and took a longer time than Logistics Regression. Hence, only Logistics Regression and Bidirectional Recurrent Neural Network with Long Short Term Memory (LSTM) are considered further.

3.2.3.3. Hyper Parameter Tuning

Logistics Regression and Bidirectional Recurrent Neural Network with Long Short Term Memory (LSTM) models are further tuned to improve their accuracy. The model tuning was performed using Grid Search Cross-Validation (GridSearchCV) to find the best hyperparameters, known as hyper-parameter tuning (Krstajic, Buturovic, Leahy, & Thomas, 2014). This model is to ensure the model will be able to perform at its best with suitable hyper-parameters. GridSearchCV runs through the possible combinations of the parameters and determines the parameters with the best performances. Due to time constraint, only several parameters were optimized. The results of GridSearchCV for both models are in Figure 5 and 6.

Figure 5. The results of GridSearchCV for Logistic Regression

Logistic Regression:

Best params: {'clf__C': 1.0, 'clf__penalty': 'l2', 'clf__solver': 'liblinear'}

Figure 6. The results of GridSearchCV for Bidirectional Recurrent Neural Network with Long-Sort Time Memory

Bidirectional Recurrent Neural Network with LSTM:

Best: 0.859594 using {'batch_size': 50, 'epochs': 6}

Best: 0.838281 using {'optimizer': 'Adam'}

After the hyper-parameter tuning, the new parameters were used to perform training and testing using the IMDB movie review dataset. The performance results of these two models are shown in Table 3. The performance for both models did not significantly increase. It was still around 89% for Logistics Regression and 85% for Bi-directional Recurrent Neural Network with LSTM.

Table 3. Performance of sentiment analytics models after parameter tuning

Method	Accuracy	Prediction Time*
Logistic Regression	89%	43.9 μs
Bi-directional Recurrent Neural Network with LSTM	85%	778 μs

*Timings may differ due to computer specifications.

To further test these models, the second dataset (serious game review from learners) was used for testing. The new parameter values from the hyper-parameter tuning were used. F1 was used to measure the performance instead of accuracy because the second dataset has data imbalance (Raschka, 2021). The number of positive sentiments and the number of negative sentiments significantly differ for the serious game review dataset. F1 score is a better indicator than accuracy when the data is imbalanced. The results are shown in Table 4. Bidirectional Recurrent Neural Network with LSTM is performing better than Logistic Regression by 1%.

Bi-directional Recurrent Neural Network with LSTM model performs better for the second dataset (serious game review dataset) compared to the first dataset (IMDB movie review dataset). It is common as the Bi-directional Recurrent Neural Network with the LSTM model has dropout layers that ignore some of the neurons during training (Brownlee, 2018). The dropout layer is used to reduce overfitting. During training, the model faces more difficulty to predict the correct answer because of the dropout layer and not all neurons are utilized. During testing, the model has all neurons utilized, thus it has the full computational power and might perform better.

Table 4. Performance of sentiment analytics models for serious game review dataset

Method	F1	Prediction Time*
Logistic Regression	85%	29.5 μs
Bi-directional Recurrent Neural Network with LSTM	86%	69.8 μs

*Timings may differ due to computer specifications.

The results indicate that the Bi-directional Recurrent Neural Network with the LSTM model performed better than Logistic Regression. Thus, Bi-directional Recurrent Neural Network with LSTM is used for the feedback analytics component.

3.3. Feedback Visualization Component

Sentiment analytics results from the second component are visualized in an interactive dashboard. It is displayed as a column chart with a red bar representing negative feedback while a green bar represents positive feedback, as illustrated in Figure 7. The X-axis of the column chart is the different categories of learners' sentiments, while the Y-axis is the count of learners having the sentiment for that question. Detailed information about the learners with positive and negative sentiments can be shown by clicking the respective bar.

This information can be used by lecturers to interpret the learners' enjoyment experience towards the topic and the game itself. Lecturers would be able to identify learners that have negative sentiments and find out the difficulties that they are encountered. A lecturer can guide them to solve their challenges and improve their learning.

4. EVALUATION OF THE ENJOYMENT ANALYTICS FRAMEWORK

To evaluate the proposed enjoyment analytics framework, seven semi-structured interviews with lecturers in Temasek Polytechnic, Singapore, were conducted. The sessions were held in December 2020 with the different lecturer for each session. During the interview sessions, the framework design was briefly described, and the lecturer's opinions regarding the framework and their suggestions were captured. The questions asked during the semi-structured interviews are listed in Table 5.

From these sessions, the lecturers think that the framework would help to monitor and evaluate the student's learning. The insights that were captured in the framework are useful for the lecturers to understand the learners' experience and learning better. Learners with positive feedback would be able to enjoy the game and, at the same time, learn new knowledge and skills. The lecturers would be able to monitor this learning through the feedback visualization. Learners with unfavorable (negative) sentiments

Figure 7. Sentiment analytics results represented in a column chart

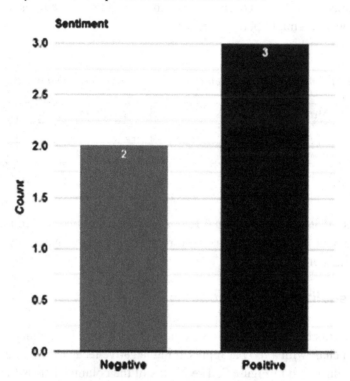

can also be identified. Negative sentiments may indicate difficulties in learning. The lecturers would be able to approach the learners and conduct follow-up discussions to improve their learning.

The lecturers also proposed additional features to improve the enjoyment analytics framework. These features include exporting the data to Ms Excel, filtering the sentiments based on the topics and filtering the sentiments based on the classes. These additional features are currently being evaluated to be added in the framework.

Table 5. Evaluation Questions

#	Question
1	Based on the current features in the enjoyment analytics framework, would the framework help you to monitor the student's learning?
2	Based on the current features in the enjoyment analytics framework, would the framework help you to evaluate the student's learning?
3	Does the current enjoyment analytics framework provide sufficient insights to understand the student's learning?
4	Does the positive and negative sentiments help you to understand the student's learning?
5	What are other features that you would like to be included in the enjoyment analytics framework?

5. FUTURE RESEARCH DIRECTIONS

A serious game for learning has received a lot of attention from educators as well as game designers. It provides a more interactive approach to engage the learners to learn new skills and knowledge. However, there are very limited works on the effectiveness of serious games as a learning tool in a different learning environment (such as problem-based learning). Most of the works focused on specific aspects of serious games or a specific serious game. More works to evaluate serious games effectiveness and to develop a generic framework to assess it are needed.

One of the approach to evaluate the effectiveness of learning is through understanding the learners' enjoyment experience. It may provide insights into the effectiveness of the serious game. These insights are proposed in the enjoyment analytics framework. There are at least two possible research opportunities to extend the enjoyment analytics framework. First, in addition, to understand the sentiments, identifying specific difficulties in a topic can also be included in the framework. Machine learning models for keyword discovery can be implemented for this purpose to the feedback text. It would be able to help the lecturers to focus their scaffolding on removing these difficulties. Second, finding and analyzing learners' learning patterns can be developed. Learners with the same enjoyable experience and learning patterns may act and perform similarly in the game. It would help the lecturers to identify a group of learners that would need more help.

6. CONCLUSION

This chapter reviews the proposed enjoyment analytics framework for a serious game using sentiment analytics. The framework aims to identify learners' sentiments to understand their enjoyable experience while learning a particular subject using a serious game. In addition to that, the framework would also help to provide insight for the lecturers to identify learners with a negative experience. It is assumed that learners with negative experience may have difficulties with the topic and the game. Lecturers would be able to pay more attention to these learners and provide more scaffolding for them.

The proposed framework consists of three main components: feedback gathering, feedback analytics and feedback visualization. The first component, feedback gathering, is embedded in the serious game itself. It allows the learners to submit text feedback regarding the topics and serious game. The second component, feedback analytics, uses machine learning models to identify learner's sentiments based on their feedback. It classifies the sentiments into two categories, positive and negative sentiments. And the third component, feedback visualization, shows the sentiment to the lecturers using an interactive dashboard where the lecturers can drill down the information to understand the sentiments and the learners better. This framework can be implemented for any serious game with different subjects with no (or limited) changes required.

ACKNOWLEDGMENT

This research is supported by the Ministry of Education, Singapore, under its Translational R&D and Innovation Fund (TIF) Grant (12th Award, MOE2019-TIF-0009). Any opinions, findings and conclusions or recommendations expressed in this material are those of the author(s) and do not reflect the views of the Ministry of Education, Singapore.

REFERENCES

Agarwal, B., & Mittal, N. (2015). Machine Learning Approach for Sentiment Analysis. In B. Agarwal & N. Mittal (Eds.), *Prominent Feature Extraction for Sentiment Analysis*. Springer.

Altrabsheh, N., Gaber, M. M., & Cocea, M. (2013). Sentiment analytics for education. In *5th KES International Conference on Intelligent Decision Technologies (KES-IDT 2013)*. Sesimbra, Portugal: IOS Press.

Amory, A. (2007). Game object model version II: A theoretical framework for educational game development. *Educational Technology Research and Development*, *55*(1), 51–77. doi:10.100711423-006-9001-x

Amory, A., & Seagram, R. (2003). Educational game models: conceptualization and evaluation: the practice of higher education. *South African Journal of Higher Education*, *17*(2), 206–217.

Barrett, L. F., Lindquist, K. A., & Gendron, M. (2007). Language as context for the perception of emotion. *Trends in Cognitive Sciences*, *11*(8), 327–332. doi:10.1016/j.tics.2007.06.003 PMID:17625952

Bellotti, F., Kapralos, B., Lee, K., Moreno-Ger, P., & Berta, R. (2013). Assessment in and of Serious Games: An Overview. *Advances in Human-Computer Interaction*, *2013*, 11. doi:10.1155/2013/136864

Blunt, R. (2009, December). *Do Serious Games Work? Results from Three Studies*. Retrieved from eLearn Magazine: https://elearnmag.acm.org/archive.cfm?aid=1661378&doi=10.1145%2F1661377.1661378

Bower, G. H. (1992). How Might Emotions Affect Learning? In S. Å. Christianson (Ed.), *The Handbook Of Emotion And Memory*. Lawrence Erlbaum Associates.

Breiman, L. (2001). Random forests. *Machine Learning*, *45*(1), 5–32. doi:10.1023/A:1010933404324

Brownlee, J. (2018, December 3). *A Gentle Introduction to Dropout for Regularizing Deep Neural Networks*. Retrieved from Machine Learning Mastery: https://machinelearningmastery.com/dropout-for-regularizing-deep-neural-networks/

Canadian Red Cross. (2021). *In Exile For A While*. Retrieved April 30, 2018, from https://www.redcross.ca/cmslib/general/inexileforawhilekit.pdf

CodeCombat. (2021). *Code Combat*. Retrieved from https://codecombat.com/

Coelho, A., Kato, E., Xavier, J., & Gonçalves, R. (2011). Serious game for introductory programming. In *International Conference on Serious Games Development and Applications* (pp. 61-71). Lisbon, Portugal: Springer. 10.1007/978-3-642-23834-5_6

Cowan, B., & Kapralos, B. (2014). A Survey of Frameworks and Game Engines for Serious Game Development. In *2014 IEEE 14th International Conference on Advanced Learning Technologies*. Athens: IEEE.

de Freitas, S., & Jarvis, S. (2008). Towards a development approach for serious games. In T. Connolly, M. Stansfield, & E. Boyle (Eds.), *Games-based learning advancements for multi-sensory human-computer interfaces: Techniques and effective practices* (pp. 215–231). IGI Global.

De Freitas, S., & Jarvis, S. (2009). Towards a development approach to serious games. In T. Connolly, M. Stansfield, & L. Boyle (Eds.), Games-based learning advancements for multi-sensory human computer interfaces: Techniques and effective practices (pp. 215-231). IGI Global. doi:10.4018/978-1-60566-360-9.ch013

De Freitas, S., & Liarokapis, F. (2011). Serious games: a new paradigm for education? In M. Ma, A. Oikonomou, & L. Jain (Eds.), *Serious Games and Edutainment Applications* (pp. 9–23). Springer. doi:10.1007/978-1-4471-2161-9_2

De Freitas, S., & Oliver, M. (2006). How can exploratory learning with games and simulations within the curriculum be most effectively evaluated? *Computers & Education*, *46*(3), 249–264. doi:10.1016/j.compedu.2005.11.007

Garcia-Ruiz, M., Tashiro, J., Kapralos, B., & Martin, M. (2011). Crouching Tangents, Hidden Danger: Assessing Development of Dangerous Misconceptions within Serious Games for Healthcare Education. In *Gaming and Simulations: Concepts, Methodologies, Tools and Applications* (pp. 1712–1749). Information Resources Management Association. doi:10.4018/978-1-60960-195-9.ch704

Giannakos, M. N., Chorianopoulos, K., Jaccheri, L., & Chrisochoides, N. (2012). *This game is girly!" Perceived enjoyment and learner acceptance of edutainment. In Edutainment 2012/GameDays 2012.* Springer.

Godsay, M. (2015). The Process of Sentiment Analysis: A Study. *International Journal of Computer Applications*.

Gómez-Rodríguez, A., González-Moreno, J., Ramos-Valcárcel, D., & Vázquez-López, L. (2011). Modeling serious games using AOSE methodologies. *11th International Conference on Intelligent Systems Design and Applications (ISDA)*, 53-58.

Gonçalves, P., Araújo, M., Benevenuto, F., & Cha, M. (2013). Comparing and combining Sentiment analytics methods. ACM conference on Online Social Networks, 27-38.

Graafland, M., Schraagen, J., & Schijven, M. (2012). Systematic review of serious games for medical education and surgical skills training. *British Journal of Surgery*, *99*(10), 1322–1330. doi:10.1002/bjs.8819 PMID:22961509

Guillén-Nieto, V., & Aleson-Carbonell, M. (2012). Serious games and learning effectiveness: The case of It's a Deal! *Computers & Education*, *58*(1), 435–448. doi:10.1016/j.compedu.2011.07.015

Hancock, J. T., Landrigan, C., & Silver, C. (2007). Expressing emotion in text-based communication. *2007 Conference on Human Factors in Computing Systems*.

Hochreiter, S., & Schmidhuber, J. (1997). Long Short-Term Memory. *Neural Computation*, *9*(8), 1735–1780. doi:10.1162/neco.1997.9.8.1735 PMID:9377276

Hosmer, D. Jr, Lemeshow, S., & Sturdivant, R. (2013). *Applied Logistic Regression* (Vol. 398). John Wiley & Sons. doi:10.1002/9781118548387

Hou, H. (2015). Integrating cluster and sequential analysis to explore learners' flow and behavioral patterns in a simulation game with situated-learning context for science courses: A video-based process exploration. *Computers in Human Behavior*, *48*, 424–435. doi:10.1016/j.chb.2015.02.010

Hutto, C., & Gilbert, E. (2014). Vader: A parsimonious rule-based model for Sentiment analytics of social media text. *International AAAI Conference on Web and Social Media*, 2-10.

IJsselsteijn, W., De Kort, Y., Poels, K., Jurgelionis, A., & Bellotti, F. (2007). Characterizing and measuring user experiences in digital games. *International conference on advances in computer entertainment technology*, *2*, 27.

Kataria, A., & Singh, M. (2013). A review of data classification using k-nearest neighbour algorithm. *International Journal of Emerging Technology and Advanced Engineering*, *3*(6), 354–360.

Kiili, K. (2006). Evaluations of an experiential gaming model. *Human Technology: An Interdisciplinary Journal on Humans in ICT Environments*, *2*(2), 187–201. doi:10.17011/ht/urn.2006518

Kiili, K. (2006). Evaluations of an Experiential Gaming Model. *An Interdisciplinary Journal on Humans in ICT Enviroments*, *2*(2), 187–201.

Kim, B., Park, H., & Baek, Y. (2009). Not just fun, but serious strategies: Using meta-cognitive strategies in game-based learning. *Computers & Education*, *52*(4), 800–810. doi:10.1016/j.compedu.2008.12.004

Knight, J., Carly, S., Tregunna, B., Jarvis, S., Smithies, R., de Freitas, S., ... Dunwell, I. (2010). Serious gaming technology in major incident triage training: A pragmatic controlled trial. *Resuscitation Journal*, *81*(9), 1174–1179. doi:10.1016/j.resuscitation.2010.03.042 PMID:20732609

Krstajic, D., Buturovic, L., Leahy, D., & Thomas, S. (2014). Cross-validation pitfalls when selecting and assessing regression and classification models. *Journal of Cheminformatics*, *6*(1), 1–15. doi:10.1186/1758-2946-6-10 PMID:24678909

Kumar, D. (2000). Pedagogical Dimensions of Game Playing. *ACM Intelligence Magazine*, *10*(10), 9–10.

Lazzaro, N. (2004). Why We Play Games: Four Keys to More Emotion in Player Experiences. *Game Developer Conference 2004*.

Lazzaro, N. (2009). Why we play: affect and the fun of games. *Human-Computer Interaction: Designing for Diverse Users and Domains*, 155.

Lim, C., & Jung, H. (2013). A study on the military Serious Game. *Advanced Science and Technology Letters*, *39*, 73–77. doi:10.14257/astl.2013.39.14

Lindquist, K. A., Satpute, A. B., & Gendron, M. (2015). Does Language Do More Than Communicate Emotion? *Current Directions in Psychological Science*, *24*(2), 99–108. doi:10.1177/0963721414553440 PMID:25983400

Lindsley, D. B. (1951). Emotion. *Handbook of experimental psychology*, 473–516.

Liu, Y., Alexandrova, T., & Nakajima, T. (2011). Gamifying intelligent environments. *Proceedings of the 2011 international ACM workshop on Ubiquitous meta user interfaces*. 10.1145/2072652.2072655

Loh, C., Sheng, Y., & Ifenthaler, D. (2015). Serious Game Analytics: Theoretical Framework. In C. Loh, Y. Sheng, & D. Ifenthaler (Eds.), *Serious Game Analytics: Methodologies for Performance Measurement, Assessment and Improvement* (pp. 3–30). Springer. doi:10.1007/978-3-319-05834-4_1

Ma, M., Oikonomou, A., & Jain, L. (2011). Innovations in Serious Games for Future Learning. In *Serious Games and Edutainment Applications* (pp. 3–7). Springer. doi:10.1007/978-1-4471-2161-9_1

Maas, A., Daly, R., Pham, P., Huang, D., Ng, A., & Potts, C. (2011). Learning Word Vectors for Sentiment Analysis. *The 49th Annual Meeting of the Association for Computational Linguistics: Human Language Technologies*, 142-150.

Manning, C., Raghavan, P., & Schütze, H. (2008). *Introduction to Information Retrieval*. Cambridge University Press. doi:10.1017/CBO9780511809071

Medhat, W., Hassan, A., & Korashy, H. (2014). Sentiment analytics algorithms and applications: A survey. *Ain Shams Engineering Journal*, *5*(4), 1093–1113. doi:10.1016/j.asej.2014.04.011

Medsker, L., & Jain, L. (2001). *Recurrent Neural Networks*. CRC Press.

Mega, C., Ronconi, L., & Beni, R. D. (2014). What Makes a Good Learner? How Emotions, Self-Regulated Learning, and Motivation Contribute to Academic Achievement. *Journal of Educational Psychology*, *106*(1), 121–131. doi:10.1037/a0033546

Miner, G., Elder, I. V. J., & Hill, T. (2012). *Practical text mining and statistical analysis for non-structured text data applications*. Academic Press.

Mishina, Y., Murata, R., Yamauchi, Y., Yamashita, T., & Fujiyoshi, H. (2015). Boosted Random Forest. *IEICE Transactions on Information and Systems*, *98*(9), 1630–1636. doi:10.1587/transinf.2014OPP0004

Muratet, M., Torguet, P., Jessel, J., & Viallet, F. (2009). Towards a serious game to help learners learn computer programming. *International Journal of Computer Games Technology*, *2009*, 1–12. doi:10.1155/2009/470590

Nagle, A., Wolf, P., Riener, R., & Novak, D. (2014). The use of player-centered positive reinforcement to schedule in-game rewards inreases enjoyment and performance in a serious game. *International Journal of Serious Games*, *1*(4), 35–47. doi:10.17083/ijsg.v1i4.47

Nasim, Z., Rajput, Q., & Haider, S. (2017). Sentiment analytics of learner feedback using machine learning and lexicon based approaches. In *2017 International Conference on Research and Innovation in Information Systems (ICRIIS)* (pp. 1-6). Langkawi: IEEE.

Noble, W. S. (2006). What is a support vector machine? *Nature Biotechnology*, *24*(12), 1565–1567. doi:10.1038/nbt1206-1565 PMID:17160063

O'Shea, K., & Nash, R. (2013). *An Introduction to Convolutional Neural Networks*. Retrieved from https://white.stanford.edu/teach/index.php/An_Introduction_to_Convolutional_Neural_Networks

Pang, B., Lee, L., & Vaithyanathan, S. (2002). *Thumbs up? Sentiment Classification using Machine Learning. In Conf. on Empirical Methods in Natural Language Processing.* EMNLP.

Pennington, J., Socher, R., & Manning, C. (2014). Glove: global vectors for word representation. *The 2014 Conference on Empirical Methods in Natural Language Processing (EMNLP)*, 1532-1543.

Raschka, S. (n.d.). *How can the F1-score help with dealing with class imbalance?* Retrieved from Sebastian Raschka: https://sebastianraschka.com/faq/docs/computing-the-f1-score.html

Rieber, L. (1996). Seriously considering play: Designing interactive learning environments based on the blending of microworlds, simulations, and games. *Educational Technology Research and Development, 44*(2), 43–58. doi:10.1007/BF02300540

Rish, I. (2001). An empirical study of the naive Bayes classifier. *IJCAI 2001 workshop on empirical methods in artificial intelligence, 3*, 41-46.

Roelleke, T. (2013). *Information Retrieval Models: Foundations and Relationships.* Morgan & Claypool.

Sommar, F., & Wielondek, M. (2015). *Combining Lexicon- and Learning-based Approaches for Improved Performance and Convenience in Sentiment Classification* (Dissertation). Retrieved from DiVA: http://urn.kb.se/resolve?urn=urn:nbn:se:kth:diva-166430

Sweetser, P., & Wyeth, P. (2005). GameFlow: a model for evaluating player enjoyment in games. *Computers in Entertainment (CIE), 3*(3), Article 3A.

Sylwester, R. (1994). How Emotions Affect Learning. *Reporting What Learners Are Learning*, 60-65.

United Nations High Commissioner for Refugees. (2005, December 7). *Surviving against the odds: a taste of life as a refugee.* Retrieved April 30, 2018, from https://www.unhcr.org/4397174b4.html

United Nations High Commissioner for Refugees. (2021). *Passages: An Awareness Game Confronting The Plight of Refugees.* Retrieved April 30, 2018, from https://www.unhcr.org/473dc1772.html

Van Staalduinen, J., & de Freitas, S. (2011). A game-based learning framework: Linking game design and learning. In M. Khine (Ed.), *Learning to play: exploring the future of education with video games* (pp. 29–54). Peter Lang.

Vapnik, V. (1995). *The Nature of Statistical Learning.* Springer. doi:10.1007/978-1-4757-2440-0

William, L. (2021). Improving Learners Programming Skills using Serious Games. *14th International Symposium on Advances in Technology Education.*

William, L., Abdul Rahim, Z., Wu, L., & de Souza, R. (2019). Effectiveness of Supply Chain Games in Problem Based Learning Environment. In D. K. Ifenthaler (Ed.), *Game-Based Assessment Revisited* (pp. 257–280). Springer. doi:10.1007/978-3-030-15569-8_13

William, L., Rahim, Z., Souza, R., Nugroho, E., & Fredericco, R. (2018). Extendable Board Game to Facilitate Learning in Supply Chain Management. *Advances in Science, Technology and Engineering Systems Journal, 3*(4), 99–111. doi:10.25046/aj030411

Yu, Z. (2019). A Meta-Analysis of Use of Serious Games in Education over a Decade. *International Journal of Computer Games Technology*, 8.

ADDITIONAL READING

Bing, L. (2015). *Opinions, sentiment, and emotion in text*. Cambridge University Press.

Dörner, R., Göbel, S., Effelsberg, W., & Wiemeyer, J. (Eds.). (2016). *Serious Games*. Springer International Publishing. doi:10.1007/978-3-319-40612-1

Ifenthaler, D., & Kim, Y. J. (Eds.). (2019). *Game-Based Assessment Revisited*. Springer International Publishing. doi:10.1007/978-3-030-15569-8

Kiili, K. (2005). *On educational game design: Building blocks of flow experience*. Tampere University of Technology.

Kiili, K., De Freitas, S., Arnab, S., & Lainema, T. (2012). The design principles for flow experience in educational games. *Procedia Computer Science*, *15*, 78–91. doi:10.1016/j.procs.2012.10.060

Kubat, M. (2017). *An Introduction to Machine Learning*. Springer International Publishing. doi:10.1007/978-3-319-63913-0

Loh, C. S., Sheng, Y., & Ifenthaler, D. (Eds.). (2015). *Serious games analytics*. Springer International Publishing. doi:10.1007/978-3-319-05834-4

KEY TERMS AND DEFINITIONS

Classification: A process of categorized the item in a dataset into predefined labels (such as positive and negative).

Flow Experience: A state during a game session where the players are fully engaged and concentrated with the game that nothing else seems to matter.

Interactive Dashboard: A visualization tool that analyzes, monitors, and visualizes key insights while allowing the users to drill down and filter the information directly.

Machine Learning: A computer algorithm that can learn and adapt without following explicit instructions by identifying and analyzing data patterns.

Neural Network: A machine learning model that mimics the human brain's neural network. It contains layers of interconnected nodes (referred to as neurons) to understand and learn from the data.

Sentiment Analytics: A method used to identify opinions, sentiments, and subjectivity from a given dataset.

Serious Game: A (digital) game designed and created not with the primary purpose of pure entertainment. It includes non-entertainment components such as learning specific skills and knowledge or building awareness on particular topics.

Supervised Learning: A machine learning model that maps an input to an output based on predefined input-output pairs (training examples). It requires a pre-labelled (with input and output) training dataset.

Chapter 9
Motivating Sustainable Recycling Practices Through Persuasive Technologies

Ricardo Santos
NOVA School of Science and Technology, Universidade NOVA de Lisboa, Portugal

Armanda Rodrigues
(iD) https://orcid.org/0000-0002-7080-5512
NOVA School of Science and Technology, Universidade NOVA de Lisboa, Portugal

Teresa Romão
NOVA School of Science and Technology, Universidade NOVA de Lisboa, Portugal

Francisco M. N. Gouveia
NOVA School of Science and Technology, Universidade NOVA de Lisboa, Portugal

ABSTRACT

Despite the importance of recycling in the current and pressing context of preserving the environment, it is still not adopted by all of us. Several mobile tools have become available with the aim of sensitizing and motivating the population towards sustainable behaviours, with limitations in information availability and in integration with formal as well as informal sources. Moreover, persuasive characteristics, such as the use of gamification also need improvement towards raising competitiveness (and awareness) in the targeted community. The authors thus propose a mobile responsive gamified application for motivating recycling attitudes centred around an interactive map, supported by the curated data of one of the reference companies of the environmental sector in the region. The app includes collaborative persuasive elements as well as validation processes for crowdsourced content proposed by the community. The results of an evaluation process, with promising results, are described.

DOI: 10.4018/978-1-7998-8089-9.ch009

INTRODUCTION

Through Recycling, used materials are transformed into new usable products. This process has gained importance in the current and pressing context of preserving the environment and reusing its natural resources (EPA, 2018). Despite the growth in the number of people who now carry out recycling, this behaviour was not yet adopted by all of us. It is necessary to act quickly in this field, educating, sensitizing, and encouraging people to a sustainable use of our planet's resources, and raising awareness for the consequences of their habits soon. In Portugal, recycling services are not standardized across the country, often because they are the result of several partnerships between city councils and a wide range of private companies. The task of informing users of the various existing services is thus complicated, due to the variety of companies operating in these markets. The lack of knowledge about recycling rules and methods can also lead to population demotivation. Thus, it is important to implement mechanisms that are able, at the same time, of informing the population about the recycling services that exist near them, as well as to keep them motivated to practice sustainable activities, such as recycling. Several digital tools have been developed with the aim of addressing this problem, lacking effectiveness in the integration of the relevant information and in maintaining long-term user interest.

We thus present, in this paper, a responsive mobile application, whose main objective is to facilitate the users' recycling process by combining information from various recycling service providers, and using persuasive and gamification techniques, as a way of keeping the users motivated to change their attitudes and behaviours regarding recycling and sustainability. This application also uses crowdsourcing techniques to include the community in the process by sharing data which will effectively contribute to maintain and improve the platform content.

Mobile Technology can play a central role in solving the issues that involve recycling, since it is used by most people in their daily lives, mainly through the use of smartphones. The availability of recycling motivational tools in these conspicuous devices can effectively persuade their owners to take an active role in caring for the environment in which we live and, through this, make recycling an activity that is sustainably part of their daily lives.

This work is a collaborative effort of NOVA LINCS - Laboratory for Computer Science and Informatics of the Department of Informatics in collaboration with the Department of Environmental Sciences and Engineering (DCEA-NOVA), at NOVA School of Science and Technology.

Since its beginning, this project has had the contribution of Amarsul[1], a company that operates in the market for the management of solid urban waste in the District of Setúbal. Amarsul provided access to the recycling spots database used in the project, which includes the geographic location of the collection spots, the supported recycling materials for each spot and the collection schedule. Amarsul updates this data daily, providing, almost in real time, updated information about its collection spots, through API access.

RELATED WORK

In this section, we analyse existing recycling applications which involve the use, to a certain extent, of a spatial context, as well as gamification and persuasive technologies, during the recycling activities led by the users. The success of the application of these approaches is analysed in the context of the state of the art in this topic, with a reflection and proposed improvements, supported by the work.

Gamified Recycling Applications

Several applications available in the Google and Apple markets aim at informing users about recycling and promoting users' recycling activities. In the context of this work, we have analysed these tools, with the aim of identifying successful approaches and missing requirements. Below we describe some of these tools.

RecycleBinGo[2] is a mobile application with the objective of educating users on the theme of recycling. It works as a game that consists of defining a recycling collection spot as "Default Spot" (recycle collectors usually used by each user), and through the geolocation of the users' mobile device, they "check-in", indicating that they have visited a specific collection spot. With this action, users collect points, which they can then exchange for real rewards, such as movie tickets or discount vouchers. The application also provides a general user ranking, which can be a way to increase the use of the platform, through competitiveness among its users.

This application is very focused on gamifying the recycling process, in order to promote sustainable practices. Sustainable user behaviour is rewarded with tangible and real prizes and checking in on your "Default Spot", is rewarded with EcoGifts, in the form of animals or flowers. The developers of the application also identified the necessity for partnerships with recycling companies, to provide worthy standing to the game, and have taken the step to contact possible partners. Moreover, although the app identifies the spatial location of the user, relating to the nearest collection spot, this cannot be verified or visualized in a map interface, which hinders the effectiveness of the app.

WasteApp's[3] main objective is to help its users to separate their garbage and to find the appropriate places for the disposal of the different types of waste to recycle. Entering the type of waste we want to recycle, we are given the location of the closest corresponding collector. In addition, the app also provides news on recent waste collection campaigns. Users can also contribute with the locations of additional collectors which are not yet part of the application's database. Although this is a significant contribution, this application is only available for a restricted region, lacking the potential to grow by integrating curated data from several partners. In fact, although WasteApp holds information regarding the recycling collectors' locations, it cannot provide an integrated view of all the waste collection sites referenced by the app. To know the location of a collection spot, it is necessary to select this collector from a list, and then request to see it, individually, overlaid on the map. This request opens Google Maps, centered on the collection spot's identified location. This application also allows users to report the existence of new collectors, but this process needs to be done outside the application, by mail, which does not facilitate the users' task and discourages them from doing so.

iRecycle's[4] main goal is to find the recycling spots closest to the user, based on the filters defined by them. This application is centred around a map that contains the available collection spots and can give the user the distance and travel time from their location to a selected collection spot. The app uses crowdsourcing to allow users to report problems at collection spots, and to submit new collection spots, providing the location and type of waste collected at that location. The collection spots entered are subsequently validated by the system administrators. The app's limitations include its limited availability (in the Greater Vancouver area, Canada). The need for new collection spot approvals by system administrators can reduce the efficiency of data updates, which could be entrusted to the user community, through crowdsourcing.

There are in fact several applications available in main online stores with the aim of facilitating and encouraging recycling and sustainable behaviours. However, our analysis has identified a few limitations which have inspired us to try and achieve a contribution in this field. Existing tools mainly cover specific geographic areas, such as a country or a district and the data that these applications provide is often out of date, as it can only be curated by system administrators. For this type of application to ensure a continuous use, it must supply a curated and continuously updated database, which must at its core be based on an official source. However, the user community may indeed provide updates, which can be based on the reputation of the contributors.

It is a necessary condition for applications that want to supply relevant information in a spatial context, in this case collectors' locations, to provide an interactive map to facilitate data visualization and access. The analysed applications, such as WasteApp or RecycleBinGo, do not provide this cartographic interface directly on the platform, and WasteApp forwards the user to an external tool to provide this functionality. The availability of an integrated cartographic interface, associated with the presentation of and interaction with the updated database is a major requirement of this type of applications, as it will allow the user to decide, based on their current spatial context or address, their preferred collection spot. Finally, these apps, although mostly innovative in terms of the use of gamification and persuasive techniques in a sustainability context, by providing various types of rewards (including tangible), do not take advantage of the potential of the user community setting. Adherence could be increased through diversifying the possibilities of a healthy competition in the community, by creating groups with common interests such as families or neighbourhoods and basing competition on the dynamics of these groups.

Technologies of Persuasion and Application of Gamification Processes

Persuasive technology aims to change the Society's attitudes and behaviours through the use of interactive technologies (Fogg, 1998). The adoption of persuasion happens when someone creates or adopts technology with the intention of changing people's attitudes and behaviours in a certain context.

In Gamification, persuasive technologies are used to influence people's behaviour, activating their individual motivations through game design elements (Petkov et al., 2011). Gamification is directly related to serious games and games with a purpose, games that are linked to a particular learning objective. In these games, the user's experience is adapted according to their actions in life, bringing their experience from the virtual to the real world. A serious game seeks not only to entertain its users, but also to convey an idea or teach something, leading them to perform certain tasks.

For users to actively engage in a game, sensors from mobile devices may be used to understand the environment surrounding the user, providing a positive and motivating experience. Taking advantage of traditional game mechanisms, such as rewards, competition, leader boards, among others, users become more involved in their context, and become motivated to perform a specific task or achieve a certain goal. These mechanisms can also be used outside gaming contexts, adding persuasive and motivational tasks and elements, without the competitive edge. In these circumstances, the use of badges or spots generates a healthy feeling of individual competition with oneself.

GAEA (Centieiro et al., 2011) is a persuasive location-based multiplayer mobile game to encourage people to recycle. Players move around and use their mobile phone to locate and collect virtual garbage spread within their surroundings. These virtual objects are linked to geographic coordinates and the players need to physically go there in order to pick them up. Once grabbed, the players must bring the garbage near a public display and place it into the right virtual recycle bin. The game also promotes physical activity and social interaction through a score system and a competitive mode with other players.

Aguiar-Castillo et al. (2018) report a study on how to encourage recycling behaviour, describing a gamified mobile application for tourists that aims at informing them about the right use of the infrastructures for the selective collection of waste, as well as the policies and ways of recycling in each city (e.g. indicating waste collection spots or collection schedules). It is also intended to collect data regarding the tourists' waste recycling behaviours and their complaints. The authors concluded that the design of this type of applications should focus on functional elements useful for the users, promoting their visibility on social networks and using low-level gaming attributes.

Gaggi et al. (2020) present a serious game intended to teach users how to select the right recycle bin for each object they want to recycle. The game has six levels, and, at each level, the player is asked which is the correct recycle bin for certain objects. Then, different types of objects fall from the top of the screen and the player has to move each object into the correct bin before it falls on the floor. The game difficulty increases at each level, as the objects become less trivial and their falling speed increases.

In the application proposed in this paper, gamification appears as a fundamental factor to keep the user motivated, whether to use the application or to carry out sustainable practices, namely recycling. The main component of the game associated with this application is the registration of deposits that users make at the collection spot that they use, in their local community. Once this deposit is made, and through the phone location sensors, users can register the materials they have recycled, such as packaging, glass, paper / card, among others, according to the type of materials accepted by the collection spot. Associated with this component is a points system, where users of the platform compete with each other, promoting entertainment and competition between them. Users collect points whenever they register a deposit, ranked by collection spot, and by neighbourhood.

In order to promote collaborative activities and increase competitiveness in the application, users can bring their families together in the application, as a group of users, promoting intra and interfamily competition in the neighbourhood. Whenever users register deposits, they are not only receiving points for themselves, but also accumulating points for their family. These points are later used for ranking families living in the same neighbourhood. In order to make people feel even more included in this process, the application also uses a crowdsourcing component where users can contribute with the collection of data, based on the users' reputation in the app community, which can improve the effectiveness of the process and of the recycling network.

SOLUTION CONCEPTION AND GAME LOGIC

The goal of this project is to provide the population with real and updated information about recycling services, and mainly to encourage the community to recycle their waste materials, contributing to improve environmental sustainability. The development of a mobile application was planned, as most people carry one mobile phone and use it frequently. Persuasion technology was used to lead to a change in attitudes and behaviour, so that the community could become more participative in activities related to environmental sustainability.

To promote users' engagement and foster recycling, gamification techniques were studied and applied. The application has an associated gamification component, which allows users to register the waste deposits they make at collection spots and earn points with this action. In addition, users can bring their families together in the application, competing with each other or competing with other families within their neighbourhood. These actions aim to encourage competitiveness and promote entertainment among users of the platform, while stimulating collaborative activities, which can influence attitudes and behaviours in their lives.

Moreover, crowdsourcing was explored to allow users to contribute to maintain the application's content updated and as complete as possible. Through crowdsourcing, users can help improve the application by contributing new information that is not yet available, such as the insertion of new collection spots or the reporting of anomalies found in collection spots. A process for the verification of these contributions was put in place, based on the reputation of the users and of the contribution itself.

The application incorporates daily updated data from Amarsul, a company that manages municipal waste, such as location, periodicity of collections and materials collected at each collection spot, providing users with real and reliable information, which contributes to keeping them motivated to participate in sustainable activities.

The main functionalities of the platform, which are detailed later in the paper, are the following:

- **Geographical display of collection spots on the map**: provide platform users with an interactive map showing the collection spots, to allow users to understand which collection spots are available around them.
- **Detailed information on collection spots:** providing detailed information on each collection spot, such as location, photo, types of material collected, periodicity of collections and their current status.
- **Insertion of new collection spots**: users can insert new collection spots that are not yet available in the application.
- **Anomalies feedback to collection spots:** in case of finding any anomaly existing in collection spots (e.g. damaged, full, dirty), users can report the problem in the application, and this information will later be transmitted to their responsible.
- **Information approval process:** according to the users' current location, they can contribute to validate or invalidate the information conveyed by other users.
- **Registration of deposits of materials for recycling:** a gamification process that aims at promoting recycling and increasing the user's engagement was implemented, involving the registration of the user's deposits of materials in the collection spots. User reports about the status of collection spots were also used to maintain this information updated.
- **Family context:** users can collaborate within their families, joining efforts to increase recycling and compete with other families in their neighbourhood.
- **Rankings:** user, collection spots and family rankings are maintained and can be visualized, encouraging competition between users, within families and between families in the same neighbourhood.
- **User's notifications:** encourage and remind the users to carry out recycling actions, such as the registration of deposits.

Design Process

The design process was based on an iterative methodology that consisted of two major phases. During the first phase, an initial prototype of the user interface was developed, using Adobe XD, and informal usability tests were performed by seven potential target users. The aim was to discover, from an early stage, potential problems that the application could encounter and gather users' feedback on new ideas and suggestions for the application.

Through the second and longest iteration, the platform was developed, and the server and the application client were implemented, according to the feedback acquired in the previous phase. Usability tests were carried out with a larger set of users. Due to the pandemic that the world experienced during the elaboration of these usability tests, they were carried out entirely online, by videoconference, which, initially, was not planned, since this application is essentially used in an outdoor context.

Application Features and User Interaction

The use of the application is conditioned by registration and login. The initial screen provides three facts/curiosities regarding recycling. The app's main screen shows the map of the users' surrounding area with the available collection spots, as well as the navigation menu at the bottom of the screen which gives users access to the main features of the application (Figure 1).

Figure 1. The application's initial page (after login).

The interactive map depicts the user's current location, as well as the locations of the collection spots closer to them. On this page, the user can also filter the collection spots by the various types of material and view unanswered notifications, whose answer may provide help to the community.

Figure 2. Collection spot details.

Figure 2 shows several screens where the users can access the details of each collection spot, such as the photo of the collection spot, its status, the materials that are collected there and the schedule for collection. This information becomes accessible by clicking on the collection spot's location on the map. As one of the objectives of the application is to improve recycling services, additional functionality is provided for this: users can read comments on the collection spot's status, made by other users; check the corresponding details, such as the type of anomaly that was found or the spot's captured photo, which motivated the report; and add a new report (the camera can be used to take a photo of the collection spot to better convey its status). Moreover, the collection spot rankings (monthly or global) can also be accessed (through the tabs on the top of the screen) showing frequent users and the collection spot's recycling champion, which promotes competitiveness among users and motivates them to recycle there.

Deposit's Registration

One of the features of the application, which helps to promote and motivate its users towards sustainable practices, is the registration of deposits of materials to be recycled, which allows the user to earn points and climb the rankings. The storyboard in Figure 3 exemplifies how this registration takes place. Users must be less than 20 meters away from a collection spot to be able to register a deposit, as the deposit registration button is only made available to the user in this case. To go further with the deposit, it is also necessary to choose the material to recycle. The deposit earns them points that support their competition on the collection spot and / or family rankings.

After the validation of the deposit, the users confirm the successful registration and are complimentarily provided with curiosity information about the type of material recycled. To prevent users from entering deposits just for the purpose of scoring points, a minimum of sixteen hours between two deposits of the same material is required.

Figure 3. Storyboard showing how to register a deposit.

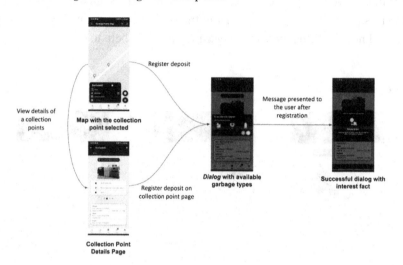

The application also detects the users' path, in order to understand if they have approached any collection spot, which may indicate they have made a recycle material disposal. When the user goes out to recycle, if they take their mobile phone with the application running open, it detects their location. Later at home, they can synchronize their most recent locations using the synchronization button located on the top bar of the map and visualize a list of all the collection spots to which they have been closer than 20 meters, or his route on the map. The user can then select one of those collection spots and register a deposit, earning the corresponding points and leading to an update of the rankings. This allows users to register a deposit when they come back home, not having to worry about it when at the collection spot.

Insert New Garbage Collection Spot

Crowdsourcing techniques are used to keep the application's data as updated as possible. Users can insert new collection spots in the application when they find them, providing data to the system such as its location, a recent photo and the type of materials allowed. This information needs to be approved by the community or system administrators to be made available to the rest of the community. Once approved, the user receives the corresponding points.

Report on Collection Points Status

Crowdsourcing techniques are also exploited to help maintaining the collection points network. Users can report anomalies they find at the collection points, conveying the type of anomaly (e.g., damaged, dirty or full), a description of the situation and a photograph. This information can be approved (or disapproved) by other users and it is then transmitted to the responsible entity in order to solve the situation.

Notifications and Pending Approvals

Users can receive three different types of notifications, which are made available in three areas of the application's notification page: collection spots status reports (pending approval), new collection spots proposals (pending approvals) and general notifications such as, for example, to alert the user that they have not made a deposit in a long time or that they have been invited to join a family.

Users are asked to verify and approve reports on the status of collection spots made by other users, as well as new collection spots inserted by other users. When doing so users earn points.

Family Context

Users can gather in groups corresponding to their household. This feature uses gamification to persuade users and encourage them to adopt sustainable attitudes and behaviours, through competition between family members and between families in the same neighbourhood. This competition is based on records of deposits made. Within the family itself, users can check the family ranking to know who the top recycler is, that is, who is registering more deposits. Points earned by family members are added to the family points. Neighbourhood competition encourages competition between families in the same neighbourhood.

Monthly and total rankings are available for users and families. The latter total ranking shows the total points acquired by the family since its creation.

Users can create a family, associating it with an address, or join a family, when invited by the family administrator. Once belonging to a family, the user can access the family details, such as the address and the list of family members and points, as well as data regarding the family neighbourhood. This includes monthly and global rankings within the neighbourhood and, on the map, the geographic distribution of families in the neighbourhood, as well as the surrounding boundaries of the neighbourhood. The storyboard in Figure 4 shows those interactions.

Figure 4. Storyboard of the family and neighbourhood context of the application

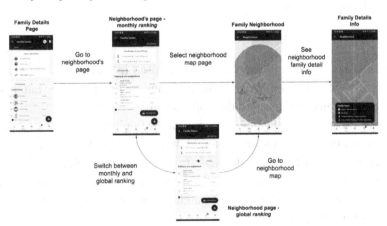

Gamified Recycling Process

As one of the main goals of this application is to motivate its users to recycle and adopt increasingly sustainable behaviours, it was important to define a way to keep users interested in using the application, while encouraging them to recycle. This was achieved through a gamification process, which consists of creating a game within the application.

Thus, a system based on points was designed which provides the user with several opportunities to enact sustainable behaviour, by which they can later be rewarded. The aim of the application thus becomes twofold, with the users relying on the application as a true source of information on the recycling process while, at the same time, playing the game. This both promotes greater use of the application and greater awareness of recycling. The points-based system also promotes competitiveness among the users of the platform, providing rankings in different contexts.

Points

There are several ways for a user to accumulate points in the application. Points can be earned by completing tasks (e.g., registering a deposit in a collection spot), by inserting new information into the application (e.g., new collection spots) or by supporting the update of the application's information, by verifying information entered by other users.

Users can, daily, register, in the application, the deposits they make at collection spots. When they physically approach a collection spot, the application recognizes it and offers the user the possibility of registering a deposit. By doing so, the user earns points that contribute to increase his own classification, as well as his family classification (if they are part of a family).

In order to prevent the user from, excessively and fraudulently, inserting deposits and thereby accumulating unreal points, the application restricts deposits of the same type of material during an interval of 16 hours.

Points earned by users are used in two ways. Firstly, these are displayed (on demand) in the user's own classification and are included in relevant rankings. Secondly, they confer reputation and reliability to the user, and thus, are used to support the credibility of the information provided by the user on the application (e.g., new collection spots).

Rankings

There are several rankings in the application, which are used to increase competitiveness at different levels. For each classification, the monthly and total rankings are provided. The latter is maintained since the initial registration of concerned users in the application.

Rankings are available at each collection spot, within the family context (as users may be aggregated in families) and between families of the same neighbourhood. Each collection spot includes a ranking that summarizes the deposits that were made there. Looking at each collection spot ranking, users can check who has registered more recycling materials in the spot. The family ranking classifies each user within their own family and the neighbourhood ranking corresponds to the sum of the points of each user, for each family of the neighbourhood.

Family and Neighbourhood Context

To diversify competitiveness, the family context was added. Family members can create a family, which allows them to join their recycling efforts contributing to the families ranking, while competing with each other for the best recycler in the family, as an intra-family ranking is available. This also promotes interaction between family members. This ranking is based on the records of deposits made by family members, and a monthly and global classification is made available for each family, according to the number and frequency of deposits made by the family members.

Based on the family concept, neighbourhoods were added. A neighbourhood refers to the set of families closest to a user's family. Families accumulate points from their members and compete with other families in their neighbourhood.

Automatic Recognition of Places Where the User Has Recently Passed

In order to prevent the user from having to register deposits only when they are at the collection spot, a mechanism has been created that allows the application to recognize the user's approaching a collection spot and allows them to register the deposit at a later time. For this mechanism to work, it is necessary for the user to keep the application open, when approaching the collection spot, so that it can access the user's location.

Once the application recognizes where the user has passed through, it notifies them of the nearest collection spots, so that they can register a deposit in one of the relevant collection spots. This mechanism prevents the user from having to directly interact with the application at the time of the deposit and allows postponement of the registration.

Approval of Collection Spots and Feedbacks

When users insert a collection spot in the application, or report existing anomalies in one the collection spot, they receive points for their actions. To validate the information provided by the users, ensuring the reliability of the application's data and preventing users from improperly earning points, a system for approving this information has been created. When a user inserts a new collection spot into the system or reports an anomaly, this information must be validated by the rest of the community (or by one of the system administrators) before it is incorporated into the application. These validations can only be made by users who are close to the collection spot in question.

Company Profile

The company profile is available only to application administrators and was created to enable insertion of new company partnerships. This feature includes the creation and management of the company profile and was evaluated only by expert users. The main functionalities of this feature are to create and/or update company data as well as supervisor information. The possibility of adding new company partnerships to the app is of relevance as it will enrich the application's content and expand its applicability to additional recycling materials and geographic regions.

SYSTEM ARCHITECTURE AND TECHNOLOGY

In this section, the technologies used in the platform are addressed, for the backend, frontend, database, and software libraries as well as other services that supported the platform's development. The technology used is also presented in the context of the platform's architecture.

Backend Technologies

For the development of the server the Spring[5] open-source framework was used, which allowed the development of a web server in Kotlin[6]. Spring offers the possibility to include several existing modules that facilitate the development. The main modules used were Spring JPA which facilitates the connection to the database and Spring Security, which deals with the platform's authentication process. The choice of Spring as the system's backend framework was primarily motivated by the ease of integration of the database system used, the ease of development due to its good documentation and very active community, and previous development experience with the framework.

The database system used was PostgreSQL[7], an open-source system, which implements the relational model and supports ACID (Atomicity, Consistency, Isolation, Durability) transactions, where the SQL language is used. Moreover, PostgreSQL supports the PostGIS[8] extension, which deals with the storage of geographic data, supporting specific functions, such as distances and areas and facilitated the implementation of the server functionality associated with the interactive map and recycling spots database.

Frontend Technologies

The application client developed was implemented in the Android[9] operating system. Android is a Linux-based operating system, with Google being one of its main contributors. The choice of this technology for customer implementation is based on the strong existing community, the ability to reach the largest number of people, as it is included in most existing smartphones, and previous development experience. One of the most important features of the application is the provision of an interactive map including the overlay of Amarsul's collection spots. To this end, and to facilitate its implementation, Mapbox[10] was chosen. This service provides customized maps for mobile and web applications, through a well-documented API (Application Programming Interface) and includes several features, such as various different maps and navigation and search functionalities. The documentation, the services offered, and the aesthetically attractive maps served as focal points for the choice of this platform.

System Architecture

The system architecture was developed to include the technologies already described and it is depicted in Figure 5.

In Figure 6 we describe the multiple layers presented in the architecture and the interactions between its different layers. The presentation layer shows all the information that is available in the application according to the user interaction. This layer was developed for the Android operating system, using Android Studio, and interacts with the database through the platform server. In addition, this client incorporates the map provided by Mapbox and handles the data entered by users, being responsible for delivering it to the server, through a REST API. The Android client also provides screen responsiveness to various types of devices/interfaces. Responsiveness was achieved through the development of the application's graphical interfaces on layouts.

Figure 5. System Architecture

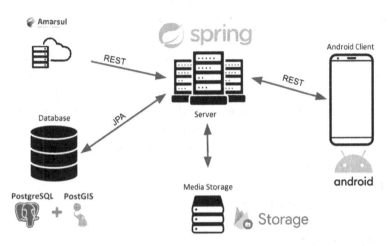

Figure 6. Interactions between architecture layers

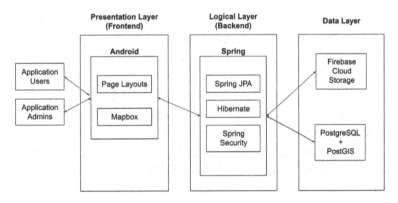

The application's server implements the backend layer of the architecture, and it was developed in Spring, which implements the MVC model. Spring is responsible for receiving requests from the client, interacting with the database to obtain the necessary data to send back to the client, and handling all the application logic which may be necessary in this process.

The application data is managed by the PostgreSQL database management system. The data layer is where all platform data is stored, such as collection spots, users, families, neighbourhoods and deposits registered by users. PostgreSQL is responsible for the persistence of all the data and uses the PostGIS extension to store and process the geographic data.

The images used in the application, such as those referring to collection spots, are stored on an external server, in Firebase Cloud Storage[11].

EVALUATION

The evaluation of the system consisted of tests carried out with volunteer users, to obtain their feedback on the developed application. These tests made it possible to find problems that existed in the application interface and which could be improved in future iterations of the platform development.

Due to the pandemic situation, which was declared during the development of this work, the evaluation of the system had to be completely rethought and adapted to the current global context. Initially, the objective was to test the application in a real context of use, that is, in a restricted location, to observe users using the application to register deposits at collection spots. In this way, it would have been possible to find the adversities that users found using the application in the real world, simulating how they would actually interact with it. As this evaluation methodology was not possible, the solution found was to carry out the users tests online through videoconference, allowing the users to remotely control the test supervisor's mobile phone, who observed the interactions that the users had with the various functionalities of the application. To simulate the presence of collection spots, close to the user's location, temporary collection spots were created according to the location of the mobile phone, which allowed users to register deposits in the application.

Evaluation Methodology

Two different types of voluntary users participated in the user's tests: the general target users of the application and expert participants, who work in recycling companies or in the environmental sector.

In the initial testing briefing, the objectives of the platform and of the test were presented to the participants, and they were asked to always comment aloud on their actions, in order to better convey possible problems that could exist on the platform. Then, the test consisted of two steps, first the participants performed a set of tasks using the application, and afterwards they answered a questionnaire related to the usability of the application and to the tasks initially proposed.

During the first step, the participants received a guide consisting of five sections each related to one of the application's navigation menu options: map, notifications, family, user's profile and rankings. In each of these sections, several tasks were presented for the participants to perform while using the application. The guide for expert participants included an exclusive section, with tasks related to the management of companies, as this feature is only intended for this type of users. The tasks completion times were collected.

After completing the tasks, the participants were presented with a google forms questionnaire, divided into 4 sections, where the first contained questions to characterize the profile of the participant, the second consisted of questions from SUS questionnaire (Brooke, 1996), a questionnaire used to measure the usability of a system, the third included questions focused on assessing the functionality of the platform, and the last section consisted of two open-ended questions, where the participants could report any difficulties they encountered during the test or provide suggestions of improvements to the application.

Participants

A total of 18 volunteers, representing the target users, participated in the user study. Their average age was 27,17 with a standard deviation of 8,10. Out of the 18 participants, 12 were male and 6 were female and all were experienced in using mobile devices, as well as interactive maps applications. 22,2% of the participants stated that they do not recycle, and the remaining ones use to recycle with different regularity. They all reported that they were concerned with environmental sustainability. However, 27,8% do not consider themselves well-informed regarding recycling, 44,4% reported being moderately informed and 27,8% well-informed. The developed mobile application can help the population become better informed about recycling, which can also contribute to improving services and increasing recycling statistics.

Two experts, an environmental engineer, working in recycling and sustainability, and a collaborator of a recycling company, in charge of the GIS services, aged 35 and 46 years old respectively, also participated in the platform evaluation. These two experts provided additional feedback from a different perspective allowing a further validation of the platform.

Results

This section presents the results of the analysis of the 18 volunteer participants' answers to the questions related to each functionality tested during the user tests. A five- point Likert-type scale was used, which ranged from totally disagree (1) to totally agree (5). The results regarding the recycling application were generally very positive, nevertheless this section focuses, in more detail, on questions related to the application's gamification component.

Deposit's Registration

Regarding the registration of deposits, the participants were able to understand and complete the task. They found it interesting to be able to register their deposits of recycling materials and earn points. Still, it was suggested that the users should be allowed to select various types of waste in a single registration action. Thus, in the case of a user wishing to recycle several types of waste on one trip to the collection spot, it should be possible to do it all at once, without having to submit several deposit registrations.

To double check whether the participants completely understood how deposits are registered in the application, a multiple-choice question was asked with four answer options (only one was correct).

- Question - Regarding the registration of deposits: Where can deposits of recycled material be made in the application?
- Correct answer - Only at collection spots that are close to the current location (or the most recent user locations)

Results were quite positive, 15 (83.3%) of the participants answered correctly, and only 3 (16.7%) gave a wrong answer. These results demonstrate that the vast majority of users understood that they can only register a deposit when they are (or were recently) close to a collection spot.

Notifications

All participants easily understood how to access and manage the notifications, as well as to approve or disapprove any new collection spot inserted by other users or any feedback report regarding a collection spot status available in their area.

To make sure the participants understood what they should do when they receive a notification, two multiple-choice questions were asked with four answer options (only one was correct).

- Question - Regarding the approval of feedback reports: What does it mean to accept a feedback?
- Correct answer - Agree with the facts reported by another user of the application by validating the information (description, photo, type of anomaly) contained in the report.
- Question - Regarding the approval of new collection spots in your area: What does it mean to validate a collection spot?
- Correct answer - Agree that there is a new collection spot, as well as validate the information associated with it, such as location, type of materials collected or state.

All participants selected the right answer for both questions.

Collection Spots Ranking

Each collection spot has an associated users' ranking which shows who is registering more deposits at that collection spot. The participants liked this feature and suggested that additional information could be included, such as what materials each user recycled at that collection spot.

Family and Neighbourhood Context

The participants were asked to join a family and perform some tasks in this context, namely viewing the family ranking, inviting new members and search for other families in their neighbourhood, using the map provided. Most of the participants enjoyed the feature which enabled competition with their family members and joined efforts to compete with other families in their neighbourhood.

The users were asked to give their opinion on whether the competition between families, in the same neighbourhood, helps to promote recycling actions. Figure 7 shows that most participants agree that competition between families helps to foster recycling by each family, where nine participants strongly agree (50%), six agree (33.3%), two neither agree or disagree (11,1%) and only one participant disagree (5,6%).

Figure 7. User opinion results on the value of family competition in promoting recycling activities

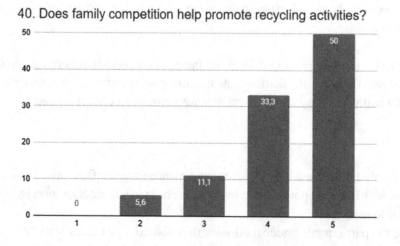

In general, all users were able to see, on the map, their family and the families in their neighbourhood. Through this functionality, it is possible to see which are the limits of our neighbourhood and which families, within those limits, are competing with the our family.

Results of Expert Evaluation

Results from the experts' evaluation were also very positive. The two participants easily performed the different tasks (same as those performed by the other participants plus those related with the management of the companies' profiles), such as the registration of deposits, notification management, visualization of rankings and family competition.

They considered that the registration of deposits and the corresponding points reward can be an asset in motivating recycling. One of the experts recommended that the users be asked for information about the capacity of the container after registering a deposit, once again using crowdsourcing to update the platform's data. Thus, the community could be informed about the current capacity of that collection spot, which would enable informed decisions on which collection spot to use for recycling.

In general, the experts were very enthusiastic about the platform and considered that it has the potential to inform the users, facilitating and encouraging recycling activities through the gamification components, as well as facilitating the maintenance of the network of collection spots based on the information reported by users.

SUS Analysis

The System Usability Scale (SUS) aims at assessing the users' overall perception of a system's usability. It is a ten-item questionnaire, developed by John Brooke, which presents the user with statements regarding several aspects of system usability. These statements are scored in a 5-point Likert scale from "strongly disagree" to "strongly agree" (Brooke, 1996). According to Tullis and Stetson (2004), SUS offers the most reliable results across sample sizes, as reported in a study comparing five questionnaires for assessing the usability of one website. Based on the participants' answers, the SUS score is calculated following a simple procedure. Based on research, a SUS score above 68 is considered above average, which means that systems whose average is higher than 68 can be considered systems with good usability.

Considering general target users, the SUS score was 85.6, a value much higher than the average global SUS value (68) previously presented. It is also interesting to note that none of the participants obtained a result weighing below the average value of 68.

The two expert users achieved SUS scores of 70 and 80. Both participants obtained a value higher than the average value of 68, despite this being lower than that recorded for general participants. Both expert users ended up classifying the general usability of the application as "Good", which is in line with the result obtained in SUS. It is worth noting that expert participants also tested the management features only available for the platform managers.

CONCLUSION AND FUTURE WORK

The work presented in this paper focuses on the development of an application that not only provides geographic information about existing recycling services, but also sought, through persuasion, crowd-sourcing and gamification, to change behaviours and attitudes in population regarding recycling.

By detecting the user's location in real time, it is possible to indicate, to the user, which collection spots are closest to them, as well as to provide relevant information about them, such as the types of materials collected on the spot and the collection schedule. Users can also contribute, in the community, to improve recycling services, by reporting problems they encounter at collection spots. The gamification component was essentially focused on the real-life registration of deposits, always trying to make this feature as less intrusive as possible.

The platform at its current development status is a clear improvement to the existing applications available in the market, since it gathers the spatial and detailed information of the collection spots, it applies gamification technology to the recycling processes and it counts on the community contribution to improve these services, which are innovative functionalities.

An iterative approach was used in the design and development of the platform, with two main iterations. The first iteration covered the first drawing of the main pages of the application. This iteration also had a small usability test based on a restricted group of users. The second iteration took into account the feedback obtained in these tests, and the entire system (backend and frontend) was implemented here, as well as its evaluation, through usability tests.

The results of the tests conducted in the second iteration were very positive, with the participants showing interest in the developed application. During the tests, the application was able to keep them motivated to fulfil the proposed tasks.

As future work we aim to fine-tune the community validation and approval model by adapting the dimension of the validation support needed to curate user submissions, to the size of the users' community in the region. This means that, in areas where the application is most used, it will be necessary that more users contribute to validate new collection spots and feedback, while in areas with less population density and / or use of the platform this number could be lower.

The gamification component used in this application will also be a factor to be analysed in future developments of the application, in order to take more advantage of these techniques. Gamification helps to entertain and motivate the users of the application, and additional gamification elements can be added to the gamified logic, such as the attribution of prizes and badges to the most active users, or to families with the best results.

In this context, a serious game is currently being developed, with the objective of educating and sensitizing the population to sustainable practices through the use of mobile applications. This game will be integrated into the platform, to create additional opportunities for the users' community to earn reward points.

REFERENCES

Aguiar-Castillo, L., Rufo-Torres, J., De Saa-Pérez, P., & Perez-Jimenez, R. (2018). How to Encourage Recycling Behaviour? The Case of WasteApp: A Gamified Mobile Application. *Journal Sustainability*, *10*(5), 1544. doi:10.3390u10051544

Brooke, J. (1996). *SUS-A quick and dirty usability scale. Usability evaluation in industry.* CRC Press.

Centieiro, P., Romão, T., & Dias, A. E. (2011). A Location-Based Multiplayer Mobile Game to Encourage Pro-Environmental Behaviours. *Proceedings of the 8th International Conference on Advances in Computer Entertainment Technology (ACE 2011).*

Fogg, B. J. (1998). Persuasive computers: Perspectives and research directions. *Conference on Human Factors in Computing Systems – Proceedings*, 225–232.

Gaggi, O., Meneghello, F., Palazzi, C., & Pante, G. (2020). Learning how to recycle waste using a game. *Proceedings of the 6th EAI International Conference on Smart Objects and Technologies for Social Good*, 144-149. 10.1145/3411170.3411251

Nielsen, J., & Landauer, J. (1993). A mathematical model of finding the usability problem. *Proceedings of ACM INTERCHI'93 Conference*, 206–213. 10.1145/169059.169166

Petkov, P., Köbler, F., Foth, M., Medland, R. C., & Krcmar, H. (2011). Engaging energy saving through motivation-specific social comparison. *Proceedings of conference on human factors in computing systems*, 1–6. 10.1145/1979742.1979855

Sauro, J. (2011). *A practical guide to the system usability scale: Background, benchmarks & best practices.* Measuring Usability LLC.

Tullis, T. S., & Stetson, J. N. (2004). A comparison of questionnaires for assessing website usability. *Usability Professional Association Conference*, 1–12.

United States Environmental Protection Agency - EPA. (2018). *Facts and Figure about Materials, Waste and Recycling.* https://www.epa.gov/facts-and-figures-about-materials-waste-and-recycling/national-overview-facts-and-figures-materials#recycling

ENDNOTES

[1]   https://www.amarsul.pt/
[2]   https://www.recyclebingo.pt/
[3]   https://www.wasteapp.pt/home
[4]   https://earth911.com/irecycle/
[5]   https://spring.io/
[6]   https://kotlinlang.org/
[7]   https://www.postgresql.org/
[8]   https://postgis.net/
[9]   https://developer.android.com/
[10]   https://www.mapbox.com/
[11]   https://firebase.google.com/docs/storage

Section 4
Gamification Novel Approaches

Chapter 10
Exploring the Possibilities of Artificial Intelligence and Big Data Techniques to Enhance Gamified Financial Services

María A. Pérez-Juárez
University of Valladolid, Spain

Javier Del-Pozo-Velázquez
University of Valladolid, Spain

Javier M. Aguiar-Pérez
University of Valladolid, Spain

Saúl Rozada-Raneros
University of Valladolid, Spain

Miguel Alonso-Felipe
University of Valladolid, Spain

Mikel Barrio-Conde
University of Valladolid, Spain

ABSTRACT

A lot of millennials have been educated in gamified schools where they played Kahoot several times per week, and where applications like Classcraft made them feel like the protagonists of a videogame in which they had to accumulate points to be able to level up. All those that were educated in a gamified environment feel it is natural and logical that gamification is used in all areas. For this reason, gamification is increasingly becoming important in different fields including financial services, bringing new challenges. Gamification allows financial institutions to provide personalized and compelling experiences. Big data and artificial intelligence techniques are called to play an essential role in the gamification of financial services. This chapter aims to explore the possibilities of using artificial intelligence and big data techniques to support gamified financial services which are essential for digital natives but also increasingly important for digital immigrants.

DOI: 10.4018/978-1-7998-8089-9.ch010

INTRODUCTION

Systems that aim to support the financial management of individuals are steadily gaining importance. Fintech is an emerging phenomenon associated with the digital transformation of financial services (Breidbach et al, 2019). Digital transformation is having an important impact on financial services. Changing customer expectations, increasing regulatory complexity, the pressure to streamline operations, and other factors are driving the push for reinvention and innovation. A new era of banking has enabled systems to quickly and seamlessly integrate with new platforms and applications. Traditional banks based in physical offices and paper documents are being replaced by robust networked digital ecosystems. As King (2017) remarks, banking is no longer somewhere you go but something you do.

Fintech is fast becoming a global phenomenon, led by innovators and followed closely by academics, and now drawing the attention of regulators (Mention, 2019). One of the main drivers of this change is mobile technologies where there is a fast-growing number of Fintech applications that offer individuals an easy access to different financial and e-banking services. Another important catalyst is being the growth of purchases made from mobile devices, a change of habit accelerated by the COVID-19 pandemic. The increasing use of technology for making purchases is making users increasingly interested in using digital tools to monitor their expenses and manage their finances. Fintech based services offer individuals the opportunity to monitor their finances in a way that was not possible until now.

At the same time, gamification is increasingly becoming important and even essential in different fields, including financial services, allowing to face new challenges. Gamification has been gaining ground in the field of financial services, largely thanks to the use of technology, and is currently being applied in many areas, ranging from budgeting to investment. Gamification allows financial institutions to use the already collected data to provide personalized and compelling experiences, and has revealed as a successful method to attract customers and help them reach their saving objectives.

In this chapter the authors aim to explore the possibilities of combining Artificial Intelligence and Big Data techniques with gamified elements and procedures to enhance financial services, which are essential for digital natives like millennials, but also increasingly important for digital immigrant generations. At the end of the chapter, the main conclusions obtained are presented, as well as a discussion about possible future lines of research.

THE IMPORTANCE OF GAMIFICATION

Gamification refers to the use of gaming elements and procedures within non-game scenarios (Deterding et al, 2011). Gamification involves applying game design techniques, game mechanics, and/or game style to non-game situations to engage and motivate users and to facilitate them the solving of problems in an easy way.

Gamification is designed to be human-centred, using the principles of basic human psychology that tap into players' needs through extrinsic (based on a reward) and intrinsic (based on a person's genuine internal desire or feeling of enjoyment or happiness) motivation. As different authors highlight (Marczewski, 2015; Growth, 2016; Playmotiv, 2019), gamification elicits a physiological reaction releasing dopamine to induce feelings of accomplishment, pleasure and reward. This, in turn, motivates players to keep coming back.

Many researchers think that gamification makes it possible to offer improved and motivating applications and services to the user in very different domains (Werbach & Hunter, 2012; Zichermann & Cunningham, 2011; Zichermann & Linder, 2013).

Millennials are the first generation that grew up surrounded by technology. Millennials are the main smartphone and social media users, and have increasingly widespread and consolidated digital habits that have created a new way of relating to financial service providers. This generation demands highly engaging solutions. According to Justin (2018), gamification can create stickiness among millennial, whose financial behaviours are affected by the memories of the global financial crisis.

A lot of millennials have been educated in gamified schools where they played Kahoot! and/or Educaplay games several times per week, and where applications like Classcraft made them feel like the protagonists of a videogame in which they had to accumulate points to be able to level up. Many authors have researched about how these applications enhance learner performance and engagement levels more than traditional teaching methods (Bonvin et al, 2017; Bawa, 2019; Charrupi et al, 2019; Sánchez-Salazar et al, 2019; Wang & Tahir, 2020).

Demkah & Bhargava (2019) highlight that gamification has evolved thanks to the growing interest shown by younger generations who are exposed to innumerable applications and educational games specially adapted for portable devices, such as smartphones, that are becoming more intelligent and capable of performing complex algorithms at unprecedented speed, backed by almost infinite memory space provided by powerful computers. For these younger generations of digital natives who have grown up surrounded by technology, and that were educated in a gamified environment, it feels as natural and logical that gamification is used in all areas from education to financial services. This phenomenon is also increasingly strong in individuals that are digital immigrants. Some authors like Autry & Berge (2011) have reviewed the characteristics associated with digital natives in comparison with digital immigrants; while other authors like Jain & Dutta (2019) have focused on analysing millennials that is the generation that is leading many technology adoption measures.

Gamification motivates and engages players using game dynamics and game mechanics. Game dynamics refer to the behaviours and emotions that motivate and engage users and include the following elements (Noble, 2021):

- Competition: It fosters genuine feelings of satisfaction for putting forth the effort to strive for excellence.
- Collaboration: Working as part of a team motivates people to take on challenges.
- Progress: It motivates players to complete levels and increases their commitment to finish the game.
- Achievement: Meeting goals leads to satisfaction, performance improvement and the confidence to tackle increasingly more difficult goals. It also boosts engagement.
- Rewards: It triggers human emotions that motivate players to complete tasks and obtain recognition.
- Surprise: It triggers engagement because of the unpredictable thrill it creates.
- Community: Team spirit helps individuals to perform better.

On the other side, game mechanics are processes, rules and visual elements that make up a game. Each type of gamification mechanic, taps back into game dynamics (Noble, 2021):

- Points shows status and help keep score (progress, achievement, reward).

- Levels indicate that certain milestones have been accomplished (competition, progress, achievement).
- Badges are awarded when players demonstrate mastery of goals (progress, achievement, competition, surprise, community).
- Unlocks are used when a series of tasks must be completed in order to reveal a new challenge, reward or tip that will help the player accelerate through the next mission (surprise, achievement).
- Leaderboards show player and team progress and how they rank against each other; all this inspires those at the top to stay at the top and motivate others to work harder to overtake the leader (achievement, competition, collaboration, community).
- Missions provide the storyline and outlines the objectives that need to be accomplished in the game (surprise, achievement, competition, community).

Individuals like to know how well they are doing in achieving specific goals or challenges. Gamification defines the milestones necessary along the road to complete a mission and provides ongoing feedback so that the player knows where he is on the road at each moment. Moreover, achievement is a powerful psychological driver for motivation and adapting to a desired behaviour. On the other side, the possibility of surprise keeps users wondering what may happen next and keeps them playing to find out. Moreover, gamification can encourage users to connect with other users to accomplish a goal. This builds a sense of community and team spirit that helps everyone to perform better and to reach their specific goals. Based on game dynamics and game mechanics different models have been proposed like the PLB (Point Leaderboards Badges) model. This model has attracted the interest of many researchers that have tried to validate it in different scenarios (Huang & Hew, 2015; Nah et al, 2015). The philosophy and elements of gaming techniques are at the base of many of the gamified applications in the financial sector that are being proposed and used today.

FINTECH AND GAMIFICATION

According to the Spanish bank BBVA's innovation team, demographic data says that about 53% of the gamers are between the ages of 18 and 49, and 55% play games on smartphones, which is actually the future of the financial sector. Hence, this represents an appreciable market opportunity for the financial firms to offer enhanced customer engagement by educating them on banking, payments, investment planning, and insurance, among others (Das, 2017).

Van der Heide & Želinský (2021) highlight that compared with domains like healthcare or education, finance gamification, arguably, is in its early days, but that there is, however, already a well-chiselled discourse that amplifies its importance for finance.

Gamification allows financial institutions to provide personalized and compelling experiences; to create digital engagement and loyalty with the final consumer; to convey information and complex procedures in a simple way; to increase participation rates and users' engagement on sites or apps, or to raise citizenship awareness towards a healthy economic and financial life-style. Gamification is revealing as a successful method to attract customers and help them reach their saving objectives.

The three key elements which have driven the financial firms to invest in gamification are the interconnected world of smart devices, the tech-savvy millennials and the mass popularity of gaming (Das, 2017).

By using gamification, financial institutions can target customers according to their specific needs. This may build a bridge over the gap between product-focused financial services and the growing need to understand the utility of these products in consumer's lives. Gamification may be a core part of financial institutions retail strategy, improving competitive positioning and building customer loyalty. It is thus expected to significantly increase the scope and scale of financial services in the future.

The scope of adopting gamification doesn't restrict itself to just offering better user engagement through gaming psychology but also presents opportunities for better product developments, proactive marketing strategies, and much more. The inception of the digital revolution has produced transformational impacts on the financial services industry and has changed perceptions to a great extent. For instance, banking which was perceived as a boring phenomenon is now a thing to do and not somewhere you go to. Gamification wave has given birth to many innovative products, enabling firms to engage more with the users (Das, 2017).

The adoption of gamification in e-banking has attracted the interest of many researchers. Rodrigues et al (2013) studied the acceptance of a gamified application in e-banking and the results showed a positive impact on the acceptance of this new concept in e-banking. Their findings presented that the perceived ease-of-use had a strong positive influence on customers' intentions. These authors also proposed a framework for gamified software in e-banking, taking a users' groups and a qualitative research approach, to check the users' design preferences in different cases of gamified banking software (Rodrigues et al, 2016).

After a review of the current existing literature regarding gamification in the banking sector, Malarout et al (2020) suggested that there is a positive relationship between motivation and the addition of gamification features in applications. These authors also identified a link between gamification and customer loyalty in banking services.

Baptista & Oliveira (2017) investigated about the potential impact of the utilization of game mechanics and game design techniques in the acceptance of mobile banking services. Findings showed that there was a direct and strong relationship between gamification and intention to use mobile banking services, supporting that, when used and designed properly, gamification can help make banking activities more exciting, more interesting and more enjoyable, and in turn increase customer acceptance, engagement and satisfaction. This also means that it is extremely important to carefully decide which elements of the user experience will be gamified.

For an e-banking financial app to stand out, it must be intuitive, highly visualized, and hassle-free. These are basic features but many fintechs go further and include some elements of gamification in daily banking experience. The idea of gamification is not about turning something into a game, but rather applying the gameplay principles and gamelike design elements. This is especially important for digital-only banks who have fewer channels of communication with their customers.

Moreover, in order to drive user incentivization, some apps use consent-based gamification models which are revolutionizing the way users think about saving. Instead of saving money in a vacuum, users can feel in control of their finances and the rewards of their efforts. In some cases, users can manually entry competitors and the app will scale and help its users to get results faster than their competitors. Additionally, gamified e-banking sites and apps need to be trendy enough to meet the standards of the emerging millennial market and the younger potential customers.

When using technology based gamified financial services, it is also very important to guarantee data security and account privacy at every time. This is very important to convince financial services users to use the new channels, because one of the biggest challenges faced by financial companies and banks that offer technology based services is customer acceptance and awareness.

Mavroeidi et al (2019) highlight that in gamified applications, protecting the privacy of users is an important aspect to consider, because the applications obtain a record of the personal information of their users. These authors examined the relationship between the set of game elements commonly applied in gamified applications and privacy requirements, in order to identify which elements conflict with the privacy requirements leading to potential privacy violations, and which elements do not. A conceptual model according to the results of this examination was designed, which presented how elements conflict with requirements. Based on the results, these authors found that there are indeed game elements which can lead to privacy violations. The results of their work provide valuable guidance to software developers, especially during the design stages of gamified applications since it helps them to consider the protection of users' privacy in parallel from the early stages of the application development onwards.

The challenge for financial institutions is not only to go digital but to be more customer-friendly. The user interface and the user experience design are very important. Even if the back end of the app is seamless and processing is quickly, what will increase the customer attraction is user experience. Today, most of the banks have their own mobile apps and they struggle hard to improve the quality of user interface and user experience (Dethe, 2020).

Many authors highlight that the success of a new technology depends on its acceptance among its potential users. Therefore, it is extremely important to understand how and why individuals decide to accept or reject new technologies (Venkatesh et al., 2003). Many research efforts have been invested in reviewing the main models and theories that have been used in previous investigations to study the adoption of innovations in different domains. According to Al-Tarawneh (2019), despite of the increasing development of technology and its incorporation into users' privacy and professional life, a decision regarding to adopt or reject it remains an open question.

According to Abraham Maslow, there are five stages of motivation (physiological, safety-security, belongingness, esteem, and self-actualization): starting with the most basic physiological and safety needs; this is followed by the psychological needs for belongingness and esteem; and finally, self-actualisation is at the top of Maslow's pyramid of needs (Taormina & Gao, 2013). Maslow's hierarchy has been modified over the years and, although the underlying principles have not changed, the pyramid has been adapted to demonstrate how gamification can address the five levels to motivate and engage customers in the case of financial services firms.

There are currently several examples of financial services that make use of different elements of game dynamics and game mechanics. The Spanish bank BBVA uses gaming techniques to encourage customers to use the digital platform, with the final goal of improving retention and online experience. Other examples of gamified financial services and experiences include Barclays who launched a social credit card and a community Barclaycard Ring where members receive incentives on sharing suggestions and ideas for credit card features; or Canada-based Sun-Life Financial who launched Money UP to educate consumers on retirement and investment decisions using a game format that requires players to pass levels by demonstrating their financial knowledge (Das, 2017).

Bayuk et al (2019) highlight that financial worry, financial literacy, subjective knowledge and expertise with money-savings/financial applications predict financial well-being. Additionally, these authors found that consumers vary in their preferences for certain financial game app features based on past financial app experience. More specifically, those who have already used a financial app tend to exhibit higher subjective (though not objective) knowledge, and want both social and economic features of financial applications, whereas those with no experience are more motivated by economic features.

Gamification of retail banking services can play an important role in educating customers. After suffering several severe financial crises, financial literacy is being recognized by modern societies as an increasingly important skill that every citizen should possess. The importance of financial literacy is perceived, not only by private financial institutions, but also by governmental organizations that are investing in financial education programs for all types of citizens. In the next decades, financial literacy is called to have as much prominence as digital literacy, from which it cannot be separated. Digital literacy is not a challenge for digital natives, but financial literacy still is. Schools are slowly taking steps in this direction, but the process is being accelerated by the private sector. By using financial literacy games, financial services and banking giants can reach younger customers, forming and shaping desired financial behaviour in the future. Justin (2018) highlights that a better education can also improve investment decision, and financial education can be effectively imparted through gamification.

Fernandes et al (2014) conducted a meta-analysis of the relationship of financial literacy and of financial education to financial behaviours in around 200 prior studies. These authors found that interventions to improve financial literacy explain only 0.1% of the variance in financial behaviours studied, with weaker effects in low-income samples. Like other education, financial education decays over time; even large interventions with many hours of instruction have negligible effects on behaviour 20 months or more from the time of intervention. The findings of these authors reinforce the need to provide ongoing or just in time financial literacy education to individuals, in which task, technology based gamified financial services can play an important role.

ARTIFICIAL INTELLIGENCE AND BIG DATA IN FINANCIAL SERVICES

Defining Artificial Intelligence is not a simple task (Wang, 2019). Artificial Intelligence can be seen as the intelligence exhibited by machines, that is, the study of the intelligent agents of any device that are capable of perceiving their environment and taking actions that allow a certain objective to be successfully carried out. Therefore, it is possible to speak of Artificial Intelligence if a machine imitates the cognitive functions of the human being to learn and solve problems.

For an Artificial Intelligence system to be able to take decisions based on the data available, different type of learning methods, such as Machine Learning (ML), need to be applied. Machine Learning is a learning technique that gives machines the ability to learn without being explicitly programmed. It addresses the study and creation of algorithms that are capable of learning from data and making predictions about it. Machine Learning algorithms can be divided into different categories including Supervised Learning (SL) and Unsupervised Learning (UL).

The main characteristic of Supervised Learning is that it uses labelled data. These algorithms are able to map an input to an output taking as a base example input-output pairs. The algorithms infer a function from a set of labelled training data examples. As a consequence, these algorithms are able to predict label values when input has unlabelled data. Unsupervised Learning, for its part, is an approach to Machine Learning used with unlabelled data. This means that the system is not told the answer, but it is given data so that the model can work on its own to discover patterns and information that was previously undetected. In this type of learning, the system does not predict the correct output, but instead, it explores the data and can draw inferences from datasets to describe hidden structures from unlabelled data. Choi et al (2020) remarks that in unsupervised algorithms the patterns that may or may not exist in a dataset are not informed by a target and are left to be determined by the algorithm.

Fast-tracking contactless, digital support across all channels generates terabytes of data a day that is essential for training supervised Machine Learning algorithms. For its part, Unsupervised Machine Learning algorithms rely on terabytes of data to discover previously unknown patterns in financial services data (Columbus, 2020).

Machine Learning can be subdivided into shallow and Deep Learning (DL), depending upon the structure and complexity of the algorithm (Cohen, 2021). For this reason, Deep Learning can be seen as subset of Machine Learning.

For its part, Big Data is the term used to refer to large amounts of data that exceed the capacity of conventional software to be captured, processed, and stored in a reasonable time.

Public interest in Artificial Intelligence has increased enormously in recent years, as there is excitement about its potential to improve our lives in domains ranging from healthcare to transportation, and of course, financial services. But at the same time, technological advances in this space have also driven uncertainty and mistrust. Artificial Intelligence is so powerful that there are growing concerns from individuals and policymakers alike that Artificial Intelligence has the potential to deeply disrupt labour markets in the incoming years (Arslanian & Fischer, 2019).

Artificial Intelligence and Big Data techniques are called to play an essential role in the design and implementation of financial services. Big Data allows to retain, process, and understand data in a way that cannot be handled by traditional database systems. Today, technology is an integral part of financial services, and challenges regarding the volume, variety, speed, and accuracy of data to handle are commonly encountered.

Big Data customer analytics drives revenue opportunities by looking at spending patterns, credit information, financial situation, and analysing social media to better understand customer behaviours, preferences and patterns, and offer them personalised gamified experiences. However, users of Artificial Intelligence analytics should have a thorough understanding of the data that has been used to train, test, retrain, upgrade and use their Artificial Intelligence systems. This is critical when analytics are provided by third parties or when proprietary analytics are built on third-party data and platforms.

Hundreds of millions of financial transactions occur in the financial world each day. Therefore, financial practitioners and analysts consider Big Data an emerging issue of the data management and analytics of different financial products and services. Identifying financial areas where Big Data has a significant influence is also an important issue to explore (Hasan, 2020).

According to Potapenko (2020), the benefits of the use of Artificial Intelligence in the field of financial services include the following:

- Personalization: By using Artificial Intelligence to make sense of customer data fintech companies can tailor their financial offering to customers' individual needs. The banking app, for example, can track users' demographics, history of spendings and transactions, and offer them financial products based on their personal needs and preferences.
- Instant tech support: By using Natural Language Processing (NLP), smart chatbots can process human queries and give immediate answers to the frequently asked customer questions. The rate of query resolution increases, and so does customer satisfaction. Moreover, apart from providing customers with comprehensive self-help solutions, smart chatbots reduce the call-centres' workload.

- Secure transactions and data protection: By analysing real-time data, Artificial Intelligence algorithms help detect non-typical activity and protect user's data from hijacking and ensure safer transactions. Machine Learning algorithms track typical user behaviour patterns. If any deviation from these patterns appears suspicious, customer accounts and data can be automatically protected from hacking and fraud.
- Loan assignment and credit scoring: Based on data they collect from various sources, including online shopping, social media, and customer's internet activity, Machine Learning algorithms evaluate if an applicant qualifies for a loan. These algorithms are self-learning. As they improve over time, they can predict the client's future spendings and possible changes in creditworthiness. Moreover, Artificial Intelligence can have a positive impact in credit decisions, as objectivity is a main benefit of Artificial Intelligence powered mechanisms that, unlike a human being, are not likely to be biased.

In relation to the above, a fundamental aspect is the issue of data collection, data quality and the bias that it might cause in Artificial Intelligence techniques (Ntoutsi et al, 2020). As mentioned before, a main benefit of Artificial Intelligence powered mechanisms is that, unlike a human being, are not likely to be biased. However, it is important to highlight that, although Artificial Intelligence will not be subjective like a human being is, the results may be biased due to the quality of the data that have been taken as a basis for learning.

Gudivada et al (2017) highlight that, although data quality issues trace back their origin to the early days of computing, the emergence of Big Data and Machine Learning has caused special attention to be paid to this issue. Data quality is important when applying Artificial Intelligence techniques, because bad quality data cannot produce good results. Without quality data, even the most sophisticated Artificial Intelligence tools will be unable to deliver good results.

In fact, data quality is paramount in analytics. As Siau et al (2021) remark data capture and cleansing are essential and can be the most time-consuming parts of a fintech analytics project, especially when Big Data is involved. Raw financial data can be extremely messy, noisy, and dirty, as it may be obtained from different sources, some of which are ill-structured and untrusted. A well-designed system architecture can enhance the accuracy, reliability, and efficiency of the data-capturing and cleansing process. As the fintech industry moves to real-time analytical processing, data quality becomes an increasingly challenging issue.

Several methods can be used to improve the data quality, including data cleaning for dealing with missing data, data normalization, feature selection, and dimensionality reduction (Huang et al, 2020).

Artificial Intelligence can also have a positive impact in trading, as intelligent trading systems can monitor both structured (databases, spreadsheets, etc.) and unstructured (social media, news, etc.) data in a fraction of the time it would take for potential investors to process it. To attract millennials, it is important to demonstrate the potential reward as well as the risks of investing. For example, allowing potential investors to learn about investing through fun, game-like processes rather than overwhelming them with technical requirements and phrases. There is a knowledge gap when it comes to financial terminology, especially amongst young people, so any communication must be simple and relatable. Once they feel confident, they can make the transition to trading real stocks (Bird, 2021).

As mentioned before, one of the main benefits of the use of Artificial Intelligence in the financial industry is customization, allowing financial firms to explore new ways to provide additional benefits and comfort to individual users, through enhanced gamified sites and apps that offer personalized advice and help individuals achieve their financial goals by using some of the elements offered by the gaming techniques like points, objectives, levels, or challenges. These intelligent systems are able to track income, essential recurring expenses or spending habits and come up with an optimized plan and financial tips including reminders to pay bills and/or taxes. These gamified sites and apps offer the customers the possibility to interact with their bank in an easier and more streamlined way, from simply getting information to completing numerous and complex transactions.

According to Das (2017), another area which could be gamified with the help of Artificial Intelligence is the tax saving decisions. At present, most of the citizens either hire a financial advisor to handle their tax savings or just follow the traditional investing patterns. This particular area of tax saving can be gamified in the form of simulations which can provide an approximate idea to the customer on where to invest, how much to invest, and for what period. The adoption of Artificial Intelligence techniques will allow to offer individuals proactive proposals regarding tax saving suggestions fully adapted to their personal situations.

Carbo-Valverde et al (2020) found that the adoption of digital banking services begins with information-based services (e.g., checking account balance), conditional on the awareness of the range of online services by customers, and then is followed by transactional services (e.g., online/mobile money transfer). According to these authors, the diversification of the use of online channels is explained by the consciousness about the range of services available and the safety perception. The results of their study suggested that banks should address the digital transformation of their customers by segmenting them according to their revealed preferences and offering them personalized digital services. This can only become fully true with the help of Artificial Intelligence and Big Data techniques.

It is also interesting that Artificial Intelligence techniques can help bank account owners to think about saving money by using pioneering technology and incentivized gamification strategies. Artificial Intelligence is able to take better decisions for customers with little to no interaction. This is one of the main reasons why the public response to such sites and apps is starting to become overwhelmingly positive, especially, but not exclusively, among digital natives. All kinds of digital assistants and apps should continue to perfect themselves thanks to Artificial Intelligence and Big Data techniques with a view to offer the possibility to manage personal finances exponentially easier. Having said that, it is also important to remark that relying on Artificial Intelligence and Big Data techniques to take the responsibility of decision making is still a challenge, and many digital assistants and apps can continue to improve without necessarily use Artificial Intelligence and Big Data techniques.

Big Data and Artificial Intelligence should be the foundation of consumer engagement, creating autonomous, real time decisions without human intervention. Because the decisions are made mostly through instant Machine Learning capabilities on an individual basis, the deployment of personalized customer engagement will be completely scalable (Marous, 2021).

Some authors like Manser Payne et al (2018) have focused on the factors that influence the attitudes and perceptions of digital natives pertaining to mobile banking and comfort interacting with Artificial Intelligence enabled mobile banking activities, taking into account the differential effects of technology-based (i.e., attitudes toward Artificial Intelligence, perceived trust and security in specific mobile banking activities) and non-technology based (i.e., need for service, quality of service) factors.

Now, financial institutions can use emerging technologies to offer new services to their prospect and customer base. These institutions can also build up new customer bases more easily, as customers are eager to buy personalized services rather than ready-made products. This digital transformation has affected both production and distribution at the same time. By statistically inferring customer's income and monthly outgoings, the system can compute the monthly saving capacity and offer suitable investment strategies. The financial institution can use this information to provide a personalized approach and an excellent customer experience (Nicoletti, 2017).

Recent technology developments have brought solutions both for the production side (databases, decision-making tools) and for distribution (digital channels, knowledge of customers, good customer experience, and flexibility of customer offerings). These advances are enabling new entrants to find a place in the industry. They allow occupying market niche offerings based on the interactivity and customization sought by younger generations, at a much lower cost than the ones offered by traditional institutions. On the production side, investment managers are increasingly using sophisticated Big Data analytics and risk management tools to create new products. However, the biggest change has been in distribution, with customers, receiving offerings personalized to their needs. To achieve this, distributors need to collect as much information as possible about their customers. In financial services, customer relationship management was for a long time thought to be the preserve of the large institutions due to the high cost of customer information acquisition, but this is no longer true (Nicoletti, 2017).

Financial services firms are increasing their adoption of Machine Learning to capitalize on the data from new digitally driven channels. According to Columbus (2020), investment banking firms are the leading adopters of Machine Learning technologies in financial services, closely followed by retail. Investment banking operations rely on Machine Learning to fine-tune algorithms and prediction models to quantify and reduce risk. Retailers rely on predictive analytics to find new insights that can help retain customers and transition them from traditional to digital channels.

Financial inclusion has attracted the attention of many researchers and practitioners. Digital financial inclusion is becoming central in the debate on how to ensure that people who are at the lower levels of the pyramid become financially active. Fintech companies are using Artificial Intelligence and its various applications to ensure that the goal of digital financial inclusion, i.e. to ensure that low-income earners or youths participate in the mainstream financial market, is realized.

According to the World Bank's Global Findex database, about 1.7 billion adults were unbanked in 2017, which means that they lacked an account with a formal financial institution or a mobile money provider (Kshetri, 2021). Artificial Intelligence and Machine Learning are rapidly developing and are bringing political, economic, and social transformation in developing economies. Artificial Intelligence based solutions are thus likely to emerge as a game-changer that have important implications for expanding financial access to unbanked individuals. This is because traditional banks are unwilling and reluctant to serve the small-scale borrowers such as low-income people and small businesses due to high transaction costs and inefficient processes associated with making small loans to these borrowers (Kshetri, 2019).

Mhlanga (2020) conducted a study to assess the impact of Artificial Intelligence on digital financial inclusion, and discovered that Artificial Intelligence has a strong influence on digital financial inclusion in areas related to risk detection, measurement and management, addressing the problem of information asymmetry, availing customer support and helpdesk through chatbots and fraud detection and cybersecurity. Therefore, it is recommended that financial institutions adopt and scale up the use of Artificial Intelligence tools and applications as they present benefits in the quest to ensure that the vulnerable groups of people who are not financially active do participate in the formal financial market with minimum challenges and maximum benefits. Guild (2017) also highlights the potential of technological innovation to increase financial inclusion. According to this author, fintech has the potential to expand financial services to hundreds of millions of people currently lacking access and to break new ground on the way finance is conducted.

FINAL DISCUSSION AND FUTURE RESEARCH DIRECTION

According to Marous (2021), the future of consumer engagement demands proactive responses to consumer needs, beliefs and behaviours in real time. Using internal and external data, as well as Artificial Intelligence and advanced analytics based on Big Data, financial institutions will be able to take advantage of opportunities and reduce risks on the consumer's behalf for an enhanced customer experience. To build a successful consumer engagement strategy, financial organizations have to better understand, and in real time, the consumer opportunities and threats that data reveals. The entire process must run seamlessly, with minimal consumer intervention required. Over time, consumers should believe in the decisions being made on their behalf, in much the same way that they would feel being handled by a financial advisor.

Kavuri & Milne (2019) highlight as some of the main research gaps regarding the future of fintech based financial services, the use of computation, Artificial Intelligence and large-scale data processing in finance, as well as all which concerns with identity, security, data privacy and their regulation.

Swanson (2021) points out that experts feel that the use of extrinsic motivational factors in gamification is not fit for long-term gamification and it can only bring immediate results. Gamification designers have to consciously in-build the intrinsic motivational factors their players need into their gamification initiatives, for which they need to thoroughly analyse the player type. Users will initially get hooked due to external factors like badges, leaderboards, etc, but will come back wanting more of it only when they enjoy the process itself. Hence, the experts believe that the future of gamification will see an inevitable shift to more intrinsic motivation and that more research on this is needed.

The financial services sector projects a promising market for gamification in the coming years with many innovations already happening such as Roboadvisory, RegTech, Artificial Intelligence and Big Data, among others. All these disruptions seek a continuous and effective customer engagement in the most interesting way. As the key players in the market are moving at a tremendous speed in providing gamification solutions all over the world, users can expect an important number of apps and websites where it would be possible to design investment or tax saving portfolios through simulations (Das, 2017). Financial stakeholders will need to understand the key role technology has to play in their core business strategy as well as which cultural attributes and organisational capabilities will create competitive advantage in this new landscape. Talent will need to be realigned with these priorities which may require to incorporate other profiles such as Artificial Intelligence experts (Bird, 2021). However, it is important to remark, that adapting business models to meet the requirements of future customers is not simply a technology bolt-on, and to be successful it will also require traditional work and talent structures to change, so efforts must also be invested in this direction.

CONCLUSION

Taking into consideration the discussion presented in this chapter, the main conclusions are the following:

- Many experts think that the philosophy of gamification can be successfully applied in very different domains, allowing to offer enhanced and motivating applications and services to the user.
- Gamification is increasingly and better accepted by society. In fact, it is essential for digital natives, but also ever more important for digital immigrants.

- Gaming techniques elements can engage customers in a real experience and efficiently support the design of financial services.
- It is extremely important to understand how and why individuals decide to accept or reject new technologies, because the success of a new technology depends on its acceptance among its potential users. Fintech based services become redundant if individuals do not want to use them.
- Financial literacy is essential to reach the acceptance of technology based financial services.
- Nowadays, financial literacy cannot be separated from digital literacy.
- Gaming and Artificial Intelligence techniques can both play a key role to reach user acceptance by providing a compelling user experience and allowing individuals to easily reach their proposed goals.
- Without the support of Artificial Intelligence and Big Data techniques it is difficult for gaming methods to achieve the degree of personalization necessary for each individual.
- Data quality is paramount when applying Artificial Intelligence and Big Data techniques, because bad quality data cannot produce good quality results.
- Artificial Intelligence and Big Data techniques can enable digital financial inclusion to allow actual unbanked adults to participate in the mainstream financial market.
- Financial information must be treated in a privacy-preserving manner, even when Big Data and Artificial Intelligence techniques are being used.
- Gamification can improve motivation in financial services. But, for gamification to reach its full potential, it is necessary to build fintech solutions on well-founded theories that exploit the core experience and psychological effects of game mechanics.
- The benefits of using gamified technology based financial services have especially been acknowledged by the millennials generation. However, digital immigrants are increasingly taking advantage of these services.

REFERENCES

Al-Tarawneh, J. M. (2019). Technology Acceptance Models and Adoption of Innovations: A Literature Review. *International Journal of Scientific Research*, 9(8), 833. doi:10.29322/IJSRP.9.08.2019.p92116

Arjen van der Heide, A., & Želinský, D. (2021). 'Level up your money game': An analysis of gamification discourse in financial services. *Journal of Cultural Economics*, 1–21. Advance online publication. doi:10.1080/17530350.2021.1882537

Arslanian, H., & Fischer, F. (2019). *The Future of Finance: The Impact of FinTech, AI, and Crypto on Financial Services*. Palgrave Macmillan. doi:10.1007/978-3-030-14533-0

Autry, A. J. Jr, & Berge, Z. (2011). Digital natives and digital immigrants: Getting to know each other. *Industrial and Commercial Training*, 43(7), 460–466. doi:10.1108/00197851111171890

Baptista, G., & Oliveira, T. (2017). Why so serious? Gamification impact in the acceptance of mobile banking services. *Internet Research*, 27(1), 118–139. doi:10.1108/IntR-10-2015-0295

Bawa, P. (2019). Using Kahoot to Inspire. *Journal of Educational Technology Systems, 47*(3), 373-390. doi:10.1177/0047239518804173

Bayuk, J., & Altobello, S. A. (2019). Can gamification improve financial behavior? The moderating role of app expertise. *International Journal of Bank Marketing, 37*(4), 951–975. doi:10.1108/IJBM-04-2018-0086

Bird, D. (2021). *Game on: the potential for gamification in asset management.* https://www.lifesight.com/ire/latest-news/game-on-the-potential-for-gamification-in-asset-management

Bonvin, G., & Sanchez, E. (2017). Social Engagement in a Digital Role-Playing Game Dedicated to Classroom Management. In J. Dias, P. Santos, & R. Veltkamp (Eds.), Lecture Notes in Computer Science: Vol. 10653. *Games and Learning Alliance. GALA.* Springer. doi:10.1007/978-3-319-71940-5_13

Breidbach, C. F., Keating, B. W., & Lim, C. (2019). Fintech: Research directions to explore the digital transformation of financial service systems. *Journal of Service Theory and Practice, 30*(1), 79–102. doi:10.1108/JSTP-08-2018-0185

Carbo-Valverde, S., Cuadros-Solas, P., & Rodríguez-Fernández, F. (2020). A machine learning approach to the digitalization of bank customers: Evidence from random and causal forests. *PLoS One, 15*(10), e0240362. Advance online publication. doi:10.1371/journal.pone.0240362 PMID:33112894

Charrupi, L., Truquez Larrahondo, C. A., & Alexis, J. (2019). *Estrategias de aprendizaje para la construcción de herramientas tecnológicas implementando la plataforma educativa Educaplay.* https://repository.usc.edu.co/handle/20.500.12421/4271

Choi, R. Y., Coyner, A. S., Kalpathy-Cramer, J., Chiang, M. F., & Campbell, J. P. (2020). Introduction to Machine Learning, Neural Networks, and Deep Learning. *Translational Vision Science & Technology, 9*(2), 14. doi:10.1167/tvst.9.2.14 PMID:32704420

Cohen, S. (2021). The basics of machine learning: strategies and techniques. In S. Cohen (Ed.), *Artificial Intelligence and Deep Learning in Pathology* (pp. 13–40). Elsevier. doi:10.1016/B978-0-323-67538-3.00002-6

Columbus, L. (2020). *The State of AI Adoption in Financial Services.* https://www.forbes.com/sites/louiscolumbus/2020/10/31/the-state-of-ai-adoption-in-financial-services/?sh=396e24702aac

Das, P. (2017). *Gamification in Financial Services: An Interesting Approach to Connect To the Financial World.* https://www.hcltech.com/blogs/gamification-financial-services-interesting-approach-connect-financial-world

Demkah, M., & Bhargava, D. (2019). Gamification in Education: A Cognitive Psychology Approach to Cooperative and Fun Learning. In *Proceedings of the Amity International Conference on Artificial Intelligence (AICAI)* (pp. 170-174). 10.1109/AICAI.2019.8701264

Deterding, S., Dixon, D., Khaled, R., & Nacke, L. (2011). From Game Design Elements to Gamefulness: Defining "Gamification". In *Proceedings of the 15th International Academic MindTrek Conference: Envisioning Future Media Environments* (pp. 9–15). 10.1145/2181037.2181040

Dethe, A. (2020). *Adding a game to banking.* https://bfsi.economictimes.indiatimes.com/news/editors-view/adding-a-game-to-banking/74387956

FernandesD.LynchJ.G.NetemeyerR.G.(2014).Financial Literacy, Financial Education and Downstream Financial Behaviors. *Management Science.* https://ssrn.com/abstract=2333898

Growth. (2016). *The Neuroscience of Gamification in Online Learning.* https://www.growthengineering.co.uk/the-neuroscience-of-gamification-in-online-learning/

Gudivada, V., Apon, A., & Ding, J. (2017). *Data Quality Considerations for Big Data and Machine Learning: Going Beyond Data Cleaning and Transformations.* Academic Press.

GuildJ. (2017). Fintech and the Future of Finance. *Asian Journal of Public Affairs*, 17-20. https://ssrn.com/abstract=3021684

Hasan, M. M., Popp, J., & Oláh, J. (2020). Current landscape and influence of big data on finance. *Journal of Big Data*, 7(1), 21. doi:10.118640537-020-00291-z

Huang, B., & Hew, K. F. (2015). Do points, badges and leaderboard increase learning and activity: A quasi-experiment on the effects of gamification. *Proceedings of the 23rd International Conference on Computers in Education.*

Huang, J., Chai, J., & Cho, S. (2020). Deep learning in finance and banking: A literature review and classification. *Frontiers of Business Research in China*, 14(13), 13. Advance online publication. doi:10.118611782-020-00082-6

Jain, A., & Dutta, D. (2019). Millennials and Gamification: Guerilla Tactics for Making Learning Fun. *SA Journal of Human Resource Management*, 6(1), 29–44. doi:10.1177/2322093718796303

Justin, E. (2018). A Study on Gamification Techniques Adopted by Financial Institutions. *Journal of Social Welfare and Management, 10*(3), 600-604. doi:10.21088/JSWM.0975.0231.10318.46

Kaur, A., & Gourav, K. (2020). A Study of Reinforcement Learning Applications & its Algorithms. *International Journal of Scientific & Technology Research*, 9(3), 4223–4228.

Kavuri, A. S., & Milne, A. (2019). *FinTech and the future of financial services: What are the research gaps?* CAMA Working Papers 2019-18, Centre for Applied Macroeconomic Analysis, Crawford School of Public Policy, The Australian National University. doi:10.2139/ssrn.3333515

King, B. (2017). *Gamification in banking: The rise of the "experiential" bank.* https://cxloyalty.dk/news-resources/gamification-banking-rise-experiential-bank/

Kshetri, N. (2019). *Global entrepreneurship: Environment and strategy* (2nd ed.). Routledge.

Kshetri, N. (2021). The Role of Artificial Intelligence in Promoting Financial Inclusion in Developing Countries. *Journal of Global Information Technology Management*, 24(1), 1–6. doi:10.1080/109719 8X.2021.1871273

Malarout, N., Jain, M., Shetty, D. K., Naik, N., Maddodi, B. S., & Perule, N. (2020). Application of Gamification in the Banking Sector: A Systematic Review. *Test Engineering and Management, 83.*

Manser Payne, L., Peltier, J. W., & Barger, V. A. (2018). Mobile banking and AI-enabled mobile banking: The differential effects of technological and non-technological factors on digital natives' perceptions and behaviour. *Journal of Research in Interactive Marketing, 12*(4), 328–346. Advance online publication. doi:10.1108/JRIM-07-2018-0087

Marczewski, A. (2015). *4 essential Neurotransmitters in gamification.* https://www.gamified.uk/2015/01/05/neurotransmitters-you-should-know-about-in-gamification/

Marous, J. (2021). *Data and AI Power the Future of Customer Engagement in Financial Services.* https://thefinancialbrand.com/86706/banking-customer-engagement-personalization-ai-trends/

Mavroeidi, A. G., Kitsiou, A., Kalloniatis, C., & Gritzalis, S. (2019). Gamification vs. Privacy: Identifying and Analysing the Major Concerns. *Future Internet, 11*(3), 67. doi:10.3390/fi11030067

Mention, A. L. (2019). The Future of Fintech. *Research Technology Management, 62*(4), 59–63. doi:10.1080/08956308.2019.1613123

Mhlanga, D. (2020). Industry 4.0 in Finance: The Impact of Artificial Intelligence (AI) on Digital Financial Inclusion. *International Journal of Financial Studies, 8*(3), 1–14.

Nah, F. F. H., Daggubati, L. S., Tarigonda, A., Nuvvula, R. V., & Turel, O. (2015). Effects of the Use of Points, Leaderboards and Badges on In-Game Purchases of Virtual Goods. In F. Fui-Hoon Nah & C. H. Tan (Eds.), Lecture Notes in Computer Science: Vol. 9191. *HCI in Business. HCIB 2015.* Springer. doi:10.1007/978-3-319-20895-4_48

Nicoletti, B. (2017). *The Future of FinTech. Integrating Finance and Technology in Financial Services.* Palgrave Macmillan. doi:10.1007/978-3-319-51415-4

Noble. (2021). *Financial Services and Gamification: Building Trust and Revenue.* https://www.noble-systems.com/resources/

Ntoutsi, E., Fafalios, P., Gadiraju, U., Iosifidis, V., Nejdl, W., Vidal, M.-E., Ruggieri, S., Turini, F., Papadopoulos, S., Krasanakis, E., Kompatsiaris, I., Kinder-Kurlanda, K., Wagner, C., Karimi, F., Fernandez, M., Alani, H., Berendt, B., Kruegel, T., Heinze, C., ... Staab, S. (2020). Bias in data-driven artificial intelligence systems - An introductory survey. *WIREs Data Mining and Knowledge Discovery, 10*(6). Advance online publication. doi:10.1002/widm.1356

Playmotiv. (2019). *Gamification and dopamine: Why games motivate us.* https://playmotiv.com/en/gamification-and-dopamine-why-games-motivate-us/

Potapenko, V. (2020). *How AI And Data Analytics Are Shaping The Future Of Fintech.* https://coruzant.com/ai/how-ai-and-data-analytics-are-shaping-the-future-of-fintech/

Rodrigues, L. F., Costa, C. J., & Oliveira, A. (2013). The adoption of gamification in e-banking. *Proceedings of the 13th International Conference on Information Systems and Design of Communication (ISDOC '13).* 10.1145/2503859.2503867

Rodrigues, L. F., Costa, C. J., & Oliveira, A. (2016). Gamification: A framework for designing software in e-banking. *Computers in Human Behavior, 62*, 620-634. doi:10.1016/j.chb.2016.04.035

Sánchez Salazar, L. A., Gallardo Pérez, H. J., & Paz Montes, L. S. (2019). The Educaplay interactive platform for the learning of mathematics in populations with special educational needs. *Journal of Physics: Conference Series*, 1329.

Siau, K., Hilgers, M., Chen, L., Liu, S., Nah, F., Hall, R., & Flachsbart, B. (2021). *Fintech Empowerment: Data Science, AI, and Machine Learning*. https://www.cutter.com/article/fintech-empowerment-data-science-ai-and-machine-learning-501881

Swanson, M. (2021). *Gamification in 2021: Future of Immersive Technologies*. https://www.gamify.com/gamification-blog/gamification-in-2021-a-more-matured-approach

Taormina, R., & Gao, J. (2013). Maslow and the Motivation Hierarchy: Measuring Satisfaction of the Needs. *The American Journal of Psychology*, *126*(2), 155–177. doi:10.5406/amerjpsyc.126.2.0155 PMID:23858951

van Engelen, J. E., & Hoos, H. H. (2020). A survey on semi-supervised learning. *Machine Learning*, *109*(2), 373–440. doi:10.100710994-019-05855-6

Venkatesh, V., Morris, M., Davis, G., & Davis, F. (2003). User Acceptance of Information Technology: Toward a Unified View. *Management Information Systems Quarterly*, *27*(3), 425–478. doi:10.2307/30036540

Wang, A. I., & Tahir, R., (2020). The effect of using Kahoot! for learning - A literature review. *Computers & Education, 149*. doi:10.1016/j.compedu.2020.103818

Wang, P. (2019). On Defining Artificial Intelligence. *Journal of Artificial General Intelligence*, *10*(2), 1–37. doi:10.2478/jagi-2019-0002

Werbach, K., & Hunter, D. (2012). *For the Win: How game thinking can revolutionize your business*. Wharton Digital Press.

Zichermann, G., & Cunningham, C. (2011). *Gamification by Design: Implementing game mechanics in web and mobile apps*. O'Reilly Media.

Zichermann, G., & Linder, J. (2013). *The gamification revolution*. McGraw-Hill Education.

KEY TERMS AND DEFINITIONS

Artificial Intelligence: A wide-ranging branch of computer science concerned with building smart machines capable of performing tasks that typically require human intelligence.

Big Data: It refers to the possibility of analyzing and systematically extracting information from, or otherwise deal with data sets that are too large or complex to be dealt with by traditional data-processing application software.

Deep Learning: Artificial Neural Networks and related Machine Learning algorithms that use multiple layers of neurons. It is seen as a subset of Machine Learning in Artificial Intelligence.

Financial Inclusion: The degree to which individuals and businesses have access to useful and affordable financial products and services that meet their needs - transactions, payments, savings, credit and insurance - delivered in a responsible and sustainable way.

Financial Literacy: The degree to which individuals have the capacity to understand and effectively use various financial skills, including personal financial management, budgeting, or investing.

Financial Well-Being: A state in which people can fully meet current and ongoing financial obligations, and have control and feel secure about their financial future.

Fintech: It refers to financial technology, i.e., technology that seeks to enhance and automate the delivery and use of financial services.

Machine Learning: A learning technique that gives machines the ability to learn without being explicitly programmed. It is seen as a subset of Artificial Intelligence.

RegTech: It refers to the management of regulatory processes within the financial industry through technology.

RoboAdvisor: It refers to digital applications that provide automated, algorithm-driven financial planning services with little to no human supervision.

Supervised Learning: It is a subcategory of Machine Learning (and Artificial Intelligence). It is characterized by the use of labelled datasets to train algorithms that classify data or predict results accurately.

Unsupervised Learning: It is a subcategory of Machine Learning (and Artificial Intelligence). It uses learning algorithms to analyze and cluster unlabelled datasets. These algorithms focus on discovering hidden patterns or data groupings without the need for human intervention.

Chapter 11
Can Artificial Intelligence and Big Data Improve Gamified Healthcare Services and Devices?

María A. Pérez-Juárez
University of Valladolid, Spain

Javier M. Aguiar-Pérez
University of Valladolid, Spain

Javier Del-Pozo-Velázquez
University of Valladolid, Spain

Miguel Alonso-Felipe
University of Valladolid, Spain

Saúl Rozada-Raneros
University of Valladolid, Spain

Mikel Barrio-Conde
University of Valladolid, Spain

ABSTRACT

Systems that aim to maintain and improve the health of citizens are steadily gaining importance. Digital transformation is having a positive impact on healthcare. Gamification motivates individuals to maintain and improve their physical and mental well-being. In the era of artificial intelligence and big data, healthcare is not only digital, but also predictive, proactive, and preventive. Big data and artificial intelligence techniques are called to play an essential role in gamified eHealth services and devices allowing to offer personalized care. This chapter aims to explore the possibilities of artificial intelligence and big data techniques to support and improve gamified eHealth services and devices, including wearable technology, which are essential for digital natives but also increasingly important for digital immigrants. These services and devices can play an important role in the prevention and diagnosis of diseases, in the treatment of illnesses, and in the promotion of healthy lifestyle habits.

DOI: 10.4018/978-1-7998-8089-9.ch011

INTRODUCTION

Systems that aim to maintain and improve the health of citizens are steadily gaining importance. The quality of health services in the society is a very important factor to individuals. Healthcare services offered for the prevention or diagnosis of diseases, or for the treatment of illnesses, are essential to maintain and improve the physical and mental well-being of the citizens.

As many experts point out, digital transformation is having a positive impact on healthcare. Telemedicine, mHealth, wearable healthcare devices, Artificial Intelligence enabled medical devices or blockchain based electronic health records are just a few examples of digital transformation in healthcare which are completely reshaping how individuals interact with healthcare professionals, how their data is shared and how decisions are made about individuals' prevention and treatment plans (Reddy, 2020).

At the same time, gamification has been gaining ground in the field of health, largely thanks to the use of technology, and is currently being applied in many areas, ranging from fitness and healthy lifestyles to diabetes control. One of the main drivers of this change is mobile technologies where there is a fast-growing number of healthcare applications offering services of preventive care.

In addition, wearable healthcare devices designed to collect data on the health and personal activity of users, are rapidly becoming everyday companions of individuals. On the one hand, these portable devices offer interesting gamification opportunities, and on the other hand individuals are increasingly concerned about their health and these devices give them the opportunity to monitor their health in a way that was not possible until now.

In this chapter the authors aim to explore the possibilities of combining Artificial Intelligence and Big Data techniques with gamified elements and procedures to enhance eHealth services and devices, including wearable technology, which are essential for digital natives like millennials, but also increasingly important for digital immigrant generations. At the end of the chapter, the main conclusions obtained are presented, as well as a discussion about possible future lines of research.

GAMIFICATION IS ALL AROUND

Gamification refers to the use of game design elements and procedures within non-game contexts (Deterding et al., 2011). Gamification involves applying game design techniques, game mechanics, and/or game style to non-game situations to engage users and to facilitate them the solving of problems in a fun way.

Many experts think that the philosophy of gamification can be successfully applied in very different domains, allowing offering enhanced and motivating applications and services to the user (Werbach & Hunter, 2012; Zichermann & Cunningham, 2011; Zichermann & Linder, 2013).

Gamification is increasingly and better accepted by society. Today's children and young people are digital natives who have grown up in homes and schools where technological devices are common and are the door to access a myriad of services, products and experiences.

In addition, many schools are carrying out digitization projects in their classrooms. Children use applications such as Kahoot, Classcraft or Educaplay, which makes them feel like absolute protagonists of a wonderful game that is the game of learning. As protagonists of their favourite videogame, students accumulate points and level up, can choose which armour to wear every day, and they even have numerous powers that allow them, for example, to save a classmate who did a math operation wrong, or to challenge their classmates with a pass word on the analysis of adjectives, or with a questionnaire on the capitals of the European countries.

The potential of these tools have rapidly attracted the interest of researchers, both in the field of technology and in the field of education. Authors like Bawa (2019) or Wang & Tahir (2020) have researched about how Kahoot! enhances learners' performance and engagement levels more than traditional teaching methods. Other researchers have focused on the potential of Educaplay to improve education (Charrupi et al., 2019), and to help students with special needs (Sánchez-Salazar et al., 2019). Bonvin et al. (2017) tried to characterize the social component of players' engagement while using the role-playing game for classroom management Classcraft, and Sanchez et al. (2017) used Classcraft to emphasize that transforming a situation into a game does not consist of using elements that have a game-like aspect, but rather of a non-essentialistic vision of play, generating a metaphor around the situation to build a reflexive space where the nature and meaning of interactions are modified.

In this way, the classroom becomes a continuation of the children play room, and many times children do not distinguish if they play for fun, or if they play to learn, because learning has become something attractive. For these digital natives, gamification is essential, and they accept it naturally in all areas of their lives. This phenomenon is also increasingly strong in individuals that are digital immigrants. Some authors like Autry & Berge (2011) have reviewed the characteristics associated with digital natives in comparison with digital immigrants, while other authors like Jain & Dutta (2019) have focused on analysing millennials that is the generation that is leading many technology adoption measures.

The PLB (Point Leaderboards Badges) Model is based on precise mechanics powered by points, objectives, levels, rankings, progress, missions, challenges, badges, notifications and obstacles, structured to engage customers in a real experience, in which motivation, participation and the amusement factor are essential. This model has attracted the interest of many researchers that have tried to validate it in different scenarios (Huang & Hew, 2015; Nah et al., 2015). The philosophy of this model is at the base of many of the gamified applications that are being proposed and used today.

Sailer et al. (2017) highlight that the main aim of gamification is to foster human motivation and performance in regard to a given activity. These authors deliberately varied different configurations of game design elements, and analysed them in regard to their effect on the fulfilment of basic psychological needs. Their study showed that badges, leaderboards, and performance graphs positively affect competence need satisfaction, as well as perceived task meaningfulness, while avatars, meaningful stories, and teammates affect experiences of social relatedness. On the other side, perceived decision freedom, however, could not be affected as intended. The authors concluded that gamification is not effective per se, but that specific game design elements have specific psychological effects and this fact must be exploited intelligently in the design of the services and applications offered to users in order to make them more efficient.

THE ACCEPTANCE OF TECHNOLOGY

Many authors highlight that the success of a new technology depends on its acceptance among its potential users. Therefore, it is extremely important to understand how and why individuals decide to accept or reject new technologies (Venkatesh et al., 2003).

Many research efforts have been invested in reviewing the main models and theories that have been used in previous investigations to study the adoption of innovations in different domains, including healthcare systems. According to Al-Tarawneh (2019), despite the increasing development of technology and its incorporation into users' privacy and professional life, the decision regarding to adopt or reject it remains an open question.

Lee & Lee (2020) examined the effects of internal and external factors on actual use behaviour, health improvement expectancy, and continuous use intention of healthcare wearable devices. These authors based their study in the Technology Acceptance Model (TAM) (Davis et al., 1989). The study results showed theoretical and practical implications regarding how healthcare wearable devices or apps can be effectively used for disease prevention and health management by the users.

Increasing interest in end users' reactions to health information technology in the latest years has elevated the importance of theories that predict and explain health information technology acceptance and use. Some authors like Holden & Karsh (2010) have reviewed the application of the Technology Acceptance Model to healthcare, and their findings showed that this model predicts a substantial portion of the use or acceptance of health information technology.

The Technology Acceptance Model has been one of the most influential models of technology acceptance, with two primary factors influencing an individual's intention to use new technology: perceived ease of use and perceived usefulness. An older adult who perceives digital games as too difficult to play or a waste of time will be unlikely to want to adopt this technology, while an older adult who perceives digital games as providing needed mental stimulation and as easy to learn will be more likely to want to learn how to use digital games (Charness & Boot, 2016). This model is frequently used as a general framework, and is consistent with a number of investigations about the factors that influence older adults' intention to use new technology systems.

Other authors like Wu & Luo (2020) also highlight the importance of user acceptance. User preferences need to be considered to design devices that will gain acceptance both in a clinical and home setting. Healthcare portable and wearable devices become redundant if individuals do not want to use them. This becomes increasingly important when the objective is to obtain measurements over long time periods, for example, in monitoring chronic diseases (Bergmann & McGregor, 2011).

Another concern is the acceptance and interest of the elderly in using wearable and portable devices and eHealth services or apps for personal health purposes. Vette et al. (2015) explain that technology based solutions can help to alleviate the increasing demand for elderly care by e.g. enabling medical professionals to remotely provide care, and activating a healthier lifestyle which extends autonomy and independence of the elderly. However, these solutions are often not sufficiently effective as adherence is low and decreases over time. Engagement in technology is important as studies have shown that use of an application significantly relates to improvement in health outcomes. According to these authors gamification offers great potential regarding the engagement and motivation of the elderly.

Finally it is important to notice that concerns about privacy can affect the acceptance of technology. Choi et al. (2017) conducted a study to investigate determinants for workers' adoption of wearable technology in the occupational work context. These researchers wanted to test hypotheses regarding workers' intention to adopt two representative wearable devices for occupational safety and health, a smart vest with an embedded indoor GPS for location tracking, and a wristband-type wearable activity tracker (i.e., wristband) with physiological sensors. The research results indicated that privacy risk was associated with workers' intention to adopt both smart vest and wristband.

HEALTHCARE AND GAMIFICATION

Taking care of one's own health is an important objective for the human being. It is for this reason that many researchers have focused on how gamification can help to motivate individuals to improve and maintain their health, which brings clear benefits to the healthcare system as a whole; and gamification techniques are being introduced with success, in different type of services and devices related to healthcare.

Some factors driving the growth of gamification in the field of eHealth include the outcomes-based medicine approach that focuses on prevention, the slow shift of digital health market to business-to-consumer model, the growth of the millennial generation that are digital natives and were grown up in gamified schools, or an increasing health consciousness as evidenced by the growing importance and popularity of health and wellness apps.

On the other side, some factors inhibiting the growth of gamification in the field of eHealth include lack of novelty in gamified features, natural limits regarding the extent to which a process can be gamified, poor correlation between gamified features and promised results, belief that gamification is solely the realm of gamers, using game mechanics to bolster a flawed system, process or product, inadequate use of game elements, or games that create systems of dependency or fatigue.

Johnson et al. (2016) highlighted that the major health challenges facing the world today are shifting from traditional, pre-modern risks like malnutrition, poor water quality and indoor air pollution to challenges generated by the modern world itself such as high blood pressure, tobacco use, high blood glucose, physical inactivity, obesity, high cholesterol, which are immediately linked to a modern lifestyle characterized by sedentary living or chronic stress, and found that gamification can have a positive impact on health and wellbeing related interventions, especially in which refers to the use of gamification to target behavioural outcomes, particularly physical activity.

Giannakis et al. (2013) found that the piece of visual information that had most impact on performance of users in a gamified sports software was average speed, which indicates a clear connection with gamification and competition.

Hamari & Koivisto (2015) showed that social influence, recognition and reciprocity have a positive impact on how much individuals are willing to exercise as well as their attitudes and willingness to use gamification services. Moreover, these authors found that the more friends a user has in the service, the larger the effects are. The findings of this type of empirical studies are important as they further provide new understanding on the phenomenon of social influence in technology adoption/use continuance in general by showing, in addition to subjective norms, how getting recognized, receiving reciprocal benefits and network effects contribute to use continuance.

The study of Sardi et al. (2017) found that gamification and serious gaming in health and wellness contexts have been mainly used for chronic disease rehabilitation, physical activity and mental health. Most of the eHealth applications and serious games investigated by these authors have been proven to yield solely short-term engagement through extrinsic rewards.

Patel et al. (2019) investigated about the best way to incorporate social incentives within a behaviourally designed gamification intervention to increase physical activity among overweight and obese adults. The researchers combined a wide range of behavioural insights, social tools such as collaboration and competition, and gamification tools such as points and levels to motivate individuals to exercise. Their study showed that small changes to the design of gamification can lead to important differences in effectiveness.

It is also important to mention that the adoption of healthcare gamified services may have some drawbacks, although in the opinion of the authors these are clearly outweighed by the benefits. Some of the possible negative outcomes of the adoption of gamification in healthcare apps and services can be competition and interactivity of gamification leading to social overload and stress. Yang & Li (2021) built a theoretical model to explore the influences of gamification characteristics on stressors (privacy invasion and social overload) and strain (gamification exhaustion) for individuals. These authors conducted a survey to test their research model collecting more than 400 questionnaires. The empirical results indicated that the competitive element and interactivity of gamification are positively associated with privacy invasion and social overload, which can cause gamification exhaustion. Moreover, the research revealed that users' health condition negatively moderates the relationship between gamification characteristics and stressors.

Another important issue is health literacy. Health literacy poses a challenge in understanding and processing health information. Health literacy, at the intersection of health and education, involves much more than reading ability. It refers to the degree to which individuals obtain, process, and understand basic health information and services that help them in decision making (Parker, Ratzan, & Lurie, 2003).

An effective and successful health literacy is important, and gamification can improve health literacy for patients, students and doctors. The growing body of knowledge on the effectiveness and usability of digital games in delivering health information to consumers reveals that the academic attention toward gaming in the field of health literacy has increased. An overabundance of health information for consumers is often very daunting. Healthcare workers need resources that focus on health literacy, and consumers demand easy to comprehend information in a user friendly format. Some authors like Faddoul (2016) have showed that games can potentially be a natural platform to deliver health information to individuals.

GAMIFIED HEALTHCARE WEARABLE TECHNOLOGY

Digital natives, that perceive technology as a strategic ally in many areas, including healthcare, are leading the use of wearable healthcare devices. These devices are designed to collect the data of users' personal health and activity. This is very useful as individuals are increasingly focused on prevention and maintenance, and demanding information about their health more frequently. Some wearable devices can even send the collected data to a healthcare platform, so that a healthcare professional can analyse the data in real time.

Wearable devices include, not only the popular exercise trackers, but also, other portable devices like heart rate sensors, oximeters (used to monitor the amount of oxygen carried in the blood), which have gained importance due to the COVID-19 pandemic (Badgujar, 2020), or sweat meters (used to monitor blood sugar levels). Wearable and portable healthcare devices can be used for medical consultation, management of medications, or close and continuous monitoring of chronic diseases. These devices give individuals a certain sense of ownership and control of the process of maintaining and improving their own health. Moreover, some of these devices offer gamification opportunities.

Some wearable and portable healthcare devices, such as fitness watches, use the approach offered by the PLB Model to create competitive goals for users to achieve through exercise, diet and nutrition. But gamification is not only used in which regards to fitness and healthy habits. For example, the Bayer's Didget blood glucose meter connects to the Nintendo DS or DS Lite gaming platform. This glucose meter, intended for use by children aged 4-14, to help them to manage and control their diabetes, has attracted the interest of many researchers (Deeb et al., 2011; Kim, 2011; Klingensmith et al., 2013). Based on the user's blood glucose testing history, points are awarded in a game called Knock 'em Downs: World's Fair. These points are used to access minigames and unlock higher levels and options within the game, exactly as it happens in the videogames children spend so many hours playing. There are leader boards with kids who collected the most points, web games and an online community as well. All this encourages children to continue using the glucose meter.

Zhao et al. (2016) discussed the feasibility and potential advantages of utilizing wearables for gamification of health and fitness. These authors also developed a pilot prototype as a case-study for this concept, and performed preliminary user studies to help further explore the proposed concept.

Finally, Kim (2016) found that having a gamified wearable device will motivate individuals to exercise willingly on regular basis, which can be helpful, especially for patients in long term rehabilitation.

ARTIFICIAL INTELLIGENCE AND BIG DATA IN HEALTHCARE SERVICES

The advances in Artificial Intelligence and Big Data are gradually transforming medical practice and healthcare. With recent progress in digitized data acquisition, machine learning and computing infrastructure, Artificial Intelligence applications are expanding into areas that were previously thought to be only the province of human experts (Yu et al., 2018).

According to Cabestany et al. (2018), the use of the Artificial Intelligence techniques can improve the management of the data generated by the eHealth activity, permitting to take more advanced decisions on the treatment and supervision of the patients.

In the era of Artificial Intelligence and Big Data, healthcare is not only digital, but also predictive, proactive, and preventive. The use of Artificial Intelligence and Big Data techniques can provide important benefits for the healthcare industry. An important field of application is medical devices, including wearable technology. Healthcare wearable devices can help individuals to make healthy life choices. The huge amount of data generated by healthcare devices is both a challenge and an opportunity for researchers to apply innovative Artificial Intelligence techniques to be able to use the collected data to identify patterns and make predictions with a preventive approach. Applying Artificial Intelligence to the right combination of data retrieved from wearable and portable technology may detect whether an individual's health is failing.

After a review of medical literature, Jiang et al. (2017) explained that Artificial Intelligence can use sophisticated algorithms to learn features from a large volume of healthcare data, and then use the obtained insights to assist clinical practice. An Artificial Intelligence system can also be equipped with learning and self-correcting abilities to improve its accuracy based on feedback. This type of systems can assist physicians by providing up-to-date medical information from journals, textbooks and clinical practices to inform proper patience care. In addition, an Artificial Intelligence system can help to reduce diagnostic and therapeutic errors that are inevitable in the human clinical practice. Moreover, these systems are able to extract useful information from a large patient population to assist in making real-time inferences for health risk alert and health outcome prediction.

Davenport & Kalakota (2019) classified the types of Artificial Intelligence of relevance to healthcare in several categories that include the following:

- Machine learning, neural networks and deep learning. The most common application of traditional machine learning is predicting what treatment protocols are likely to succeed on a patient based on various patient attributes and the treatment context. On the other side, a possible application of deep learning in healthcare is recognition of potentially cancerous lesions in radiology images. Deep learning is increasingly being applied to the detection of clinically relevant features in imaging data beyond what can be perceived by the human eye.

- Natural Language Processing (NLP). The most common application of Natural Language Processing is the creation, understanding and classification of clinical documentation and published research. These systems can analyse unstructured clinical notes on patients, prepare reports (e.g. on radiology examinations), transcribe patient interactions and conduct conversational Artificial Intelligence.

- Rule based expert systems. These systems that have traditionally been employed for clinical decision support are slowly being replaced in healthcare by approaches based on data and machine learning algorithms, because if the knowledge domain changes, changing the rules with traditional techniques can be difficult and time-consuming.

- Physical (surgical) robots which provide valuable help to surgeons, improving their ability to see, create precise and minimally invasive incisions or stitch wounds. Common surgical procedures using robotic surgery include gynaecologic surgery, prostate surgery and head and neck surgery. More recently, robots are becoming more collaborative and intelligent, as Artificial Intelligence capabilities are being embedded in their operating systems.

The potential of Artificial Intelligence and Big Data techniques to improve eHealth services and devices is immense. Some authors like Ramirez (2020) highlight that Artificial Intelligence techniques may assist clinicians with imaging based diagnosis, for example, skin cancer. And according to Makhlysheva et al. (2018), the use of machine learning will lead to disruptions in different healthcare areas, with different time horizons, including interpretation of medical images, where many projects have already proven their effectiveness, showing results as good or even better than medical specialists; and prognostics, and diagnostics, where algorithms are not so developed yet, and it will take some years before solutions are ready for use in practice.

Artificial Intelligence wearable health technology has made it viable for patients to monitor heart rhythm anywhere anytime. Using deep learning algorithms in wireless electrocardiogram devices, it is possible to identify rhythmic irregularities and mechanical dysfunctions and assist with healthcare decisions. Barrett et al. (2019) combined the state of the art heart failure care, Artificial Intelligence, serious gaming and patient coaching to develop a virtual doctor to advance and personalise self-care, where standard care tasks are performed by the patients themselves, in principle without involvement of healthcare professionals, the latter being able to focus on complex conditions. This new vision on care significantly reduces costs per patient while improving outcomes to enable long-term sustainability of top-level heart failure care. This is a promising result in a field that refers to one of the most complex chronic disorders with high prevalence, mainly due to the ageing population and better treatment of underlying diseases.

Another case are Artificial Intelligence based stethoscopes to assist clinicians by, for example, offering them real-time help in identifying respiratory sounds, categorizing the lung sounds into groups based upon the duration, frequency, and strength of the sound. Cabestany et al. (2018) have developed a solution to be applied to the management of Parkinson Disease. And Iwendi et al. (2020) have used

Artificial Intelligence to propose a fine-tuned random forest model that uses the COVID-19 pandemic patient's geographical, travel, health, and demographic data to predict the severity of the case and the possible outcome, recovery, or death. The data analysis revealed a positive correlation between patients' gender and deaths, and also indicated that the majority of patients were aged between 20 and 70 years, leading to important findings thanks to Artificial Intelligence techniques.

Makhlysheva et al. (2018) highlight that if machine learning is going to be used for clinical decision support, a ready-trained model and access to individual patient data is needed. This means that the system must be integrated with electronic health records or other systems where data is stored. This can be done in several ways, either by incorporating with the electronic health record system or radiology system, as a cloud service provided by a third party, or as a service in a private cloud. In any case, personal health information must be treated in a privacy-preserving manner. According to General Data Protection Regulation, data must be sufficient, relevant and limited to what is necessary to achieve the purpose for which the data is processed. Patients must be fully informed about the cause of data processing to be able to choose whether or not they allow the use of their data in an algorithm.

FINAL DISCUSSION AND FUTURE RESEARCH DIRECTIONS

Some authors point out that the combined use of Gamification and Artificial Intelligence would allow obtaining benefits not achieved so far. In this sense, Yordanova (2020) highlights that intelligence refers to the ability to learn and apply knowledge in new situations, and games have proven their capacity to support the process of learning. Following this logical reasoning, gamification would probably be in use for Artificial Intelligence development and Artificial Intelligence may probably support and enhance Gamification techniques.

The possibility of combining Artificial Intelligence techniques and Gamification has attracted the interest of many researchers in different fields of knowledge and action like Sotoca-Orgaz (2020).

It is interesting to analyse how the various apps, platforms, and other services that we use on a daily basis, use the concept of Gamification to a greater or lesser extent with the ultimate goal of collecting the greatest amount of user information. All these data would not be of much use if they were not treated simultaneously by an Artificial Intelligence algorithm that ends up generating new information that is usually used to offer a better service.

A common denominator in Artificial Intelligence is the possibility of customizing services or products according to the needs, circumstances, interests or preferences of each user.

Therefore, it is important to highlight the advantages of introducing gaming elements in the context of eHealth services, but it is even more interesting to highlight how these services can be improved through the use of Artificial Intelligence and Big Data techniques, since without the support of these techniques, it is difficult to achieve the degree of personalization necessary for each patient, which will be key for the acceptance of the service by said patient.

In relation to the above, several studies have indicated the need for personalizing gamified systems to users' personalities. However, mapping user personality onto design elements is difficult. More research efforts should be invested in this direction. For example by combining the Hexad gamification user types model (Tondello et al., 2016, 2019) with Artificial Intelligence and Big Data techniques that allow to obtain detailed information of users.

According to Davenport & Kalakota (2019), a growing focus in healthcare is on effectively designing the choice architecture to nudge patients' behaviour in a more anticipatory way based on real-world evidence. Through information provided by biosensors, watches, smartphones, conversational interfaces and other instrumentation, Artificial Intelligence powered software can tailor recommendations by comparing patient data to other effective treatment pathways for similar cohorts.

According to El-Gayar et al. (2020), common underlying risk factors for chronic diseases include physical inactivity accompanying modern sedentary lifestyle, unhealthy eating habits, and tobacco use which are modifiable behavioural risk factors, emphasizing the importance of self-care to improve wellness and prevent the onset of many debilitating conditions. Advances in wearable devices capable of pervasively collecting data about oneself, coupled with the analytic capability provided by Artificial Intelligence, and with the motivation provided by gaming techniques, can potentially upend how individuals care for themselves.

As previously described in this chapter, many authors highlight the importance of user acceptance, and different models such as the Theory of Reasoned Action (TRA), the Technology Acceptance Model (TAM), the Theory of Planned Behavior (TPB), or the Unified Theory of Acceptance and Use of Technology (UTAUT), have been widely studied (Venkatesh et al., 2003; Al-Tarawneh, 2019; Lee & Lee, 2020). Gamification and Artificial Intelligence techniques can both play a key role to reach user acceptance, even in the case of the elderly.

These authors also highlight that messaging alerts and relevant targeted content that provoke actions at moments that matter is a promising field in research. This is clearly integrated with the gaming techniques. The support provided by models such as PLB has proven to have an impact on individuals' behaviour in very diverse areas including eHealth. On the other hand, maintaining good physical and mental health is a very valuable objective for individuals. For this reason, the combination of Artificial Intelligence techniques with gamification techniques has an enormous probability of success in the field of eHealth, since it allows the user to offer significant tools and dynamics that allow them to obtain the proposed goals.

Davenport & Kalakota (2019) highlighted that patient engagement and adherence have long been seen as the 'last mile' problem of healthcare – the final barrier between ineffective and good health outcomes. The more patients proactively participate in their own well-being and care, the better the outcomes – utilisation, financial outcomes and member experience. According to these authors, these factors are increasingly being addressed by Artificial Intelligence and Big Data. There is growing emphasis on using machine learning and business rules engines to drive nuanced interventions along the care continuum.

Sailer et al. (2017) concluded that gamification is not effective per se, but that specific game design elements have specific psychological effects. In this way, it would be interesting to invest research efforts in determining the effects of each gaming element.

The study of Sardi et al. (2017) found that most of the eHealth applications and serious games investigated have been proven to yield solely short-term engagement. For gamification to reach its full potential, it is therefore necessary to research and build eHealth solutions on well-founded theories that exploit the core experience and psychological effects of game mechanics.

Although gamification is a popular approach to increase engagement, motivation, and adherence to behavioural interventions, empirical studies have rarely focused on this topic. There is a need to empirically evaluate gamification models to increase the understanding of how to integrate gamification into interventions (Floryan et al., 2020). This aspect is crucial, because if gamification is not adequately integrated into the processes of disease prevention, diagnosis and treatment, it will be useless. In addition, it must be taken into account that this knowledge must be acquired in a differentiated way for the different processes related to health, and for the different types of users, taking into account various factors, such as their age or preferences, since a general and unique solution for everyone regardless of circumstances, interests, needs and preferences will not be helpful.

Finally, the benefits of using gamification in healthcare have especially been acknowledged by the millennials generation both as a personal and social motivator within fields like training and food/nutrition as well as mental health and therapy. However, digital immigrants are also increasingly taking advantage of gamified healthcare digital services and efforts must be invested to make this a reality.

CONCLUSION

Taking into consideration the discussion presented in this chapter, the main conclusions are the following:

- Many experts think that the philosophy of gamification can be successfully applied in very different domains, allowing offering enhanced and motivating applications and services to the user.
- Gamification is increasingly and better accepted by society. In fact, it is essential for digital natives, but also increasingly important for digital immigrants.
- Some interesting models like the PLB (Point Leaderboards Badges) model based on precise mechanics powered by points, objectives, levels, rankings, progress, missions, challenges, badges, notifications and obstacles can engage users in a real experience and efficiently support the design of gamified services.
- It is extremely important to understand how and why individuals decide to accept or reject new technologies, because the success of a new technology depends on its acceptance among its potential users. Healthcare technology becomes redundant if individuals do not want to use it.
- Health literacy is essential to reach the acceptance of technology based healthcare services.
- The adoption of healthcare gamified services may have some possible negative outcomes in health, such as competition and interactivity of gamification leading to social overload and stress, which must not be underestimated.
- Gamification and Artificial Intelligence techniques can both play a key role to reach user acceptance by providing a compelling user experience and allowing individuals to easily reach their proposed goals.
- Without the support of Artificial Intelligence and Big Data techniques it is difficult for gaming techniques to achieve the degree of personalization necessary for each individual, which will be key to the acceptance of the service by said patient.
- In the era of Artificial Intelligence and Big Data, healthcare must not only be digital, but also predictive, proactive, and preventive.
- The potential of Artificial Intelligence and Big Data techniques to improve eHealth services and devices is immense in very different areas, as for example, heart failure care or imaging based diagnosis.
- Personal health information must be treated in a privacy-preserving manner, even when Big Data and Artificial Intelligence techniques are being used.

- Gamification can improve motivation in eHealth services. But, for gamification to reach its full potential, it is necessary to build eHealth solutions on well-founded theories that exploit the core experience and psychological effects of game mechanics.
- The benefits of using gamified technology based healthcare services have especially been acknowledged by the millennials generation. However, digital immigrants are increasingly taking advantage of these services.

REFERENCES

Al-Tarawneh, J. M. (2019). Technology Acceptance Models and Adoption of Innovations: A Literature Review. *International Journal of Scientific Research*, *9*(8), 833. doi:10.29322/IJSRP.9.08.2019.p92116

Autry, A. J. Jr, & Berge, Z. (2011). Digital natives and digital immigrants: Getting to know each other. *Industrial and Commercial Training*, *43*(7), 460–466. doi:10.1108/00197851111171890

Badgujar, K. C., Badgujar, A. B., Dhangar, D. V., & Badgujar, V. C. (2020). *Importance and use of pulse oximeter in COVID-19 pandemic: general factors affecting the sensitivity of pulse oximeter*. Indian Chemical Engineer. doi:10.1080/00194506.2020.1845988

Barrett, M., Boyne, J., Brandts, J., Brunner-La Rocca, H.-P., De Maesschalck, L., De Wit, K., Dixon, L., Eurlings, C., Fitzsimons, D., Golubnitschaja, O., Hageman, A., Heemskerk, F., Hintzen, A., Helms, T. M., Hill, L., Hoedemakers, T., Marx, N., McDonald, K., Mertens, M., ... Zippel-Schultz, B. (2020). Artificial intelligence supported patient self-care in chronic heart failure: A paradigm shift from reactive to predictive, preventive and personalised care. *The EPMA Journal*, *10*(4), 445–464. doi:10.100713167-019-00188-9 PMID:31832118

Bawa, P. (2019). Using Kahoot to Inspire. *Journal of Educational Technology Systems*, *47*(3), 373-390. doi:10.1177/0047239518804173

Bergmann, J., & McGregor, A. (2011). Body-worn sensor design: What do patients and clinicians want? *Annals of Biomedical Engineering*, *39*(9), 2299–2312. doi:10.100710439-011-0339-9 PMID:21674260

Bonvin, G., & Sanchez, E. (2017). Social Engagement in a Digital Role-Playing Game Dedicated to Classroom Management. In J. Dias, P. Santos, & R. Veltkamp (Eds.), Lecture Notes in Computer Science: Vol. 10653. *Games and Learning Alliance. GALA*. Springer. doi:10.1007/978-3-319-71940-5_13

Cabestany, J., Rodriguez-Martín, D., Pérez, C., & Sama, A. (2018). Artificial Intelligence Contribution to eHealth Application. In *Proceedings of 25th International Conference "Mixed Design of Integrated Circuits and System" (MIXDES)* (pp. 15-21). 10.23919/MIXDES.2018.8436743

Charness, N., & Boot, W. R. (2016). Technology, Gaming, and Social Networking. In Handbook of the Psychology of Aging (8th ed.). Academic Press.

Charrupi, L., Truquez Larrahondo, C. A., & Alexis, J. (2019). *Estrategias de aprendizaje para la construcción de herramientas tecnológicas implementando la plataforma educativa Educaplay*. https://repository.usc.edu.co/handle/20.500.12421/4271

Choi, B., Hwang, S., & Lee, S. (2017). What drives construction workers' acceptance of wearable technologies in the workplace? Indoor localization and wearable health devices for occupational safety and health. *Automation in Construction, 84*, 31–41. doi:10.1016/j.autcon.2017.08.005

Davenport, T., & Kalakota, R. (2019). The Potential for Artificial Intelligence in Healthcare. *Future Healthcare Journal, 6*(2), 94–98. doi:10.7861/futurehosp.6-2-94 PMID:31363513

Davis, F. D., Richard, B., & Warshaw, P. R. (1989). User Acceptance of Computer Technology: A Comparison of Two Theoretical Models. *Management Science, 35*(8), 982–1003. doi:10.1287/mnsc.35.8.982

Deeb, L. C., Parkes, J. L., Pardo, S., Schachner, H. C., Viggiani, M. T., Wallace, J., & Bailey, T. (2011). Performance of the DIDGET blood glucose monitoring system in children, teens, and young adults. *Journal of Diabetes Science Technology, 5*(5), 1157-63. doi:10.1177/193229681100500518

Deterding, S., Dixon, D., Khaled, R., & Nacke, L. (2011). From Game Design Elements to Gamefulness: Defining "Gamification". In *Proceedings of the 15th International Academic MindTrek Conference: Envisioning Future Media Environments* (pp. 9–15). 10.1145/2181037.2181040

El-Gayar, O. F., Ambati, L. S., & Nawar, N. (2020). Wearables, Artificial intelligence, and the Future of Healthcare. In M. Strydom & S. Buckley (Eds.), *AI and Big Data's Potential for Disruptive Innovation* (pp. 104–129). IGI Global. doi:10.4018/978-1-5225-9687-5.ch005

Faddoul, B. (2016). Gamification and Health Literacy. In D. Novák, B. Tulu, & H. Brendryen (Eds.), *Handbook of Research on Holistic Perspectives in Gamification for Clinical Practice* (pp. 35–46). IGI Global. doi:10.4018/978-1-4666-9522-1.ch003

Floryan, M., Chow, P. I., Schueller, S. M., & Ritterband, L. M. (2020). The Model of Gamification Principles for Digital Health Interventions: Evaluation of Validity and Potential Utility. *Journal of Medical Internet Research, 22*(6), e16506. https://www.jmir.org/2020/6/e16506 doi:10.2196/16506

Giannakis, K., Chorianopoulos, K., & Jaccheri, M. L. (2013). User requirements for gamifying sports software. In *Proceedings of 2013 3rd International Workshop on Games and Software Engineering: Engineering Computer Games to Enable Positive, Progressive Change (GAS)* (pp. 22-26). Academic Press.

Hamari, J. & Koivisto, J. (2015). "Working out for likes": An empirical study on social influence in exercise gamification. *Computers in Human Behavior, 50*, 333-347. doi:10.1016/j.chb.2015.04.018

Holden, R. J., & Karsh, B. T. (2010). The Technology Acceptance Model: Its past and its future in health care. *Journal of Biomedical Informatics, 43*(1), 159-172. doi:10.1016/j.jbi.2009.07.002

Huang, B., & Hew, K. F. (2015). Do points, badges and leaderboard increase learning and activity: A quasi-experiment on the effects of gamification. *Proceedings of the 23rd International Conference on Computers in Education.*

Iwendi, C., Bashir, A. K., Atharva, P., Sujatha, R., Chatterjee, J. M., Pasupuleti, S., Mishra, R., Pillai, S., & Jo, O. (2020). COVID-19 Patient Health Prediction Using Boosted Random Forest Algorithm. *Frontiers in Public Health, 8*, 357. https://www.frontiersin.org/article/10.3389/fpubh.2020.00357 doi:10.3389/fpubh.2020.00357

Jain, A., & Dutta, D. (2019). Millennials and Gamification: Guerilla Tactics for Making Learning Fun. *SA Journal of Human Resource Management, 6*(1), 29–44. doi:10.1177/2322093718796303

Jiang, F., Jiang, Y., Zhi, H., Dong, Y., Li, H., Ma, S., Wang, Y., Dong, Q., Shen, H., & Wang, Y. (2017). Artificial intelligence in healthcare: past, present and future. *Stroke and Vascular Neurology Journal, 21*(4), 230-243. doi:10.1136/svn-2017-000101

Johnson, D., Deterding, S., Kuhn, K. A., Staneva, A., Stoyanov, S., & Hides L. (2016). Gamification for health and wellbeing: A systematic review of the literature. *Internet Interventions, 6*, 89-106. doi:10.1016/j.invent.2016.10.002

Kim, S. (2011). Analysis article: Accuracy of the DIDGET glucose meter in children and young adults with diabetes. *Journal of Diabetes Science and Technology, 5*(5), 1164–1166. doi:10.1177/193229681100500519 PMID:22027311

Kim, T. (2016). *Gamification of Wearable Devices in the Healthcare Industry*. Academic Press.

Klingensmith, G. J., Aisenberg, J., Kaufman, F., Halvorson, M., Cruz, E., Riordan, M. E., Varma, C., Pardo, S., Viggiani, M. T., Wallace, J. F., Schachner, H. C., & Bailey, T. (2013). Evaluation of a combined blood glucose monitoring and gaming system (Didget®) for motivation in children, adolescents, and young adults with type 1 diabetes. *Pediatric Diabetes, 14*(5), 350–357. doi:10.1111/j.1399-5448.2011.00791.x PMID:21699639

Lee, S. M., & Lee, D. (2020). Healthcare wearable devices: an analysis of key factors for continuous use intention. *Service Business, 14*, 503-531. doi:10.1007/s11628-020-00428-3

Makhlysheva, A., Bakkevoll, P. A., Nordsletta, A. T., & Linstad, L. H. (2018). *Artificial Intelligence and Machine Learning in Healthcare*. Norwegian Center for e-Health Research. https://ehealthresearch.no/en/fact-sheets/artificial-intelligence-and-machine-learning-in-healthcare

Nah, F. F. H., Daggubati, L. S., Tarigonda, A., Nuvvula, R. V., & Turel, O. (2015). Effects of the Use of Points, Leaderboards and Badges on In-Game Purchases of Virtual Goods. In F. Fui-Hoon Nah & C. H. Tan (Eds.), Lecture Notes in Computer Science: Vol. 9191. *HCI in Business. HCIB 2015*. Springer. doi:10.1007/978-3-319-20895-4_48

Parker, R. M., Ratzan, S. C., & Lurie, N. (2003). Health Literacy: A Policy Challenge for advancing high-quality Health care. *Health Affairs (Project Hope), 22*(4), 147–153. doi:10.1377/hlthaff.22.4.147 PMID:12889762

Patel, M. S., Small, D. S., Harrison, J. D., Fortunato, M. P., Oon, A. L., Rareshide, C. A. L., Reh, G., Szwartz, G., Guszcza, J., Steier, D., Kalra, P., & Hilbert, V. (2019). Effectiveness of Behaviorally Designed Gamification Interventions with Social Incentives for Increasing Physical Activity among Overweight and Obese Adults Across the United States. *JAMA Internal Medicine, 179*(12), 1624–1632. doi:10.1001/jamainternmed.2019.3505 PMID:31498375

Ramirez, N. (2020). *How AI and ML Technology is Transforming Medical Devices*. https://techbullion.com/

Reddy, M. (2021). *Digital Transformation in Healthcare in 2021: 7 Key Trends*. https://www.digitalauthority.me/resources

Sailer, M., Hense, J. U., Mayr, S. K., & Mandl, H. (2017). How gamification motivates: An experimental study of the effects of specific game design elements on psychological need satisfaction. *Computers in Human Behavior, 69*, 371-380. doi:10.1016/j.chb.2016.12.033

Sanchez, E., Young, S., & Jouneau-Sion, C. (2017). Classcraft: From Gamification to Ludicization of Classroom Management. *Journal of Education and Information Technologies, 22*(2), 497–513. doi:10.100710639-016-9489-6

Sánchez Salazar, L. A., Gallardo Pérez, H. J., & Paz Montes, L. S. (2019). The Educaplay interactive platform for the learning of mathematics in populations with special educational needs. *Journal of Physics: Conference Series*, 1329.

Sardi, L., Idri, A., & Fernández-Alemán, J. L. (2017). A Systematic Review of Gamification in e-Health. *Journal of Biomedical Informatics, 71*, 31-48. doi:10.1016/j.jbi.2017.05.011

Sotoca-Orgaz, P. (2020). *Gamificación e Inteligencia artificial (IA). Cuando Sherlock conoció a Watson* [Paper presentation]. Encuentro de Innovación de Docencia Universitaria (XII EIDU UAH). Madrid, España. doi:10.13140/RG.2.2.22895.25760

Tondello, G. F., Mora, A., Marczewski, A., Nacke, L. E. (2019). Empirical validation of the Gamification User Types Hexad scale in English and Spanish. *International Journal of Human-Computer Studies, 127*, 95-111. doi:10.1016/j.ijhcs.2018.10.002

Tondello, G. F., Wehbe, R. R., Diamond, L., Busch, M., Marczewski, A., & Nacke, L. E. (2016). The Gamification User Types Hexad Scale. In *Proceedings of the 2016 Annual Symposium on Computer-Human Interaction in Play* (pp. 229-243). 10.1145/2967934.2968082

Venkatesh, V., Morris, M., Davis, G., & Davis, F. (2003). User Acceptance of Information Technology: Toward a Unified View. *Management Information Systems Quarterly, 27*(3), 425–478. doi:10.2307/30036540

Vette, D. F., Tabak, M., & Vollenbroek-Hutten, M. (January, 2015). *Increasing motivation in eHealth through gamification* [Paper presentation]. *Fifth Dutch Conference on Bio-Medical Engineering*. Egmond aan Zee, The Netherlands.

Wang, A. I., & Tahir, R., (2020). The effect of using Kahoot! for learning - A literature review. *Computers & Education, 149*. doi:10.1016/j.compedu.2020.103818

Werbach, K., & Hunter, D. (2012). *For the Win: How game thinking can revolutionize your business*. Wharton Digital Press.

Wu, M., & Luo, J. (2020). *Wearable Technology Applications in Healthcare: A Literature Review*. https://www.himss.org/resources/

Yang, H., & Li, D. (2021). Understanding the dark side of gamification health management: A stress perspective. *Information Processing & Management, 58*(5), 1–19. doi:10.1016/j.ipm.2021.102649

Yordanova, Z. (2020). Gamification as a Tool for Supporting Artificial Intelligence Development – State of Art. In M. Botto-Tobar, M. Zambrano Vizuete, P. Torres-Carrión, S. Montes León, G. Pizarro Vásquez, & B. Durakovic (Eds.), *Applied Technologies. ICAT 2019. Communications in Computer and Information Science* (Vol. 1193). Springer. doi:10.1007/978-3-030-42517-3_24

Yu, K. H., Beam, A. L., & Kohane, I. S. (2018). Artificial Intelligence in Healthcare. *Nature Biomedical Engineering*, 2(10), 719–731. doi:10.103841551-018-0305-z PMID:31015651

Zhao, Z., Ali Etemad, S., & Arya, A. (2016). Gamification of Exercise and Fitness using Wearable Activity Trackers. In P. Chung, A. Soltoggio, C. Dawson, Q. Meng, & M. Pain (Eds.) In *Proceedings of the 10th International Symposium on Computer Science in Sports (ISCSS). Advances in Intelligent Systems and Computing* (vol. 392). Springer. 10.1007/978-3-319-24560-7_30

Zichermann, G., & Cunningham, C. (2011). *Gamification by Design: Implementing game mechanics in web and mobile apps*. O'Reilly Media.

Zichermann, G., & Linder, J. (2013). *The gamification revolution*. McGraw-Hill Education.

KEY TERMS AND DEFINITIONS

Artificial Intelligence: A wide-ranging branch of computer science concerned with building smart machines capable of performing tasks that typically require human intelligence.

Big Data: It refers to the possibility of analyzing and systematically extracting information from, or otherwise deal with data sets that are too large or complex to be dealt with by traditional data-processing application software.

Deep Learning: It refers to Artificial Neural Networks and related machine learning algorithms that uses using multiple layers of neurons. It is seen as a subset of machine learning in artificial intelligence.

Health Literacy: It refers to the degree to which individuals have the capacity to obtain, process, and understand basic health information and services needed to make appropriate health decisions.

Health Monitoring: It is the tracking of any aspect of an individual's health. It is very important for illness prevention.

Healthcare Wearable Devices: Portable devices designed to collect the data of individuals' personal health and activity.

Machine Learning: It refers to the study of computer algorithms that improve automatically through experience. It is seen as a subset of artificial intelligence.

PLB (Point Leaderboards Badges) Model: A model based on precise mechanics powered by points, objectives, levels, rankings, progress, missions, challenges, badges, notifications, and obstacles, structured to engage users in a real experience, in which motivation, participation and the amusement factor are essential.

TAM (Technology Acceptance Model): A theory that models how users come to accept and use a technology. It has been one of the most influential models of technology acceptance, according to what there are two primary factors influencing an individual's intention to use new technology: perceived ease of use and perceived usefulness.

Chapter 12
Augmented Reality Games

Baris Atiker

https://orcid.org/0000-0002-4622-7409

Bahcesehir University, Turkey

ABSTRACT

Augmented reality strengthens its ties with the gaming world every day. The fact that smartphones can be used as an augmented reality tool, in particular, shows this interest as a remarkable phenomenon for both gamers and game producers. The development of augmented reality applications is of great importance for the future of the gaming world, as it is not only limited to mobile phones but also covers more sophisticated devices. This research intends to evaluate how augmented reality games interpret gaming concepts and principles, through field research methods, new applications, and studies that deal with gamification, presence, immersion, and game transfer phenomena. It is also aimed to make inferences about how our daily life can be gamified in the near future thanks to augmented reality.

INTRODUCTION

One of the fastest-growing areas of digital technologies is undoubtedly the gaming industry. In addition to hardware and software developments, subjects such as digital storytelling, character design, realistic simulations, artificial intelligence, and user experience increase the connection of technology with the concept of gaming day by day.

The relationship between gaming technologies and the concept of reality has been one of the most challenged areas throughout history. Computer visualization is one of the most essential parts of the gaming experience and has become competitive with cinematic visual effects thanks to software and hardware advancements that require high processing power. In addition, the ability of computer games to make this visualization simultaneously within the experience itself has made it more effective and persuasive than the cinema.

Video games often prefer to separate the user from the real world. This isolated world, where imagination and actions are limitless, is one of the main motivations for most players to play the game, even if they are not aware of it. Because this virtual world is more exciting, fun, passionate, and competitive than the ordinary lives of the gamers.

DOI: 10.4018/978-1-7998-8089-9.ch012

Augmented Reality technology offers never-before-seen experiences in terms of matching the immersive gaming world with real life. Removing the boundaries between the virtual and real world means making these unique experiences a reality, not just for gaming, but for gamification as well.

AUGMENTED REALITY GAMES

Augmented Reality, under the umbrella of Extended Reality (XR), is an interdisciplinary subject of artificial intelligence and human-computer interaction. Augmented Reality is a technology that organically integrates physical (visual and auditory) information between the real and virtual world through computer simulation, which is difficult or impossible to experience in a certain time and place in the real world. Augmented Reality devices instantly calculate the user's position and angle framed by the camera and superimpose the digital images by matching them with the real objects in the three-dimensional environment.

Virtual and Augmented Reality games, which have become increasingly popular in recent years, have led to the need to look at the concept of reality from a different perspective. In virtual reality games, the user is fully surrounded by an artificial image, while in Augmented Reality real world is still visible. In Augmented Reality games, players can only partially disconnect from the real world. At this point, the player's presence is challenged not only mentally but also physically.

Augmented Reality uses three-dimensional motion graphics to blend digital images with the user's point of view. Unlike Virtual Reality, which creates a completely artificial environment, Augmented Reality aims to keep the user inside by creating add-ons to the real world. Because of this feature, Augmented Reality is a subset of virtual reality that is rapidly gaining ground among app developers, businesses, and gamers alike.

Augmented Reality applications have been able to overcome many technological obstacles in recent years, thanks to mobile phones that can integrate face and voice recognition technologies. Also factors such as artificial intelligence and machine learning, the Internet of Things, 5G, and cloud computing are driving the growth of Augmented Reality in coming years, making those technologies an indispensable part of the gaming industry of the future.

Augmented Reality and Gamification

Gamification refers to the use of game design elements in non-game contexts (Deterding et al., 2011). Gamification can be easily applied to almost any industry, such as entertainment and media, gaming, aerospace, defense, manufacturing, retail, education, and healthcare.

According to Alsawaier (2018), gamification is the adoption of game mechanics and dynamics to engage people, solve problems and improve the learning process. Gamification involves the use of elements traditionally found in games such as narrative, feedback, reward system, conflict, cooperation, competition, clear goals and rules, levels, trial and error, fun, interaction, interaction.

Education, which is one of the most widely used areas of gamification, contains very concrete methods both in terms of approach and goals. These concrete approaches are one of the main reasons why Augmented Reality applications have become widespread in the field of education. The relative readiness of educational content allows them to be prioritized in Augmented Reality and digital transformation.

JFK Moonshot (2019), for example, relives the Apollo 11 experience that first set foot on the moon in 1969 as an Augmented Reality game and documentary (Fig. 1).

Figure 1. JFK Moonshot AR (2019)
Source: www.jfkmoonshot.org

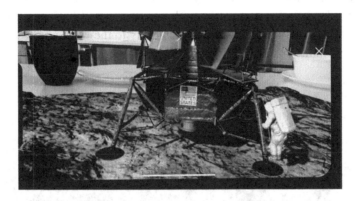

According to Kapp (2012), gamification can be broadly divided into two types: (a) Structural Gamification; (b) Content Gamification. Structural Gamification is characterized by the use of game mechanics such as badges, scoreboards, and leaderboards. In general, awards are an incentive to engage students and encourage them to continue. The content of the learning material is not like a game, only the structure around the content is gamified. The learning objectives should be clear from the start because that's how rewards can be earned. Structural Gamification "drags" the learner through the content and tries to engage it by handing out rewards.

Content gamification, on the other hand, takes advantage of game mechanics such as challenge, storytelling, feedback loops, freedom to fail, to involve students from the beginning and even without knowing their learning goals in advance. It is also perfectly possible to add these game mechanics to increase interaction and learning without designing an entire game (Kapp, 2012).

According to Barker (2017), four key components are needed to gamify any task: (a) winnable (b) promises new challenges (c) sets clear achievable goals, and (d) provides performance feedback. It is seen that Augmented Reality games easily respond to these four basic components. In particular, the interaction in form of transferring the information to the user is much more convincing and efficient, since it also contains elements from real life.

Conceptually, many games contain real-life simulations. This is the reason why gamification can be adapted to almost any real-life scenarios. These simulations have evolved from just verbal expression simulations to sensory simulations with today's technologies. Especially the proficiency of Augmented Reality games in terms of abstract, stylized, realistic, and unreal simulations brings it to the center of game and gamification studies. Of course, not only the game itself but also the player's relationship with the content and context is a simulation. This relationship determines the continuation of the game. Here, player motivation is one of the most basic tools handled in Augmented Reality games, both psychologically and physiologically.

Self-Determination theory, which is an important study on human motivation, guides us in our view of Augmented Reality games. This theory considers three basic psychological needs: (a) having meaningful choices, referring to the need for freedom and autonomy; (b) the desire to gain mastery and success rate; and (c) connecting with others who need interaction and relationships. It is very important for the player to understand what (content) and why (process) goal pursuit and goal-directed behavior is. (Deci and Ryan, 2000).

Photonlens company synthesizes the concept of physical exercise with gamification by using Augmented Reality glasses and Fighting Fit (2021) application (Fig. 2). It is a known situation that people who have exercise habits have higher motivation for being fit and healthy. Users who are separated from the gym due to Covid 19 are adding some fun and sociability to their lives by redesigning their exercise routines in a safer way in their home environment.

Figure 2. Photonlens Fighting Fit (2021)
Source: www.photonlens.com

What makes augmented reality games more advantageous than other games is that they respond to these psychological and physiological needs while increasing them in a sensory sense. Augmented reality is undoubtedly an excellent tool for gamification, not just for gaming but for all types of industries.

Serious Games and Gamification

The concept of gamification is often confused with serious games. Both terms share many common elements but it is necessary to distinguish them. Gamification uses game codes and other elements commonly found in games, for example, to make an existing training more interesting and fun. Elements such as awards, recognition, and competition are added to the training.

A serious game, on the other hand, is an education offered in the form of a game or simulation created to meet the specific needs of a group and serve a non-entertainment purpose. (Deterding et al., 2011; Laamarti et al., 2014). Serious games can be seen as games that involve targeted missions, with both real-world and non-real scenarios aimed at improving the gamers' performance and cognitive abilities (Shi and Shih, 2015).

A significant proportion of simulation-based Augmented Reality applications are seen in the serious games category. These applications that mainly focus on medicine, military, and industry are preferred because they minimize the cost, risks, margin of error and user concerns of training in a basic sense. Augmented Reality games, which can be evaluated in the field of gamification, mainly aim to entertain, focus, compete and share during training. In a comparative analysis of gamified and non-gamified balance exercises, gamified versions outperformed traditional ones. (Brumels et al., 2008)

In 2021, Microsoft signed an agreement with the US Army for five years and 21 billion dollars over the HoloLens II platform (Palladino, 2021). The use of Augmented Reality technology by military personnel both off the field and during the operation is a remarkable development within the scope of serious games (Fig. 3).

Figure 3. Microsoft HoloLens II for Military Use (2021)
Source: Microsoft

According to Deterding et al. (2011) gamification depends on four semantic components. (a) rule-based or goal-oriented structure, (b) elements as game building blocks in a real-world context, (c) design as elements of technology, and (d) non-game contexts in which gamification can be applied.

Augmented Reality games are preferred because they are one of the most suitable environments for these four components. It is seen that the training given in Augmented Reality Games, especially for educational purposes, fully overlaps with the rules and objectives of the game, real-world objects can be used as game elements, interface and digital graphics are integrated into the real world, and the place where the players are in is a part of the interaction as a non-game context.

The incorporation of gamification methods into educational context known as 'Serious Games' is still the subject of much debate, particularly among educators and society. It is used to reinforce certain learning behaviors with game elements and mechanics such as points, badges, and leaderboards (Werbach & Hunter, 2012). Particularly, the risk of falling behind the weight of educational content in general interaction compared to factors such as entertainment, competition, and immersion is the focus of discussions on this subject. However, while the personalization of the learning experience with Augmented Reality applications provides great advantages in terms of high focus and development while competing, the training content should be at the forefront as much as these factors.

CatchyWords AR (2018) is an incredibly simple yet unique and immersive word game made specifically with the Augmented Reality approach in mind (Fig. 4). To form a word, all the player has to do is move around with the device and tap the virtual objects with their phone to catch the letters.

Figure 4. Catchywords AR (2018)

Augmented Reality in the Gaming Industry

Due to social isolation along with Covid-19, Augmented and Virtual Reality tools are spreading at an accelerating rate from online shopping to entertainment and gaming. Augmented Reality technologies are facing an unprecedented demand for product imaging, interactive clothing, and games. Gamified marketing activities and even the games themselves, which are offered to consumers under the name of a pleasant experience during shopping, have started to take a much more place in our daily lives as Augmented Reality products.

Augmented Reality games are cheaper and more common in terms of accessibility than other reality (VR and MR) approach. Mobile phones, which became widespread after the 2000s, started to be used as powerful Augmented Reality tools with their visual, auditory, and tactile responses, and with this a different experience gate was opened to the game world.

Augmented Reality games promise to make this world more interesting and fun without isolating the user from the real world. Released in 2016, Pokémon Go (2016) is perhaps one of the most popular games in the Augmented Reality world. Pokémon Go became an overnight sensation, with a record 7.2 million downloads in its first week. One of the main reasons for this interest is that it not only brings an already beloved game to the world of Augmented Reality but also makes it possible to experience it simultaneously with millions of players in different parts of the real world.

Robbins (2016) has pointed out that it is so rare for a game that fundamentally changed the way we socialize and use technology to be defined as a real game. Poké Stops and Pokémon Gyms that Pokémon players use while developing their Pokémon characters with various tools, items, and training are actually physical places such as the library and gym on the maps, and the necessity of the player to walk close to these places helps to strengthen his relationship with the game and the real place (Fig.

5). The relationship between the game and the real spaces can be considered as a match rather than an overlap. Pokémon Go is an excellent example of looking at this potential for making learning fun, as it has already shown that emerging technology creates opportunities to connect and educate users in unexpected ways (Spina, 2016).

Figure 5. Pokémon Go (2016)
Source: Niantic

The increasing use of Augmented Reality technology in the gaming industry increases the market size on an accelerating scale. According to research by Facts & Factors (2021), the global Augmented and Virtual Reality Market is expected to reach US$305 Billion by 2026.

The use of Augmented Reality in gaming applications, with the inclusion of visual, auditory, and even tactile content, allows users to interact with the physical environment in different ways and further improve their gamification experience. Technology is the key driver for the Augmented Reality gaming market. Major technology providers collaborate with device and game manufacturers to provide users with immersive gaming features and experiences.

Digital Presence

In Augmented Reality games, the matching between the real and virtual worlds takes place both by tracking the user's physical movements and by the simultaneous response of digital objects to these movements. According to Riva and Mantovani (2012), it is possible to exist in the virtual environment as well as in the physical environment, because "presence" is a neurocognitive phenomenon in which the cognitive system plans actions, performs these actions, and examines the degree to which these actions are completed as intended.

In this case, the person's location is the first key to the numeric entity. These games, categorized as Location-Based Mobile Games (LBMG), mostly use the GPS features of mobile phones to act according to the user's location (de Souza e Silva, 2006).

According to Lombard and Ditton (1997), presence can be considered from six different perspectives. (a) Being as Social Wealth is primarily concerned with notions of intimacy and intimacy applied to unmediated interpersonal communication. (b) Being as realism; It concerns the degree to which an environment can produce seemingly accurate representations of objects, events, and people. (c) Being as transportation; moving the user to another location or moving the location and its contents to the user; It's about taking two or more users to a place they share. (d) Being as immersion; perceptually and psychologically related to the idea of diving (e) Being in the environment as a social actor; (f) The presence of the environment as a social actor; it is about involving users' social reactions to cues (not people or computer characters) provided by a medium itself.

The concept of presence in Augmented Reality games can be easily applied to the approach of Lombard and Ditton. First of all, social interaction in Augmented Reality games has reached great potential, although it is still in its infancy. The fact that users are in communication and interaction at the same time gives great speed to network games in terms of social wealth. In terms of realism, the concept of being is the closest environment to reality because Augmented Reality games consist of virtual interfaces superimposed on the real world. From a transportation perspective, Augmented Reality games have the power to convincingly change the look of the environment, both with virtual portals and overlay graphics. From an immersion perspective, as the user gets used to the virtual images in their world, they tend to accept them as part of reality after a while. In terms of social interaction, players from different locations can affect each other's status simultaneously. Finally, in terms of the social actor, presence can be observed as the feeling of comfort and confidence that comes from being in the actor's environment in Augmented Reality games.

Of course, the most fundamental reason for the success of Augmented Reality applications is the perfect alignment and mapping between the real and virtual worlds. Objects in the real and virtual worlds must be properly aligned with each other, otherwise, the illusion that the two worlds will coexist is jeopardized (Azuma, 1997). Augmented Reality applications rely on several matching technologies to ensure this alignment is perfect.

Similarly, the development of application contents in the field of Augmented Reality brings along the design principles of this world. Vuforia's Augmented Reality System Development Kit (SDK) uses computer vision technology for real-time detection and monitoring of image targets and three-dimensional objects (Fig. 6). The three-dimensional tracking feature uses images such as cubes, blocks, or cylinders as targets. The quick installation method is one of the main advantages of Vuforia AR SDK. This feature makes it possible to create an easy development environment for the designer and get results quickly.

Figure 6. Vuforia AR Interface.
Source: https://www.ptc.com/en/products/vuforia

Mediation Theory

The physical world is a unique source of information that provides humans with a continuous stream of images, sounds, and emotions that cannot be fully simulated by the computers yet. Mainstream games aim to fully exploit the richness of the physical world as a game resource by interlacing digital media with our daily experiences (Broll et al., 2006).

Ihde's (1993) conceptualization of technological mediation has led to a discussion of technology in mediated experiences. So, technology transforms experiences between people and the real world, and creates that subjectivity. In this respect, technology cannot be said to be neutral, but it is thought to have a subjective role in mediated experiences.

Lombard and Ditton (1997) define the concept of presence as 'the illusion of non-mediation'. This illusion effectively redefines what it means to be in one's own body. This redefinition places the virtual world and the real physical world of natural perception on an equal playing field. At this point, the artificiality of Augmented Reality images does not create any negative perception in experiencing it, and on the contrary, it ensures that it is adopted more as a means of adding the difference to the mediocrity of real life.

Many factors promote a sense of presence, such as variables related to the perception of motion, color and size of visual screens, fields of view created by various camera techniques, image quality, size, and viewing distance. Several new technologies, including Virtual and Augmented Reality, simulation rides, video conferencing, home theater, and high-definition television, are designed to provide media users with the illusion that a mediated experience is not mediated.

The "illusion of non-mediation" arises when a person cannot perceive or accept the presence of a tool in the communication environment or react as if the tool has changed there. In a sense, although all our experiences are driven by our internal sensory and perceptual systems, they are defined here as experiences without "agents", that is, without man-made technology. According to this definition, even hearing aids and glasses are "interfering" environments.

The illusion of mediation can occur in two different ways: (a) the media can be invisible or transparent and act as a large window through which the media user and media content are shared in the same physical environment; (b) the environment may seem to have changed from being a social entity to something other than a tool (Lombard & Ditton, 1997).

Augmented Reality games have started to show themselves in two different ways. Especially applications such as Google Glass are built on the principle of hiding themselves as much as possible. Augmented Reality games allow the user to react naturally to the interaction, with maximum harmony with physical environment in terms of social presence.

Although Augmented Reality becomes widespread in our lives with smartphones, it will accelerate its real development with wearable technologies. Google Glass experiences show that we are not ready yet, but soon an inclusive world is waiting to open its doors. The recent evolution of Augmented Reality tools from heavy glasses to contact lens sizes is also part of this trend.

Wearable technologies play an important role in the future of augmented reality, with their shrinking size and increasing processing power as portable computers. Contactless Augmented Reality devices such as glasses, lenses, or motion tracking devices are gradually making Augmented Reality tools invisible and unnoticeable. This will undoubtedly result in much more inclusive, inseparable, and "non-mediated experiences" in Augmented Reality games.

Physical Perception and Shared Experiences

Because interaction is an essential part of the definition of Augmented Reality, an efficient and easy-to-use experience must be provided. Augmented Reality improves a user's perception and interaction with the real world. Virtual objects show information that the user cannot perceive directly with the senses. Information transmitted by virtual objects helps a user perform real-world tasks (Azuma, 1997: 3).

Augmented Reality applications use three different approaches to provide bridging between the virtual and real-world in terms of physical perception. (a) Sign-based Augmented Reality applications use image recognition technology that relies on beacons to overlay and display Augmented Reality content in user's real-life environments. For example, MaxST Augmented Reality platform, uses two- and three-dimensional image tracking technology while superimposing virtual images on the real world through signs placed on real maps (Fig. 7).

Figure 7. MaxST Interface
Source: www.maxst.com

(b) Location-based Augmented Reality applications, operating without signs, use GPS, accelerometer, or digital compass to detect the user's location and then overlay the digital data in physical locations. They include additional features that allow them to send user notifications about new Augmented Reality content available based on their location.

Available only for iOS devices, ARKit is one of the powerful Augmented Reality creation tools. The tool uses Visual Inertial Odometry (VIO) to accurately monitor the environment (Fig. 8). Powerful face and object tracking capabilities allow 3D features and facial effects. The system also includes methods for detecting objects with simultaneous image rendering tools such as Unreal and Unity.

(c) Real-time location system (RTLS) is a location and technology-based application that operates based on technologies such as Wi-Fi, Bluetooth, Ultra-wideband UWB, and other radio frequency identification (RFID). These platforms are used in fleet tracking, navigation, inventory and asset tracking, personnel tracking, network security, and other applications.

Figure 8. ARKit 5 Demo.
Source: Apple

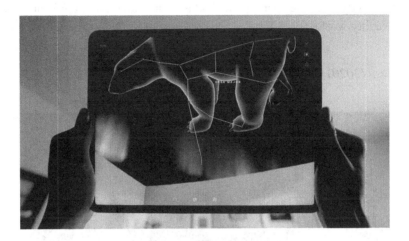

In fact, Augmented Reality games also have to consider the user's interaction with their physical environment. There is already a concern that the use of Augmented Reality games in physical spaces, and especially in public spaces, can cause distraction and unwanted accidents.

Augmented Reality games can be defined as an uninterrupted flow of user experience somewhere between real and virtual environments. This is one of the important factors that allow players to perceptually stay in the flow between physical and virtual reality.

Csikszentmihalyi (1990) defined flow as a state of mind of absolute concentration and absorption in the task at hand. In those moments when time, worries are forgotten and integrated into an activity, the flow appears. Csikszentmihalyi also discussed what facilitates flow formation and what keeps it alive, and proposed nine dimensions that should represent the optimal psychological flow state. (a) the challenge-skill balance as a challenge to the user; (b) the action-awareness dimension that combines activity with a sense of effortlessness as perceiving spontaneously or automatically; (c) clear objectives stating what users should do; (d) precise feedback that allows people to check their progress; (e) Concentration on the task, forgetting all the unpleasant aspects of life; (f) A sense of control as a release from the fear of failure; (g) Loss of self-consciousness due to not worrying about self-evaluation; (h) Time transformation as a perception of time; and (i) the autotelic experience as a fun experience at the end.

Augmented Reality games can be more advantageous than video games or virtual reality games in all nine dimensions of the flow concept. These advantages increase especially in terms of feedback, concentration, and sense of control.

Meaningful interaction in games like Neyon Clash (2020) cannot be achieved through ordinary user interfaces due to the nature of Augmented Reality experiences (Fig. 9). As a team game, Neyon Clash creates the opportunity for gamers to experience virtual interaction in the real world simultaneously. Players struggle to capture target areas in open spaces such as parks, and not being alone during this experience is an important part of the flow.

Azuma (1997) envisioned two similar approaches about Augmented Reality applications and flow connectivity, which inspired many applications in use today. Navigation systems, as one of the first approaches that come to mind for Augmented Reality, make it easier to find a way by automatically performing the virtual and real-world association step. If the user's location and direction are known, and the system has access to a digital map of the space, the Augmented Reality system can draw the map in three dimensions directly from the user's view. Today, many navigation applications are transitioning to the Augmented Reality world.

Figure 9. Neyon Clash (2020)
Source: Reaktor Berlin

The second approach is to visualize locations and events as they were in the past or as they will be after future changes have been made. They are apps available to tourists visiting historical sites such as the site of the Civil War or the Acropolis in Athens (Azuma, 1997).

The MauAR (2019) application has a documentary-like structure that conveys the Berlin Wall, which was destroyed in 1989, along with the important events of the period. Users can experience the Berlin wall, watchtowers, and military vehicles in their real size and location on a location-based basis via their mobile phones and tablets (Fig 10).

Figure 10. MauAR (2019)
Source: ZDF

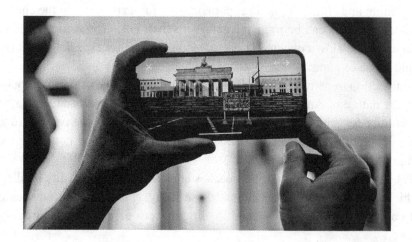

Flow is also essential in learning activities. Goerner points out that augmented reality "can attract users to experience in a way that makes learning more meaningful" (Goerner, 2016).

The experience of the user in Augmented Reality games gains a significant depth when combined with the purpose of learning. Zhu et al. (2016) defines ten characteristics that an intelligent learning environment should have: (a) location sensitive; (b) context-sensitive; (c) social awareness; (d) interoperability; (e) seamless connectivity; (f) adaptable; (g) is ubiquitous; (h) the entire record; (i) natural interaction; and (j) high interaction properties.

All of these components are available in Ingress Prime AR (2018). It is the current version of the Ingress game released by the Niantic company in 2012. The game, which has the same logic as Pokémon Go, aims to transform players into heroes instead of virtual characters. (Fig. 11) Ingress is a game that pioneered the concept of Augmented Reality and location-based games, and its success has allowed Niantic to work on two of the world's largest popular culture brands.

Figure 11. Ingress Prime AR (2018)
Source: Niantic

Transformation

Augmented Reality applications can capture the perfect transition between the real and virtual worlds, with the perfect transformation of the two worlds into each other. Although this transformation may seem to be one-sided from the virtual world to the real world, the transformation is two-way. Making this calculation in two-sided transformation also includes converting the real world into digital data.

Mobile inertial measurement units (IMUs) consist of 9D sensors (acceleration, gyroscope, magnetic field) that can be worn with their small size or can be directly integrated into the auxiliary device and can detect the horizontal and vertical deviation or possible bending of the user. In this way, the user's position and viewpoint can be calculated very precisely. This transformation enables the creation of numerical graphics that will affect the user's field of view.

One of the transformations from the real world to the virtual world is the transformation of gestures as interfaces and interaction tools. Motion and gesture tracking technologies have an important place in the future of Augmented Reality games. Instead of clicking virtual buttons, users can use body language with more natural responses, simplifying the interaction interface. The ability of devices such as Microsoft Kinect and Nintendo Wii Remote to track the player's movements will be one of the biggest needs for Augmented Reality games in terms of a natural interface that changes according to the instant movements and gestures of the player. Transformation to digital media will increase both the quality of the matched object and the interaction positively.

Tokuyama et al. (2019) developed a simple and experimental Augmented Reality mirror game using a Kinect device for the activation of the brain and the exercise of the lower limbs, especially for the elderly, (Fig. 12). The game acts when the user presses virtual buttons created with Augmented Reality. The player's movements are monitored simultaneously, and the foot and button relationships are evaluated and converted into points.

Figure 12. Tokuyama AR Game (2019)

Another transformation in Augmented Reality games is the increase of the photorealistic effect of digital images. Photorealism in digital graphics is successfully achieved in movies and computer games through visual effects, but this is much more difficult to achieve in an interactive and simultaneous application. Lighting conditions, surface reflections, shadow values, and other properties should be measured automatically and in real-time. The physical properties of the real-world environment such as light, shadow, texture, and depth should be calculated digitally and immediately reflected on the user. More sophisticated lighting, texture rendering, and shading capabilities should run at interactive speeds in future scene generators (Azuma, 1997).

The capacity of today's image processors is not yet sufficient to create full realistic images simultaneously. Instead, low-quality images are deliberately and acceptably stylized and used over a small number of polygons and shading features.

Three-dimensional scanning technologies are a great way to combine real-world objects in digitized, even low resolution. LiDAR scanner technology provides ultra-detailed three-dimensional mapping that allows Augmented Reality systems to place their data in a precise and reliable location. Seeing what's going on with a smartphone is not the same as having a full 3D map of the area. The point cloud scanner created by LiDAR greatly improves the accuracy of the Augmented Reality experience. It may even be a step towards a fully developed 3D user interface.

Apple specializes in two key areas such as shrouding and motion capture, with a brand-new set of tools focused on three-dimensional Augmented Reality, called RealityKit. This technology places a virtual three-dimensional object in a real space, allowing the application to understand and evaluate where the actors are on the stage. This feature is of great importance in multiplayer scenarios of Augmented Reality games. The motion capture feature of RealityKit also makes it possible to track the joints and even facial expressions of the players, thus maximizing the interaction between the application and the user.

The speed of transformation between the virtual and real-world is just as important as the interaction itself. The emergence of 5G technology has brought with it the ideal three main features of Augmented Reality devices, namely high speed, large capacity, and low latency. These features enable the system to establish a fast and stable connection to the cloud network and provide a foundation for large-scale commercial use of augmented reality equipment and completing tasks that require high-performance computing.

Immersion

The concept of immersion experienced by many users in virtual environments refers to a user's level of physical or psychological immersion in a virtual space relative to the user's awareness of the real-world environment (Emma-Ogbangwo et al., 2014). While VR applications are undoubtedly much more advantageous in terms of immersion, they also provide important clues for Augmented Reality games.

First of all, although this concept is thought of as the abstraction of the user from his real environment, the level of immersion should be considered together with the concept of flow. While most users use a virtual reality application, they first adapt to the new environment, and the user's awareness of the environment decreases as the experience time increases. The immersion experience here is therefore not only due to the perception of being in a different environment but also to concentrate more on the experience itself after getting used to the new environment.

The continuity of the flow is directly proportional to the isolation of the actor from real space and time. The necessity of virtual and real-world matching in Augmented Reality games comes from this continuity. Any disruption greatly disrupts the immersion effect along with the flow.

Harry Potter: Wizards Unite is an Augmented Reality game that continues the success of its novels and movies, and brings reality to fantastic experiences. In the highly immersive game, players can personalize their selfies with Wizarding World-inspired lenses, frames, deformations, accessories, stickers, and many more customizable features to take their place as an official member of the wizarding world and the Stealth Statute Task Force (Fig. 13).

When we look at the basic tools of the concept of immersion, it is seen that the psychological elements are much more dominant than the physical elements. Even the experience of reading a book is counted as an active immersion experience, although it does not contain any physical elements in itself. Similarly, the psychological immersion effect of Augmented Reality games is much greater than media such as books or movies. This is because both the psychological and physical elements match together, enriching and deepening the experience.

Figure 13. Harry Potter: Wizards Unite (2019)

Another advantage of Augmented Reality games is the emphasis on personalized experience. Especially, users who experience Augmented Reality games in their natural environment are under the influence of the psychological sensations created by a safe and comfortable environment without being aware of it. This naturally strengthens the immersion experience in Augmented Reality games.

One of the important elements that increase the immersion effect is that the actions of the player find their response in the virtual world without any delay. As mentioned before, the users' facial expressions and body language as an interaction tool simplifies and facilitates both the interaction and the environment interface. Tracking hand movements, such as the user touching a virtual object in Augmented Reality games, can be seen as both guidance and a control system. In perfect match scenarios, the user will more easily adopt the illusion that virtual objects belong to the real world. Body/system feedback establishes a perceptual continuity in a relationship where the body feels in an area that "feels" the body (Domingues & Miranda, 2019).

Matching Augmented Reality applications with the real world in terms of immersion concept is possible by calculating depth perception. If the virtual object is positioned behind the real object, the real object must cover the virtual object. Visualization of occluded objects often misleads users' perception if this situation is not properly addressed (Kasapakis and Gavalas, 2017). In other words, the positions of the objects on the depth axis reveal the concept of occlusion in the matching of virtual and real-world objects.

The concept of occlusion is related to the fact that the interaction between two different worlds is in a continuous flow and cannot be separated from each other, just like immersion. With occlusion, digital images are placed not only on top of real-world images but also between them. Google ARCore can calculate the distance between objects using its computer visualization (Raw Depth API) to perfectly place virtual objects between real objects (Fig. 14). This means that a virtual object is created not only from the user's point of view but also associated with real objects.

Figure 14. Google ARCore Occlusion (2020)
Source: Google

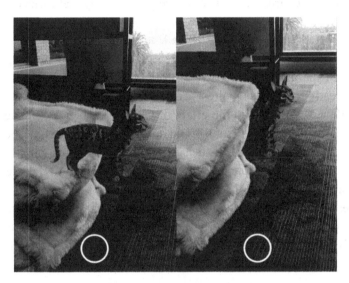

The approach to addressing the problem of covering virtual objects in Augmented Reality consists of three steps. The first step is the selection of an object to cover the virtual object. Here, all pixels in the image are divided into two classes, object, and background. In the second step, the edge boundaries of the object are tracked and averaged based on the displacement of the tracking points. In the third and final step, all pixels within the object boundaries are redrawn according to the position between the real and virtual object (Tian, Guan, & Wang, 2010).

Game Transfer Phenomenon

The effects of the transformation between the virtual and real-world on the user indicate an interesting phenomenon both during and after the experience. In terms of simulations of real-world environments, there is an integration between Augmented Reality games and the use of Virtual Reality headsets. This integration challenges our perceptions of reality for two important reasons: (a) virtuality allows us to live parallel lives in unreal worlds by embracing virtual identities and materializing fantasies (Ryan, 1999) and (b) the results of virtual immersion, seeing or hearing elements in the game after playing may facilitate and/or promote post-game phenomena that occur as hallucinatory-like experiences (Ortiz de Gortari and Griffiths, 2017).

The Game Transfer Phenomenon (GTP) is the habit of bringing gaming experiences to the real-world. It is a psychological phenomenon encountered by the reflection of audio-visual and even scripted elements in the player's real life after an intense and long gaming experience. According to many studies conducted since the 1990s, when the human mind encounters a different situation after intense activity, it cannot quickly adapt to the new situation. In addition, while the natural conditioning reflex of the human brain is shown as one of the reasons for this phenomenon, the similarities between the game and the real-world can trigger some behaviors in users.

In Augmented Reality games, the probability of experiencing GTP is greatly increased due to the interaction with the digital world without leaving the real world completely. The user may not be fully aware of the distinction between the two worlds subconsciously. Even with advancing technologies, the perfect match of more realistic virtual objects to the real world may make this phenomenon even more uncertain.

One of the most important factors for GTP is the level of physical or psychological immersion in a virtual space relative to the user's awareness of the real-world environment. Augmented Reality applications offer the closest experience to reality as they contain digital elements placed in the real world. This experience also greatly facilitates the presence and immersion experience.

Gortari and Griffiths (2014) revealed the effect of GTP on behaviors such as visual and auditory perceptions such as images, visual effects, sounds and music related to the game, bodily perceptions such as acting as in a game, and mental processes such as automated thoughts, impulses or repetitive tasks; LaViola (2000) stated that these perceptual effects are directly related to the use of highly immersive technologies such as simulators and head-mounted displays.

Virtual experiences like Augmented Reality have proven to be commonplace in the lives of many gamers. The interplay of physiological, perceptual, and cognitive processes is evident among the different manifestations of GTP experiences. This is particularly important given the gradual proliferation of highly immersive technologies that are expected to amplify the effects of the GTP (Ortiz de Gortari, 2015).

CONCLUSION

Despite the increasing interest in recent years, there are still significant challenges for Augmented Reality applications to overcome. One of the most important factors hindering the development of Augmented Reality applications is ergonomic problems. Devices that are being developed in the field of wearable technologies such as augmented reality glasses, which have a much greater impact and efficiency compared to the limited interaction of mobile phones, struggle with a number of problems in terms of both hardware and accessibility on the ergonomic axis.

Pribeanu (2012) describes the ergonomics quality of augmented reality applications; it deals with 3 aspects on the axis of usability; ease of understanding, ease of learning how to operate, and ease of operating with a software system. In this case, physical, mental and software issues that affect usability should always be considered.

The most important physical problem is that the weight of augmented reality devices is not yet at an acceptable level. This weight reveals physical discomforts such as pain, dizziness and nausea in long-term use. This problem will begin to disappear as the sizes of components such as processor and ram, which are required for the conversion of HMD and glasses into image processing devices, become smaller.

The bridging feature of AR applications between the real and virtual worlds brings along many ergonomic mental problems. These AR experiences, which are much more "interesting" than real life, can cause addiction due to the level of immersion. The length of time users stay in the AR world will increase as wearable AR devices become more and more common in our lives. In fact, Game Transfer Phenomenon, which is the situation where virtual objects continue to be detected after leaving the augmented reality world, contains important determinations about this problem. (Ortiz de Gortari, 2017)

Finally, the interface design and software features of augmented reality applications can have a negative impact on the instinctive behavior of users. If the system does not warn the user of these dangers, it is very likely that unwanted accidents will occur. Security is a vital issue in placing users of Augmented Reality applications between the real and virtual world. In the perfect immersion experience, which is indistinguishable from the real, especially in theoretical matters, the user may think that real items are virtual. Such applications must be strictly controlled by security and various regulations.

Sharks in the Park (2016) is the first release of Geo AR Games' world's first geospatial Augmented Reality game for kids. By enclosing the real playground with virtual borders, it prevents children from encountering dangerous situations such as getting on the road. (Fig. 15).

Figure 15. Shark in the Park Game Warning Screen

Another problem regarding the accessibility of AR is the high prices of devices such as glasses and lenses, which offer a more immersive and high-quality experience. The main reason for this is hardware features such as high-capacity processors and display, which are mandatory to match the application with the real world.

The fact that Augmented Reality technologies still have a limited number and variety of content is one of the biggest challenges for society to realize its Augmented Reality use potential. Although face-altering applications such as Instagram filters, aging, and Snapchat are attracting a lot of attention, they provide a one-way experience that is far from gamification.

Augmented Reality for the gaming industry, which has accelerated in recent years, will not be limited to a few new technology use cases as in previous years. Augmented Reality will undoubtedly be everywhere and will touch every sector. Beyond its default application in the gaming and entertainment industries, Augmented Reality has groundbreaking potential in healthcare, education, marketing, business, as well as government and non-governmental sectors.

One of Azuma's (1997) predictions is that Augmented Reality applications are perceived as technological innovations that will replace employees in many companies. Augmented Reality can do a good job in this respect when it is designed as a tool to facilitate the user's work rather than a phenomenon that completely replaces the human worker. At this point, social and political concerns should not be ignored before many experimental applications reach the end-user.

In terms of future developments, the use of Augmented Reality environments that can allow collaborative and spatial learning everywhere through computer simulations, games, models, and virtual objects in real environments may become strongly widespread (Broll et al. 2008). 5G technology, especially in mobile-based Augmented Reality games, with shorter latency, less vibration, and less data loss, can bring the world closer together and provide a more realistic perception of real cloud gaming services.

A great development is observed around cloud computing and the Internet of Things. Average consumers own between five and eight mobile-connected devices. In the gaming world, this means that the number of devices that can be directly connected to the network, from smartwatches to Augmented Reality glasses will increase, the wire will be cut forever, and three-dimensional games will bring people much closer together. In addition, cloud network technology will significantly alleviate Augmented Reality devices, as it can solve the need for hardware with high processing power through remotely accessed powerful computers.

The next decade will begin to see some significant developments that will allow cloud computing and cloud-based Augmented Reality games to become more general opportunities for end-users and companies. With the development of Cloud Augmented Reality technology, it is expected that wearable Augmented Reality devices will be rapidly developed and become popular. The mobility demand of AR technology will increase immediately and the demand for 5G technology will grow.

In the future, Augmented Reality will reshape the way people interact with computers, such as holographic graphical user interfaces that will completely change the relationship between the real and digital worlds. Tilt Five AR (2021) is one of the prototypes for the future of Augmented Reality games. It transforms traditional tabletop games through the Augmented Reality and hologram approach, uniting all players at the same table regardless of location (Fig. 16).

Figure 16. Tilt Five AR (2021)
Source: www.tiltfive.com

Sheridan (1992) has asked "What do new technological interfaces add beyond the ways in which our imaginations (our mental models) have been mobilized by writers and artists for centuries, and how do they affect this emotion? His answers given to the questions also give us important clues about the future of Augmented Reality games. The first answer is the degree of sensory information, namely resolution, colors, sound quality, naturalness of movement, etc. elements are reaching new levels of reality that have never been before. Second, the player can control the actions in the game, react to certain changes in the environment and respond to stimuli created by the environment or expressions as simulated figures. Thirdly, the player can control not only his movements but also all the parameters of the virtual environment, so that he can even play against himself.

Artificial intelligence and the Internet of Things will play a major role in overcoming today's obstacles in terms of Augmented Reality games. Torres Vega et al. (2020) state that there are two challenges in combining AR/VR applications with the Internet of Things. Integration and management of direct connections between two AR/VR devices and the semantification of AR/VR data for its interoperability as offered by appropriate IoT platforms. Current peer-to-peer connections are far from allowing the management of both Iot and AR/VR devices. They also state that there is need for a holistic solution that combines data from traditional IoT devices (sensors) with AR/VR data in a single platform, combining semantic interoperability with state-of-the-art techniques for achieving a high quality of service at the connection layer. Applications that can perform more and more successful predictive analysis will be able to offer users much more reliable interactions through Augmented Reality devices. In addition, computer vision will increase human vision more than ever by analyzing real-world objects around the user more thoroughly.

REFERENCES

Alsawaier, R. (2018). The effect of gamification on motivation and engagement. *International Journal of Information and Learning Technology*, *35*(1), 56–79. doi:10.1108/IJILT-02-2017-0009

Azuma, R. T. (1997). A survey of augmented reality. *Presence (Cambridge, Mass.)*, *6*(4), 355–385. doi:10.1162/pres.1997.6.4.355

Barker, E. (2017). *Barking up the wrong tree: The surprising science behind why everything you know about success is (mostly) wrong*. HarperCollins.

Broll, W., Lindt, I., Herbst, I., Ohlenburg, J., Braun, A. K., & Wetzel, R. (2008). Toward next-gen mobile AR games. *IEEE Computer Graphics and Applications*, *28*(4), 40–48. doi:10.1109/MCG.2008.85

Broll, W., Ohlenburg, J., Lindt, I., Herbst, I., & Braun, A. K. (2006). Meeting technology challenges of pervasive augmented reality games. *Proc 5th ACM SIGCOMM Workshop Network System Support Games*, 28–39. 10.1145/1230040.1230097

Brumels, K. A., Blasius, T., Cortright, T., Daniel, O., & Brent, S. (2008). Comparison of efficacy between traditional and video game based balance programs. *Clin Kinesiol*, *62*, 26–31.

Csikszentmihalyi, M. (1990). *The psychology of optimal experience*. HarperCollins.

de Souza e Silva, A., & Delacruz, G. C. (2006). Hybrid reality games reframed: Potential uses in educational contexts. *Games and Culture*, *1*(3), 231–251. doi:10.1177/1555412006290443

Deci, E. L., & Ryan, R. M. (2000). The "what" and "why" of goal pursuits: Human needs and the self-determination of behavior. *Psychological Inquiry*, *11*(4), 227–268. doi:10.1207/S15327965PLI1104_01

Deterding, S., Dixon, D., Khaled, R., & Nacke, L. (2011). From game design elements to gamefulness: defining "Gamification". *15th International Academic MindTrek Conference*. 10.1145/2181037.2181040

Domingues, D. M., & Miranda, M. R. (2019). Affective presence in enactive immersive space: Sensorial and mobile technologies reengineering life. In E. Simão & C. Soares (Eds.), *Trends, Experiences, and Perspectives in Immersive Multimedia and Augmented Reality* (pp. 23–51). IGI Global. doi:10.4018/978-1-5225-5696-1.ch002

Emma-Ogbangwo, C., Cope, N., Behringer, R., & Fabri, M. (2014). Enhancing user immersion and virtual presence in interactive multiuser virtual environments through the development and integration of a gesture- centric natural user interface developed from existing virtual reality technologies. *HCI International*. https://bit.ly/3w5uzIn

Goerner, P. (2016). Augmented reality: What's next? *School Library Journal*, *62*(9), 19–20.

Ihde, D. (1993). *The philosophy of technology*. Paragon House.

Kapp, K. (2012). *The Gamification of Learning and Instruction: Game-based Methods and Strategies for Training and Education*. Pfeiffer.

Kasapakis, V., & Gavalas, D. (2017). Revisiting design guidelines for pervasive games. *International Journal of Pervasive Computing and Communications*, *13*(4), 386–407. doi:10.1108/IJPCC-D-17-00007

Laamarti, F., Eid, M., & Saddik, A. (2014). An overview of serious games. *International Journal of Computer Games Technology*, *2014*, 1–15. doi:10.1155/2014/358152

LaViola, J. A. Jr. (2000). Discussion of cybersickness in virtual environments. *SIGCHI Bulletin*, *32*(1), 47–56. doi:10.1145/333329.333344

Lombard, M., & Ditton, T. (1997). At the Heart of It All: The Concept of Presence. *Journal of Computer-Mediated Communication*, *3*(2), 0. Advance online publication. doi:10.1111/j.1083-6101.1997.tb00072.x

Ortiz de Gortari, A. B. (2015). What can game transfer phenomena tell us about the impact of highly immersive gaming technologies? In *Proceedings from ITAG'15:2015 International conference on interactive technologies and games* (pp. 84–89). 10.1109/iTAG.2015.15

Ortiz de Gortari, A. B. (2017). *Game Transfer Phenomena and the Augmented Reality Game Pokémon Go: The prevalence and the relation with benefits, risks, immersion and motivations*. 22nd Annual Cyber Psychology, Cyber Therapy & Social Networking.

Ortiz De Gortari, A. B., & Griffiths, M. (2017). Beyond the Boundaries of the Game: The Interplay Between In-Game Phenomena, Structural Characteristics of Video Games, and Game Transfer Phenomena. In Boundaries of Self and Reality Online. Academic Press.

Ortiz de Gortari, A. B., & Griffiths, M. D. (2014). Automatic mental processes, automatic actions and behaviours in game transfer phenomena: An empirical self-report study using online forum data. *International Journal of Mental Health and Addiction*, *12*(4), 432–452. doi:10.100711469-014-9476-3

Palladino, T. (2021). *Microsoft emerges from the trenches with more details behind the army edition of Hololens 2*. Retrieved from https://hololens.reality.news/news/microsoft-emerges-from-trenches-with-more-details-behind-army-edition-hololens-2-0384713/

Pribeanu, C. (2012). Specification and Validation of a Formative Index to Evaluate the Ergonomic Quality of an AR-based Educational Platform. *International Journal of Computers, Communications & Control*, 7(4), 721–732. doi:10.15837/ijccc.2012.4.1370

Riva, G., & Mantovani, F. (2012). Being There: Understanding the Feeling of Presence in a Synthetic Environment and Its Potential for Clinical Change. *Virtual Reality in Psychological, Medical and Pedagocical Applications. IntechOpen.*, 28. Advance online publication. doi:10.5772/46411

Robbins, M. B. (2016). The future of gaming. *Library Journal*, 141(15), 59.

Ryan, M. L. (1999). Immersion vs. interactivity: Virtual reality and literary theory. *SubStance*, 28(2), 110–137. doi:10.1353ub.1999.0015

Sheridan, T. B. (1992). Musings on telepresence and virtual presence. *Presence (Cambridge, Mass.)*, 1(1), 120–126. doi:10.1162/pres.1992.1.1.120

Shi, Y., & Shih, J. (2015). Game factors and game-based learning design model. *International Journal of Computer Games Technology. Article ID, 549684*, 1–11.

Spina, C. (2016). Libraries embrace Pokémon Go. *School Library Journal*, 62(8), 12–13.

Tian, Y., Guan, T., & Wang, C. (2010). Real-time occlusion handling in augmented reality based on an object tracking approach. *Sensors (Basel)*, 10(4), 2885–2900. doi:10.3390100402885 PMID:22319278

Tokuyama, Rajapakse, Yamabe, Konno, & Hung. (2019). A kinect-based augmented reality game for lower limb exercise. *Proc. - 2019 Int. Conf. Cyberworlds*, 399–402.

Torres Vega, M., Liaskos, C., Abadal, S., Papapetrou, E., Jain, A., Mouhouche, B., Kalem, G., Ergüt, S., Mach, M., Sabol, T., Cabellos-Aparicio, A., Grimm, C., De Turck, F., & Famaey, J. (2020). Immersive Interconnected Virtual and Augmented Reality: A 5G and IoT Perspective. *Journal of Network and Systems Management*, 28(4), 796–826. doi:10.100710922-020-09545-w

Werbach, K., & Hunter, D. (2012). *For the win: How game thinking can revolutionize your business.* Wharton Digital Press.

Zhu, Z., Yu, M., & Riezebos, P. (2016). A research framework of smart education. *Smart Learning Environments*, 3(1), 1–17. doi:10.118640561-016-0026-2

Compilation of References

Abegaz, T., Smatt, C., Oakley, R., & Freeman, M. (2019). Win Or Lose: A Study On The Effects Of Video Game Violence. *QRBD, 79.*

Abt, C. C. (1987). *Serious Games.* University Press of America.

Abu, A., Jusmawati, J., Makmur, Z., Jumliadi, J., & Yusuf, M. (2020). Problems Faced by IAIN Palu Students in Online Learning in the Middle of the COVID-19 Pandemic. *International Colloquium on Environmental Education (ICEE).*

Accord, L. M. S. (n.d.). *Accord LMS.* https://evaluate.accordlms.com/learning-management-system/

Adachi, P. J. C., & Willoughby, T. (2013). More than just fun and games: The longitudinal relationships between strategic video games, self reported problem solving skills, and academic grades. *Journal of Youth and Adolescence, 42*(7), 1041–1052. doi:10.100710964-013-9913-9 PMID:23344653

Adukaite, A., van Zyl, I., Er, Ş., & Cantoni, L. (2017). Teacher perceptions on the use of digital gamified learning in tourism education: The case of South African secondary schools. *Computers & Education, 111,* 172–190. doi:10.1016/j.compedu.2017.04.008

Agarwal, B., & Mittal, N. (2015). Machine Learning Approach for Sentiment Analysis. In B. Agarwal & N. Mittal (Eds.), *Prominent Feature Extraction for Sentiment Analysis.* Springer.

Aguiar-Castillo, L., Rufo-Torres, J., De Saa-Pérez, P., & Perez-Jimenez, R. (2018). How to Encourage Recycling Behaviour? The Case of WasteApp: A Gamified Mobile Application. *Journal Sustainability, 10*(5), 1544. doi:10.3390u10051544

Ajzen, I. (2012). Values, attitudes, and behavior. In *Methods, theories, and empirical applications in the social sciences* (pp. 33–38). VS Verlag für Sozialwissenschaften. doi:10.1007/978-3-531-18898-0_5

Alabbasi, D. (2018). Exploring Teachers' Perspectives towards Using Gamification Techniques in Online Learning. *Turkish Online Journal of Educational Technology-TOJET, 17*(2), 34–45.

Aldemir, T., Celik, B., & Kaplan, G. (2018). A qualitative investigation of student perceptions of game elements in a gamified course. *Computers in Human Behavior, 78,* 235–254. doi:10.1016/j.chb.2017.10.001

Aledo, S. G., & Gómez, R. C. (2016). GAMIFICATION: A NEW APPROACH FOR. *Human Resource Management, 60.*

Alharthi, S., & Parrish, J. (2017). The Role of Gamification in Motivating User Participation in Requirements Determinations. *Proceedings of the 12th SAIS, 7.*

Alkawsi, G. A., Ali, N., Mustafa, A. S., Baashar, Y., Alhussian, H., Alkahtani, A., Tiong, S. K., & Ekanayake, J. (2021a). A hybrid SEM-neural network method for identifying acceptance factors of the smart meters in Malaysia: Challenges perspective. *Alexandria Engineering Journal, 60*(1), 227–240. doi:10.1016/j.aej.2020.07.002

Alkawsi, G. A., & Baashar, Y. (2020). An empirical study of the acceptance of IoT-based smart meter in Malaysia: The effect of electricity-saving knowledge and environmental awareness. *IEEE Access: Practical Innovations, Open Solutions, 8*, 42794–42804. doi:10.1109/ACCESS.2020.2977060

Alkawsi, G., Ali, N. A., & Baashar, Y. (2021b). The Moderating Role of Personal Innovativeness and Users Experience in Accepting the Smart Meter Technology. *Applied Sciences (Basel, Switzerland), 11*(8), 3297. doi:10.3390/app11083297

Almeida, F., & Simoes, J. (2019). The Role of Serious Games, Gamification and Industry 4.0 Tools in the Education 4.0 Paradigm. *Contemporary Educational Technology, 10*(2), 120–136. doi:10.30935/cet.554469

Al-Okaily, A., Al-Okaily, M., Shiyyab, F., & Masadah, W. (2020). Accounting information system effectiveness from an organizational perspective. *Management Science Letters, 10*, 3991–4000. doi:10.5267/j.msl.2020.7.010

Alsawaier, R. (2018). The effect of gamification on motivation and engagement. *International Journal of Information and Learning Technology.* doi:10.1108/IJILT-02-2017-0009

Al-Tarawneh, J. M. (2019). Technology Acceptance Models and Adoption of Innovations: A Literature Review. *International Journal of Scientific Research, 9*(8), 833. doi:10.29322/IJSRP.9.08.2019.p92116

Altrabsheh, N., Gaber, M. M., & Cocea, M. (2013). Sentiment analytics for education. In *5th KES International Conference on Intelligent Decision Technologies (KES-IDT 2013).* Sesimbra, Portugal: IOS Press.

Alzahrani, M. G., & O'Toole, J. M. (2017). The Impact of Internet Experience and Attitude on Student Preference for Blended Learning. *Journal of Curriculum and Teaching, 6*(1), 65–78. doi:10.5430/jct.v6n1p65

Amini, P., Zahiri Motlagh, S. A., & Nezhadpour, M. (2018). A large-scale infrastructure for serious games services. *2018 2nd National and 1st International Digital Games Research Conference: Trends, Technologies, and Applications (DGRC),* 27-33. 10.1109/DGRC.2018.8712040

Amory, A. (2007). Game object model version II: A theoretical framework for educational game development. *Educational Technology Research and Development, 55*(1), 51–77. doi:10.100711423-006-9001-x

Amory, A., & Seagram, R. (2003). Educational game models: conceptualization and evaluation: the practice of higher education. *South African Journal of Higher Education, 17*(2), 206–217.

Anand, G., & Kodali, R. (2008). Benchmarking the benchmarking models. *Benchmarking, 15*(3), 257–291. doi:10.1108/14635770810876593

Anand, V. (2007). A study of time management: The correlation between video game usage and academic performance markers. *Cyberpsychology & Behavior, 10*(4), 552–559. doi:10.1089/cpb.2007.9991 PMID:17711364

Anderson, C. A., Shibuya, A., Ihori, N., Swing, E. L., Bushman, B. J., Sakamoto, A., Rothstein, H. R., & Saleem, M. (2010). Violent video game effects on aggression, empathy, and prosocial behavior in Eastern and Western countries: A meta-analytic review. *Psychological Bulletin, 136*(2), 151–173. doi:10.1037/a0018251 PMID:20192553

Anderson, L. W., & Krathwohl, D. R. (Eds.). (2001). *A taxonomy for learning, teaching, and assessing: A revision of Bloom's taxonomy of educational objectives.* Longman.

Antin, J., & Churchill, E. F. (2011). Badges in Social Media: A Social Psychological Perspective. In *Proceedings of ACM CHI Conference on Human Factors in Computing Systems.* (pp. 1-4). ACM.

Antonaci, A., Klemke, R., & Specht, M. (2019, September). The effects of gamification in online learning environments: A systematic literature review. In Informatics (Vol. 6, No. 3, p. 32). Multidisciplinary Digital Publishing Institute. doi:10.3390/informatics6030032

Appleton, J. J. Christenson, S. L, Kim, D., & Reschly, A. L. (2006). *Measuring cognitive and psychological engagement: Validation of the Student Engagement Instrument.* doi:10.1016/j.jsp.2006.04.002

Arjen van der Heide, A., & Želinský, D. (2021). 'Level up your money game': An analysis of gamification discourse in financial services. *Journal of Cultural Economics*, 1–21. Advance online publication. doi:10.1080/17530350.2021.1882537

Arslanian, H., & Fischer, F. (2019). *The Future of Finance: The Impact of FinTech, AI, and Crypto on Financial Services.* Palgrave Macmillan. doi:10.1007/978-3-030-14533-0

Ašeriškis, D., Blazauskas, T., & Damasevicius, R. (2017). UAREI: A model for formal description and visual representation/software gamification. *DYNA (Colombia)*, *84*(200), 326–334. doi:10.15446/dyna.v84n200.54017

Attali, Y., & Arieli-Attali, M. (2015). Gamification in assessment: Do points affect test performance? *Computers & Education*, *83*, 57–63. doi:10.1016/j.compedu.2014.12.012

Autry, A. J. Jr, & Berge, Z. (2011). Digital natives and digital immigrants: Getting to know each other. *Industrial and Commercial Training*, *43*(7), 460–466. doi:10.1108/00197851111171890

Axonify. (n.d.). *Axonify*. https://axonify.com/

Azuma, R. T. (1997). A survey of augmented reality. *Presence (Cambridge, Mass.)*, *6*(4), 355–385. doi:10.1162/pres.1997.6.4.355

Badgujar, K. C., Badgujar, A. B., Dhangar, D. V., & Badgujar, V. C. (2020). *Importance and use of pulse oximeter in COVID-19 pandemic: general factors affecting the sensitivity of pulse oximeter.* Indian Chemical Engineer. doi:10.1080/00194506.2020.1845988

Baisheva, M., Golikov, A., Prokopieva, M., Popova, L., Zakharova, A., & Kovtun, T. (2017). The potential of folk tabletop games in the development of the intelligence and creativity of children. *Journal of Social Studies Education Research*, *8*(3), 128–138.

Baptista, G., & Oliveira, T. (2017). Why so serious? Gamification impact in the acceptance of mobile banking services. *Internet Research*, *27*(1), 118–139. doi:10.1108/IntR-10-2015-0295

Barker, E. (2017). *Barking up the wrong tree: The surprising science behind why everything you know about success is (mostly) wrong.* HarperCollins.

Barna, B., & Fodor, S. (2019). A Data-Driven Approach to Analyze User Behavior on a Personalized Gamification Platform. In *International Conference on Games and Learning Alliance.* Springer. 10.1007/978-3-030-34350-7_26

Barrett, L. F., Lindquist, K. A., & Gendron, M. (2007). Language as context for the perception of emotion. *Trends in Cognitive Sciences*, *11*(8), 327–332. doi:10.1016/j.tics.2007.06.003 PMID:17625952

Barrett, M., Boyne, J., Brandts, J., Brunner-La Rocca, H.-P., De Maesschalck, L., De Wit, K., Dixon, L., Eurlings, C., Fitzsimons, D., Golubnitschaja, O., Hageman, A., Heemskerk, F., Hintzen, A., Helms, T. M., Hill, L., Hoedemakers, T., Marx, N., McDonald, K., Mertens, M., ... Zippel-Schultz, B. (2020). Artificial intelligence supported patient self-care in chronic heart failure: A paradigm shift from reactive to predictive, preventive and personalised care. *The EPMA Journal*, *10*(4), 445–464. doi:10.100713167-019-00188-9 PMID:31832118

Barr, M. (2017). Video games can develop graduate skills in higher education students: A randomised trial. *Computers & Education*, *113*, 86–97. doi:10.1016/j.compedu.2017.05.016

Barr, M. (2018). Student attitudes to games-based skills development: Learning from video games in higher education. *Computers in Human Behavior*, *80*, 283–294. doi:10.1016/j.chb.2017.11.030

Bartle, R. (1996). Hearts, clubs, diamonds, spades: Players who suit MUDs. *Journal of MUD Research, 1*(1), 19.

Bartle, R. (1996). Hearts, clubs, diamonds, spades: Players who suit MUDs. *Journal of MUD Research, 1*(1).

Bateman, J., Allen, M. E., Kidd, J., Parsons, N., & Davies, D. (2012). Virtual patients design and its effect on clinical reasoning and student experience: A protocol for a randomised factorial multi-center study. *BMC Medical Education, 12*(1), 62. Advance online publication. doi:10.1186/1472-6920-12-62 PMID:22853706

Bawa, P. (2019). Using Kahoot to Inspire. *Journal of Educational Technology Systems, 47*(3), 373-390. doi:10.1177/0047239518804173

Bayuk, J., & Altobello, S. A. (2019). Can gamification improve financial behavior? The moderating role of app expertise. *International Journal of Bank Marketing, 37*(4), 951–975. doi:10.1108/IJBM-04-2018-0086

Bellotti, F., Kapralos, B., Lee, K., Moreno-Ger, P., & Berta, R. (2013). Assessment in and of Serious Games: An Overview. *Advances in Human-Computer Interaction, 2013*, 11. doi:10.1155/2013/136864

Beranuy, M., Chamarro, A., Graner, C., & Carbonell, X. (2009). Validación de dos escalas breves para evaluar la adicción a Internet y el abuso de móvil. *Psicothema, 21*, 480–485.

Bergmann, J., & McGregor, A. (2011). Body-worn sensor design: What do patients and clinicians want? *Annals of Biomedical Engineering, 39*(9), 2299–2312. doi:10.100710439-011-0339-9 PMID:21674260

Biddiss, E., & Irwin, J. (2010). Active video games to promote physical activity in children and youth: A systematic review. *Archives of Pediatrics & Adolescent Medicine, 164*(7), 664–672. PMID:20603468

Bioulac, S., Arfi, L., & Bouvard, M. P. (2008). Attention deficit/hyperactivity disorder and video games: A comparative study of hyperactive and control children. *European Psychiatry, 23*(2), 134–141. doi:10.1016/j.eurpsy.2007.11.002 PMID:18206354

Bird, D. (2021). *Game on: the potential for gamification in asset management.* https://www.lifesight.com/ire/latest-news/game-on-the-potential-for-gamification-in-asset-management

Bíró, G. I. (2014). Didactics 2.0: A pedagogical analysis of gamification theory from a comparative perspective with a special view to the components of learning. *Social and Behavioral Sciences, 141*, 148–151.

Blunt, R. (2009, December). *Do Serious Games Work? Results from Three Studies.* Retrieved from eLearn Magazine: https://elearnmag.acm.org/archive.cfm?aid=1661378&doi=10.1145%2F1661377.1661378

Bobokhujaev, S. I. (2019). The role of ICT and the problems of organizing distance education in Uzbekistan. *2019 International Conference on Information Science and Communications Technologies (ICISCT)*, 1-4. 10.1109/ICISCT47635.2019.9011876

Bonvin, G., & Sanchez, E. (2017). Social Engagement in a Digital Role-Playing Game Dedicated to Classroom Management. In J. Dias, P. Santos, & R. Veltkamp (Eds.), Lecture Notes in Computer Science: Vol. 10653. *Games and Learning Alliance. GALA.* Springer. doi:10.1007/978-3-319-71940-5_13

Boot, W. R., Kramer, A. F., Simons, D. J., Fabiani, M., & Gratton, G. (2008). The effects of video game playing on attention, memory, and executive control. *Acta Psychologica, 129*(3), 387–398. doi:10.1016/j.actpsy.2008.09.005 PMID:18929349

Bower, G. H. (1992). How Might Emotions Affect Learning? In S. Å. Christianson (Ed.), *The Handbook Of Emotion And Memory.* Lawrence Erlbaum Associates.

Breidbach, C. F., Keating, B. W., & Lim, C. (2019). Fintech: Research directions to explore the digital transformation of financial service systems. *Journal of Service Theory and Practice, 30*(1), 79–102. doi:10.1108/JSTP-08-2018-0185

Breiman, L. (2001). Random forests. *Machine Learning, 45*(1), 5–32. doi:10.1023/A:1010933404324

Broeckhoven, F., & Troyer, O. (2013). ATTAC-L: A modeling language for educational virtual scenarios in the context of preventing cyber bullying. *2013 IEEE 2nd International Conference on Serious Games and Applications for Health (SeGAH)*, 1-8. 10.1109/SeGAH.2013.6665300

Broll, W., Lindt, I., Herbst, I., Ohlenburg, J., Braun, A. K., & Wetzel, R. (2008). Toward next-gen mobile AR games. *IEEE Computer Graphics and Applications, 28*(4), 40–48. doi:10.1109/MCG.2008.85

Broll, W., Ohlenburg, J., Lindt, I., Herbst, I., & Braun, A. K. (2006). Meeting technology challenges of pervasive augmented reality games. *Proc 5th ACM SIGCOMM Workshop Network System Support Games*, 28–39. 10.1145/1230040.1230097

Brooke, J. (1996). *SUS-A quick and dirty usability scale. Usability evaluation in industry.* CRC Press.

Brownlee, J. (2018, December 3). *A Gentle Introduction to Dropout for Regularizing Deep Neural Networks.* Retrieved from Machine Learning Mastery: https://machinelearningmastery.com/dropout-for-regularizing-deep-neural-networks/

Brumels, K. A., Blasius, T., Cortright, T., Daniel, O., & Brent, S. (2008). Comparison of efficacy between traditional and video game based balance programs. *Clin Kinesiol, 62*, 26–31.

Buabeng-Andoh, C. (2018). Predicting students' intention to adopt mobile learning: A combination of theory of reasoned action and technology acceptance model. *Journal of Research in Innovative Teaching & Learning.*

Buelow, M. T., Okdie, B. M., & Cooper, A. B. (2015). The influence of video games on executive functions in college students. *Computers in Human Behavior, 45*, 228–234. doi:10.1016/j.chb.2014.12.029

Buhagiar, T., & Leo, C. (2018). Does Gamification Improve Academic Performance? *Journal of Instructional Pedagogies, 20.*

Cabada, R. Z., Estrada, M. L. B., Hernández, F. G., Bustillos, R. O., & Reyes-García, C. A. (2018). An affective and Web 3.0-based learning environment for a programming language. *Telematics and Informatics, 35*(3), 611–628. doi:10.1016/j.tele.2017.03.005

Cabestany, J., Rodriguez-Martín, D., Pérez, C., & Sama, A. (2018). Artificial Intelligence Contribution to eHealth Application. In *Proceedings of 25th International Conference "Mixed Design of Integrated Circuits and System" (MIXDES)* (pp. 15-21). 10.23919/MIXDES.2018.8436743

Cable, J., & Cheung, C. (2017). Eight principles of effective online teaching: A decade-long lessons learned in project management education. *PM World Journal, 6*(7), 1–16.

Calantone, R. J., Chan, K., & Cui, A. S. (2006). Decomposing product innovativeness and its effects on new product success. *Journal of Product Innovation Management, 23*(5), 408–421. doi:10.1111/j.1540-5885.2006.00213.x

Camacho Vásquez, G., & Camilo Ovalle, J. (2019). The Influence of Video Games on Vocabulary Acquisition in a Group of Students from the BA in English Teaching. *GIST: Education & Learning Research Journal*, (19).

Canadian Red Cross. (2021). *In Exile For A While.* Retrieved April 30, 2018, from https://www.redcross.ca/cmslib/general/inexileforawhilekit.pdf

Carbo-Valverde, S., Cuadros-Solas, P., & Rodríguez-Fernández, F. (2020). A machine learning approach to the digitalization of bank customers: Evidence from random and causal forests. *PLoS One, 15*(10), e0240362. Advance online publication. doi:10.1371/journal.pone.0240362 PMID:33112894

Castro, M., Martínez, A., Zurita, F., Chacón, R., Espejo, T., & Cabrera, A. (2015). Uso de videojuegos y su relación con las conductas sedentarias en una población escolar y universitaria. *Journal for Educators, Teachers and Trainers*, *6*(1), 40–51.

Castro-Sánchez, M., Rojas-Jiménez, M., Zurita-Ortega, F., & Chacón-Cuberos, R. (2019). Multidimensional Self-Concept and Its Association with Problematic Use of Video Games in Spanish College Students. *Education Sciences*, *9*(3), 206. doi:10.3390/educsci9030206

Centieiro, P., Romão, T., & Dias, A. E. (2011). A Location-Based Multiplayer Mobile Game to Encourage Pro-Environmental Behaviours. *Proceedings of the 8th International Conference on Advances in Computer Entertainment Technology (ACE 2011)*.

Chacón Cuberos, R., Ortega, F. Z., Sánchez, M. C., & Espejo, T. (2018). The association of Self-concept with Substance Abuse and Problematic Use of Video Games in University Students: A Structural Equation Model Relación entre autoconcepto, consumo de sustancias y uso problemático de videojuegos en universitarios. *Adicciones*, *30*(3), 179–188. PMID:28492955

Chacón Cuberos, R., Zurita Ortega, F., Martínez Martínez, A., Castro Sánchez, M., Espejo Garcés, T., & Pinel Martínez, C. (2017). Relación entre factores académicos y consumo de videojuegos en universitarios. Un modelo de regresión. *Pixel-Bit. Revista de Medios y Educación*, *50*, 109–121.

Chamarro, A., Carbonell, X., Manresa, J. M., Munoz-Miralles, R., Ortega-Gonzalez, R., Lopez-Morron, M. R., Batalla-Martinez, C., & Toran-Monserrat, P. (2014). El Cuestionario de Experiencias Relacionadas con los Videojuegos (CERV): Un instrumento para detectar el uso problemático de videojuegos en adolescentes españoles. *Adicciones*, *26*(4), 303–311. doi:10.20882/adicciones.31 PMID:25578001

Chang, V., & Guetl, C. (2010). Generation Y Learning in the 21st Century: Integration of Virtual Worlds and Cloud Computing Services. In *Proceedings of Global Learn Asia Pacific 2010 –Global Conference on Learning and Technology* (vol. 1, pp. 1888-1897). Association for the Advancement of Computing in Education (AACE).

Chao, C. M. (2019). Factors determining the behavioral intention to use mobile learning: An application and extension of the UTAUT model. *Frontiers in Psychology*, *10*, 1652. doi:10.3389/fpsyg.2019.01652 PMID:31379679

Charness, N., & Boot, W. R. (2016). Technology, Gaming, and Social Networking. In Handbook of the Psychology of Aging (8th ed.). Academic Press.

Charrupi, L., Truquez Larrahondo, C. A., & Alexis, J. (2019). *Estrategias de aprendizaje para la construcción de herramientas tecnológicas implementando la plataforma educativa Educaplay*. https://repository.usc.edu.co/handle/20.500.12421/4271

Chen, C. Y., Shih, B. Y., & Yu, S. H. (2012). Disaster prevention and reduction for exploring teachers' technology acceptance using a virtual reality system and partial least squares techniques. *Natural Hazards*, *62*(3), 1217–1231. doi:10.100711069-012-0146-0

Cherry, S. (2017). *Transforming behaviour: Pro-social modelling in practice*. Taylor & Francis. doi:10.4324/9781315084633

Chiu, S.-I., Lee, J.-Z., & Huang, D.-H. (2004). Video game addiction in children and teenagers in Taiwan. *Cyberpsychology & Behavior*, *7*(5), 571–581. doi:10.1089/cpb.2004.7.571 PMID:15667052

Choi, B., Hwang, S., & Lee, S. (2017). What drives construction workers' acceptance of wearable technologies in the workplace? Indoor localization and wearable health devices for occupational safety and health. *Automation in Construction*, *84*, 31–41. doi:10.1016/j.autcon.2017.08.005

Choi, R. Y., Coyner, A. S., Kalpathy-Cramer, J., Chiang, M. F., & Campbell, J. P. (2020). Introduction to Machine Learning, Neural Networks, and Deep Learning. *Translational Vision Science & Technology*, *9*(2), 14. doi:10.1167/tvst.9.2.14 PMID:32704420

Chong, D. Y. K. (2019). Benefits and challenges with gamified multi-media physiotherapy case studies: A mixed method study. *Archives of Physiotherapy*, *9*(1), 1–11. doi:10.118640945-019-0059-2 PMID:31139434

Chou, Y. (2015). *Actionable gamification - beyond points, badges, and leaderboards. Technical report*. Octalysis Media.

CodeCombat. (2021). *Code Combat*. Retrieved from https://codecombat.com/

Coelho, A., Kato, E., Xavier, J., & Gonçalves, R. (2011). Serious game for introductory programming. In *International Conference on Serious Games Development and Applications* (pp. 61-71). Lisbon, Portugal: Springer. 10.1007/978-3-642-23834-5_6

Cohen, S. (2021). The basics of machine learning: strategies and techniques. In S. Cohen (Ed.), *Artificial Intelligence and Deep Learning in Pathology* (pp. 13–40). Elsevier. doi:10.1016/B978-0-323-67538-3.00002-6

Columbus, L. (2020). *The State of AI Adoption in Financial Services*. https://www.forbes.com/sites/louiscolumbus/2020/10/31/the-state-of-ai-adoption-in-financial-services/?sh=396e24702aac

Connolly, T., Boyle, E., MacArthur, E., Hainey, T., & Boyle, J. (2012). A systematic literature review of empirical evidence on computer games and serious games. *Computers & Education*, *59*(2), 661–686. doi:10.1016/j.compedu.2012.03.004

Consorti, F., Mancuso, R., Nocioni, M., & Piccolo, A. (2012). Efficacy of virtual patients in medical education: A meta-analysis of randomized studies. *Computers & Education*, *59*(3), 1001–1008. doi:10.1016/j.compedu.2012.04.017

Cook, D. A., & Triola, M. M. (2009, April). Virtual patients: A critical literature review and proposed next steps. *Medical Education*, *43*(4), 303–311. doi:10.1111/j.1365-2923.2008.03286.x PMID:19335571

Copenhaver, A. (2020). Violent Video Games as Scapegoat After School Shootings in the United States. In *Handbook of Research on Mass Shootings and Multiple Victim Violence* (pp. 243–266). IGI Global. doi:10.4018/978-1-7998-0113-9.ch014

Cowan, B., & Kapralos, B. (2014). A Survey of Frameworks and Game Engines for Serious Game Development. In *2014 IEEE 14th International Conference on Advanced Learning Technologies*. Athens: IEEE.

Crawford, C. (1984). *The Art of Computer Game Design*. McGraw-Hill, Inc.

Cruz-Cunha, M. M. (2012). *Handbook of Research on Serious Games as Educational, Business and Research Tools*. IGI Global. doi:10.4018/978-1-4666-0149-9

Csíkszentmihályi, M. (1975). *Beyond Boredom and Anxiety: Experiencing Flow in Work and Play*. Jossey-Bass.

Csikszentmihalyi, M. (1990). *The psychology of optimal experience*. HarperCollins.

Darden, C. A., Ginter, E. J., & Gazda, G. M. (1996). Life-skills development scale – adolescent form: The theoretical and therapeutic relevance of life-skills. *Journal of Mental Health Counseling*, *18*, 142–163.

Das, P. (2017). *Gamification in Financial Services: An Interesting Approach to Connect To the Financial World*. https://www.hcltech.com/blogs/gamification-financial-services-interesting-approach-connect-financial-world

Davenport, T., & Kalakota, R. (2019). The Potential for Artificial Intelligence in Healthcare. *Future Healthcare Journal*, *6*(2), 94–98. doi:10.7861/futurehosp.6-2-94 PMID:31363513

Davis, F. D. (1989). Perceived usefulness, perceived ease of use, and user acceptance of information technology. *Management Information Systems Quarterly, 13*(3), 319–340. doi:10.2307/249008

Davis, F. D., Bagozzi, R. P., & Warshaw, P. R. (1989). User acceptance of computer technology: A comparison of two theoretical models. *Management Science, 35*(8), 982–1003. doi:10.1287/mnsc.35.8.982

de Aldama, C., & Pozo, J.-I. (2020). Do you want to learn physics? please play angry birds (but with epistemic goals). *Journal of Educational Computing Research, 58*(1), 3–28. doi:10.1177/0735633118823160

De Freitas, S., & Jarvis, S. (2009). Towards a development approach to serious games. In T. Connolly, M. Stansfield, & L. Boyle (Eds.), Games-based learning advancements for multi-sensory human computer interfaces: Techniques and effective practices (pp. 215-231). IGI Global. doi:10.4018/978-1-60566-360-9.ch013

de Freitas, S., & Jarvis, S. (2008). Towards a development approach for serious games. In T. Connolly, M. Stansfield, & E. Boyle (Eds.), *Games-based learning advancements for multi-sensory human-computer interfaces: Techniques and effective practices* (pp. 215–231). IGI Global.

De Freitas, S., & Liarokapis, F. (2011). Serious games: a new paradigm for education? In M. Ma, A. Oikonomou, & L. Jain (Eds.), *Serious Games and Edutainment Applications* (pp. 9–23). Springer. doi:10.1007/978-1-4471-2161-9_2

De Freitas, S., & Oliver, M. (2006). How can exploratory learning with games and simulations within the curriculum be most effectively evaluated? *Computers & Education, 46*(3), 249–264. doi:10.1016/j.compedu.2005.11.007

de la Peña, D., Lizcano, D., & Martínez-Álvarez, I. (2021). Learning through play: Gamification model in university-level distance learning. *Entertainment Computing, 39*, 100430. doi:10.1016/j.entcom.2021.100430

de Souza e Silva, A., & Delacruz, G. C. (2006). Hybrid reality games reframed: Potential uses in educational contexts. *Games and Culture, 1*(3), 231–251. doi:10.1177/1555412006290443

Deci, E. L., & Ryan, R. M. (2000). The "what" and "why" of goal pursuits: Human needs and the self-determination of behavior. *Psychological Inquiry, 11*(4), 227–268. doi:10.1207/S15327965PLI1104_01

Deci, E. L., & Ryan, R. M. (2002). Overview of self-determination theory: An organismic-dialectical perspective. In E. L. Deci & R. M. Ryan (Eds.), *Handbook of self-determination research* (pp. 3–33). University of Rochester Press.

Deeb, L. C., Parkes, J. L., Pardo, S., Schachner, H. C., Viggiani, M. T., Wallace, J., & Bailey, T. (2011). Performance of the DIDGET blood glucose monitoring system in children, teens, and young adults. *Journal of Diabetes Science Technology, 5*(5), 1157-63. doi:10.1177/193229681100500518

De-Marcos, L., Domínguez, A., Saenz-de-Navarrete, J., & Pagés, C. (2014). An empirical study comparing gamification and social networking on e-learning. *Computers & Education, 75*, 82–91. doi:10.1016/j.compedu.2014.01.012

Demkah, M., & Bhargava, D. (2019). Gamification in Education: A Cognitive Psychology Approach to Cooperative and Fun Learning. In *Proceedings of the Amity International Conference on Artificial Intelligence (AICAI)* (pp. 170-174). 10.1109/AICAI.2019.8701264

Deterding, S., Dixon, D., Khaled, R., & Nacke, L. (2011, September). From game design elements to gamefulness: defining "gamification". In *Proceedings of the 15th international academic MindTrek conference: Envisioning future media environments* (pp. 9-15). Academic Press.

Deterding, S., Dixon, D., Khaled, R., & Nacke, L. (2011). From Game Design Elements to Gamefulness: Defining "Gamification". In *Proceedings of the 15th International Academic MindTrek Conference: Envisioning Future Media Environments* (pp. 9–15). 10.1145/2181037.2181040

Deterding, S., Sicart, M., Nacke, L., O'Hara, K., & Dixon, D. (2011, May). Gamification: Toward a definition. *Proceedings of the CHI 2011 Gamification Workshop.*

Dethe, A. (2020). *Adding a game to banking.* https://bfsi.economictimes.indiatimes.com/news/editors-view/adding-a-game-to-banking/74387956

Díaz-Ramírez, J. (2020). Gamification in engineering education–An empirical assessment on learning and game performance. *Heliyon, 6*(9), e04972. doi:10.1016/j.heliyon.2020.e04972 PMID:32995639

Dickerman, C., Christensen, J., & Kerl-McClain, S. B. (2008). Big breasts and bad guys: Depictions of gender and race in video games. *Journal of Creativity in Mental Health, 3*(1), 20–29. doi:10.1080/15401380801995076

Dishaw, M. T., & Strong, D. M. (1999). Extending the technology acceptance model with task–technology fit constructs. *Information & Management, 36*(1), 9–21. doi:10.1016/S0378-7206(98)00101-3

Domingues, D. M., & Miranda, M. R. (2019). Affective presence in enactive immersive space: Sensorial and mobile technologies reengineering life. In E. Simão & C. Soares (Eds.), *Trends, Experiences, and Perspectives in Immersive Multimedia and Augmented Reality* (pp. 23–51). IGI Global. doi:10.4018/978-1-5225-5696-1.ch002

Domínguez, A., de Navarrete, J. S., de Marcos, L., Fernández-Sanz, L., Pagés, C., & Martínez-Herráiz, J.-J. (2013). Gamifying learning experiences: Practical implications and outcomes. *Computers & Education, 63*, 380–392. doi:10.1016/j.compedu.2012.12.020

Dragomir, C. C., & Munteanu, A. (2020). Impact of online education on economic students' professional training in the context of Covid-19 pandemic. *Review of General Management, 31*(1).

Drummond, A., & Sauer, J. D. (2014). Video-games do not negatively impact adolescent academic performance in science, mathematics or reading. *PloS One, 9*(4).

El-Gayar, O. F., Ambati, L. S., & Nawar, N. (2020). Wearables, Artificial intelligence, and the Future of Healthcare. In M. Strydom & S. Buckley (Eds.), *AI and Big Data's Potential for Disruptive Innovation* (pp. 104–129). IGI Global. doi:10.4018/978-1-5225-9687-5.ch005

Emma-Ogbangwo, C., Cope, N., Behringer, R., & Fabri, M. (2014). Enhancing user immersion and virtual presence in interactive multiuser virtual environments through the development and integration of a gesture- centric natural user interface developed from existing virtual reality technologies. *HCI International.* https://bit.ly/3w5uzIn

Faddoul, B. (2016). Gamification and Health Literacy. In D. Novák, B. Tulu, & H. Brendryen (Eds.), *Handbook of Research on Holistic Perspectives in Gamification for Clinical Practice* (pp. 35–46). IGI Global. doi:10.4018/978-1-4666-9522-1.ch003

Fagan, M. H., Neill, S., & Wooldridge, B. R. (2008). Exploring the intention to use computers: An empirical investigation of the role of intrinsic motivation, extrinsic motivation, and perceived ease of use. *Journal of Computer Information Systems, 48*(3), 31–37.

Fathali, S., & Okada, T. (2018). Technology acceptance model in technology-enhanced OCLL contexts: A self-determination theory approach. *Australasian Journal of Educational Technology, 34*(4). Advance online publication. doi:10.14742/ajet.3629

Ferguson, C. J. (2007). The good, the bad and the ugly: A meta-analytic review of positive and negative effects of violent video games. *The Psychiatric Quarterly, 78*(4), 309–316. doi:10.100711126-007-9056-9 PMID:17914672

Ferguson, C. J. (2011). The influence of television and video game use on attention and school problems: A multivariate analysis with other risk factors controlled. *Journal of Psychiatric Research*, *45*(6), 808–813. doi:10.1016/j.jpsychires.2010.11.010 PMID:21144536

Ferguson, C. J., & Wang, J. C. K. (2019). Aggressive video games are not a risk factor for future aggression in youth: A longitudinal study. *Journal of Youth and Adolescence*, *48*(8), 1439–1451. doi:10.100710964-019-01069-0 PMID:31273603

FernandesD.LynchJ. G.NetemeyerR. G. (2014). Financial Literacy, Financial Education and Downstream Financial Behaviors. *Management Science*. https://ssrn.com/abstract=2333898

Floryan, M., Chow, P. I., Schueller, S. M., & Ritterband, L. M. (2020). The Model of Gamification Principles for Digital Health Interventions: Evaluation of Validity and Potential Utility. *Journal of Medical Internet Research, 22*(6), e16506. https://www.jmir.org/2020/6/e16506 doi:10.2196/16506

Fogg, B. J. (1998). Persuasive computers: Perspectives and research directions. *Conference on Human Factors in Computing Systems – Proceedings*, 225–232.

Fong, C., Ooi, K., Tan, B., Lee, V., & Yee-Loong Chong, A. (2011). HRM practices and knowledge sharing: An empirical study. *International Journal of Manpower*, *32*(5/6), 704–723. doi:10.1108/01437721111158288

Forsberg, E., Georg, C., Ziegert, K., & Fors, U. (2011). Virtual patients for assessment of clinical reasoning in nursing - A pilot study. *Nurse Education Today*, *31*(8), 757–762. doi:10.1016/j.nedt.2010.11.015 PMID:21159412

Franco, A. A. (2013). El uso de la tecnología: Determinación del tiempo que los jóvenes de entre 12 y 18 años dedican a los equipos tecnológicos. *RIED*, *16*(2), 107–125.

Fulton, J. N. (2019). *Theory of Gamification – Motivation* (PhD dissertation). William Howard Taft University.

Fuster, H., Chamarro, A., Carbonell, X., & Vallerand, R. J. (2014). Relationship between Passion and Motivation for Gaming in Massively Multiplayer Online Role-Playing Games. *Cyberpsychology, Behavior, and Social Networking*, *17*(5), 292–297. doi:10.1089/cyber.2013.0349 PMID:24611801

Gachkova, M., & Somova, E. (2016). Game Approach e-learning. In *Proceedings of IX National Conference Education and Research in Information Society*. (pp. 143-152). Institute of Mathematics and Informatics, Bulgarian Academy of Sciences.

Gachkova, M., & Somova, E. (2019). Plug-in for creation of gamified courses in the e-learning environment Moodle. *IOP Conference Series. Materials Science and Engineering*, *618*(012079), 1–7. doi:10.1088/1757-899X/618/1/012079

Gachkova, M., & Somova, E. (2020). Moodle plug-ins for design and development of gamified courses. In *Proceedings of 14th Annual International Technology, Education and Development Conference – INTED'2020*. (pp. 2187-2195). IATED Digital Library. 10.21125/inted.2020.0676

Gachkova, M., Somova, E., & Gaftandzhieva, S. (2020). Gamification of learning course in the e-learning environment. *IOP Conference Series. Materials Science and Engineering*, *878*(012035), 1–9.

Gachkova, M., Takev, M., & Somova, E. (2018). Learning and Assessment Based on Gamified e-Course in Moodle. *Journal Mathematics and Informatics*, *61*(5), 444–454.

Gaggi, O., Meneghello, F., Palazzi, C., & Pante, G. (2020). Learning how to recycle waste using a game. *Proceedings of the 6th EAI International Conference on Smart Objects and Technologies for Social Good*, 144-149. 10.1145/3411170.3411251

García, F., & Musitu, G. (1999). *Autoconcepto forma 5*. Madrid: Tea.

Garcia, M. B. (2017). E-Learning Technology Adoption in the Philippines: An Investigation of Factors Affecting Filipino College Students' Acceptance of Learning Management Systems. *The International Journal of E-Learning and Educational Technologies in the Digital Media*, 3(3), 118–130. doi:10.17781/P002374

Garcia-Ruiz, M., Tashiro, J., Kapralos, B., & Martin, M. (2011). Crouching Tangents, Hidden Danger: Assessing Development of Dangerous Misconceptions within Serious Games for Healthcare Education. In *Gaming and Simulations: Concepts, Methodologies, Tools and Applications* (pp. 1712–1749). Information Resources Management Association. doi:10.4018/978-1-60960-195-9.ch704

Gee, J. P. (2005). Learning by design: Good video games as learning machines. *E-learning*, 2(1), 5–16.

Gentile, D. A., Choo, H., Liau, A., Sim, T., Li, D., Fung, D., & Khoo, A. (2011). Pathological video game use among youths: A two-year longitudinal study. *Pediatrics*, 127(2), e319–e329. doi:10.1542/peds.2010-1353 PMID:21242221

Gentile, D. A., Swing, E. L., Lim, C. G., & Khoo, A. (2012). Video game playing, attention problems, and impulsiveness: Evidence of bidirectional causality. *Psychology of Popular Media Culture*, 1(1), 62–70. doi:10.1037/a0026969

Giannakis, K., Chorianopoulos, K., & Jaccheri, M. L. (2013). User requirements for gamifying sports software. In *Proceedings of 2013 3rd International Workshop on Games and Software Engineering: Engineering Computer Games to Enable Positive, Progressive Change (GAS)* (pp. 22-26). Academic Press.

Giannakos, M. N., Chorianopoulos, K., Jaccheri, L., & Chrisochoides, N. (2012). *This game is girly!" Perceived enjoyment and learner acceptance of edutainment. In Edutainment 2012/GameDays 2012.* Springer.

Gikas, J., & Grant, M. M. (2013). Mobile computing devices in higher education: Student perspectives on learning with cellphones, smartphones & social media. *The Internet and Higher Education*, 19, 18–26. doi:10.1016/j.iheduc.2013.06.002

Gloria, A., Bellotti, F., & Berta, R. (2014). Serious Games for education and training. *International Journal of Serious Games*, 1(1). Advance online publication. doi:10.17083/ijsg.v1i1.11

Glover, I. (2013, June). Play as you learn: gamification as a technique for motivating learners. In Edmedia+ innovate learning (pp. 1999-2008). Association for the Advancement of Computing in Education (AACE).

Gnauk, B., Dannecker, L., & Hahmann, B. (2012). Leveraging gamification in demand dispatch systems. In *EDBT-ICDT '12: Proceedings of the 2012 Joint EDBT/ICDT Workshops* (pp. 103-110). ACM Digital Library.

Godsay, M. (2015). The Process of Sentiment Analysis: A Study. *International Journal of Computer Applications*.

Goerner, P. (2016). Augmented reality: What's next? *School Library Journal*, 62(9), 19–20.

Goethe, O. (2019). *Gamification Mindset*. Springer International Publishing. doi:10.1007/978-3-030-11078-9

Gómez-Rodríguez, A., González-Moreno, J., Ramos-Valcárcel, D., & Vázquez-López, L. (2011). Modeling serious games using AOSE methodologies. *11th International Conference on Intelligent Systems Design and Applications (ISDA)*, 53-58.

Gonçalves, P., Araújo, M., Benevenuto, F., & Cha, M. (2013). Comparing and combining Sentiment analytics methods. ACM conference on Online Social Networks, 27-38.

Goodhue, D. L., & Thompson, R. L. (1995). Task-technology fit and individual performance. *Management Information Systems Quarterly*, 19(2), 213–236. doi:10.2307/249689

Gordon, S., Todder, D., Deutsch, I., Garbi, D., Alkobi, O., Shriki, O., Shkedy-Rabani, A., Shahar, N., & Meiran, N. (2019). Effects of neurofeedback and working memory-combined training on executive functions in healthy young adults. *Psychological Research*, 1–24. doi:10.100700426-019-01170-w PMID:31053887

Graafland, M., Schraagen, J., & Schijven, M. (2012). Systematic review of serious games for medical education and surgical skills training. *British Journal of Surgery*, *99*(10), 1322–1330. doi:10.1002/bjs.8819 PMID:22961509

Granic, I., Lobel, A., & Engels, R. C. M. E. (2014). The benefits of playing video games. *The American Psychologist*, *69*(1), 66–78. doi:10.1037/a0034857 PMID:24295515

Green, C. S., & Bavelier, D. (2007). Action-video-game experience alters the spatial resolution of vision. *Psychological Science*, *18*(1), 88–94. doi:10.1111/j.1467-9280.2007.01853.x PMID:17362383

Green, C. S., & Bavelier, D. (2012). Learning, attentional control, and action video games. *Current Biology*, *22*(6), 197–206. doi:10.1016/j.cub.2012.02.012 PMID:22440805

Growth Engineering Academy. (n.d.). *Academy LMS*. https://www.growthengineering.co.uk/academy-lms/

Growth Engineering GENIE. (n.d.). *GENIE Authoring Tool*. https://www.growthengineering.co.uk/genie-content-authoring-tool/

Growth. (2016). *The Neuroscience of Gamification in Online Learning*. https://www.growthengineering.co.uk/the-neuroscience-of-gamification-in-online-learning/

Gudivada, V., Apon, A., & Ding, J. (2017). *Data Quality Considerations for Big Data and Machine Learning: Going Beyond Data Cleaning and Transformations*. Academic Press.

GuildJ. (2017). Fintech and the Future of Finance. *Asian Journal of Public Affairs*, 17-20. https://ssrn.com/abstract=3021684

Guillén-Nieto, V., & Aleson-Carbonell, M. (2012). Serious games and learning effectiveness: The case of It's a Deal! *Computers & Education*, *58*(1), 435–448. doi:10.1016/j.compedu.2011.07.015

Hair, J. F., Hult, G. T. M., Ringle, C. M., & Sarstedt, M. (2016). *A Primer on Partial Least Squares Structural Equation Modeling (PLS-SEM)*. Sage Publications.

Hair, J. F., Ringle, C. M., & Sarstedt, M. (2011). PLS-SEM: Indeed a silver bullet. *Journal of Marketing Theory and Practice*, *19*(2), 139–151. doi:10.2753/MTP1069-6679190202

Hall, J., Stickler, U., Herodotou, C., & Iacovides, I. (2020). Player conceptualizations of creativity in digital entertainment games. *Convergence*, *26*(5-6), 1226–1247. doi:10.1177/1354856519880791

Hamari, J., Koivisto, J., & Sarsa, H. (2014). Does gamification work? A literature review of empirical studies on gamification. *2014 47th Hawaii International Conference on System Sciences*, 3025-3034.

Hamari, J., & Koivisto, J. (2015). "Working out for likes": An empirical study on social influence in exercise gamification. *Computers in Human Behavior*, *50*, 333–347. doi:10.1016/j.chb.2015.04.018

Ham, M., Jeger, M., & Frajman Ivković, A. (2015). The role of subjective norms in forming the intention to purchase green food. Economic research-. *Ekonomska Istrazivanja*, *28*(1), 738–748. doi:10.1080/1331677X.2015.1083875

Hancock, J. T., Landrigan, C., & Silver, C. (2007). Expressing emotion in text-based communication. *2007 Conference on Human Factors in Computing Systems*.

Hanna, P. (2016). Java Games Programming. Queen's University.

Harbert, T. (2013, Setembro 18). *Case study: 3 heavyweights give Gamification a go*. Computerworld. https://www.computerworld.com/article/2485087/emerging-technology-case-study-3-heavyweights-give-gamification-a-go.html

Hasan, M. M. (2018). Design and Implementation of Gamified Course Contents. Handbook of Research on Mobile Devices and Smart Gadgets in K-12 Education, 32-44. doi:10.4018/978-1-5225-2706-0.ch003

Hasani, L. M., & Adnan, H. R. (2020). *Factors affecting student's perceived readiness on abrupt distance learning adoption: Indonesian Higher-Education Perspectives.* doi:10.13140/RG.2.2.22908.16008

Hasan, M. M., Popp, J., & Oláh, J. (2020). Current landscape and influence of big data on finance. *Journal of Big Data, 7*(1), 21. doi:10.118640537-020-00291-z

Henrick, G. (2013). *Gamification – What is it and what it is in Moodle.* http://classroom-aid.com/2013/11/18/gamifying-learning-with-moodle-gbl/

Henseler, J., Ringle, C. M., & Sarstedt, M. (2015). A new criterion for assessing discriminant validity in variance-based structural equation modeling. *Journal of the Academy of Marketing Science, 43*(1), 115–135. doi:10.100711747-014-0403-8

Herzig, P., Jugel, K., Momm, C., Ameling, M., & Schill, A. (2013). Gaml - A modeling language for gamification. *2013 IEEE/ACM 6th International Conference on Utility and Cloud Computing*, 494-499.

Herzig, P., Srahringer, S., & Ameling, M. (2012). Gamification of ERP systems – Exploring gamification effects on user acceptance constructs. *Proceedings of the Multikonferenz Wirtschaftsinformatik MKWI, 12*, 793–804.

Hetherinton, D. (2014). Sysml requirements for training game design. *17th International IEEE Conference on Intelligent Transportation Systems (ITSC)*, 162-167.

Hettrick, J. (2012). *Online Video Games: Leadership Development for the Millennial College Student.* Johnson & Wales University.

Hochreiter, S., & Schmidhuber, J. (1997). Long Short-Term Memory. *Neural Computation, 9*(8), 1735–1780. doi:10.1162/neco.1997.9.8.1735 PMID:9377276

Holden, R. J., & Karsh, B. T. (2010). The Technology Acceptance Model: Its past and its future in health care. *Journal of Biomedical Informatics, 43*(1), 159-172. doi:10.1016/j.jbi.2009.07.002

Hosmer, D. Jr, Lemeshow, S., & Sturdivant, R. (2013). *Applied Logistic Regression* (Vol. 398). John Wiley & Sons. doi:10.1002/9781118548387

Hou, H. (2015). Integrating cluster and sequential analysis to explore learners' flow and behavioral patterns in a simulation game with situated-learning context for science courses: A video-based process exploration. *Computers in Human Behavior, 48*, 424–435. doi:10.1016/j.chb.2015.02.010

Huang, B., & Hew, K. F. (2015). Do points, badges and leaderboard increase learning and activity: A quasi-experiment on the effects of gamification. *Proceedings of the 23rd International Conference on Computers in Education.*

Huang, C. K., Chen, C. D., & Liu, Y. T. (2019). To stay or not to stay? Discontinuance intention of gamification apps. *Information Technology & People, 32*(6), 1423–1445. doi:10.1108/ITP-08-2017-0271

Huang, J., Chai, J., & Cho, S. (2020). Deep learning in finance and banking: A literature review and classification. *Frontiers of Business Research in China, 14*(13), 13. Advance online publication. doi:10.118611782-020-00082-6

Huang, W., & Soman, D. (2013). *A Practitioner's Guide To Gamification Of Education.* University of Toronto.

Huang, X., & Mayer, R. E. (2016). Benefits of adding anxiety-reducing features to a computer-based multimedia lesson on statistics. *Computers in Human Behavior, 63*, 293–303. doi:10.1016/j.chb.2016.05.034

Hung, H. T., Yang, J. C., Hwang, G. J., Chu, H. C., & Wang, C. C. (2018). A scoping review of research on digital game-based language learning. *Computers & Education, 126*, 89–104. doi:10.1016/j.compedu.2018.07.001

Hunicke, R., Leblanc, M., & Zubek, R. (2004). Mda: A formal approach to game design and game research. *AAAI Workshop - Technical Report, 1.*

Huotari, K., & Hamari, J. (2012). Defining Gamification: A Service Marketing Perspective. In *Proceeding of the 16th International Academic MindTrek Conference.* ACM. 10.1145/2393132.2393137

Hutto, C., & Gilbert, E. (2014). Vader: A parsimonious rule-based model for Sentiment analytics of social media text. *International AAAI Conference on Web and Social Media,* 2-10.

Ibanez, M. B., Di-Serio, A., & Delgado-Kloos, C. (2014). Gamification for engaging computer science students in learning activities: A case study. *IEEE Transactions on Learning Technologies, 7*(3), 291–301. doi:10.1109/TLT.2014.2329293

Igbaria, M., & Parasuraman, S. (1989). A path analytic study of individual characteristics, computer anxiety and attitudes toward microcomputers. *Journal of Management, 15*(3), 373–388. doi:10.1177/014920638901500302

Ihde, D. (1993). *The philosophy of technology.* Paragon House.

IJsselsteijn, W., De Kort, Y., Poels, K., Jurgelionis, A., & Bellotti, F. (2007). Characterizing and measuring user experiences in digital games. *International conference on advances in computer entertainment technology, 2,* 27.

Intelligence, M. (2020). *Gaming Market - Growth, Trends, Forecasts (2020 - 2025).* https://www.researchandmarkets.com/reports/4845961/gaming-market-growth-trends-forecasts-2020

Iwendi, C., Bashir, A. K., Atharva, P., Sujatha, R., Chatterjee, J. M., Pasupuleti, S., Mishra, R., Pillai, S., & Jo, O. (2020). COVID-19 Patient Health Prediction Using Boosted Random Forest Algorithm. *Frontiers in Public Health, 8,* 357. https://www.frontiersin.org/article/10.3389/fpubh.2020.00357 doi:10.3389/fpubh.2020.00357

Jackson, L. A., von Eye, A., Fitzgerald, H. E., Witt, E. A., & Zhao, Y. (2011). Internet use, videogame playing and cell phone use as predictors of children's body mass index (BMI), body weight, academic performance and social and overall self-esteem. *Computers in Human Behavior, 27,* 599–604.

Jackson, L. A., von Eye, A., Witt, E. A., Zhao, Y., & Fitzgerald, H. E. (2011). A longitudinal study of the effects of Internet use and videogame playing on academic performance and the roles of gender, race and income in these relationships. *Computers in Human Behavior, 27*(1), 228–239. doi:10.1016/j.chb.2010.08.001

Jackson, L. A., Witt, E. A., Games, A. I., Fitzgerald, H. E., von Eye, A., & Zhao, Y. (2012). Information technology use and creativity: Findings from the Children and Technology Project. *Computers in Human Behavior, 28*(2), 370–376. doi:10.1016/j.chb.2011.10.006

Jain, A., & Dutta, D. (2019). Millennials and Gamification: Guerilla Tactics for Making Learning Fun. *SA Journal of Human Resource Management, 6*(1), 29–44. doi:10.1177/2322093718796303

Janssens, O., Samyny, K., Van de Walle, R., & Van Hoecke, S. (2014). Educational virtual game scenario generation for serious games. *2014 IEEE 3rd International Conference on Serious Games and Applications for Health (SeGAH),* 1-8. 10.1109/SeGAH.2014.7067106

Jensen, G., Resnik, L., & Haddad, A. (2008). Expertise and clinical reasoning. *Clinical Reasoning in the Health Professions, 3,* 123–136.

Jiang, F., Jiang, Y., Zhi, H., Dong, Y., Li, H., Ma, S., Wang, Y., Dong, Q., Shen, H., & Wang, Y. (2017). Artificial intelligence in healthcare: past, present and future. *Stroke and Vascular Neurology Journal, 21*(4), 230-243. doi:10.1136/svn-2017-000101

Johnson, D., Deterding, S., Kuhn, K. A., Staneva, A., Stoyanov, S., & Hides L. (2016). Gamification for health and wellbeing: A systematic review of the literature. *Internet Interventions, 6*, 89-106. doi:10.1016/j.invent.2016.10.002

Joo, Y. J., Kim, N., & Kim, N. H. (2016). Factors predicting online university students' use of a mobile learning management system (m-LMS). *Educational Technology Research and Development, 64*(4), 611–630. doi:10.100711423-016-9436-7

Joy, M., & Assistant, J. (2017). An investigation into Gamification as a tool for enhancing recruitment process. *Ideal Research, 3*.

Julius, K., & Salo, J. (2013). *Designing gamification. Technical report.* Marketing.

Jull, G., Wright, A., Joan, M., Norman, M., Rivett, D., Blackstock, F., … Neads, P. (2011). *Health Workforce Australia National Simulated Learning Project Report for Physiotherapy.* Health Workforce Australia.

Junco, R., & Cotten, S. R. (2011). *A decade of distraction? How multitasking affects student outcomes.* Academic Press.

Justin, E. (2018). A Study on Gamification Techniques Adopted by Financial Institutions. *Journal of Social Welfare and Management, 10*(3), 600-604. doi:10.21088/JSWM.0975.0231.10318.46

Kapp, K. M. (2012). *The gamification of learning and instruction: Game-based methods and strategies for training and education.* Pfeiffer.

Kapp, K. M. (2012). *The Gamification of Learning and Instruction: Game-based Methods and Strategies for Training and Education.* Pfeiffer.

Kapp, K. M. (2013). *The Gamification of Learning and Instruction. In Fieldbook: Ideas into Practice.* John Wiley & Sons.

Kapustina, L. V., & Martynova, I. A. (2020). Training Employees in the Digital Economy with the Use of Video Games. In *Digital Transformation of the Economy: Challenges, Trends and New Opportunities* (pp. 444–454). Springer.

Kasapakis, V., & Gavalas, D. (2017). Revisiting design guidelines for pervasive games. *International Journal of Pervasive Computing and Communications, 13*(4), 386–407. doi:10.1108/IJPCC-D-17-00007

Kataria, A., & Singh, M. (2013). A review of data classification using k-nearest neighbour algorithm. *International Journal of Emerging Technology and Advanced Engineering, 3*(6), 354–360.

Kaur, A., & Gourav, K. (2020). A Study of Reinforcement Learning Applications & its Algorithms. *International Journal of Scientific & Technology Research, 9*(3), 4223–4228.

Kavuri, A. S., & Milne, A. (2019). *FinTech and the future of financial services: What are the research gaps?* CAMA Working Papers 2019-18, Centre for Applied Macroeconomic Analysis, Crawford School of Public Policy, The Australian National University. doi:10.2139/ssrn.3333515

Keller, J. M. (2010). *Motivational Design for Learning and Performance.* Springer. doi:10.1007/978-1-4419-1250-3

Kerr, C., Francis, B., Cross, K., & Guide, G. C. (2020). *Video games, violence, and common sense.* https://www.gamasutra.com/blogs/NicholasMatthews/20130402/189739/Video_games_violence_and_common_sense.php

Kiili, K. (2006). Evaluations of an Experiential Gaming Model. *An Interdisciplinary Journal on Humans in ICT Enviroments, 2*(2), 187–201.

Kiili, K. (2006). Evaluations of an experiential gaming model. *Human Technology: An Interdisciplinary Journal on Humans in ICT Environments, 2*(2), 187–201. doi:10.17011/ht/urn.2006518

Kim, T. (2016). *Gamification of Wearable Devices in the Healthcare Industry.* Academic Press.

Kim, B., Park, H., & Baek, Y. (2009). Not just fun, but serious strategies: Using meta-cognitive strategies in game-based learning. *Computers & Education*, *52*(4), 800–810. doi:10.1016/j.compedu.2008.12.004

Kim, S. (2011). Analysis article: Accuracy of the DIDGET glucose meter in children and young adults with diabetes. *Journal of Diabetes Science and Technology*, *5*(5), 1164–1166. doi:10.1177/193229681100500519 PMID:22027311

King, B. (2017). *Gamification in banking: The rise of the "experiential" bank.* https://cxloyalty.dk/news-resources/gamification-banking-rise-experiential-bank/

King, D. L., Delfabbro, P. H., & Griffiths, M. D. (2013). Trajectories of problem video gaming among adult regular gamers: An 18-month longitudinal study. *Cyberpsychology & Behavior*, *16*(1), 72–76. doi:10.1089/cyber.2012.0062 PMID:23098213

Kirkpatrick, D. (1959). Techniques for Evaluating Training Programs. *Journal of American Society for Training and Development*, *13*(11-12).

Kiselicki, M., Josimovski, S., Pulevska Ivanovska, L., & Kirovska, Z. (2020). Digital transformation of learning process due to Covid19 crisis in the Republic of North Macedonia. *Journal of Sustainable Development, 10*(25), 53-66. http://fbe.edu.mk/images/stories/JSDv25.pdf

Klimmt, C., & Hartmann, T. (2006). Effectance, self-efficacy, and the motivation to play video games. *Playing video games: Motives, responses, and consequences*, 133-145.

Klingensmith, G. J., Aisenberg, J., Kaufman, F., Halvorson, M., Cruz, E., Riordan, M. E., Varma, C., Pardo, S., Viggiani, M. T., Wallace, J. F., Schachner, H. C., & Bailey, T. (2013). Evaluation of a combined blood glucose monitoring and gaming system (Didget®) for motivation in children, adolescents, and young adults with type 1 diabetes. *Pediatric Diabetes*, *14*(5), 350–357. doi:10.1111/j.1399-5448.2011.00791.x PMID:21699639

Klopping, I. M., & McKinney, E. (2004). Extending the technology acceptance model and the task-technology fit model to consumer e-commerce. *Information Technology, Learning and Performance Journal*, *22*(1).

Knight, J., Carly, S., Tregunna, B., Jarvis, S., Smithies, R., de Freitas, S., ... Dunwell, I. (2010). Serious gaming technology in major incident triage training: A pragmatic controlled trial. *Resuscitation Journal*, *81*(9), 1174–1179. doi:10.1016/j.resuscitation.2010.03.042 PMID:20732609

Kolb, A. Y., & Kolb, D. A. (2005). Learning Styles and Learning Spaces: Enhancing Experiential Learning in Higher Education. *Academy of Management Learning & Education*, *4*(2), 193–212. doi:10.5465/amle.2005.17268566

Kononowicz, A. A., Woodham, L. A., Edelbring, S., Stathakarou, N., Davies, D., Saxena, N., Tudor Car, L., Carlstedt-Duke, J., Car, J., & Zary, N. (2019). Virtual patient simulations in health professions education: Systematic review and meta-analysis by the Digital Health Education Collaboration. *Journal of Medical Internet Research*, *21*(7), e14676. doi:10.2196/14676 PMID:31267981

Kostick, M. (1977). *Kostick's Perception and Preference Inventory.* Applied Psychology Associates.

Krishnamurthy, S. (2020). The future of business education: A commentary in the shadow of the Covid-19 pandemic. *Journal of Business Research, Elsevier, 117*(C), 1–5. doi:10.1016/j.jbusres.2020.05.034 PMID:32501309

Krstajic, D., Buturovic, L., Leahy, D., & Thomas, S. (2014). Cross-validation pitfalls when selecting and assessing regression and classification models. *Journal of Cheminformatics*, *6*(1), 1–15. doi:10.1186/1758-2946-6-10 PMID:24678909

Kshetri, N. (2019). *Global entrepreneurship: Environment and strategy* (2nd ed.). Routledge.

Kshetri, N. (2021). The Role of Artificial Intelligence in Promoting Financial Inclusion in Developing Countries. *Journal of Global Information Technology Management, 24*(1), 1–6. doi:10.1080/1097198X.2021.1871273

Kühn, S., Kugler, D. T., Schmalen, K., Weichenberger, M., Witt, C., & Gallinat, J. (2019). Does playing violent video games cause aggression? A longitudinal intervention study. *Molecular Psychiatry, 24*(8), 1220–1234. doi:10.103841380-018-0031-7 PMID:29535447

Kumar, D. (2000). Pedagogical Dimensions of Game Playing. *ACM Intelligence Magazine, 10*(10), 9–10.

Kurfalı, M., Arifoğlu, A., Tokdemir, G., & Paçin, Y. (2017). Adoption of e-government services in Turkey. *Computers in Human Behavior, 66*, 168–178. doi:10.1016/j.chb.2016.09.041

Laamarti, F., Eid, M., & Saddik, A. (2014). An overview of serious games. *International Journal of Computer Games Technology, 2014*, 1–15. doi:10.1155/2014/358152

Landers, R. N. (2014). Developing a theory of gamified learning: Linking serious games and gamification of learning. *Simulation & Gaming, 45*(6), 752–768. doi:10.1177/1046878114563660

Landers, R. N., Auer, E. M., Collmus, A. B., & Armstrong, M. B. (2018). Gamification science, its history and future: Definitions and a research agenda. *Simulation & Gaming, 49*(3), 315–337. doi:10.1177/1046878118774385

Landers, R. N., & Callan, R. C. (2011). Casual social games as serious games: The psychology of gamification in undergraduate education and employee training. In *Serious games and edutainment applications* (pp. 399–423). Springer. doi:10.1007/978-1-4471-2161-9_20

Landers, R. N., & Landers, A. K. (2014). An empirical test of the theory of gamified learning: The effect of leaderboards on time-on-task and academic performance. *Simulation & Gaming, 45*(6), 769–785. doi:10.1177/1046878114563662

Langendah, P. A., Cook, M., & Mark-Herbert, C. (2016). Gamification in higher education. Toward a pedagogy to engage and motivate. In *Working Paper Series* (vol. 6, pp. 1-43). Swedish University of Agricultural Sciences.

Larson, R., Csikszentmihalyi, M., & Graef, R. (1980). Mood variability and the psychosocial adjustment of adolescents. *Journal of Youth and Adolescence, 9*(6), 469–490. doi:10.1007/BF02089885 PMID:24318310

Lau, J. (2008). *Students' experience of using electronic textbooks in different levels of education.* Academic Press.

Lau, L. (2014, Fevereiro 5). How Cisco Drives Social Media Training with Gamification. *Gamification Co.* https://www.gamification.co/2014/02/05/cisco-drives-social-media-training-gamification/

LaViola, J. A. Jr. (2000). Discussion of cybersickness in virtual environments. *SIGCHI Bulletin, 32*(1), 47–56. doi:10.1145/333329.333344

Lazzaro, N. (2009). Why we play: affect and the fun of games. *Human-Computer Interaction: Designing for Diverse Users and Domains,* 155.

Lazzaro, N. (2004). Why We Play Games: Four Keys to More Emotion in Player Experiences. *Game Developer Conference 2004.*

Lee, S. M., & Lee, D. (2020). Healthcare wearable devices: an analysis of key factors for continuous use intention. *Service Business, 14*, 503-531. doi:10.1007/s11628-020-00428-3

Lee, J., & Hammer, J. (2011). Gamification in education: What, how, why bother? *Academic Exchange Quarterly, 15*(2), 146.

Lim, C., & Jung, H. (2013). A study on the military Serious Game. *Advanced Science and Technology Letters, 39*, 73–77. doi:10.14257/astl.2013.39.14

Lindquist, K. A., Satpute, A. B., & Gendron, M. (2015). Does Language Do More Than Communicate Emotion? *Current Directions in Psychological Science, 24*(2), 99–108. doi:10.1177/0963721414553440 PMID:25983400

Lindsley, D. B. (1951). Emotion. Handbook of experimental psychology, 473–516.

Lisk, T. C., Kaplancali, U. T., & Riggio, R. E. (2012). Leadership in multiplayer online gaming environments. *Simulation & Gaming, 43*(1), 133–149. doi:10.1177/1046878110391975

Liu, N. H., Chiang, C. Y., & Chu, H. C. (2013). Recognizing the degree of human attention using EEG signals from mobile sensors. *Sensors, 13*(8), 10273-10286.

Liu, Y., Alexandrova, T., & Nakajima, T. (2011). Gamifying intelligent environments. *Proceedings of the 2011 international ACM workshop on Ubiquitous meta user interfaces.* 10.1145/2072652.2072655

Loh, C., Sheng, Y., & Ifenthaler, D. (2015). Serious Game Analytics: Theoretical Framework. In C. Loh, Y. Sheng, & D. Ifenthaler (Eds.), *Serious Game Analytics: Methodologies for Performance Measurement, Assessment and Improvement* (pp. 3–30). Springer. doi:10.1007/978-3-319-05834-4_1

Lombard, M., & Ditton, T. (1997). At the Heart of It All: The Concept of Presence. *Journal of Computer-Mediated Communication, 3*(2), 0. Advance online publication. doi:10.1111/j.1083-6101.1997.tb00072.x

Lowry, P. B., Gaskin, J., Twyman, N., Hammer, B., & Roberts, T. (2012). Taking 'fun and games' seriously: Proposing the hedonic-motivation system adoption model (HMSAM). *Journal of the Association for Information Systems, 14*(11), 617–671. doi:10.17705/1jais.00347

Lyubomirsky, S., Dickerhoof, R., Boehm, J. K., & Sheldon, K. M. (2011). Becoming happier takes both a will and a proper way: An experimental longitudinal intervention to boost well-being. *Emotion (Washington, D.C.), 11*(2), 391–402. doi:10.1037/a0022575 PMID:21500907

Maas, A., Daly, R., Pham, P., Huang, D., Ng, A., & Potts, C. (2011). Learning Word Vectors for Sentiment Analysis. *The 49th Annual Meeting of the Association for Computational Linguistics: Human Language Technologies*, 142-150.

Macauley, K. (2018). Evaluating changes in clinical decision-making in physical therapy students after participating in simulation. *Health Profession Education, 4*(4), 278–286. doi:10.1016/j.hpe.2018.06.001

Mak, H. W. (2013, Janeiro 11). Deloitte Leadership Academy Leads with the Gamification of Training. *Gamification Co.* https://www.gamification.co/2013/01/11/deloitte-leadership-academy-leads-with-the-gamification-of-training/

Makhlysheva, A., Bakkevoll, P. A., Nordsletta, A. T., & Linstad, L. H. (2018). *Artificial Intelligence and Machine Learning in Healthcare.* Norwegian Center for e-Health Research. https://ehealthresearch.no/en/fact-sheets/artificial-intelligence-and-machine-learning-in-healthcare

Malarout, N., Jain, M., Shetty, D. K., Naik, N., Maddodi, B. S., & Perule, N. (2020). Application of Gamification in the Banking Sector: A Systematic Review. *Test Engineering and Management, 83.*

Malone, T. W. (1981). Toward a Theory of Intrinsically Motivating Instruction. *Cognitive Science, 5*(4), 333–369. doi:10.120715516709cog0504_2

Ma, M., Oikonomou, A., & Jain, L. (2011). Innovations in Serious Games for Future Learning. In *Serious Games and Edutainment Applications* (pp. 3–7). Springer. doi:10.1007/978-1-4471-2161-9_1

Manning, C., Raghavan, P., & Schütze, H. (2008). *Introduction to Information Retrieval*. Cambridge University Press. doi:10.1017/CBO9780511809071

Manser Payne, L., Peltier, J. W., & Barger, V. A. (2018). Mobile banking and AI-enabled mobile banking: The differential effects of technological and non-technological factors on digital natives' perceptions and behaviour. *Journal of Research in Interactive Marketing*, *12*(4), 328–346. Advance online publication. doi:10.1108/JRIM-07-2018-0087

Manzano-León, A., Camacho-Lazarraga, P., Guerrero, M. A., Guerrero-Puerta, L., Aguilar-Parra, J. M., Trigueros, R., & Alias, A. (2021). Between level up and game over: A systematic literature review of gamification in education. *Sustainability*, *13*(4), 2247.

Marczewski, A. (2015). *4 essential Neurotransmitters in gamification*. https://www.gamified.uk/2015/01/05/neurotransmitters-you-should-know-about-in-gamification/

Marczewski, A. (2015). User Types. In Even Ninja Monkeys Like to Play: Gamification, Game Thinking and Motivational Design (pp. 65-80). CreateSpace Independent Publishing Platform.

Marczewski, A. (2015). *Even Ninja Monkeys like to play*. Blurb Inc.

Marous, J. (2021). *Data and AI Power the Future of Customer Engagement in Financial Services*. https://thefinancialbrand.com/86706/banking-customer-engagement-personalization-ai-trends/

Marshall, M. (2020). Covid Virus Pushing Education to Online Learning/Teaching Creates Big Challenges: Ethical, Practical & Financial Issues for Teachers/Professors and Administration Leadership; Commentary. *PM World Journal*, 1-4.

Martínez-Martínez, A., Zurita-Ortega, F., Castro-Sánchez, M., Chacón-Cuberos, R., Hinojo-Lucena, M. A., & Espejo-Garcés, T. (2016). La elección de estudios superiores universitarios en estudiantes de último curso de bachillerato y ciclos formativos. *Revista Electrónica Educare*, *20*(1), 304–321.

Martín, M. D. M. B., Muntada, M. C., Busquets, C. G., Pros, R. C., & Sáez, T. D. (2015). Videojuegos, televisión y rendimiento académico en alumnos de primaria. Pixel-Bit. *Revista de Medios y Educación*, (46), 25–38.

Martí-Parreño, J., Seguí-Mas, D., & Seguí-Mas, E. (2016). Teachers' attitude towards and actual use of gamification. *Procedia: Social and Behavioral Sciences*, *228*, 682–688. doi:10.1016/j.sbspro.2016.07.104

Masie, E. (2006). The blended learning imperative. The handbook of blended learning: Global perspectives, local designs, 22-26.

Mavroeidi, A. G., Kitsiou, A., Kalloniatis, C., & Gritzalis, S. (2019). Gamification vs. Privacy: Identifying and Analysing the Major Concerns. *Future Internet*, *11*(3), 67. doi:10.3390/fi11030067

McKenney, J. L., & Dill, W. R. (1966). Influences on Learning in Simulation Games. *The American Behavioral Scientist*, *10*(2), 28–32. doi:10.1177/000276426601000205

Meade, J. A., & Parthasaranthy, K. (2020). Did COVID-19 Impact Student Learning in an Introductory Accounting Course? *Business Education Innovation Journal*, *12*(2), 18–23.

Medhat, W., Hassan, A., & Korashy, H. (2014). Sentiment analytics algorithms and applications: A survey. *Ain Shams Engineering Journal*, *5*(4), 1093–1113. doi:10.1016/j.asej.2014.04.011

Medsker, L., & Jain, L. (2001). *Recurrent Neural Networks*. CRC Press.

Mega, C., Ronconi, L., & Beni, R. D. (2014). What Makes a Good Learner? How Emotions, Self-Regulated Learning, and Motivation Contribute to Academic Achievement. *Journal of Educational Psychology*, *106*(1), 121–131. doi:10.1037/a0033546

Meister, J. C. (2013, Janeiro 2). How Deloitte Made Learning a Game. *Harvard Business Review*. https://hbr.org/2013/01/how-deloitte-made-learning-a-g

Mella, E. R., & Bravo, P. R. (2011). Análisis Psicométrico confirmatorio de la medida multidimensional del Test de Autoconcepto Forma 5 en Español (AF5), en estudiantes Universitarios de Chile. *Psicologia, Saúde & Doenças*, *12*(1), 91–103.

Melzer, P. (2019). A conceptual framework for task and tool personalisation in IS education. In *A conceptual framework for personalised learning* (pp. 47–76). Springer Gabler.

Mensah, I. K. (2019). Factors influencing the intention of university students to adopt and use e-government services: An empirical evidence in China. *SAGE Open*, *9*(2).

Mention, A. L. (2019). The Future of Fintech. *Research Technology Management*, *62*(4), 59–63. doi:10.1080/0895630 8.2019.1613123

Meyniel, F., Goodwin, G. M., Deakin, J. W., Klinge, C., MacFadyen, C., Milligan, H., Mullings, E., Pessiglione, M., & Gaillard, R. (2016). A specific role for serotonin in overcoming effort cost. *eLife*, 5. PMID:27824554

Mhlanga, D. (2020). Industry 4.0 in Finance: The Impact of Artificial Intelligence (AI) on Digital Financial Inclusion. *International Journal of Financial Studies, 8*(3), 1–14.

Michael, D., & Chen, S. (2005). *Serious Games: Games That Educate, Train, and Inform*. Muska & Lipman/Premier-Trade.

Milani, L., Grumi, S., & Di Blasio, P. (2019). Positive Effects of Videogame Use on Visuospatial Competencies: The Impact of Visualization Style in Preadolescents and Adolescents. *Frontiers in Psychology*, 10. PMID:31231275

Miner, G., Elder, I. V. J., & Hill, T. (2012). *Practical text mining and statistical analysis for non-structured text data applications*. Academic Press.

Mishina, Y., Murata, R., Yamauchi, Y., Yamashita, T., & Fujiyoshi, H. (2015). Boosted Random Forest. *IEICE Transactions on Information and Systems*, *98*(9), 1630–1636. doi:10.1587/transinf.2014OPP0004

Mo, D., Xiang, M., Luo, M., Dong, Y., Fang, Y., Zhang, S., ... Liang, H. (2019). Using gamification and social incentives to increase physical activity and related social cognition among undergraduate students in Shanghai, China. *International Journal of Environmental Research and Public Health*, *16*(5), 858.

Moodle Plugins. (n.d.). *Moodle plugins database*. https://moodle.org/plugins

Moodle. (n.d.). *Moodle*. https://moodle.com/

Mora, A., Riera, D., Gonzalez, C., & Arnedo-Moreno, J. (2015). A literature review of gamification design frameworks. *2015 7th International Conference on Games and Virtual Worlds for Serious Applications (VS-Games)*, 1-8. 10.1109/VS-GAMES.2015.7295760

Mullins, J. K., & Sabherwal, R. (2020). Gamification: A cognitive-emotional view. *Journal of Business Research*, *106*, 304–314. doi:10.1016/j.jbusres.2018.09.023

Muratet, M., Torguet, P., Jessel, J., & Viallet, F. (2009). Towards a serious game to help learners learn computer programming. *International Journal of Computer Games Technology*, *2009*, 1–12. doi:10.1155/2009/470590

Murphy, S., Imam, B., & Macintyre, D. L. (2015). Standardized patients versus volunteer patients for physical therapy students' interviewing practice: A pilot study. *Physiotherapy Canada. Physiotherapie Canada, 67*(4), 378–384. doi:10.3138/ptc.2014-50E PMID:27504038

Mustafa, A. S., & Karimi, K. (2021). Enhancing Gamified Online Learning User Experience (UX): A Systematic Literature Review of Recent Trends. In Human-Computer Interaction and Beyond-Part I (pp. 74-99). Bentham Science Publishers.

Mustafa, A. S., Ali, N., & Dhillon, J. S. (2021). A Systematic Review of the Integration of Motivational and Behavioural Theories in Gamified Health Interventions. In F. Saeed, F. Mohammed, & A. Al-Nahari (Eds.), *Innovative Systems for Intelligent Health Informatics. IRICT 2020. Lecture Notes on Data Engineering and Communications Technologies* (Vol. 72). Springer.

Myers, J. (2016). *The world's 10 youngest populations are all in Africa.* Retrieved from: https://www.weforum.org/agenda/2016/05/the-world-s-10-youngest-countries-are-all-in-africa/

Nabar, M. J. M. Y., Algieri, R. D., & Tornese, E. B. (2018). Gamification or gaming techniques applied to pedagogy: Foundations of the cognitive neuroscience applied to the education. *Global Journal of Human-Social Science: Linguistics & Education, 18*(2).

Nagle, A., Wolf, P., Riener, R., & Novak, D. (2014). The use of player-centered positive reinforcement to schedule in-game rewards inreases enjoyment and performance in a serious game. *International Journal of Serious Games, 1*(4), 35–47. doi:10.17083/ijsg.v1i4.47

Nah, F. F. H., Daggubati, L. S., Tarigonda, A., Nuvvula, R. V., & Turel, O. (2015). Effects of the Use of Points, Leaderboards and Badges on In-Game Purchases of Virtual Goods. In F. Fui-Hoon Nah & C. H. Tan (Eds.), Lecture Notes in Computer Science: Vol. 9191. *HCI in Business. HCIB 2015.* Springer. doi:10.1007/978-3-319-20895-4_48

Nah, F., Eschenbrenner, B., Claybaugh, C., & Koob, P. (2019). Gamification of Enterprise Systems. *Systems., 7*(1), 13. doi:10.3390ystems7010013

Nah, S., & Saxton, G. D. (2013). Modeling the adoption and use of social media by nonprofit organizations. *New Media & Society, 15*(2), 294–313. doi:10.1177/1461444812452411

Nasim, Z., Rajput, Q., & Haider, S. (2017). Sentiment analytics of learner feedback using machine learning and lexicon based approaches. In *2017 International Conference on Research and Innovation in Information Systems (ICRIIS)* (pp. 1-6). Langkawi: IEEE.

Nestel, D., & Tierney, T. (2007). Role-play for medical students learning about communication: Guidelines for maximising benefits. *BMC Medical Education, 7*(1), 3. doi:10.1186/1472-6920-7-3 PMID:17335561

Nicoletti, B. (2017). *The Future of FinTech. Integrating Finance and Technology in Financial Services.* Palgrave Macmillan. doi:10.1007/978-3-319-51415-4

Nielsen, J., & Landauer, J. (1993). A mathematical model of finding the usability problem. *Proceedings of ACM INTERCHI'93 Conference*, 206–213. 10.1145/169059.169166

Noble. (2021). *Financial Services and Gamification: Building Trust and Revenue.* https://www.noblesystems.com/resources/

Noble, W. S. (2006). What is a support vector machine? *Nature Biotechnology, 24*(12), 1565–1567. doi:10.1038/nbt1206-1565 PMID:17160063

Ntoutsi, E., Fafalios, P., Gadiraju, U., Iosifidis, V., Nejdl, W., Vidal, M.-E., Ruggieri, S., Turini, F., Papadopoulos, S., Krasanakis, E., Kompatsiaris, I., Kinder-Kurlanda, K., Wagner, C., Karimi, F., Fernandez, M., Alani, H., Berendt, B., Kruegel, T., Heinze, C., ... Staab, S. (2020). Bias in data-driven artificial intelligence systems - An introductory survey. *WIREs Data Mining and Knowledge Discovery, 10*(6). Advance online publication. doi:10.1002/widm.1356

O'Shea, K., & Nash, R. (2013). *An Introduction to Convolutional Neural Networks.* Retrieved from https://white.stanford.edu/teach/index.php/An_Introduction_to_Convolutional_Neural_Networks

Ofosu-Ampong, K., & Anning-Dorson, T. (2020). Gamification Research: Preliminary Insights Into Dominant Issues, Theories, Domains, and Methodologies. In Handbook of Research on Managing Information Systems in Developing Economies (pp. 397-412). IGI Global.

Ofosu-Ampong, K., Boateng, R., Anning-Dorson, T., & Kolog, E. A. (2020). Are we ready for Gamification? An exploratory analysis in a developing country. *Education and Information Technologies, 25*(3), 1723–1742. doi:10.100710639-019-10057-7

Oluwajana, D., Idowu, A., Nat, M., Vanduhe, V., & Fadiya, S. (2019). The adoption of students' hedonic motivation system model to gamified learning environment. *Journal of Theoretical and Applied Electronic Commerce Research, 14*(3), 156–167. doi:10.4067/S0718-18762019000300109

Onyemaka, S. B., Igbokwe, D. O., Adekeye, O. A., & Agbu, J. F. (2017). "I failed because I was Playing Video games": An Examination of Undergraduate Males Videogame Addiction and Academic Performance. *Covenant International Journal of Psychology, 2*(1).

Ortiz de Gortari, A. B. (2015). What can game transfer phenomena tell us about the impact of highly immersive gaming technologies? In *Proceedings from ITAG'15:2015 International conference on interactive technologies and games* (pp. 84–89). 10.1109/iTAG.2015.15

Ortiz De Gortari, A. B., & Griffiths, M. (2017). Beyond the Boundaries of the Game: The Interplay Between In-Game Phenomena, Structural Characteristics of Video Games, and Game Transfer Phenomena. In Boundaries of Self and Reality Online. Academic Press.

Ortiz de Gortari, A. B. (2017). *Game Transfer Phenomena and the Augmented Reality Game Pokémon Go: The prevalence and the relation with benefits, risks, immersion and motivations. 22nd Annual Cyber Psychology, Cyber Therapy & Social Networking.*

Ortiz de Gortari, A. B., & Griffiths, M. D. (2014). Automatic mental processes, automatic actions and behaviours in game transfer phenomena: An empirical self-report study using online forum data. *International Journal of Mental Health and Addiction, 12*(4), 432–452. doi:10.100711469-014-9476-3

Ortiz-Rojas, M., Chiluiza, K., & Valcke, M. (2019). Gamification through leaderboards: An empirical study in engineering education. *Computer Applications in Engineering Education, 27*(4), 777–788. doi:10.1002/cae.12116

Paiva, Haraszczuk, Queiros, Leal, Swacha, & Kosta. (2021). *FGPE Gamification Service: A GraphQL Service to Gamify Online Education.* . doi:10.1007/978-3-030-72654-6_46

Paiva, J. C., Leal, J. P., & Queirós, R. (2015). Odin: A service for gamification of learning activities. In *Languages, Applications and Technologies - 4th International Symposium, SLATE 2015.* Springer. 10.1007/978-3-319-27653-3_19

Paiva, J. C., Leal, J. P., & Queirós, R. A. P. (2016). Enki: A pedagogical services aggregator for learning programming languages. In *Proceedings of the 2016 ACM Conference on Innovation and Technology in Computer Science Education, ITiCSE 2016.* ACM. 10.1145/2899415.2899441

Palladino, T. (2021). *Microsoft emerges from the trenches with more details behind the army edition of Hololens 2.* Retrieved from https://hololens.reality.news/news/microsoft-emerges-from-trenches-with-more-details-behind-army-edition-hololens-2-0384713/

Pallavicini, F., Ferrari, A., & Mantovani, F. (2018). Video games for well-being: A systematic review on the application of computer games for cognitive and emotional training in the adult population. *Frontiers in Psychology, 9,* 2127. doi:10.3389/fpsyg.2018.02127 PMID:30464753

Pang, B., Lee, L., & Vaithyanathan, S. (2002). *Thumbs up? Sentiment Classification using Machine Learning. In Conf. on Empirical Methods in Natural Language Processing.* EMNLP.

Paparella-Pitzel, S., Edmond, S., & DeCaro, C. (2009). The use of standardized patients in physical therapist education programs. *Journal of Physical Therapy Education, 23*(2). https://journals.lww.com/jopte/Fulltext/2009/07000/The_Use_of_Standardized_Patients_in_Physical.3.aspx

Parker, R. M., Ratzan, S. C., & Lurie, N. (2003). Health Literacy: A Policy Challenge for advancing high-quality Health care. *Health Affairs (Project Hope), 22*(4), 147–153. doi:10.1377/hlthaff.22.4.147 PMID:12889762

Pasch, M., Bianchi-Berthouze, N., van Dijk, B., & Nijholt, A. (2009). Movement-based sports video games: Investigating motivation and gaming experience. *Entertainment Computing, 1*(2), 49–61. doi:10.1016/j.entcom.2009.09.004

Pastor Pina, H., Satorre Cuerda, R., Molina-Carmona, R., Gallego-Durán, F. J., & Llorens Largo, F. (2015). Can Moodle be used for structural gamification? *INTED2015: Proceedings of the 9th International Technology, Education and Development Conference*, 1014-1021.

Patel, M. S., Small, D. S., Harrison, J. D., Fortunato, M. P., Oon, A. L., Rareshide, C. A. L., Reh, G., Szwartz, G., Guszcza, J., Steier, D., Kalra, P., & Hilbert, V. (2019). Effectiveness of Behaviorally Designed Gamification Interventions with Social Incentives for Increasing Physical Activity among Overweight and Obese Adults Across the United States. *JAMA Internal Medicine, 179*(12), 1624–1632. doi:10.1001/jamainternmed.2019.3505 PMID:31498375

Peffers, K., Tuunanen, T., Rothenberger, M. A., & Chatterjee, S. (2007). A Design Science Research Methodology for Information Systems Research. *Journal of Management Information Systems, 24*(3), 45–77. doi:10.2753/MIS0742-1222240302

Pennington, J., Socher, R., & Manning, C. (2014). Glove: global vectors for word representation. *The 2014 Conference on Empirical Methods in Natural Language Processing (EMNLP)*, 1532-1543.

Pérez-Fuentes, M. C., Álvarez-Bermejo, J. A., Molero, M. M., Gázquez, J. J., & López Vicente, M. A. (2015). Violencia Escolar y Rendimiento Académico (VERA): Aplicación de realidad aumentada. *European Journal of Investigation in Health, Psychology and Education, 1*(2), 71–84. doi:10.30552/ejihpe.v1i2.19

Petkov, P., Köbler, F., Foth, M., Medland, R. C., & Krcmar, H. (2011). Engaging energy saving through motivation-specific social comparison. *Proceedings of conference on human factors in computing systems*, 1–6. 10.1145/1979742.1979855

Phillips, A. C., Mackintosh, S. F., Bell, A., & Johnston, K. N. (2017). Developing physiotherapy student safety skills in readiness for clinical placement using standardised patients compared with peer-role play: A pilot non-randomised controlled trial. *BMC Medical Education, 17*(1), 133. doi:10.118612909-017-0973-5 PMID:28797260

Pirker, J., Riffnaller-Schiefer, M., Tomes, L. M., & Guetl, C. (2016). Motivational Active Learning in Blended and Virtual Learning Scenarios: Engaging Students in Digital Learning. In Handbook of Research on Engaging Digital Natives in Higher Education Settings. IGI Global.

Playmotiv. (2019). *Gamification and dopamine: Why games motivate us.* https://playmotiv.com/en/gamification-and-dopamine-why-games-motivate-us/

Poels, Y., Annema, J. H., Verstraete, M., Zaman, B., & De Grooff, D. (2012). Are you a gamer? A qualititive study on the parameters for categorizing casual and hardcore gamers. *Iadis International Journal*, (1), 1–16.

Ponto, J. (2015). Understanding and evaluating survey research. *Journal of the Advanced Practitioner in Oncology, 6*(2), 168. PMID:26649250

Potapenko, V. (2020). *How AI And Data Analytics Are Shaping The Future Of Fintech.* https://coruzant.com/ai/how-ai-and-data-analytics-are-shaping-the-future-of-fintech/

Prensky, M. (2001). The games generations: How learners have changed. *Digital Game-Based Learning, 1*(1), 1-26.

Pribeanu, C. (2012). Specification and Validation of a Formative Index to Evaluate the Ergonomic Quality of an AR-based Educational Platform. *International Journal of Computers, Communications & Control, 7*(4), 721–732. doi:10.15837/ijccc.2012.4.1370

Pritchard, S. A., Blackstock, F. C., Nestel, D., & Keating, J. L. (2016). Simulated patients in physical therapy education: Systematic review and meta-analysis. *Physical Therapy, 96*(9), 1342–1353. doi:10.2522/ptj.20150500 PMID:26939603

Prochnow, T., Patterson, M. S., & Hartnell, L. (2020). *Social support, depressive symptoms, and online gaming network communication.* Mental Health and Social Inclusion.

Puerta, D. X., & Carbonell, X. (2013). Uso problemático de Internet en una muestra de estudiantes universitarios co-lombianos. *Avances en Psicología Latinoamericana, 31*(3), 620–631.

Putz, L. M., & Treiblmaier, H. (2019). Increasing Knowledge Retention through Gamified Workshops: Findings from a Longitudinal Study and Identification of Moderating Variables. *Proceedings of the 52nd Hawaii International Conference on System Sciences.*

Queirós, R. A. P. (2017). A survey on game backend services. In Gamification- Based E-Learning Strategies for Computer Programming Education. IGI Global.

Queirós, R. (2017). A Survey on Game Backend Services. In R. Alexandre Peixoto de Queirós & M. Pinto (Eds.), *Gamification-Based E-Learning Strategies for Computer Programming Education* (pp. 1–13). IGI Global. doi:10.4018/978-1-5225-1034-5.ch001

Radianti, J., Majchrzak, T. A., Fromm, J., & Wohlgenannt, I. (2020). A systematic review of immersive virtual reality applications for higher education: Design elements, lessons learned, and research agenda. *Computers & Education, 147,* 103778. doi:10.1016/j.compedu.2019.103778

Raftopoulos, M. (2014). Towards gamification transparency: A conceptual framework for the development of responsible gamified enterprise systems. *Journal of Gaming and Virtual Worlds., 6*(2), 159–178. doi:10.1386/jgvw.6.2.159_1

Rahman, R. A., Ahmad, S., & Hashim, U. R. (2018). The effectiveness of gamification technique for higher education students engagement in polytechnic Muadzam Shah Pahang, Malaysia. *International Journal of Educational Technology in Higher Education, 15*(1), 1–16. doi:10.118641239-018-0123-0

Ramirez, N. (2020). *How AI and ML Technology is Transforming Medical Devices.* https://techbullion.com/

Raschka, S. (n.d.). *How can the F1-score help with dealing with class imbalance?* Retrieved from Sebastian Raschka: https://sebastianraschka.com/faq/docs/computing-the-f1-score.html

Ray, M., & Jat, K. R. (2010). Effect of electronic media on children. *Indian Pediatrics, 47*(7), 561–568. doi:10.100713312-010-0128-9 PMID:20683108

Reddy, M. (2021). *Digital Transformation in Healthcare in 2021: 7 Key Trends.* https://www.digitalauthority.me/resources

Reiners, T., & Wood, L. C. (Eds.). (2015). *Gamification in Education and Business.* Springer International Publishing., doi:10.1007/978-3-319-10208-5

Restrepo Escobar, S. M., Taborda, A., Magdaly, L., & Arboleda Sierra, W. (2019). School Performance and Video Games among Middle School Students in the Municipality of La Estrella-Antioquia (Colombia). *Review of Education*, *43*(2), 122–134.

Ribeiro, M. T., Singh, S., & Guestrin, C. (2016). Model-agnostic interpretability of machine learning. *2016 ICML Workshop on Human Interpretability in Machine Learning*.

Rieber, L. (1996). Seriously considering play: Designing interactive learning environments based on the blending of microworlds, simulations, and games. *Educational Technology Research and Development*, *44*(2), 43–58. doi:10.1007/BF02300540

Ringle, C. M., Wende, S., & Becker, J. M. (2015). *SmartPLS 3*. http://www.smartpls.com

Rish, I. (2001). An empirical study of the naive Bayes classifier. *IJCAI 2001 workshop on empirical methods in artificial intelligence*, *3*, 41-46.

Riva, G., & Mantovani, F. (2012). Being There: Understanding the Feeling of Presence in a Synthetic Environment and Its Potential for Clinical Change. *Virtual Reality in Psychological, Medical and Pedagocical Applications. IntechOpen.*, *28*. Advance online publication. doi:10.5772/46411

Rizun, M., & Strzelecki, A. (2020). Students' acceptance of the Covid-19 impact on shifting higher education to distance learning in Poland. *International Journal of Environmental Research and Public Health*, *17*(18), 6468. doi:10.3390/ijerph17186468 PMID:32899478

Robbins, M. B. (2016). The future of gaming. *Library Journal*, *141*(15), 59.

Robson, K., Plangger, K., Kietzmann, J., McCarthy, I., & Pitt, L. (2015). Is it all a game? Understanding the principles of gamification. *Business Horizons*, *58*(4), 411–420. Advance online publication. doi:10.1016/j.bushor.2015.03.006

Rodrigues, L. F., Costa, C. J., & Oliveira, A. (2016). Gamification: A framework for designing software in e-banking. *Computers in Human Behavior, 62*, 620-634. doi:10.1016/j.chb.2016.04.035

Rodrigues, L. F., Costa, C. J., & Oliveira, A. (2013). The adoption of gamification in e-banking. *Proceedings of the 13th International Conference on Information Systems and Design of Communication (ISDOC '13)*. 10.1145/2503859.2503867

Rodrigues, L., Toda, A. M., Oliveira, W., Palomino, P. T., Avila-Santos, A. P., & Isotani, S. (2021, March). Gamification Works, but How and to Whom? An Experimental Study in the Context of Programming Lessons. In *Proceedings of the 52nd ACM Technical Symposium on Computer Science Education* (pp. 184-190). 10.1145/3408877.3432419

Rodríguez, F., & Santiago, R. (2015). *Cómo motivar a tu alumnado y mejorar el clima en el aula*. Digital-Text.

Rodríguez, H. G., & Sandoval, M. (2011). Consumo de videojuegos y juegos para computador: Influencias sobre la atención, memoria, rendimiento académico y problemas de conducta. *Suma Psicologica*, *18*(2), 99–110.

Roelleke, T. (2013). *Information Retrieval Models: Foundations and Relationships*. Morgan & Claypool.

Routledge, H. (2016). *SpringerLink (Online service)*. Why Games Are Good for Business How to Leverage the Power of Serious Games, Gamification and Simulations.

Ruhi, U. (2015). Level Up Your Strategy: Towards a Descriptive Framework for Meaningful Enterprise Gamification. *Technology Innovation Management Review*, *5*(8), 5–16. doi:10.22215/timreview/918

Ryan, M. L. (1999). Immersion vs. interactivity: Virtual reality and literary theory. *SubStance*, *28*(2), 110–137. doi:10.1353ub.1999.0015

Saadé, R. G., & Kira, D. (2007). Mediating the impact of technology usage on perceived ease of use by anxiety. *Computers & Education, 49*(4), 1189–1204. doi:10.1016/j.compedu.2006.01.009

Sailer, M., & Homner, L. (2020). *The gamification of learning: A meta-analysis*. Academic Press.

Sailer, M., Hense, J. U., Mayr, S. K., & Mandl, H. (2017). How gamification motivates: An experimental study of the effects of specific game design elements on psychological need satisfaction. *Computers in Human Behavior, 69*, 371-380. doi:10.1016/j.chb.2016.12.033

Sánchez Salazar, L. A., Gallardo Pérez, H. J., & Paz Montes, L. S. (2019). The Educaplay interactive platform for the learning of mathematics in populations with special educational needs. *Journal of Physics: Conference Series*, 1329.

Sánchez-Alcaraz Martinez, B. J., Sánchez-Díaz, A., Alfonso-Asencio, M., Courel-Ibáñez, J., & Sánchez-Pay, A. (2020). Relationship between physical activity level, use of video games and academic performance in university students. *Espiral-Cuadernos Del Profesorado, 13*(26), 64–73. doi:10.25115/ecp.v13i26.2900

Sanchez, E., Young, S., & Jouneau-Sion, C. (2017). Classcraft: From Gamification to Ludicization of Classroom Management. *Journal of Education and Information Technologies, 22*(2), 497–513. doi:10.100710639-016-9489-6

Sánchez-Mena, A., & Martí-Parreño, J. (2016, June). Gamification in higher education: teachers' drivers and barriers. In *Proceedings of the International Conference the Future of Education* (pp. 180-184). Academic Press.

Sardi, L., Idri, A., & Fernández-Alemán, J. L. (2017). A Systematic Review of Gamification in e-Health. *Journal of Biomedical Informatics, 71*, 31-48. doi:10.1016/j.jbi.2017.05.011

Sauro, J. (2011). *A practical guide to the system usability scale: Background, benchmarks & best practices*. Measuring Usability LLC.

Sawahel, W. (2020, November 26). *Gamification of education could engage students during COVID-19*. Available at: https://www.universityworldnews.com/post.php?story=20201123063309960

Sawangchai, A., Prasarnkarn, H., Kasuma, J., Polyakova, A. G., & Qasim, S. (2020). Effects of Covid-19 on digital learning of entrepreneurs. *Polish Journal of Management Studies, 22*(2), 502–517. doi:10.17512/pjms.2020.22.2.33

Scheiner, C., Witt, M., Voigt, K., & Robra-Bissantz, S. (2012). Einsatz von Spielemechaniken in Ideewettbewerben. *Proceedings of the Multikonferenz Wirtschaftsinformatik MKWI, 12*, 781–792.

Schmitt, Z. L., & Livingston, M. G. (2015). Video game addiction and college performance among males: Results from a 1 year longitudinal study. *Cyberpsychology, Behavior, and Social Networking, 18*(1), 25–29. doi:10.1089/cyber.2014.0403 PMID:25584728

Scott, S., Niemand, T., Kraus, S., & Oberreiner, R. (2020). Let the Games Begin: Finding The Nascent Entrepreneurial Mindset of Video Gamers. *Proceedings of the 53rd Hawaii International Conference on System Sciences*.

Seaborn, K., & Fels, D. I. (2015). Gami_cation in theory and action: A survey. *International Journal of Human-Computer Studies, 74*, 14–31. doi:10.1016/j.ijhcs.2014.09.006

Sharkova, D., Somova, E., & Gachkova, M. (2020). Gamification in cloud-based collaborative learning. *Journal Mathematics and Informatics, 63*(5), 471–483.

Sheridan, T. B. (1992). Musings on telepresence and virtual presence. *Presence (Cambridge, Mass.), 1*(1), 120–126. doi:10.1162/pres.1992.1.1.120

Shih, Y. Y., & Chen, C. Y. (2013). The study of behavioral intention for mobile commerce: Via integrated model of TAM and TTF. *Quality & Quantity, 47*(2), 1009–1020. doi:10.100711135-011-9579-x

Shi, Y., & Shih, J. (2015). Game factors and game-based learning design model. *International Journal of Computer Games Technology. Article ID, 549684*, 1–11.

Shliakhovchuk, E., & Muñoz García, A. (2020). Intercultural Perspective on Impact of Video Games on Players: Insights from a Systematic Review of Recent Literature. *Educational Sciences: Theory and Practice, 20*(1).

Siau, K., Hilgers, M., Chen, L., Liu, S., Nah, F., Hall, R., & Flachsbart, B. (2021). *Fintech Empowerment: Data Science, AI, and Machine Learning.* https://www.cutter.com/article/fintech-empowerment-data-science-ai-and-machine-learning-501881

Silvia, P. J. (2008). Interest—The curious emotion. *Current Directions in Psychological Science, 17*(1), 57–60. doi:10.1111/j.1467-8721.2008.00548.x

Silvia, P. J., Winterstein, B. P., Willse, J. T., Barona, C. M., Cram, J. T., Hess, K. I., Martinez, J. L., & Richard, C. A. (2008). Assessing creativity with divergent thinking tasks: Exploring the reliability and validity of new subjective scoring methods. *Psychology of Aesthetics, Creativity, and the Arts, 2*(2), 68–85. doi:10.1037/1931-3896.2.2.68

Skoric, M. M., Teo, L. L. C., & Neo, R. L. (2009). Children and video games: Addiction, engagement, and scholastic achievement. *Cyberpsychology & Behavior, 12*(5), 567–572. doi:10.1089/cpb.2009.0079 PMID:19624263

Smutny, P., & Shreiberova, P. (2020). Chatbots for learning: A review of educational chatbots for the Facebook Messenger. *Computers & Education, 151*, 103–862. doi:10.1016/j.compedu.2020.103862

Soderstrom, N. C., & Bjork, R. A. (2015). Learning Versus Performance: An Integrative Review. *Perspectives on Psychological Science, 0*(2), 176–199. doi:10.1177/1745691615569000 PMID:25910388

Sommar, F., & Wielondek, M. (2015). *Combining Lexicon- and Learning-based Approaches for Improved Performance and Convenience in Sentiment Classification* (Dissertation). Retrieved from DiVA: http://urn.kb.se/resolve?urn=urn:nbn:se:kth:diva-166430

Somova, E., & Gachkova, M. (2016). An Attempt for Gamification of Learning in Moodle. In *Proceedings of International Conference on e-Learning (e-Learning'16).* (pp. 201-207). Slovak University of Technology in Bratislava.

Sotoca-Orgaz, P. (2020). *Gamificación e Inteligencia artificial (IA). Cuando Sherlock conoció a Watson* [Paper presentation]. Encuentro de Innovación de Docencia Universitaria (XII EIDU UAH). Madrid, España. doi:10.13140/RG.2.2.22895.25760

Spina, C. (2016). Libraries embrace Pokémon Go. *School Library Journal, 62*(8), 12–13.

Steinkuehler, C., & Duncan, S. (2008). Scientific habits of mind in virtual worlds. *Journal of Science Education and Technology, 17*(6), 530–543. doi:10.100710956-008-9120-8

Stuart, H., Serna, A., Marty, J. C., & Lavoué, E. (2019). Adaptive gamification in education: A literature review of current trends and developments. *European Conference on Technology, Enhanced Learning (EC-TEL), 294-307.

Susi, T., Johannesson, M., & Backlund, P. (2007). Serious games: An overview - Taiwan. *Cyberpsychology & Behavior, 7*(5), 571–581.

Swacha, J., Paiva, J. C., Leal, J. P., Queirós, R., Montella, R., & Kosta, S. (2020). GEdIL—Gamified Education Interoperability Language. *Information, 11*(6), 287. doi:10.3390/info11060287

Swacha, J., Queirós, R., Paiva, J. C., Leal, J. P., Kosta, S., & Montella, R. (2020b). A roadmap to gamify programming education. In *First International Computer Programming Education Conference, ICPEC 2020.* Schloss Dagstuhl - Leibniz-Zentrum fur Informatik.

Swacha, J. (2018). Representation of events and rules in gamification systems. *Procedia Computer Science, 126*, 2040–2049. doi:10.1016/j.procs.2018.07.248

Swanson, M. (2021). *Gamification in 2021: Future of Immersive Technologies.* https://www.gamify.com/gamification-blog/gamification-in-2021-a-more-matured-approach

Sweetser, P., & Wyeth, P. (2005). GameFlow: a model for evaluating player enjoyment in games. *Computers in Entertainment (CIE), 3*(3), Article 3A.

Sylwester, R. (1994). How Emotions Affect Learning. *Reporting What Learners Are Learning*, 60-65.

Talent, L. M. S. (n.d.). *TalentLMS.* http://www.talentlms.com/

Tandon, T. (2017). A Study on Relationship between Self Efficacy and Flow at Work. *International Journal of Indian Psychology, 4*(4), 87–100. doi:10.25215/0404.069

Tan, M., & Hew, K. F. (2016). Incorporating meaningful gamification in a blended learning research methods class: Examining student learning, engagement, and affective outcomes. *Australasian Journal of Educational Technology, 32*(5). Advance online publication. doi:10.14742/ajet.2232

Taormina, R., & Gao, J. (2013). Maslow and the Motivation Hierarchy: Measuring Satisfaction of the Needs. *The American Journal of Psychology, 126*(2), 155–177. doi:10.5406/amerjpsyc.126.2.0155 PMID:23858951

Taylor, S., & Todd, P. (1995). An integrated model of waste management behavior: A test of household recycling and composting intentions. *Environment and Behavior, 27*(5), 603–630. doi:10.1177/0013916595275001

Tejeiro, R., Pelegrina, M., & Gómez, J. L. (2009). Efectos psicosociales de los videojuegos. *Comunicación (Cartago), 17*(1), 235–250.

Tian, Y., Guan, T., & Wang, C. (2010). Real-time occlusion handling in augmented reality based on an object tracking approach. *Sensors (Basel), 10*(4), 2885–2900. doi:10.3390100402885 PMID:22319278

Tokuyama, Rajapakse, Yamabe, Konno, & Hung. (2019). A kinect-based augmented reality game for lower limb exercise. *Proc. - 2019 Int. Conf. Cyberworlds*, 399–402.

Tondello, G. F., Mora, A., Marczewski, A., Nacke, L. E. (2019). Empirical validation of the Gamification User Types Hexad scale in English and Spanish. *International Journal of Human-Computer Studies, 127*, 95-111. doi:10.1016/j.ijhcs.2018.10.002

Tondello, G. F., Wehbe, R. R., Diamond, L., Busch, M., Marczewski, A., & Nacke, L. E. (2016). The Gamification User Types Hexad Scale. In *Proceedings of the 2016 Annual Symposium on Computer-Human Interaction in Play* (pp. 229-243). 10.1145/2967934.2968082

Torres Vega, M., Liaskos, C., Abadal, S., Papapetrou, E., Jain, A., Mouhouche, B., Kalem, G., Ergüt, S., Mach, M., Sabol, T., Cabellos-Aparicio, A., Grimm, C., De Turck, F., & Famaey, J. (2020). Immersive Interconnected Virtual and Augmented Reality: A 5G and IoT Perspective. *Journal of Network and Systems Management, 28*(4), 796–826. doi:10.100710922-020-09545-w

Trick, L. M., Jaspers-Fayer, F., & Sethi, N. (2005). Multiple-object tracking in children: The "Catch the Spies" task. *Cognitive Development, 20*(3), 373–387. doi:10.1016/j.cogdev.2005.05.009

Tsai, Y. Y., Chao, C. M., Lin, H. M., & Cheng, B. W. (2018). Nursing staff intentions to continuously use a blended e-learning system from an integrative perspective. *Quality & Quantity, 52*(6), 2495–2513. doi:10.100711135-017-0540-5

Tullis, T. S., & Stetson, J. N. (2004). A comparison of questionnaires for assessing website usability. *Usability Professional Association Conference*, 1–12.

United Nations High Commissioner for Refugees. (2005, December 7). *Surviving against the odds: a taste of life as a refugee*. Retrieved April 30, 2018, from https://www.unhcr.org/4397174b4.html

United Nations High Commissioner for Refugees. (2021). *Passages: An Awareness Game Confronting The Plight of Refugees*. Retrieved April 30, 2018, from https://www.unhcr.org/473dc1772.html

United States Environmental Protection Agency - EPA. (2018). *Facts and Figure about Materials, Waste and Recycling*. https://www.epa.gov/facts-and-figures-about-materials-waste-and-recycling/national-overview-facts-and-figures-materials#recycling

Utomo, A. Y., & Santoso, H. B. (2015). Development of gamification-enriched pedagogical agent for e-learning system based on community of inquiry. *Proceedings of the International HCI and UX Conference in Indonesia*, 1-9. 10.1145/2742032.2742033

Uttal, D. H., Meadow, N. G., Tipton, E., Hand, L. L., Alden, A. R., Warren, C., & Newcombe, N. S. (2013). The malleability of spatial skills: A meta-analysis of training studies. *Psychological Bulletin*, *139*(2), 352–402. doi:10.1037/a0028446 PMID:22663761

Van der Heijden, H. (2004). User acceptance of hedonic information systems. *Management Information Systems Quarterly*, *28*(4), 695–704. doi:10.2307/25148660

van Engelen, J. E., & Hoos, H. H. (2020). A survey on semi-supervised learning. *Machine Learning*, *109*(2), 373–440. doi:10.100710994-019-05855-6

Van Staalduinen, J., & de Freitas, S. (2011). A game-based learning framework: Linking game design and learning. In M. Khine (Ed.), *Learning to play: exploring the future of education with video games* (pp. 29–54). Peter Lang.

Vanduhe, V. Z., Nat, M., & Hasan, H. F. (2020). Continuance intentions to use gamification for training in higher education: Integrating the technology acceptance model (TAM), social motivation, and task technology Fit (TTF). *IEEE Access: Practical Innovations, Open Solutions*, *8*, 21473–21484. doi:10.1109/ACCESS.2020.2966179

Vapnik, V. (1995). *The Nature of Statistical Learning*. Springer. doi:10.1007/978-1-4757-2440-0

Venkatesh, V., & Davis, F. D. (2000). A theoretical extension of the technology acceptance model: Four longitudinal field studies. *Management Science*, *46*(2), 186–204. doi:10.1287/mnsc.46.2.186.11926

Venkatesh, V., Morris, M. G., Davis, G. B., & Davis, F. D. (2003). User acceptance of information technology: Toward a unified view. *Management Information Systems Quarterly*, *27*(3), 425–478. doi:10.2307/30036540

Ventura, M., Shute, V., & Kim, Y. J. (2012). Video gameplay, personality and academic performance. *Computers & Education*, *58*(4), 1260–1266. doi:10.1016/j.compedu.2011.11.022

Vette, D. F., Tabak, M., & Vollenbroek-Hutten, M. (January, 2015). *Increasing motivation in eHealth through gamification* [Paper presentation]. *Fifth Dutch Conference on Bio-Medical Engineering*. Egmond aan Zee, The Netherlands.

Villani, D., Carissoli, C., Triberti, S., Marchetti, A., Gilli, G., & Riva, G. (2018). Video games for emotion regulation: A systematic review. *Games for Health Journal*, *7*(2), 85–99. doi:10.1089/g4h.2017.0108 PMID:29424555

Von der Heiden, J. M., Braun, B., Müller, K. M., & Egloff, B. (2019). The Association Between Video Gaming and Psychological Functioning. *Frontiers in Psychology*, *10*, 17–31. doi:10.3389/fpsyg.2019.01731 PMID:31402891

Wang, A. I., & Tahir, R., (2020). The effect of using Kahoot! for learning - A literature review. *Computers & Education, 149*. doi:10.1016/j.compedu.2020.103818

Wang, P. (2019). On Defining Artificial Intelligence. *Journal of Artificial General Intelligence, 10*(2), 1–37. doi:10.2478/jagi-2019-0002

WCPT-ER. (2013). *WCPT Glossary: Terms Used in WCPT's Policies*. Author.

Weis, R., & Cerankosky, B. C. (2010). Effects of Video-Game Ownership on Young Boys' Academic and Behavioral Functioning: A Randomized, Controlled Study. *Psychological Science, 21*(4), 463–470. doi:10.1177/0956797610362670 PMID:20424084

Werbach, K., & Hunter, D. (2012). *For the win: How game thinking can revolutionize your business*. Wharton Digital Press.

Werbach, K., & Hunter, D. (2012). *For the win: How game thinking can revolutionize your business*. Wharton Digital Press.

Werbach, K., & Hunter, D. (2012). *For the Win: How game thinking can revolutionize your business*. Wharton Digital Press.

William, L. (2021). Improving Learners Programming Skills using Serious Games. *14th International Symposium on Advances in Technology Education*.

William, L., Abdul Rahim, Z., Wu, L., & de Souza, R. (2019). Effectiveness of Supply Chain Games in Problem Based Learning Environment. In D. K. Ifenthaler (Ed.), *Game-Based Assessment Revisited* (pp. 257–280). Springer. doi:10.1007/978-3-030-15569-8_13

William, L., Rahim, Z., Souza, R., Nugroho, E., & Fredericco, R. (2018). Extendable Board Game to Facilitate Learning in Supply Chain Management. *Advances in Science, Technology and Engineering Systems Journal, 3*(4), 99–111. doi:10.25046/aj030411

Wolf, D. (2007). *Prepared and Resolved: The Strategic Agenda for Growth, Performance, and Change*. Dsb Pub.

Wolf, M. J. (2001). *The medium of the video game*. University of Texas Press.

Wong, D., Liu, H., Meng-Lewis, Y., Sun, Y., & Zhang, Y. (2021). Gamified money: Exploring the effectiveness of gamification in mobile payment adoption among the silver generation in China. *Information Technology & People*. Advance online publication. doi:10.1108/ITP-09-2019-0456

Wu, M., & Luo, J. (2020). *Wearable Technology Applications in Healthcare: A Literature Review*. https://www.himss.org/resources/

Wu, B., & Chen, X. (2017). Continuance intention to use MOOCs: Integrating the technology acceptance model (TAM) and task technology fit (TTF) model. *Computers in Human Behavior, 67*, 221–232. doi:10.1016/j.chb.2016.10.028

Wu, J., & Lu, X. (2013). Effects of extrinsic and intrinsic motivators on using utilitarian, hedonic, and dual-purposed information systems: A meta-analysis. *Journal of the Association for Information Systems, 14*(3), 1. doi:10.17705/1jais.00325

Yakubu, M. N., & Dasuki, S. I. (2019). Factors affecting the adoption of e-learning technologies among higher education students in Nigeria: A structural equation modelling approach. *Information Development, 35*(3), 492–502. doi:10.1177/0266666918765907

Yang, H., & Li, D. (2021). Understanding the dark side of gamification health management: A stress perspective. *Information Processing & Management, 58*(5), 1–19. doi:10.1016/j.ipm.2021.102649

Yen, D. C., Wu, C. S., Cheng, F. F., & Huang, Y. W. (2010). Determinants of users' intention to adopt wireless technology: An empirical study by integrating TTF with TAM. *Computers in Human Behavior, 26*(5), 906–915. doi:10.1016/j.chb.2010.02.005

Yordanova, Z. (2020). Gamification as a Tool for Supporting Artificial Intelligence Development – State of Art. In M. Botto-Tobar, M. Zambrano Vizuete, P. Torres-Carrión, S. Montes León, G. Pizarro Vásquez, & B. Durakovic (Eds.), *Applied Technologies. ICAT 2019. Communications in Computer and Information Science* (Vol. 1193). Springer. doi:10.1007/978-3-030-42517-3_24

Yuan, S., Liu, Y., Yao, R., & Liu, J. (2016). An investigation of users' continuance intention towards mobile banking in China. *Information Development, 32*(1), 20–34. doi:10.1177/0266666914522140

Yu, K. H., Beam, A. L., & Kohane, I. S. (2018). Artificial Intelligence in Healthcare. *Nature Biomedical Engineering, 2*(10), 719–731. doi:10.103841551-018-0305-z PMID:31015651

Yu, Z. (2019). A Meta-Analysis of Use of Serious Games in Education over a Decade. *International Journal of Computer Games Technology, 8*.

Zainuddin, Z., Chu, S. K. W., Shujahat, M., & Perera, C. J. (2020). The impact of gamification on learning and instruction: A systematic review of empirical evidence. *Educational Research Review, 30*, 100326. doi:10.1016/j.edurev.2020.100326

Zhao, Z., Ali Etemad, S., & Arya, A. (2016). Gamification of Exercise and Fitness using Wearable Activity Trackers. In P. Chung, A. Soltoggio, C. Dawson, Q. Meng, & M. Pain (Eds.) In *Proceedings of the 10th International Symposium on Computer Science in Sports (ISCSS). Advances in Intelligent Systems and Computing* (vol. 392). Springer. 10.1007/978-3-319-24560-7_30

Zhu, Z., Yu, M., & Riezebos, P. (2016). A research framework of smart education. *Smart Learning Environments, 3*(1), 1–17. doi:10.118640561-016-0026-2

Zichermann, G., & Cunningham, C. (2011). *Gamification by Design*. Academic Press.

Zichermann, G., & Cunningham, C. (2011). *Gamification by design: Implementing game mechanics in web and mobile apps*. O'Reilly Media, Inc.

Zichermann, G., & Cunningham, C. (2011). *Gamification by Design: Implementing game mechanics in web and mobile apps*. O'Reilly Media.

Zichermann, G., & Linder, J. (2013). *The gamification revolution*. McGraw-Hill Education.

Zielke, M. A., Evans, M. J., Dufour, F., Christopher, T. V., Donahue, J. K., Johnson, P., Jennings, E. B., Friedman, B. S., Ounekeo, P. L., & Flores, R. (2009). Serious games for immersive cultural training: Creating a living world. *IEEE Computer Graphics and Applications, 29*(2), 49–60. doi:10.1109/MCG.2009.30 PMID:19462634

About the Contributors

Filipe Portela went to the University of Minho in Guimarães, where he studied information systems and obtained his degree in 2007 (Lic), 2009 (MSc) and 2013 (PhD). He held a PhD in Information Systems and Technologies in 2013. He is an integrated researcher at ALGORITMI Centre, where he developed his post-doctoral research work on "Pervasive Intelligent Decision Support Systems". Filipe Portela started his research in the INTCare R&D project (Intensive Medicine area), participated in other projects and was also Principal Investigator of ioCOVID19 and ioCity. He already has relevant indexed publications in the main research topics: Data Science, Intelligent Decision Support Systems, Intelligent Systems, Pervasive Data, Business Intelligence, Data Mining and Knowledge Discovery. He is (co)organizer of several workshops and conferences and a reviewer and editor of many indexed journals and conferences on these topics. Currently, he is also an Invited Assistant Professor of the Information Systems Department, School of Engineering, University of Minho, Portugal, where he supervises several masters and PhD students in the areas mentioned above. Filipe Portela founded IOTech - Innovation on Technology in 2018, through which he is transferring and applying scientific knowledge for the benefit of the citizens.

Ricardo Queirós holds a PhD on Computer Science and is an assistant professor of Computer Science at the Polytechnic Institute of Porto. He is also a researcher in the field of e-learning interoperability and programming languages learning at the Center for Research in Advanced Computing Systems (CRACS) research group of INESC TEC Porto. He is also the author of 5 books regarding Android development and has almost 100 scientific publications focused on computer science education.

* * *

Javier M. Aguiar is Associate Professor at University of Valladolid, and Head of the Data Engineering Research Unit. His research is focused on Big Data, Artificial Intelligence, and Internet of Things. He has managed international research projects and he has contributed to the standardisation field as expert at the European Telecommunications Standards Institute. He serves as editor, guest editor and reviewer, and author in several international journals, books, and conferences. Furthermore, he has been involved as reviewer and rapporteur in several international research initiatives.

Gamal Abdulnaser Alkawsi was born in Yemen. He received the B.S. degree in software engineering and the master's degree in management information systems from Coventry University, and the Ph.D. degree in information communication technology from The Energy University (UNITEN), Malaysia, in 2019. He was a lecturer at Thamar University (2008-2013). He is currently a Postdoctoral Researcher with The Energy University (UNITEN). He has published in journals and conferences. His research interests include emerging technology acceptance, user behavior, adoption of information systems in organizations, ICT in renewable energy, and artificial intelligence.

Miguel Alonso Felipe received his M.S. degrees in telecommunication engineering from the University of Valladolid, Spain. In addition, he is PhD Candidate at University of Valladolid and Researcher of the Data Engineering Research Unit. His research is mainly focused on Big Data, Artificial Intelligence and Internet of Things. Besides, he is co-author of some publications in journals, dealing with topics related to his lines of research.

Yahia Baashar received the B.S. degree in network computing and the master's degree in management information systems from Coventry University, INTI International University, Malaysia. He is currently pursuing the Ph.D. degree in industrial science with The Energy University (UNITEN), Malaysia. He has published in journals and conferences. His research interests include technology acceptance, medical informatics, e-health, artificial intelligence, and machine learning.

Pedro Branco is Assistant Professor at the Department of Information Systems, University of Minho where he is currently the director of the Master Program in Technology and Digital Art. He graduated in Computer Science from University of Porto, participated in the first joint Fraunhofer Center for Research in Computer Graphics/ Rhode Island School of Design New Media program. He joined Fraunhofer's U.S. operations as Researcher/3D Software Engineer in the development of virtual reality interaction techniques. He worked at IMEDIA, Providence, RI, studying user interface usability based on physiological monitoring. He received his doctorate degree in Information Systems from University of Minho with the topic: "Computer-based Facial Expression Analysis for Assessing User Experience". More recently he co-founded engageLab where he is working closely with students from a wide range of backgrounds developing interactive systems that explore a synergy of technology and aesthetics, exploring future directions for our interaction with technology.

María Buenadicha-Mateos is Assistant Professor of Human Resources, based at the Department of Business, University of Extremadura, Badajoz, Spain. She is specialist on e-recruitment and virtual teams.

Mikel Barrio Conde is a PhD candidate at University of Valladolid, who received his M.S. degrees in telecommunication engineering from the University of Valladolid, Spain. He is researcher of the Data Engineering Research Unit and his research is focused on Artificial Intelligence, and Internet of Things. Also, he is co-author of some publications in journals, dealing with topics related to his lines of his research.

Javier del Pozo Velázquez received his M.S. degrees in telecommunication engineering from the University of Valladolid, Spain. In addition, he is PhD Candidate at University of Valladolid and Researcher of the Data Engineering Research Unit. His research is mainly focused on Big Data, Artificial Intelligence and Internet of Things. Besides, he is co-author of some publications in journals, dealing with topics related to his lines of research.

Mariya Gachkova graduated a PhD degree in Plovdiv University in Computer Science Department. Gamification in education is her main field of research.

Manuel B. Garcia is a licensed professional teacher and a professor of information technology at FEU Institute of Technology, Philippines. His research interests include topics that, individually or collectively, cover the disciplines of education and information technology.

Francisco Gouveia is a student at FCT-UNL, taking a Master's Degree in Computer Science.

Abdulsalam S. Mustafa completed his BSc and MSc Computer Science from the University of Hertfordshire, UK, and is currently pursuing a PhD in Information & Communication Technology at UNITEN, Malaysia. He currently works for NILDS and is previously an instructor and researcher at Khazar University. His research interests include gamification, mHealth, e-learning technologies, e-democracy adoption, and informatics.

María A. Pérez received her M.S. and Ph.D. degrees in telecommunication engineering from the University of Valladolid, Spain, in 1996 and 1999, respectively. She is presently Associate Professor at University of Valladolid, and member of the Data Engineering Research Unit. Her research is focused on Big Data, Artificial Intelligence, Internet of Things, and the application of technology to the learning process. She has managed or participated in numerous international research projects. She is author or co-author of many publications in journals, books, and conferences. In addition, she has been involved as reviewer in several international research initiatives.

Armanda Rodrigues is an Associate Professor at the Computer Science Department, NOVA School of Science and Technology and an integrated member of the Multimodal Systems Group of NOVA LINCS. Armanda is interested in providing models, methods, tools and infrastructures that may enable improvements in the use of Web/Mobile GIS (Geographic Information Systems), focusing in changes in context and in collaborative environments. She has been involved in several International and national research projects related with GIS, Simulation, Web-GIS and Geo-Collaborative Systems with case studies in Emergency Management, Digital Heritage and Agronomy. Armanda Rodrigues supervised more than 30 postgraduate theses already completed and currently supervises several doctoral and master dissertations. She is the author and co-author of several GI Science and Computer Science peer reviewed publications. She also reviews and serves in the program committee of various GI national and international conferences as well as peered review journals.

Teresa Romão is an Assistant Professor at NOVA University of Lisbon, where she teaches and develops research work in the area of Human-Computer Interaction. She studied computer science at FCT/UNL and received her PhD degree from the same University in 2001. She is also an integrated member of the research center NOVA LINCS (Multimodal Systems group). She has been coordinating and participating in several national and European research projects related with computer entertainment, augmented reality, mobile storytelling, ubiquitous computing and persuasive technology. She is a member of the Digital Media PhD Scientific Committee in the scope of UT/Austin-Portugal Program. She has authored and co-authored many publications in books, peer reviewed journals and conferences (e.g. CHI, UIST, INTERACT, MobileHCI, ACE). Teresa Romão has been involved in the organization and served on the program committees of various national and top international conferences (e.g. INTERACT, ACM EICS, ACE, IEEE VR). She was member of the Steering Committee of the International Conference on Advances in Computer Entertainment Technology – ACE (2012-2017).

Saúl Rozada Raneros is a PhD candidate at University of Valladolid, who received his M.S. degrees in telecommunication engineering from the University of Valladolid, Spain. He is researcher of the Data Engineering Research Unit and his research is focused on Internet of Things, and Virtual Reality. Also, he is co-author of some publications in journals, dealing with topics related to his lines of his research.

Alberto Simões, with a PhD on Artificial Intelligence, area of Natural Language Processing, is a lecturer at Polytechnic Institute of Cávado and Ave, in Barcelos, and a researcher at Algoritmi Center and Center for Humanistic Studies, both from University of Minho. Main Interests: Natural Language Processing: Bilingual Resources Extraction, Machine Translation and Ontologies; Languages Processing, Domain Specific Languages; Digital Preservation, namely music scores; Artificial Intelligence in Computer Games Development.

Elena Somova is a Professor in Computer Science. She is a head of Computer Science Department at the University of Plovdiv "Paisii Hilendarski". Her research interests are in the fields of gamification of learning, e-learning, game-based learning, green technologies, sustainability, etc.

Vanye Vanduhe got Ph.D. degree in management information systems with the School of Applied Sciences, Cyprus International University. He is currently a Researcher and IT staff Uner Insaat. He is also involved in researching on gamification for instructor training with blended learning environment in higher education. He is also a co founder of the Student Engagement Research Group (SERG) called SEngagement. He aims at designing learning management platforms that could be gamified for students learning and instructor training. He has authored some journals and conferences. His areas of research include designing gamification training environment using game elements, game principles and theories, and game mechanics. Notwithstanding current research on machine learning, virtual reality, and Human Interactive Systems.

Linda William is a Senior Lecturer in School of Informatics and IT, Temasek Polytechnic. She obtained her PhD (Information Systems) from the School of Information Systems, Singapore Management University. Her research interests are in Intelligent Systems, Decisions & Data Analytics, Machine Learning, Metaheuristics Algorithm, and Serious Game in Education. She has published a book and articles in international conferences and academic journals such as the Journal of the Operation Research Society and Journal of Urban Sciences.

Ruan Yang is a 3rd year student from Diploma of Big Data Management & Governance in School of Informatics and IT, Temasek Polytechnic. Her interests include Data Analytics as well as Machine Learning.

Index

H

I

L

M

N

O

P

R

S

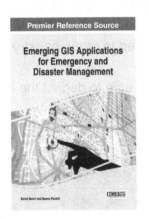

Printed in the United States
by Baker & Taylor Publisher Services